Ashkelon 5

HARVARD SEMITIC MUSEUM PUBLICATIONS
Lawrence E. Stager, General Editor
Michael D. Coogan, Director of Publications

FINAL REPORTS

OF THE

LEON LEVY EXPEDITION

TO

ASHKELON

Series Editors
Lawrence E. Stager, Daniel M. Master, and J. David Schloen

1. *Ashkelon 1: Introduction and Overview (1985–2006)*
   edited by Lawrence E. Stager, J. David Schloen, and Daniel M. Master
2. *Ashkelon 2: Imported Pottery of the Roman and Late Roman Periods*
   by Barbara L. Johnson
3. *Ashkelon 3: The Seventh Century B.C.*
   by Lawrence E. Stager, Daniel M. Master, and J. David Schloen
4. *Ashkelon 4: The Iron Age Figurines of Ashkelon and Philistia*
   by Michael D. Press
5. *Ashkelon 5: The Land behind Ashkelon*
   by Yaakov Huster, with contributions by Daniel M. Master, George A. Pierce, and Michael D. Press

THE LEON LEVY EXPEDITION TO ASHKELON

ASHKELON 5

The Land behind Ashkelon

By

Yaakov Huster

With contributions by

Daniel M. Master, George A. Pierce, and Michael D. Press

Winona Lake, Indiana
EISENBRAUNS
2015

Ashkelon 5:
The Land behind Ashkelon

by Yaakov Huster
With contributions by
Daniel M. Master, George A. Pierce, and Michael D. Press

Printed in the U.S.A.

Distributed by
Eisenbrauns
PO Box 275
Winona Lake, IN 46590-0275

http://eisenbrauns.com

Library of Congress Cataloging-in-Publication Data

Huster, Yaakov, author.
  Ashkelon 5 : the land behind Ashkelon / by Yaakov Huster ; with contributions by
    Daniel M. Master, George A. Pierce, and Michael D. Press.
      pages ; cm. — (Final reports of the Leon Levy expedition to Ashkelon ; 5)
      Includes bibliographical references and index.
      ISBN 978-1-57506-952-4 (hardback : alk. paper)
  1. Ashkelon (Israel)—Antiquities. 2. Excavations (Archaeology)—Israel—
    Ashkelon. 3. Material culture—Israel—Ashkelon. I. Master, Daniel M., 1971–
    author. II. Pierce, George A., author. III. Press, Michael D., author. IV. Title.
    V. Title: Ashkelon five.
  DS110.A76H88   2015
  956.94'9—dc23
                                                                    2015006352

The paper used in this publication meets the minimum requirements of the American National
Standard for Information Sciences—Permanence of Paper for Printed Library Materials, ANSI
Z39.48-1984.♾™

Shelby White and Leon Levy

The Leon Levy Expedition to Ashkelon is indebted to the vision and support of Leon Levy and Shelby White. Its ongoing publications are underwritten by a grant from the Leon Levy Foundation.

CONTENTS

Editors' Preface   ix

Author's Preface   xi

Abbreviations   xiii

List of Tables   xv

1. **Introduction**   *Yaakov Huster*   1
   Previous Research   1
   Goals and Methods   2
   Conclusion   11

2. **Survey of Settlement Patterns by Period**   *Yaakov Huster*   13
   Paleolithic   13
   Neolithic and Chalcolithic   15
   Early Bronze Age   17
   Middle Bronze Age   20
   Late Bronze Age   24
   Iron Age I   25
   Iron Age II   30
   Persian (539–312 B.C.) and Hellenistic (332–37 B.C.) Periods   36
   Roman Period   40
   Byzantine Period   40
   Early Islamic Period (A.D. 638–1099)   55
   Medieval Period   57

3. **Identification of Ottoman Sites**   *Michael D. Press*   89
   Corrections to Earlier Surveys   92
   Appendix A: Identification of Ottoman Sites in Hütteroth/Abdulfattah   95
   Appendix B: Discussion of Ottoman Site Identification   102

4. **Ashkelon as Maritime Gateway and Central Place**   *George A. Pierce and Daniel M. Master*   109
   Settlement Theories   109
   The Rise of the Gateway (Early Bronze–Iron I)   110
   The Dynamic Gateway (Iron II–Byzantine)   115
   The Demise of the Gateway (Early Islamic–Mamluk)   120
   Conclusion   122

5. **Regional Archaeological Survey: Map of Sderot (96)**   *Yaakov Huster*   125
   Geological and Geographical Overview   125
   History of Research   126
   Excavations   127
   Archaeological Overview   127
   Appendix C: Index of Site Names   148
   Appendix D: Index of Sites Listed by Period   150
   Appendix E: Index of Map of Sderot (96) Sites   151
   Appendix F: Catalogue of Map of Sderot (96) Sites   157

Bibliography   209

EDITORS' PREFACE

From the outset, the Leon Levy Expedition has been committed to placing the excavations at Tel Ashkelon within a wider regional context. From 1986 to 1990, we supported Mitchell Allen's survey of the area southeast of modern Ashkelon (IAA map 92), but we looked for a chance to do more. One of the impediments has always been the scale of the task. Since Allen's survey, the city of Ashkelon has grown considerably, and that growth has been accompanied by extensive salvage excavations undertaken by the Israel Antiquities Authority (IAA). If we were to understand the land behind Ashkelon, we needed not only to revisit the older surveys but also to take into account an enormous amount of new information collected by the archaeologists of the IAA.

In 2009, we met with Yigael Yisrael and Yaakov Huster of the IAA who suggested a solution. Yaakov Huster, who had been working in the Ashkelon region for many years, was about to retire. He had completed his work on another survey area close to Ashkelon (IAA map 96) and, as inspector for the Ashkelon region, had seen all of the ongoing salvage work for the last decade or more. Yigael and Yaakov suggested that the Leon Levy Expedition fund a publication project, overseen by Yaakov, to pull together all of the new data, to revisit the entire area around Ashkelon, and to publish the new data from map 96. We were enthusiastic. Not only would this allow us to fulfill one of our core research goals, but Yaakov's firsthand experience would add particular expertise. Too many times, local IAA inspectors are not given their due. They are not afforded the time to articulate the type of regional perspective that their work has uniquely afforded them. This was our chance to rectify this oversight at Ashkelon.

Yaakov began his work in 2009 and carefully worked through a large body of earlier materials. His work was facilitated by the Ashkelon laboratory, directed in turn by Michael Press (2009–2010), Rona Avissar Lewis (2010–2012), and Rafael (Rafi) Lewis (2012–2013). In particular, Michael Press was a close confidant of Yaakov, working through many of the details of site identification. As the project progressed, and the final prose was being constructed, Michael agreed to join the project in an official capacity. Michael undertook most of the editing for chapters 1 and 2. In addition, Michael asked whether he might write up the conclusions for the Ottoman period (chapter 3). His positive contributions to the volume were indispensable.

This project was also aided by many others. Elise Jakoby Laguier constructed the maps from tables supplied by Yaakov Huster. She also produced several analyses of the key spatial relationships through time in ArcGIS. While these analyses are not graphically relayed in the volume, many of the concepts that she uncovered are reflected upon in chapter 4. George Pierce provided a synthetic reflection that builds on his previous studies of the Dothan Valley and Sharon Plain. His is just the first of what we hope will be many attempts to reflect on the relationship between Ashkelon as a site and this rich dataset assembled by Yaakov Huster. Finally, Megan Sauter completed the layout and copy editing, a core task which makes our job as series editors much simpler.

The Land behind Ashkelon represents a fundamental contribution to the goals of the Leon Levy Expedition, but more than this, it is a distillation of numerous excavations by many talented archaeologists, brought together by Yaakov Huster, a man who has devoted his life to preserving the cultural heritage of the Ashkelon region.

The writing and publication of this volume have been made possible by a grant from the Leon Levy Foundation. The Leon Levy Expedition has also been sponsored by Harvard University, the Semitic Museum, and later by Boston College, Wheaton College, and Troy University.

Daniel M. Master
Wheaton, Illinois

Lawrence E. Stager
Concord, Massachusetts   February 2015

AUTHOR'S PREFACE

THE present work builds in no small measure on that of previous researchers. In particular, the surveys of Berman and Allen are fundamental to any analysis of settlement patterns in the Ashkelon region. These studies, however, looked primarily at small, 10 x 10 km areas while largely ignoring the surrounding region. For many years, as district inspector of the Ashkelon region for the Israel Antiquities Authority, I had the chance to study the Ashkelon region as a whole and was able to observe excavations and surveys as they occurred. In addition, I have come to know the archaeologists who conducted the surveys and excavations, as well as their published reports and unpublished data. The opportunity to pull together all of this information into a comprehensive regional study is the culmination of a lifetime of observation.

I would like to thank Lawrence E. Stager and Daniel M. Master for providing us with the opportunity to conduct this study. Thanks are also due to Alon Shavit, who generously gave his time to discuss aspects of his survey of the southern coastal plain and provided a copy of his unpublished Ph.D. dissertation, and to Benjamin Felker and Elise Jakoby Laugier for producing the maps.

Above all, this work is a tribute to the long line of travelers and researchers that worked in the area, starting in the nineteenth century: from Victor Guérin, the team who worked on the Survey of Western Palestine, and British surveyors and mapmakers through to the Archaeological Survey of Israel teams, Hütteroth and Abdulfattah, and countless others that we do not have space to mention here. Without the accumulation of their knowledge, the present study would in no way be possible.

Yaakov Huster
Ashkelon, Israel   February 2015

ABBREVIATIONS

AmAnt	*American Antiquity*
ANET³	*Ancient Near Eastern Texts Relating to the Old Testament,* 3d ed. [= Pritchard 1969]
Ashkelon 1	*Ashkelon,* vol. 1, *Introduction and Overview (1985–2006)* [= Stager, Schloen, and Master 2008]
Ashkelon 2	*Ashkelon,* vol. 2, *Imported Pottery of the Roman and Late Roman Periods* [= Johnson 2008]
Ashkelon 3	*Ashkelon,* vol. 3, *The Seventh Century B.C.* [= Stager, Master, and Schloen 2011]
Ashkelon 4	*Ashkelon,* vol. 4, *The Iron Age Figurines of Ashkelon and Philistia* [= Press 2012]
BA	*Biblical Archaeologist*
BARIS	British Archaeological Reports, International Series
BASOR	*Bulletin of the American Schools of Oriental Research*
CA	*Current Anthropology*
CCEM	Contributions to the Chronology of the Eastern Mediterranean
EA	el-Amarna text [as numbered in Knudtzon 1915]
EB	Early Bronze Age
EI	*Eretz-Israel*
ESI	*Excavations and Surveys in Israel*
HA	*Hadashot Arkheologiyot*
HA-ESI	*Hadashot Arkheologiyot-Excavations and Surveys in Israel*
IAA	Israel Antiquities Authority
IEJ	*Israel Exploration Journal*
JAS	*Journal of Archaeological Science*
JEA	*Journal of Egyptian Archaeology*
JESHO	*Journal of the Economic and Social History of the Orient*
JFA	*Journal of Field Archaeology*
LB	Late Bronze Age
MB	Middle Bronze Age
NEAEHL	*New Encyclopedia of Archaeological Excavations in the Holy Land*
NIG	New Israel Grid
OIG	Old Israel Grid
PEFQS	*Palestine Exploration Fund Quarterly Statement*
PEQ	*Palestine Exploration Quarterly* [continues *PEFQS*]
QDAP	*Quarterly of the Department of Antiquities in Palestine*
TA	*Tel Aviv*
UF	*Ugarit-Forschungen*
ZAW	*Zeitschrift für die alttestamentliche Wissenschaft*
ZDPV	*Zeitschrift des Deutschen Palästina-Vereins*

LIST OF TABLES

1.1 Sites and Non-Sites in Surveys of the Ashkelon Region and Its Vicinity   11

2.1 Late Bronze Age and Iron Age I Sites in the Ashkelon Region, within a radius of c. 18 km   28

2.2 Winepresses in the Ashkelon Region   44

2.3 Byzantine Churches in the Ashkelon Region   49

2.4 Number of Early Islamic Sites in the Surveyed Maps   55

2.5 Crusader Villages and Their Identifications with Archaeological Sites   60

2.6 Number of Sites from the Medieval Period   61

2.7 Sheikh Tombs in the Ashkelon Region   64

2.8 Location of Coastal *Welis* and Umayyad/Abbasid *Ribāṭs*   67

2.9 Table of All Survey Sites   69

1. INTRODUCTION

by Yaakov Huster

THE maritime networks of Tel Ashkelon extended across the ancient Mediterranean,
reaching peoples and markets from Cyprus to
Spain. However, Tel Ashkelon's hinterland, a region extending some 15–20 km inland from the
site, has received little attention. This volume attempts to fill that lacuna by describing the region
of Ashkelon across its entire premodern history of
human occupation.

Previous Research

The Ashkelon region, like the rest of Israel, has been
extensively surveyed since the nineteenth century
(for a brief survey, see Schloen in *Ashkelon 1*, pp.
143–52). At that time, most interest in the region
was due to its role in the Bible and, secondarily,
its historical role in the Crusades (Rey 1871; also
1862). Of the various early explorers and travelers,
the most systematic was Victor Guérin, who conducted two detailed surveys of Tel Ashkelon and
its vicinity (1857; 1869); his work approached that
of a scientific survey. Despite this early interest,
however, detailed survey work for both the identification of archaeological sites and the production
of a high-quality, accurate map of the country did
not take place until the 1870s when work began
on the Survey of Western Palestine under Claude
Conder and Horatio Kitchener (1881–83). While
the PEF's conduct of this survey was driven by
biblical interest, its ultimate sponsorship and the
production of the map itself—by the Ordnance
Survey of the UK—was not for biblical but for
military reasons (Goren 2002).

With World War I, the recognition came that the
Survey of Western Palestine map—while highly
accurate compared to other nineteenth-century
maps—did not meet current standards or needs
(i.e., it was not accurate enough for directing artillery). Although the British army had mapped large
parts of the country during the war (see Collier and
Inkpen 2001), the Mandate began a comprehensive
topographic survey of the country in the 1920s,
leading to a highly accurate series of map sheets
produced from the 1930s by the Survey of Palestine
(printed in both 1:20,000 and 1:100,000 scales; see
Gavish 2005). Among the features noted on these

maps were archaeological sites (listed as "ruin,"
cistern, well, etc.), including many not previously
noted by Conder and Kitchener or other surveyors
and explorers.

A strictly archaeological survey of the country, meanwhile, was planned and started in the
mid-1930s by P. L. O. Guy, then Director of the
British School of Archaeology in Jerusalem (Guy
1937; 1938; Green 2009:176–79). This survey
used the new British maps—not the large-scale
1:20,000 map sheets, however, but the smaller-
scale 1:100,000 sheets (contra Green 2009:177,
who mistakenly states that Guy used the Survey
of Western Palestine map sheets). Guy himself began a survey on map sheet 7, covering the coastal
plain from Tel Aviv south—but only as far as the
region of Ashdod. Unfortunately, due to lack of
funds and manpower, and increasing disturbances
caused by the Arab Revolt, this survey was sus-
pended in 1938 before being extended farther
south toward Ashkelon.

The newly established state of Israel expressed
renewed interest in a systematic archaeological
survey of the country. Therefore, it organized the
Archaeological Survey of Israel in 1964 (Dagan
n.d.). This survey followed the British large-scale
1:20,000 map sheets. The modern city of Ashkelon
itself was covered by four of these 10 x 10 km
maps: Ascalon (2 sheets: Sheets 10-11 and 10-12),
Hamame (Sheet 11-12), and El Majdal (Sheet 11-
11). Each of these map sheets was surveyed and
published by the Archaeological Survey. A team
under Ariel Berman surveyed Ascalon Sheet
10-11 (Map 91 of the Archaeological Survey,
called Ziqim), Ascalon Sheet 10-12 (Map 87,
Nizzanim West), and Hamame Sheet 11-12 (Map
88, Nizzanim East) between 1971 and 1973; the
publications of these survey maps (Berman,
Stark, and Barda 2004; Berman and Barda 2005)
are revised versions of his work, as these areas
were resurveyed under Leticia Barda in the 1990s.
The El Majdal sheet (Map 92, Ashkelon) was surveyed by Mitchell Allen in the Ashkelon Regional
Archaeological Survey between 1986 and 1990
(Allen 1997; *Ashkelon 1*, pp. 21–66). An additional
survey was conducted by Alon Shavit (from 1994
to 1998) of the southern coastal plain of Israel,

including the Ashkelon region (Shavit 2003; 2008); Shavit's survey, however, focused only on sites inhabited in the Iron Age II.

The Ashkelon region has been extensively excavated over the last hundred years. Among tell sites, the major focus has been Tel Ashkelon itself (for a brief summary, see Schloen in *Ashkelon 1*, pp. 153–64). Tel Ashkelon was first excavated by the Palestine Exploration Fund under John Garstang and William J. Phythian-Adams between 1920 and 1922 (Garstang 1921a; 1921b; 1922; 1924; Phythian-Adams 1921; 1923). The major result of these excavations was the exposure of a major public building from the Roman and Byzantine periods in the center of the ancient city, while a series of probes and sections revealed the occupational history of the site along the sea cliff and the site's western side. Since 1985, the Leon Levy Expedition to Ashkelon (directed first by Lawrence E. Stager, now joined by Daniel M. Master) has more systematically and broadly exposed the occupational sequence, from Middle Bronze (with occasional Early Bronze pottery and stratigraphic units, as well as Chalcolithic pottery) to Crusader (see *Ashkelon 1*).

Beyond Tel Ashkelon, however, there has been little excavation of large mounded sites (in part due to the relative absence of such sites in the area; note that we are not counting Tel Ashdod here as part of the area of interest). The only example of any systematic (non-salvage) work has been at Tel Poran (Gophna 1977; 1992b); salvage work, meanwhile, has been conducted at Netiv Ha-ᶜAsara (Yasur-Landau and Shavit 1999; Shavit and Yasur-Landau 2005) and Khirbet Bakkita (see Berman, Stark, and Barda 2004). A number of (generally small-scale) excavations of non-tell sites have also been conducted in the region, mostly by the Mandatory Department of Antiquities, the Israel Department of Antiquities and Museums, and the latter's successor, the Israel Antiquities Authority (IAA). In particular, in the last 15 years the IAA has conducted a series of salvage digs in and around the modern city of Ashkelon.

Goals and Methods

The present study has two basic goals:

1. To investigate the general settlement patterns in the Ashkelon region—period by period—and attempt to understand how and why these patterns changed over time.

2. To provide information on the relationship between the central site of the region, Tel Ashkelon, and the sites that constitute its hinterland.

Our main tools will necessarily be archaeological surface surveys, especially those of the Archaeological Survey of Israel (but also Shavit's survey). These surveys consisted (for Allen at least!) of a full-coverage site-based surface survey (with team members typically walking 30–40 meters apart) (Allen in *Ashkelon 1*, p. 24). Given this type of survey and the techniques used by the surveyors, the collected data cover the entire area and do not suffer from sample bias—either toward particular subsets of the area or types of sites.

Nevertheless, surface survey via fieldwalking ("pedestrian techniques" after Schiffer, Sullivan, and Klinger 1978), as with any method, has its own set of limitations: the complex nature of the relationship between surface and subsurface materials; overrepresentation of larger materials on the surface; overrepresentation of later periods on the surface, with corresponding underrepresentation of earlier periods; and problems of visibility (see Schiffer, Sullivan, and Klinger 1978; Cherry 1983; Leibner 2009:84; Snodgrass 1987:101–2). As a result, some archaeologists have come to see this technique in general as unreliable (cf. Snodgrass 1987:102). A particularly relevant situation concerning the effects of *sebakh*—the decomposed organic material that forms the ancient mounds—on site survey in Egypt (see below) caused Bailey (1999) to question the value of fieldwalking in Egypt.

Therefore, for our project we are fortunate to have, in addition to extensive survey data, results from a large series of salvage excavations conducted in and around the modern city of Ashkelon, particularly in the last 15 years. These excavations are invaluable for exposing "windows" into the occupational history of the region, allowing us to test the results of systematic surface survey. In addition, one of the major benefits of our study is, therefore, a new synthesis of data: a combination of excavation and survey data, including the results of multiple excavations and multiple surveys, as well as inspection work, which has not always been reported or registered. Moreover, for each dataset we cover a larger region than that in one of the 100-square-kilometer survey maps, thereby presenting a more regional outlook than most survey work. This unprecedented integration of data sources will also allow us to update and correct previous work.

Size of the Study Area

This study, as mentioned above, covers the area in the Archaeological Survey of Israel map sheets 87, 88, 91, and 92. The general size of the study area is related in part to models of site systems and the relationship between their sizes and transport costs and travel times. How large can the settlement system of a site be if it is to maintain continual contact for political and economic purposes? Thus Ehud Weiss, Mordechai Kislev, and Yael Maher-Slansky (2008:606–7; see also Weiss and Kislev 2004:11), in their analysis of ancient Ashkelon's food supply sources, suggest that the agricultural hinterland of Ashkelon would have formed a radius of approximately 7 km. This estimate is based on Michael Chisholm's (1968) study of rural settlement. In fact, Chisholm's analysis (1968:131) suggests 7 km as an approximate distance between settlements, meaning that the maximum radius of a town's fields would have been around 3–4 km, while the diameter of the hinterland would have been approximately 7 km. Meanwhile, Colin Renfrew's "Early State Module" suggested a distance of approximately 40 km between centers, resulting in a radius of about 20 km for the administrative boundary of the center, although Renfrew noted that environmental and social factors could lead to a range in the distance between centers of 20 to 100 km (1975:14). Similarly, Gregory Johnson's work on the Uruk administration in Iran (based on settlement density around major sites) suggests a distance of a half-day's journey—approximately 20 km in the pre-modern Near East—between sites and the main city that controlled them (1987:115–16). This is the figure used by Shavit (2008:138):

> Satellite sites had to be within a half-day walking distance from central sites, to allow village residents to make their way to and from the central site in a day. Therefore, the distance between them could not exceed 10–15 km. These conditions are necessary for sustaining continuous commercial relations between a central settlement and the surrounding villages.

The applicability of these studies to the Ashkelon region may be limited: After all, Tel Ashkelon was not a small farming village but a large international port, with an estimated population in various periods (see, e.g., *Ashkelon 1*, pp. 3–4) much greater than that of a typical rural settlement (following

discussion in Bunce 1982:13). However, while these studies may not be useful for exact definitions of a hinterland (agricultural or otherwise), we may use them to provide a general approximation; thus our study should cover the area in a 10–20 km radius from Tel Ashkelon. In fact, the evidence suggests that, at least at certain points in the region's history, this radius approximates or even overestimates the extent of Ashkelon's hinterland. For example, Tel Ashdod, on the edge of Map 88 (Nizzanim East) and at a distance of approximately 15 km from Tel Ashkelon, was not strictly a part of the Ashkelon sphere but a major site in its own right. Similarly, there is evidence that the site of Netiv Ha-ᶜAsara, roughly 10 km south of Tel Ashkelon, may have belonged to the sphere of Gaza and not of Ashkelon (see discussion in chapter 2).

As a result, we have adopted a 15 km radius from Tel Ashkelon to represent the hinterland of ancient Ashkelon. In order to best approximate this radius, we have included survey data from four of the Archaeological Survey of Israel map sheets: Maps 87 (Nizzanim West), 88 (Nizzanim East), 91 (Ziqim), and 92 (Ashkelon). In addition,

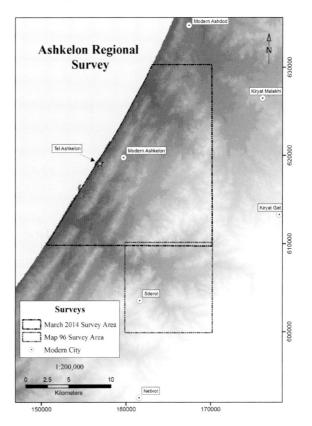

Figure 1.1. Map of Ashkelon Regional Survey, with coordinates in NIG.

reference will be made periodically to neighboring map sheets, in particular Map 96—immediately to the south of Map 92—published as chapter 5 of this volume. Tel Ashkelon falls near the boundary of Maps 87 and 91, although the exact distance of the edge of the study area from the tell varies (as the shape is not circular but rectangular); also, note that Ziqim and especially Nizzanim West largely fall over the water, and so the area is not a full 20 x 20 km square. This layout also allows us to use both the Berman and the Allen surveys and, therefore, to assess their conclusions more completely.

Organization of the Study

The study itself consists of two main sections. In the first, we present a survey of settlement patterns in the Ashkelon region by period. This discussion follows the general format of the archaeological overviews in the Archaeological Survey of Israel map sheet publications, although it is more extensive in length and covers a larger area than a single 10 x 10 km map sheet. The second section includes a more diachronic analysis of settlement patterns. In the discussion, we try to identify longer-term trends (following the concept of *la longue durée*) in settlement patterns, considering environmental and economic factors among others. We also try to place the Ashkelon region within its wider context in Palestine in order to determine whether the Tel Ashkelon system is typical of larger patterns in the country or is a special case.

The settlement pattern survey by period uses, for the most part, the nomenclature of the Archaeological Survey of Israel, including the survey work of Mitchell Allen in Map 92. The periods, then, are the following:

- Paleolithic (encompassing the Lower Paleolithic to the Epipaleolithic)
- Neolithic
- Chalcolithic to Early Bronze (EB) (treated together)
- Middle Bronze (MB)
- Late Bronze (LB)
- Iron Age (Iron I and II treated together)
- Persian and Hellenistic (treated together, as Hellenistic sites appear to be a continuation of the Persian period sites)
- Roman (Early Roman [ER] and Late Roman [LR])
- Byzantine

- Early Islamic
- Medieval
- Ottoman

Two periods require special comment. In the literature there is often confusion in the terms "Late Roman" and "Byzantine," resulting from different usages. In typical usage, Late Roman is seen as synonymous with Byzantine and used to cover the third or fourth to early seventh centuries A.D. (see, e.g., *Ashkelon 2*, p. 463; Allen in *Ashkelon 1*, esp. Fig. 3.21). Among Israeli archaeologists, however, Late Roman and Byzantine are usually treated as distinct periods. Our usage follows that of the *NEAEHL* (Stern 1993:1529), which is also that generally in use in the Archaeological Survey of Israel (e.g., Berman and Barda 2005; Berman, Stark, and Barda 2004). Thus, in the current study, the Roman period is divided into Early Roman (first century B.C. to first century A.D.) and Late Roman (second to third centuries A.D.). The Byzantine period, meanwhile, covers the fourth through early seventh centuries. In our period by period survey, the description of the Byzantine period—despite the fact that this period marks, by far, the premodern height of settlement in the region—will be relatively brief. There has been an abundant discussion of this period in previous studies, and we will, as a result, make only a brief reference to earlier work.

The second period that needs elaboration is "medieval." This is the term we are using (like M. Allen) to cover both the Crusader and Mamluk periods. Crusader and Mamluk pottery often poses a problem of differentiation; for any attempt at finer distinctions we will rely on historical sources.

Sites and Non-Sites

One important topic directly related to the method of the current study is the existence of a number of questionable sites in the study area. These sites, localized in the sand dunes along the coast, consist almost entirely of artifact scatters, especially pottery, with little or no evidence of structures or building stones. Both Berman and Allen (see Allen in *Ashkelon 1*, pp. 25, 33–34) were reluctant to characterize these scatters as actual sites. Nevertheless, in the final publication of the Nizzanim West, Nizzanim East, and Ziqim survey maps (Maps 87, 88, and 91; Berman and Barda 2005; Berman, Stark, and Barda 2004), they are

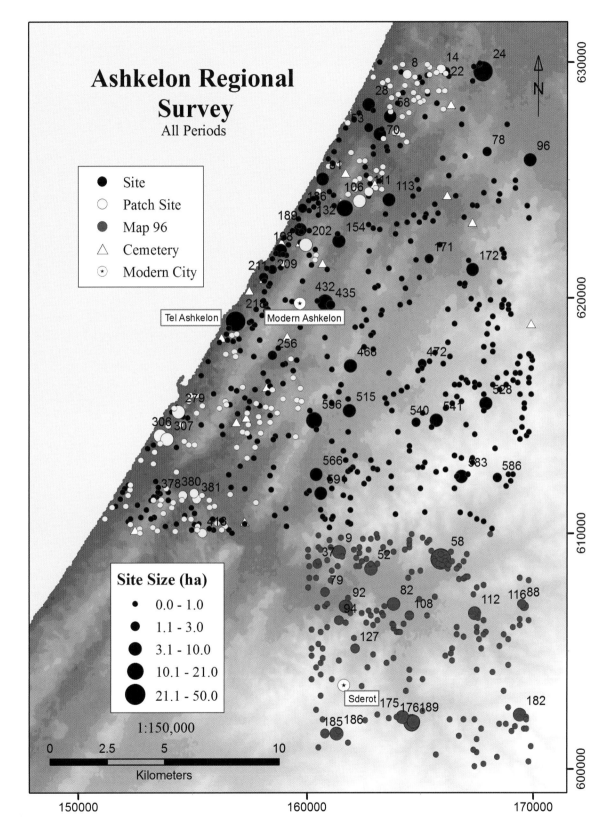

Figure 1.2. Map of Ashkelon Regional Survey with all periods shown, with coordinates in NIG.

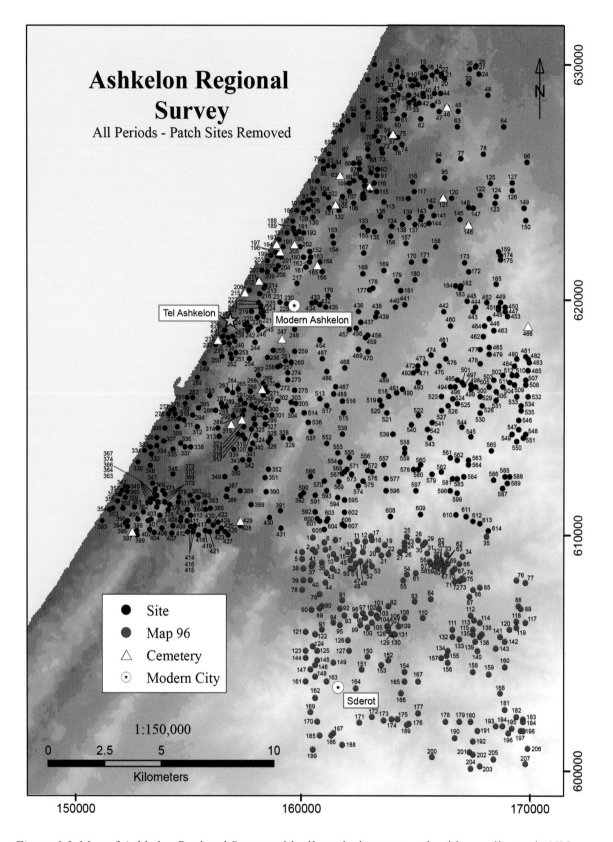

Figure 1.3. Map of Ashkelon Regional Survey with all patch sites removed, with coordinates in NIG.

not differentiated from other sites. Given that the classification of these scatters will greatly affect any regional study in the coastal plain, an extended discussion is in order here.

When Berman directed his surveys from 1971 to 1973, large parts of Nizzanim West and Ziqim were covered by sand dunes. The very recent age of the dunes was deduced from the Byzantine and Early Islamic finds on the soil below the sand (Issar 1968:25; Issar and Zohar 2007:15–16). Notably, many of Berman's sites were found in depressions between the dunes. Most of these sites consisted chiefly of pottery scatters from various periods and were almost devoid of structural remains. Berman listed these sites as "patches" of pottery in his original manuscript, as well as in his communication with Mitchell Allen (*Ashkelon 1*, p. 25). Berman himself hesitated to assert that these "patches" were in fact sites. However, in the final publication of both maps, after Berman's sites had been resurveyed by teams in the 1990s to confirm the original data (mainly the location of the sites but also the nature of their remains), Berman's doubts were not clearly reflected. Instead, the "patches" are numbered and registered together with the other sites in Nizzanim West and Ziqim. We believe, however, that Berman's original determination was correct: Many of these "patches" were not true sites, and the regional analysis therefore needs to be adjusted to reflect this.

Berman's descriptions of several of the "patches," particularly as they appear in the final publication of Map 91 (Ziqim), are quite consistent:

> Scatter of potsherds and fragments of glass vessels (c.5 dunams), in long valley between sandy hills. At the site are ruinous structures, built a few generations ago, surrounded by agricultural plots. Finds: Roman, Mamluk and Ottoman pottery; a coin, 14th century C.E., and four perforated silver coins from the late Ottoman period. (Berman, Stark, and Barda 2004 [Site 78. Holot Ashkelon, coordinates 15955-61565])

> Ruins of a structure built a few generations ago on low sandy spur. Ancient building stones, some of them dressed, and ancient architectural elements, were observed in the walls of the structure and in the debris. Surrounding the remains—agricultural terraces and stone clearance piles. Pottery: Iron, Roman, Byzantine, and Ottoman. (Berman, Stark, and Barda 2004 [Site 115. Holot Ziqim, coordinates 15775-61365])

> Ruins of a structure (c. 10 x 35 m) built during the last few generations, on moderate sandy slope, NE of Nahal Shiqma. In the courtyard is a well. Scattered on the sand are building stones and potsherds (c. 1 dunam). Pottery: Iron II, Byzantine, Early Islamic, Mamluk, and Ottoman. (Berman, Stark, and Barda 2004 [Site 158. Holot Karmiyya, coordinates 15667-61165])

From these descriptions, the basic features of Berman's "patches" can be detailed as follows: They consist primarily of artifact scatters located among the sand dunes. These scatters may be associated with terraces or other traces of agriculture, as well as with recent buildings (other descriptions of "patches," not reproduced here, make no mention of recent structures); otherwise structural remains are generally absent. Sherds from various periods are most common, but finds also include small metal objects, coins, tesserae, and glass. The late Ottoman period is particularly well represented by pottery, clay pipes, and coins.

The association of these "patches" with agricultural traces within the sand dunes, sometimes adjacent to recent (late Ottoman or Mandatory) buildings, is remarkably closely paralleled by Charles Warren's description a century earlier of fruit trees within the sand dunes of the southern coastal plain:

> It is curious in traversing these sand hills to come upon the site of some orchard which has been covered perhaps for hundreds of years. You suddenly come upon a sort of crater in the sand, 40ft. deep, at the bottom of which flourishes an apple tree; then you come upon a fig tree growing in the same manner, and lastly upon a little patch of ground, quite below the level of the sand, with a house attached; but even this patch of ground has several feet of sand over it. The husbandman's chief duty appears to consist in dragging up the sand in baskets from the bottom of the craters to the surface. The trees growing in these little hollows are very fruitful, and no wonder, for they have no wind, plenty of sun, and good moist earth to grow in; the superincumbent sand, being a non-conductor, prevents evaporation from the soil below and keeps it moist through the summer. (Warren 1871:84)

Both Berman and Warren's accounts, in turn, are excellent illustrations of a phenomenon known as *mawasi* agriculture. In this system of agriculture—or, more properly, horticulture—either

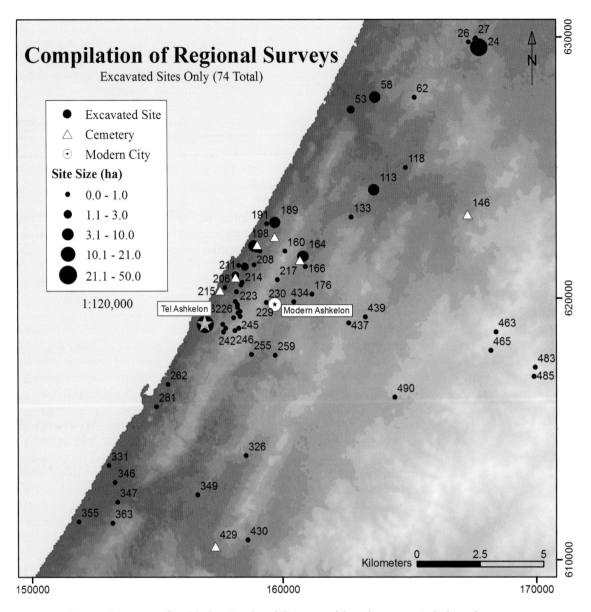

Figure 1.4. Map of Ashkelon Regional Survey with only excavated sites shown,
with coordinates in NIG.

natural or man-made depressions between sandy hills are used for growing crops, fruit trees in particular (see Tsoar 2000:193; Pye and Tsoar 2009:356). While nowadays irrigation and fertilization are most commonly practiced in the southern coastal plain, during the late Ottoman and Mandatory periods the *mawasi* fields reached from the southern Gaza strip to the north of Yavneh on a relatively narrow strip running parallel to the sea. (In fact, they probably extended well north of modern Tel Aviv: Evidence exists for the practice of this system hundreds of years

ago in the Sharon plain, in the vicinity of Caesarea [Porat 1975].) *Mawasi* agriculture was developed to exploit the existence of a high aquifer along the seashore and to make use of every available patch of sandy ground. Mandatory maps and especially later, more accurate Israeli maps of the southern coastal plain are dotted with graphic representations of these fields, most of them vineyards. The 1948 war and the driving out of the population of the Arab villages put an end to this traditional system throughout the territory held by the State of Israel. It continued, however, to be practiced in the

Gaza Strip; moreover, many of the now-defunct *mawasi* fields in Israel are still visible today.[1]

Berman's descriptions of sherd and other artifact scatters have added to our knowledge of *mawasi* agriculture. These scatters, in our opinion, are the remains of the manuring of the *mawasi* fields, a process during which fertilizer was purposely brought from tell sites. In the *mawasi* system, fertilizer such as animal manure was added to the soil which contained naturally high levels of nitrogen and phosphorus because of the fresh water supply (Pye and Tsoar 2009:356). Shimon Gibson (1995:83–84) emphasizes that during the Ottoman period sown fields were very rarely manured; following George Post (1891:116), he states that manure was mainly kept for use in vegetable gardens and orchards. Manuring, then, would have been widely practiced in the *mawasi* system of the coastal plain, which was used specifically to grow vegetables and fruit trees (Pye and Tsoar 2009:356). Thus travelers' accounts of fields surrounding Tel Ashkelon from the nineteenth century frequently note the predominance of orchards, vineyards, and vegetable gardens (e.g., Porter 1858:267–69; Guérin 1857:83; Guérin 1869:134–35; Conder and Kitchener 1883:237).

The use of organic material taken from archaeological sites as fertilizer is seen in a variety of regions throughout the Mediterranean and Middle East (e.g., Crete, mainland Greece, Egypt, and Iraq) and throughout a range of periods (from at least the third millennium B.C. to the twentieth century A.D.; see, e.g., Wilkinson 1982; 1989; Bintliff and Snodgrass 1988; Bailey 1999; Bull, Betancourt, and Evershed 2001). In Egypt, the use of *sebakh* as fertilizer (and for the manufacture of gunpowder) over many generations caused the destruction of ancient cities, villages, and cemeteries (Bailey 1999). In 1990, Huster witnessed the manuring of fields north of the city of Gaza with a sort of dark soil, very rich in organic material, containing many small sherds, probably brought from a tell. The soil was spread on only part of

the field.[2] Avner Raban described a similar situation at Tel Sham and Hurvat Tzror in the Jezreel Valley: "Surveyors found some of the sites to be almost totally wiped out either from land reclamation or because the tel's soil had been carried away for fertilizer in nearby fields" (Raban 1991:19, also 21–22). Shimon Gibson (1995:311), who conducted a landscape archaeology project at Sataf, near Jerusalem, also noted "evidence proving that during the Mamluk and Ottoman periods many of the terraces had been artificially elevated with khirbet soils (organic soils containing potsherds) brought from ruins of ancient settlements located in the vicinity."

The studies cited above suggest manuring as an explanation for low-density sherd carpeting of the entire landscape (cf. Allen in *Ashkelon 1*, p. 25). In the case of the southern coastal plain dunes, however, the situation is quite different: Here, instead of a light scattering over the entire landscape, there are higher-density clusters of artifacts. We believe that difference is because of the unique characteristics of *mawasi* agriculture. It seems that in the southern coastal plain the manuring of fields was concentrated in relatively small areas ("patches") between the dunes, likely because of the composition of the soil below them. While the soil contains *hamra* in certain places, it mainly consists of loam and (older) sand. These components have a very low percentage of organic material, although some nutrients are provided by the fresh water supply (see Pye and Tsoar 2009:356). East of the dune belt, where the land is composed of terrestrial source deposits (meaning a mixture of all the soils of the region), the soil contains mainly redeposited loess; this is the "fat" land, used primarily for grain crops.[3] Here, after crops were harvested, flocks of sheep and goats and herds of cattle dropped dung while they grazed. It is not surprising, then, that the number of sherds between sites east of the dune belt was much lower: The testing of non-site artifact density by Mitchell Allen (*Ashkelon 1*, p. 25) in the area of Map 92 also revealed places entirely devoid of pottery. However, while Allen acknowledged the use of organic soil

---

[1] The *mawasi* fields have often been misunderstood by recent observers and taken for the remains of ancient fields. This seems to be the case with Warren's description above; compare Weiss, Kislev, and Maher-Slasky 2008:606: "Relatively recent sand dunes now cover these ancient fields, so it is impossible to locate them precisely. However, scattered old vines, apparently rooted in fertile soil underneath the sand and still producing fleshy grapes, are visible in the sand-covered depressions"; see also Weiss and Kislev 2004:11.

[2] Manuring fields with soil brought from ancient mounds was not the only agent reason why sherds were scattered over wide areas. In the same year, a small tell named el Fuhari in the south of the Gaza Strip vanished almost completely. Its soil was used to pave a road, several kilometers long, on sand dunes.

[3] For more information on "zoning" for ecological and other reasons in antiquity, see Faust and Weiss 2005.

from tells to fertilize agricultural land and recognized it as a phenomenon of the coastal plain of Palestine, he did not identify any distinctions in this activity between the dune belt and the land to the east.

A more detailed analysis of Berman's "patches" (than provided above) reveals the following characteristics:

- Sites are located in low areas within the dunes.
- Their size varies from a few square meters to several thousand square meters.
- They are almost devoid of structural remains, although remains of recent structures are occasionally found.
- The most common finds are sherds from various periods; small metal objects, coins, tesserae, and glass have also been found.
- The late Ottoman period is particularly well represented, with finds including pottery, clay pipes, and coins.
- Sherd size is very small (an average of 5–6 cm); larger sherds were apparently left at the tell site.
- Finds have been polished by sand and wind.
- The depth of the remains does not exceed 10–15 cm.

These features permit us to identify "patches" of pottery in the sand dunes and to distinguish them from real sites. In addition, recent work in the city of Ashkelon has allowed this proposed distinction to be tested. While development works and sand quarrying have uncovered both known and unknown real sites, they have also revealed additional "patches" covered by the shifting sand dunes over the last few decades.

It is clear, then, that a large number of these scatters in the sand dunes were misidentified as ancient sites in the published survey maps. As a result, the total number of sites in Nizzanim West and Ziqim needs to be reduced. For our analysis, it is essential to be able to identify sites properly so that we can remove non-sites from consideration. Unfortunately, reevaluating the data by conducting a new ground survey is not feasible. The shifting of sand dunes over the four decades since Berman's surveys has made it impossible to locate many of his sites; this difficulty was already noted in the 1980s and 1990s when Allen and Barda tried to revisit Berman's sites (*Ashkelon 1*, p. 25). It is therefore necessary to develop a system to calibrate the existing data as accurately as possible. While the above list of features of Berman's "patches" serves as a basic guideline, many of these characteristics

are not consistently noted in the site descriptions. It appears that the best formal yardstick at our disposal is the density of stone observed at the sites covered by the survey.

This method of testing stone density can be employed on sites that are still visible (north of Ashkelon, in a Nature Reserve) and—even more significantly—on destroyed or covered sites by using the files, records, and descriptions of the surveys. At the same time, this method should be employed cautiously since, as noted above, several "patches" contain structural remains from recent generations, which incorporate some ancient architectural elements. In the archaeological overview of the Map of Ziqim (Map 91), the total number of sites by period are given alongside the proportion of sites with building remains (see table 1.1). In general, only one-quarter to one-third of sites had structural remains, while the rest contained only artifact scatters. Although the archaeological overview of the Nizzanim West and East maps (Maps 87 and 88) does not provide the proportion of sites with building remains, it supplies information that indicates a similar pattern. Our analysis of the Iron Age II, Persian, Hellenistic, and Roman period site descriptions for each map reveals the same picture. The results are given in table 1.1: The total number of sites for each period is provided, along with the number of sites containing structural remains (given in parentheses). In order to compare these four consecutive periods in Berman's Ziqim and Nizzanim maps with an area of similar size to the east (i.e., outside of the coastal dune belt), the table also supplies the results of the surveys of the Maps of Ashkelon (92) and Sderot (96).[4]

In the table we have also provided the total number of Iron II sites listed by Shavit (2003) in the results of his survey, for each corresponding Archaeological Survey of Israel map area. Shavit's survey was based on his own conception of site definition and therefore merits brief discussion.

---

[4] Note that Allen, in his publication of Map 92 (Ashkelon), provides a number of definite sites as well as a number of possible sites for each period (*Ashkelon 1*, p. 21, table 2). As Allen notes (*Ashkelon 1*, p. 26), the listing of possible sites indicates only a tentative suggestion in an attempt to be inclusive; thus the identification of possible sites is often based on the presence of only one or two sherds collected in the survey. In addition, Huster—in revisiting the sites in part of Allen's map—did not identify pre-Roman sherds at any of these possible sites. As a result, we believe that the minimum number of sites in these periods is the more accurate number and the number we have chosen to use in table 1.1.

Table 1.1: Sites and Non-Sites in Surveys of the Ashkelon Region and Its Vicinity

Period	Map 91 Ziqim (Berman and Barda 2004) c. 60 km²	Map 91 Ziqim (Shavit 2003)	Map 88 Nizzanim (Berman, Stark, and Barda 2005) c. 65 km²	Map 88 Nizzanim (Shavit 2003)	Map 92 Ashkelon (Allen 2008) 100 km²	Map 92 Ashkelon (Shavit 2003)	Map 96 Sderot (Huster this volume) 100 km²	Map 96 Sderot (Shavit 2003)
Iron II	40 (10)*	10**	26 (10)	10	4	1	3	1
Persian	35 (12)		33 (14)		10		3	
Hellenistic	46 (16)		30 (14)		8		7	
Roman	97		150		41		44	

* The archaeological overview of the Iron Age II sites at Ziqim emphasized that building remains were observed at only one-fourth of the sites, meaning 10 sites out of 40. Our count reveals more than 10. The above numbers in parentheses indicate the sites with structural remains.

** Four more sites were discerned outside of but close to the southern border of the Map of Ziqim.

The number of Iron Age II sites in the table is taken from Shavit's map of Iron II sites (Shavit 2003:154). In Shavit's study, sites with unclear Iron II presence were counted as settlements with an area of one dunam (1000 square meters) in order not to skew his demographic assessments. Shavit recognized that this approach might alter the count of small villages in the surveyed regions, meaning that the actual number of sites would be even lower. On the other hand, he emphasized that, in certain areas, geological and environmental processes could have covered small sites, thereby preventing their location by survey. This is true mainly of the sand dunes along the Mediterranean seashore. Since the quantity of sites listed in the uncertain Iron II category is very low, a certain statistical balance is created. In our opinion, then, his survey generally reflects the true number of sites from this period. It is therefore noteworthy that, as indicated in the table, Shavit's totals largely confirm our own use of structural remains as a baseline criterion for identifying actual sites in the sand dunes.

Two other aspects of the table are worthy of note. First the number of archaeological sites ascribed to the Roman period in Berman's maps of Ziqim and Nizzanim is much larger than the number of sites from this period in the neighboring areas of Ashkelon and Sderot. This fact again suggests that non-sites have been improperly reported and registered for Ziqim and Nizzanim. Second, it is also important to note that the total area of the Maps of Ziqim and Nizzanim is much smaller than the area of the Maps of Ashkelon and Sderot, further emphasizing the anomaly of high site counts in Ziqim and Nizzanim.

Conclusion

The existence of a high sweet water aquifer on a northeast-southwest strip parallel to the coast is an insufficient explanation for such a dense concentration of sites in a small area. Very similar hydrological conditions prevailed in areas just to the east, in the wide flood plains of Nahal Evtah in the north, and of Nahal Shiqma in the south. Also, the suggestion that these sites were apparently close to the "Way of the Sea" and trade routes (Berman and Barda 2005:x) does not provide a satisfactory explanation for the high density of sites north and south of Ashkelon. Furthermore, Allen (*Ashkelon 1*, p. 37) has already noted that, within the area of the surveyed Map of Nizzanim, there are surprisingly few sites along the assumed route of the main north-south road during the Bronze and Iron Ages. Our conclusion, then, is that the real site distribution is correctly represented in the area located east of the sand belt region, while the number of sites within the sand dunes should be drastically reduced, according to the results presented in table 1.1.

2. Survey of Settlement Patterns by Period

by Yaakov Huster

The region around Ashkelon is a palimpsest of human activity over many millennia. From the Paleolithic through the Mamluk period, the people lived along the same coast and among the same dunes but exploited the landscape in diverse ways. This summary attempts to describe some of the distinctive ways in which people related to their landscape through a focus on the size, placement, and function of settlements around Ashkelon over time.

Paleolithic

One of the first prehistoric investigations in the southern coastal plain was carried out during the First World War, near the Arab village of Huleiqat, located c. 12 km southeast of Ashkelon. In 1917, Josef Bayer, an Austrian officer serving in the Turkish army and stationed in the area, had the opportunity to collect and study hundreds of stone tools (Bayer 1919:168; Antl-Weiser 2007). Based on Bayer's notes, it appears that the lithics do not derive from a single site but rather were collected from a number of findspots over a wide area, precisely the same method employed by later surveyors. Bayer used this assemblage of tools to define a new "Askalonian" culture, seen by him as a transition between the Lower Paleolithic and the Neolithic (Bayer 1919:171–72; Antl-Weiser 2007:145). Alfred Rust, who visited Huleiqat in 1931, found that Bayer's assumptions derived from the mixing of two flint industries, the Late Acheulean from the Lower Paleolithic period and the Microlithic from the Epipaleolithic period (which Rust calls Mesolithic, 1936:12–15).

Northwest of Huleiqat, on the same *kurkar* ridge, and also farther to the east, on the Negba-Sde Yoav *hamra* outcrops, more tools (235 items), were collected and studied by Ytzchak Eshel (unpublished 1973 seminar paper [in Hebrew]: Negba Collection—Flint Tools from the Lower Paleolithic). This study extended the survey area and confirmed that Lower Paleolithic flint implements in this region were clearly connected to the *hamra* deposits.

Most recently, Mitchell Allen surveyed the region and collected the remaining known flint implements; by this time, however, only a small

number of mostly undiagnostic flints remained. Most of Map 92's (Ashkelon) prehistoric sites (*Ashkelon 1*, p. 29, fig. 3.7) are located in exactly the same area surveyed previously by Bayer and Rust. Allen's Paleolithic flint collections were too small to enable him to determine the exact phases represented at his findspots, their identification instead being presented as questionable. Fortunately, Bayer and Rust's drawings and notes are of sufficient quality to allow for identification. On their basis, we can conclude that the Huleiqat region was dotted with Lower Paleolithic flints as well as Epipaleolithic remains.

Directly to the south, a comprehensive prehistoric survey of a large region on both banks of the Nahal Shiqma (Wadi Hesi) and adjacent areas contributed additional data (Lamdan et al. 1977).

The conclusion reached from all of the above-mentioned studies points to intensive human activity in the region during the Lower Paleolithic period, and specifically at the cultural-industrial Late Acheulean phase, but without notable signs of occupation. The findspots are located in what would have been humid environments, specifically *hamra* layers, probably the Holon Hamra Member that crops out in the region. An excavation of this *hamra* in Holon (Noy 1967) revealed a Late Acheulean assemblage, as well as large mammal bones.

Despite the fact that intensive use of the Levallois technique was noted at some sites and that dominant and Mousterian points were also occasionally found at others, whole handaxes and handaxe fragments are clearly attributable to a lithic industry of the Lower Paleolithic period. Distinct Middle Paleolithic sites or Upper Paleolithic sites have not been found in the region.

Allen (*Ashkelon 1*, p. 27) notes that most of the Map 92's sites are "along the spine of the easternmost *kurkar* ridge, at the highest elevations of the survey area." The recognition that sites were concentrated on the elevations of the *kurkar* ridges—but not on the youngest ridges, which postdate the Lower Paleolithic industries—was paralleled by the work of the Lamdan survey, especially on slopes facing north or northwest, and of Bayer (see Antl-Weiser 2007:Abb. 4) and Eshel. It is important to emphasize that there is no evidence of

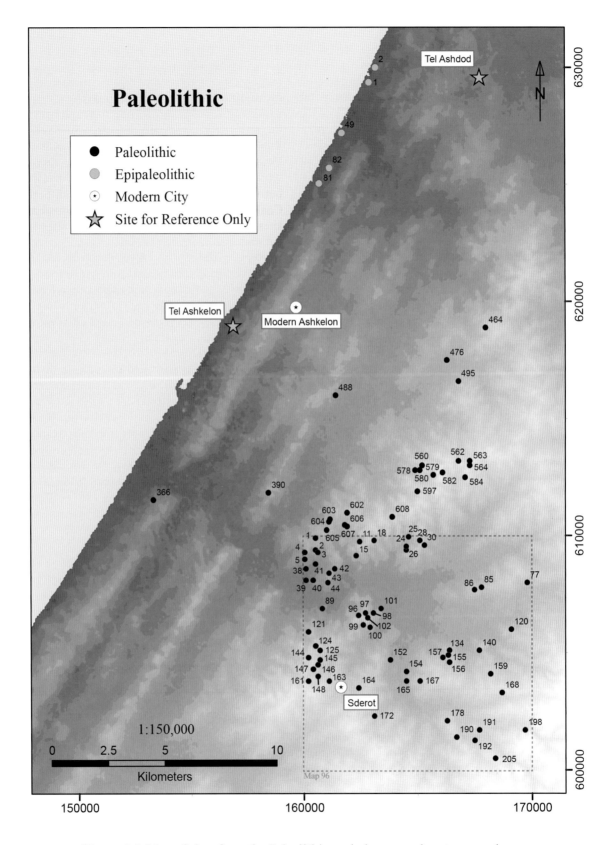

Figure 2.1: Map of sites from the Paleolithic period over modern topography.

settlement, only of human activity, and therefore we cannot establish any pattern of settlement. The association of lithics with elevated locations may be significant but may simply be due to environmental factors: The upper *kurkar* layer has eroded on these ridges, revealing the *hamra* soils below that contain stone tools. On the other hand, the consistent discovery of Lower Paleolithic tools in the *hamra* paleosols is certainly significant, indicating a link between human activity in this period with a more humid, lush environment.

The pattern for the Epipaleothic, meanwhile, is quite distinct. In the entirety of the surveyed region included in this study, amounting to 225 km^2, a total of five Epipaleolithic sites have been noted. All of these, in Map 88, are located on a strip close to the Mediterranean coast, either on the first *kurkar* ridge or on flat ground nearby. A similar pattern is noticeable farther north in Map 84. There, 11 sites were identified near the coast, generally on sandy hills topping the *kurkar* ridges. (These sites were surveyed by Berman in 1970 [Berman et al. 2005] and published in 2005; some of these had been previously identified by Ofer Bar-Yosef in a survey conducted in 1965–66 [Bar-Yosef 1970a; 1970b].) Elsewhere, the identification of Epipaleothic sites is questionable, as in the area of Huleiqat surveyed by Rust.

Neolithic and Chalcolithic

In the Neolithic period, settlement was concentrated in the southwest part of the study area. The Map of Ziqim included 26 sites identified by survey; one of these (site 347,[1] see below) was excavated by T. Noy on the banks of the Nahal Shiqma (Noy 1976, 1993). Elsewhere, very few sites were noted: two in Nizzanim East—site 1, tentatively ascribed to this period, and site 53 (E. Yeivin and Olami 1979; 1980; see below)—and one in Nizzanim West (site 207, in the Afridar neighborhood of modern Ashkelon; see Perrot 1955; Perrot and Gopher 1996; Garfinkel 1999; Garfinkel and Dag 2008). No clearly identifiable sites were located in Map 92, nor were they in Map 96 to the south: In Map 96, only two findspots were discerned, each represented by a single flint arrowhead. This site distribution can be explained by a pattern of settlement along the wadis—in particular, along the Nahal Shiqma or in its large drainage basin in Map

91 (cf. Berman et al. 2004:10*).[2] The excavation of site 347 yielded several flint tools, including sickle blades and arrowheads. In light of the finds, T. Noy (1993) suggested it could have been a seasonal settlement, situated in a high groundwater area, where the inhabitants' subsistence was based on hunting, fishing, and herding.

Although most of the sites in the area consist largely of artifact scatters, we can conclude that—unlike scatters of later material in the sand dunes—these are likely to be real sites. Scatters taken from tells would have Bronze, Iron, and later material, but we would not expect Neolithic (and, perhaps, Chalcolithic), as this material is not found at tell sites.[3] Indeed, some twenty Neolithic sites in the westernmost area of the Nahal Shiqma contain artifacts ascribed to the Chalcolithic (see below) and later periods as well. Berman observed these sites particularly in flat depressions, the only localities free of sand, which paradoxically are also included in the "patches" category. Probably one of the best examples of a Neolithic site containing scatters of later material is site 308 (Map 91). Here, remnants of Neolithic flint tools were found side by side with a ruin built in a recent period and with irrigated agricultural fields. Only eight Neolithic/Chalcolithic sites were devoid of later remains. We assume that one of them, excavated site 347, represents the majority: Several occupation levels dated to the Pottery Neolithic period followed by a thin layer from the Chalcolithic period. Site 53 is the only Neolithic settlement in the northern part of the study area. Its original area was estimated at 30 dunams, but only a very small portion was excavated. Seven occupational layers were exposed, all of them from the Pottery Neolithic period. A larger excavation (c. 1 dunam) took place in the Afridar neighborhood. Its activity area was estimated to be about 20 dunams. Finds permitted the site to be ascribed to the Pre-Pottery Neolithic and suggested it to be a pastoral camp. The location,

---

[1] Note that all site numbers refer to the number in our site table; please refer to table 2.9 on pp. 69–88 for references.

[2] Compare a similar pattern of prehistoric sites in the Map of Urim (125), where the relatively large number of Paleolithic and Chalcolithic sites are almost all concentrated along the Nahal Besor; in this case there are very few Neolithic sites, but they are also concentrated along the Besor (Gazit 1996:10*–11*, maps 1–2).

[3] The published Map of Ziqim claims that Neolithic remains were found at Tel Ashkelon or its "margins" (site 1; Berman et al. 2004:23*). To our knowledge, however, no Neolithic remains have been found on the tell. This confusion may have arisen because a Neolithic site "on the shore"—which is in fact the Afridar site (site 207)—is mentioned in the Encyclopedia entry for Ashkelon (Stager 1993:150).

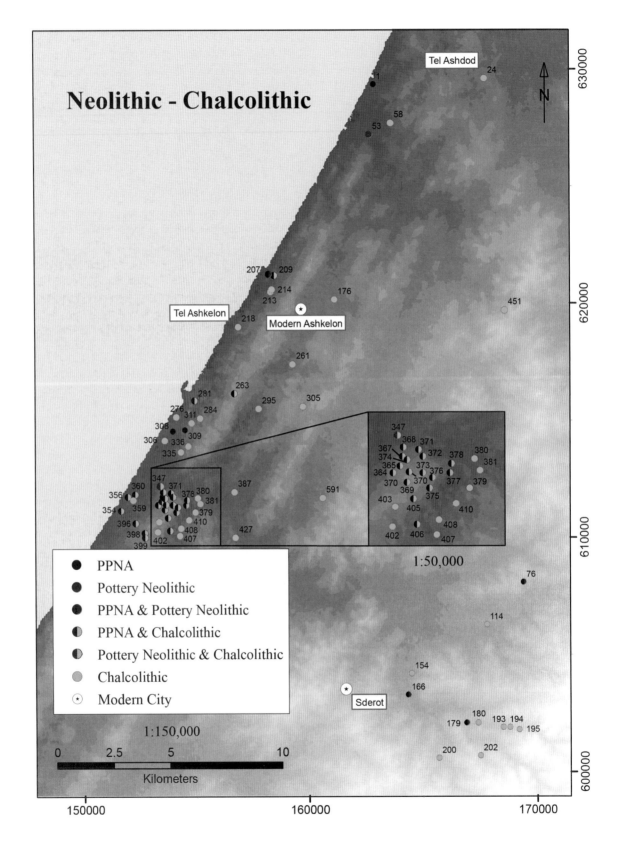

Figure 2.2: Map of sites from the Neolithic and Chalcolithic periods over modern topography.

close to the shoreline of the Mediterranean, is likely because of the existence of the high aquifer.

Flint tools assigned to the Late Neolithic period were sporadically found near the bedrock (not in situ) in Area G of the EB I site of Afridar (site 209) located east of the Pre-Pottery Neolithic site (Braun and Gophna 2004; Zbenovich 2004).

The Chalcolithic period is represented mainly in the southern area of the study. Here, site distribution follows the settlement pattern that had already begun in the Neolithic period, i.e., it was directly connected to the wide drainage system of the Nahal Shiqma. Some 30 Chalcolitic sites are located south of the wadi in a relatively small area (2 x 2 km); of these, 20 are located exactly where Neolithic settlements were discerned (as noted by Berman et al. 2004:11*). This dense concentration of sites in a small area can be explained in two different ways. First, these settlements were almost continuously occupied since the Neolithic period. This assumption is reinforced by the results of the excavation of the Neolithic site, where the uppermost layer was ascribed to the Chalcolithic period as mentioned above. In this case, the possibility that the Chalcolithic finds could have been intrusive was not considered. Second, as in other places within the dune belt, the finds here were encountered mainly in depressions, on the top of the soil that preceded the sand infiltration. The relatively numerous small sites and findspots are merely windows, reflecting a large occupational zone[4] composed of settlements of varying sizes, near water sources whether permanent or seasonal. Quite the same settlement pattern was observed along the banks of the Nahal Besor (Gazit 1996, esp. Map 2). These suggestions do not negate the idea that the depressions containing Chalcolithic in situ material could have served in the late Ottoman and Mandatory periods as *mawasi* agricultural plots. Most of the Chalcolithic sites also yielded later material and displayed the characteristic features attributed to "patches" (see chapter 1).

North of Tel Ashkelon, Chalcolithic pottery and flint tools were only sporadically found, consistent with excavated Early Bronze Age I assemblages. In Area E (site 212) of the Ashkelon-Afridar site, the EB I cultural horizon contained Chalcolithic elements, among them cornet bases, suggesting

[4] For example, when Berman conducted the survey of the Map of Ziqim in 1972–73, a large area of c. 1 km² on the southern bank of the wadi had been flooded or covered by a layer of silt due to the Nahal Shiqma dam construction in 1958. Many additional sites were therefore not visible to the survey team.

the site was occupied during this period (Golani 2004). In Area F (site 213) of the same large site, the lower EB I stratum also contained typical Chalcolithic flint artifacts and pottery (Khalaily 2004). An identical stratification was observed farther to the north, at the Nizzanim site from the EB I period (site 58, Yekutieli and Gophna 1994). Meanwhile, at both Tel Ashdod and Tel Ashkelon scattered sherds dating to the Chalcolithic period were found in fill layers (for Ashkelon, see Stager 1993:105). It is quite clear that settlements at Tel Ashdod and Tel Ashkelon were much smaller in the Chalcolithic period than they would later become, but there is no way to accurately estimate the size of the Chalcolithic sites. The identification of so few Chalcolithic sites in the Nahal Evtah (Wadi el Ibtah) area, as opposed to the long-term occupation of Tel Poran in later periods, suggests that not all the sites of the Chalcolithic period were discerned. This wadi, while small, likely played an important role as a water source.

Both Neolithic and Chalcolithic concentrations of sites are located close to the seashore and in the vicinity of the Nahal Shiqma and its tributaries. The banks of the Nahal Evtah (Wadi el Ibtah) also formed an environment conducive to settlement in these periods.

The description of the 26 sites in Ziqim varies: Sometimes they include small light scatters of flint (e.g., sites 263, 368), while in other cases there is also processed shell (site 354) or proof of a borer industry (as in the excavated site 281; Noy and Berman 1974). The nature of the excavated sites seems to be completely different from the Paleolithic findspots in maps 96 and 92.

Early Bronze Age

Since 1968 we have known that the vicinity of Tel Ashkelon was occupied during the Early Bronze Age. Soundings conducted that year by Ram Gophna (2002a) revealed EB IB building remains in the Afridar neighborhood, 1.5 km north of the tell. Since then, a series of salvage excavations has been conducted at the Afridar site, revealing mainly EB IA remains (sites 209, 211–14; Brandl and Gophna 1993; Braun and Gophna 2004; Baumgarten 2004; 2006; Golani 2004; 2005b; 2008; Khalaily 2004). At Tel Ashkelon, pottery collection indicates a long-term occupation sporadically attested in EB I—but more extensively recovered in EB III across Ashkelon's north tell, which is roughly 9 hectares (Stager 1993:105–6; *Ashkelon 1*, pp. 215, 251). The various excavations

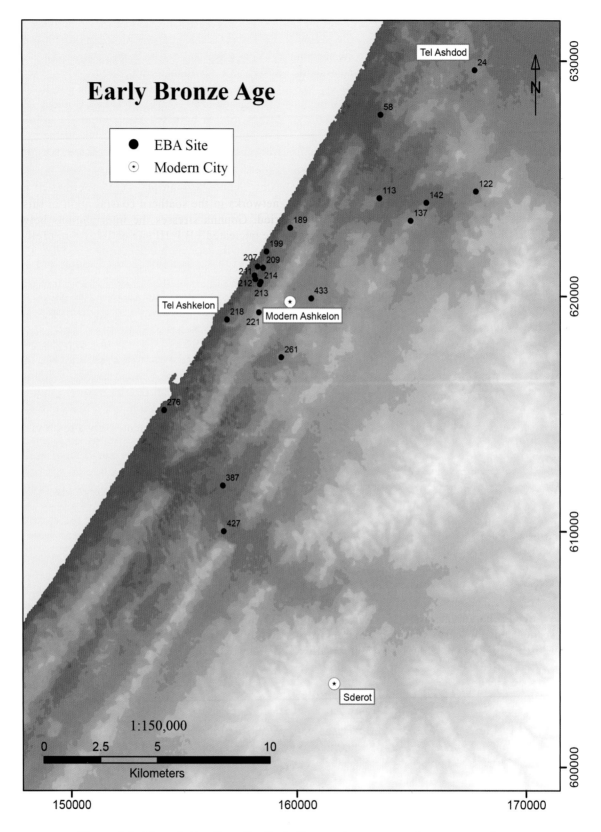

Figure 2.3: Map of sites from the Early Bronze Age over modern topography.

of the Afridar site, as well as recent unpublished soundings in the most northern part of the Afridar neighborhood, the excavation of industrial facilities south of the Sheikh Awad tomb (site 199; Toueg 2010), and the exposure of c. 8 dunams in the northernmost part of the Barnea region, the Barnea B-C quarter (site 189), all revealed large areas of an extensive settled zone. This remarkable occupation reached its peak during the late EB IA to early EB IB period when it was dispersed intermittently over a length of c. 4 km along the Mediterranean coast. The settlement characteristics are almost the same at each site, comprising clusters of residential structures, storage facilities (mudbrick silos for grain storage), and industrial areas used for copper processing.

Other Early Bronze Age excavated sites within the bounds of this study are found north of Ashkelon, at Tel Poran (Tell el-Farāni; site 113), where fortifications from this period were uncovered (Gophna 1992b), and at Nizzanim (Yekutieli and Gophna 1994; site 58, Holot Ashdod). A small number of EB pottery sherds were found at Tel Ashdod (Er-Ras) and at two small surveyed findspots in the valley of Nahal Evtah; these sites were likely seasonal camps near periodic water sources, a pattern that can still be seen today. In the Map of Ziqim, at a distance of c. 2 km south of Tel Ashkelon, large quantities of EB I pottery were noted during inspection work of an already disturbed area near the remains of a well, probably from the same period (site not in table, Yoram Haimi, pers. comm.). Farther to the south, the surveyed site of Saknat Muhammad Mahmud (site 276) is the only potential EB settlement. Other sites are merely findspots consisting of potsherds, flint tools, and bones. Before the construction of the Nahal Shiqma dam, water would puddle in the valley during the winter rains, surviving through the spring and into early summer. This environment, then, as with that of the Nahal Evtah valley, was perfect pasture land and might have been suitable for shepherds in the past (as far back as the Chalcolithic) with these findspots the remains of their encampments.

Turning to the east, no Early Bronze Age remains are known from either surveys or inspection work. Allen (*Ashkelon 1*, p. 33) ascribes the lack of Bronze Age (and Iron I) settlements to the possibility that the area was wooded or swampy and therefore not conducive to settlement. In fact, swamp remains and deposits should be easily distinguishable. They were noted in deep sections between the neighborhoods of Majdal and Afridar, where an enormous swamp existed until 1991, but no remains were found farther east.

Searching for other reasons to explain the lack of settlements, Allen also emphasizes the geographical and economic importance of the north-south route running parallel to the coast, contrasting it with the relative unimportance of east-west contacts (*Ashkelon 1*, p. 33). This concept of insignificant connections between Tel Ashkelon on the coast and interior settlements, however, runs counter to multiple reconstructions of trade networks in the southern coastal plain in this period. Gophna stresses the interrelations between the nucleated EB I–III site of Tel ʿErani (Tell esh-Sheikh Ahmed el-ʿAreini), situated about 23 km to the east, and the Afridar/Tel Ashkelon site, defining the latter as the "maritime counterpart" of and "sea gate" to the former (2004:7). Another EB site, Horvat Ptora (Petura), a sizeable settlement of c. 7 dunams dated to the Early Bronze Age I and located only 4 km east of Tel ʿErani, has been partly excavated (Milevski and Baumgarten 2008; Baumgarten et al. 2008). Here, a later phase of the Early Bronze Age I, equivalent to stratum C at Tel ʿErani, was exposed, but—unlike at ʿErani— Egyptian pottery was absent. Only a tomb yielded pottery from the end of the Early Bronze Age I, during which there was no settlement at the site (Baumgarten et al. 2008:1995). Similarly, Stager (2001), in his application of the "port power" model, has suggested (following Fargo 1979) that inland sites (such as ʿErani) located along the wadi systems in the southern part of the country (especially the Nahal Lachish [Nahr Sukreir] and the Nahal Shiqma) would have funneled goods to the seaport at Tel Ashkelon for overseas shipment. In addition, Stager sees Tel Ashkelon as part of a larger trading network in the Near East in this period, a major stop on the route between Egypt and Byblos, and thereby a link between Egypt and Mesopotamia, as well as a way station on the overland route to Egypt (Stager 2001; 1993:105–6; cf. Gophna and Liphschitz 1996; Gophna 2002b). Indeed, one might expect some sort of contact between Tel ʿErani or Ptora and Ashkelon, since Ashkelon is located on the coast almost due west, but there are no decisive data pointing toward direct links between the eastern settlements and Ashkelon. While the Egyptian pottery at ʿErani demonstrates its role in part of a larger trade network, the river valleys of Nahal Shiqma and Nahal Besor (Wadi Ghazzeh) could have served as overland transport arteries, thereby explaining the Egyptian pottery findings at Tel ᶜErani. There is no clear evidence directly linking these probable east-west connections to the Ashkelon region itself, however attractive the hypothesis.

One other aspect of the EB settlement patterns in the Ashkelon region is worthy of note. While the stretch of settlements along the coast is restricted to EB I, occupation of Tel Ashkelon is most pronounced in EB III. In EB III, then, Tel Ashkelon stood nearly alone as a settlement, with Tel Ashdod, Tel Poran, and site 58—Tel Poran's satellite site (although farther to the east, Tel ᶜErani displays the same occupational sequence; see Kempinski and Gilead 1991; Yeivin and Kempinski 1993). This pattern suggests two different stages: a large stretch of settlements in the EB I, followed by the consolidation of settlements at Tel Ashkelon in the later EB. If this is true, this pattern may follow the rise of maritime trade in the EB I, which appears to have superseded overland trade as the principal avenue of transport between Egypt and the Levantine coast by the EB II (see, e.g., Stager 2001:631, 633).

Middle Bronze Age

Middle Bronze Age I
(EB IV or Intermediate Bronze)

The existence of the remains of mudbrick buildings from the MB I period, extending over 40 dunams at a distance of 4.5 km northeast of Tel Ashkelon (site 164), was noted by Allen (*Ashkelon 1*, p. 33). In the course of a salvage excavation, small circular and oval structures were exposed (Israel 1995a). These data are repeated here first and foremost because this is the only recognized settlement of this period within a large surveyed area of 225 km². Another site with remains ascribed to MB I contains merely a scatter of pottery sherds in an area of 90 m² located c. 6 km northeast of Tel Ashkelon (site 169). Similarly, in the 100 km² of Map 96 (Sderot), only two small MB I cemeteries were surveyed (see chapter 5, sites 61, 138).

It appears that the region was mostly uninhabited in this period, with EB settlements having been abandoned. At Tel Ashkelon, probes have revealed a thick sand layer beneath the MB levels in Grid 38; the continual appearance of EB sherds in later fills in this area, however, hints at possible EB occupation below the sand (*Ashkelon 1*, p. 251). The sand layer may be related to the Taᶜaruha Sand Member, an Early to Intermediate Bronze sedimentary phase dated by Netser (1994) from 5580 to 4110 B.P. The EB I Afridar

site, Area E (site 212), was covered by a layer of sand from the first phase of this sand member (Barzilay 2004). These sand layers might be more noticeable at sites located close to the seashore, hence their discovery at Tel Ashkelon and Afridar.

Middle Bronze Age II

While a large city flourished at Tel Ashkelon during the Middle Bronze Age II (*Ashkelon 1*, pp. 217, 234–36, 251, 303), few remains of this period have been discovered beyond the tell. At Netiv Ha-ᶜAsara (Shavit and Yasur-Landau 2005), c. 10 km south of Tel Ashkelon, salvage excavations revealed fills with MB IIA–B sherds, but no occupation levels were observed (Yasur-Landau and Shavit 1999; Shavit and Yasur-Landau 2005:67–69). A survey of Netiv Ha-ᶜAsara revealed a tell of c. 30 dunams, settled from the Middle Bronze Age until the Persian period at an advantageous location (on an elevated place on the second *kurkar* ridge just south of a potential water source, the Nahal Shiqma, and set strategically close to the main road leading to Gaza); however, in the Bronze and Iron Ages it was probably a small settlement, as it appears to have covered only two dunams until its expansion in the Persian period (Shavit and Yasur-Landau 2005:60). On the northern slope of the tell, sand dunes were removed during development work, exposing collapsed walls built of dressed *kurkar* stones, pointing to the existence of a large fortified structure situated on the summit of the tell. Here, too, MB sherds were retrieved, but the Bronze Age finds were mainly from the Late Bronze Age. Netiv Ha-ᶜAsara is probably the southern equivalent of Tel Poran (site 113), north of Ashkelon. At Tel Poran, the archaeological excavated remains included both EB fortifications (see above) and an earth and gravel glacis attributed to the MB II period (Gophna 1977; 1992b), suggesting a long-term fortified settlement. (Both of these sites will be mentioned again in relation to the LB period.) It is also worth mentioning Tel Ashdod, located at the northeastern edge of the area included in this study, where an occupation level of this period was exposed during excavations (Dothan and Porath 1993:9; Dothan 1993:95). Berman (survey of Map 91) also discovered identifiable MB II pottery at a distance of c. 2 km southeast of Tel Ashkelon and other evidence for MB II occupation there (site 254). Berman mentions three more pottery scatters containing MB sherds south of Nahal Shiqma (sites 361, 362, and 402), but in our opinion these sites are questionable: They may be seasonal camps or "patches" resulting from modern *mawasi* agriculture. Allen also mentions MB sherds in the area of Map 92 but notes that their identification is

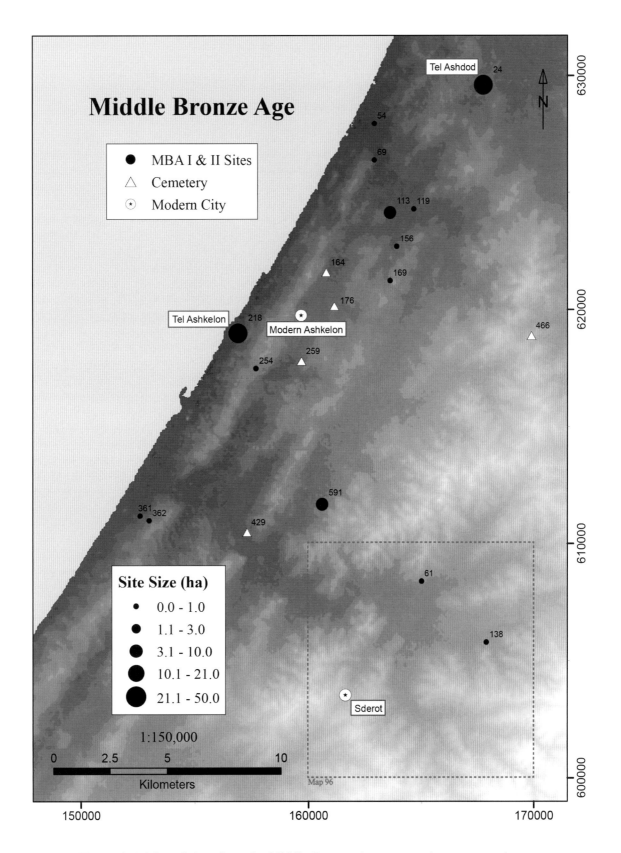

Figure 2.4: Map of sites from the Middle Bronze Age over modern topography.

questionable since no habitation sites from this period have been identified in that region (*Ashkelon 1*, p. 30; site 490). The situation is identical to that of Map 96 to the south, where no Middle Bronze Age habitation sites have been discovered.

Instead, other MB sites in the region consist of burial grounds: the cemetery in the Migdal (Majdal) district (site 176; Gershuny 1996; 1997) and the cemetery located north of Migdal and east of Barnea (site 164; Israel 1995a). In the latter case, an additional excavation proved site 164's large dimensions. The ceramic finds in the graves date to the end of MB IIA and MB IIB (Zelin 2002). Both sites, together with a single MB tomb at Negba (site 466), were mentioned by Allen (*Ashkelon 1*, p. 30); in addition to these, a set of graves were excavated at Kh. Ma^craba (site 429), and another single shaft tomb was found in the neighborhood of Giv^cat Ziyyon (site 259; Gershuny 1999). These data, in turn, lead us to reconsider the geographical link between cemeteries and habitation sites in this period. While a cemetery should indicate the existence of a settlement, we have no evidence of MB II occupation near the cemeteries. The only exception to this pattern is at Tel Ashkelon: In the excavation area of Grid 50, a large cemetery composed of rock-cut chamber tombs was unearthed (*Ashkelon 1*, pp. 300–3). The tombs were cut into the *kurkar* bedrock beneath the Bronze Age habitation level. Four distinct phases of the use of these tombs were distinguished, spanning the MB IIB–C (and LB I). Here, the direct link between the cemetery and the population of the flourishing city was obvious, with abundant evidence for occupation on the tell throughout MB II.

For Migdal, Frank Koucky (*Ashkelon 1*) and Aaron Burke (2007) have argued that there was an ancient settlement at the site of the Arab village and modern Israeli neighborhood going back as far as the Middle Bronze Age.[5] Both have suggested an association between sites with the Arabic name *Majdal* (or Hebrew *Migdal*) and ancient watchtowers; Burke has demonstrated a general pattern of association between such names and MB sites throughout the Levant. Both also note Migdal's placement near the coastal road, an expected location for a watchtower (Burke 2007:52; Koucky in *Ashkelon 1*, p. 17). While Burke (2007:39) and Koucky (*Ashkelon 1*, p. 19) argue that the MB cemetery at Migdal proves or at least supports the idea of settlement at Migdal in this period, the situation is in fact far less clear. In the survey of Map 92, the earliest pottery found at Majdal was Persian (Allen in

Ashkelon 1, p. 59). While surface survey does tend to result in underrepresentation of earlier periods (as discussed in chapter 1), recent salvage excavations have not revealed any traces of settlement in the Middle Bronze Age. Thus, while there may be circumstantial evidence of a settlement at Migdal, there are no concrete data to support this idea.

Instead, we seem to have a pattern in the Ashkelon region, and perhaps in the southern coastal plain more generally, of cemeteries located at some distance from settlements. Thus Allen (*Ashkelon 1*, p. 30) tentatively connected the cemeteries of Migdal and east Barnea to ancient Ashkelon. Meanwhile, Zelin (2002:87*), who conducted the salvage excavation in the northern cemetery east of Barnea (site 164), assumed that it served a rural settlement located in the vicinity of Ashkelon. Zelin also noted that the cemetery lies on the road to Tel Poran, c. 5 km to the north, where an MB II settlement is known to have existed. This same phenomenon of an MB II cemetery located relatively far from any sizeable settlement was noted at Rishon le-Ziyyon, the largest cemetery excavated in the central coastal plain (Levy 2005; 2008). Again, as in the Ashkelon region, it is located on a *kurkar* ridge that runs parallel to the coast. The cemetery originally extended over an area of c. 100 dunams and included about 1,000 graves. It is not known to what settlement the cemetery belonged, despite the fact that the remains of a Middle Bronze Age II settlement, whose extent is unknown, were uncovered nearby. Levy assumes that it may have functioned as a central cemetery for the many settlements scattered in a wide area around it or for a nomadic population, while at the same time expressing doubts about whether it seems feasible that this large and rich cemetery could have served such a population (Levy 2008:2020). The attribution of cemeteries containing grave goods and vessels used during funeral ceremonies to a substantial and wealthy sedentary population only seems unjustified, however. It is certainly reasonable to think that in a region around a powerful port center such as Ashkelon, trade and commerce with surrounding pastoral populations would have been common. The existence of a pastoral population around Ashkelon may also explain both the lack of settlements and the light scatters of MB II pottery in the western valleys and riverbanks of the Nahal Evtah in the north and of Nahal Shiqma in the south, which are typical pasture environments even up to the present. (Unfortunately, at present there are not enough data to test these ideas by comparing material from Migdal, east Barnea, and Rishon le-Ziyyon with the Grid 50 tombs at Ashkelon.)

---

[5] This suggestion had already been made by Abel (1938:218).

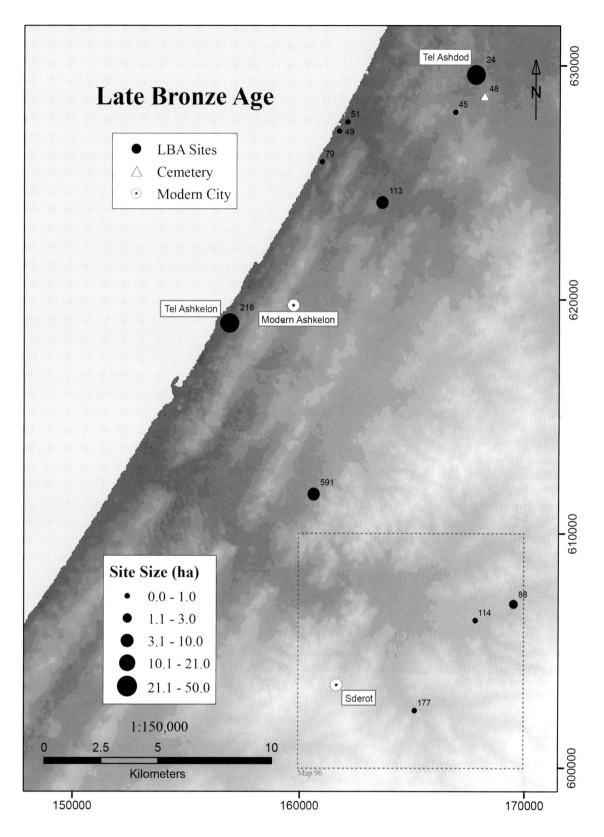

Figure 2.5: Map of sites from the Late Bronze Age over modern topography.

Late Bronze Age

The Late Bronze Age is well attested at the major tell sites of the region: At Tel Ashkelon, remains dating to this period reveal a prosperous port city, and at Tel Ashdod a public building from this period was uncovered. However, there are few traces of the LB in the surrounding areas. South of Ashkelon (with the exception of Tel Ashkelon, mentioned above), remains from the Late Bronze Age were not recorded by Berman in 1972–73, nor by the later team, within the entire 60 km² surveyed area of the Ziqim map (Berman et al. 2004). LB remains were not discovered until 1997, when a survey and salvage excavation conducted on the precincts of Netiv Ha-ᶜAsara, near a location already identified as an LB site (Finkelstein 1996b:238), uncovered evidence of a Late Bronze I–II settlement and part of a large Late Bronze II structure (Yasur-Landau and Shavit 1999; Shavit and Yasur-Landau 2005). The finds included a number of vessels imported from Cyprus—among them "bilbils" (Base Ring Ware I–II) and "milk bowls" (White Slip II). North of Ashkelon, at Tel Poran (site 113), Late Bronze II pottery sherds were collected, and included fragments of imported Cypriot and Mycenaean vessels. Northwest of Tel Poran, close to the Mediterranean coast on the first *kurkar* ridge, three Late Bronze sites containing structural remains were surveyed (sites 49, 51, and 79). One of them, El ᵓAbtah (site 79), was tentatively identified as a possible fortress (Berman and Barda 2005:51*). At three other locations within the Nizzanim map (sites 21, 45, and 156), the identification of sherds ascribed to the Late Bronze period is questionable. In Map 92, the survey conducted by Mitchell Allen identified only one Late Bronze Age site southeast of Ashkelon at Tel Obed (Beit Jirja; site 591), a mound of ashy soil containing a dense scatter of ceramics (*Ashkelon 1*, p. 58). A similar scarcity of sites was found in the survey of the Map of Sderot (96), directly south of Allen's survey region: A total of three small sites, all of them in proximity to possible water sources, were attributed to the LB. Two are located on the northern bank of Nahal Shiqma (Wadi Hesi) at a distance of c. 3 km apart (chapter 5, sites 88 and 114). It is worth noting that Mandatory surveyors named an area on the southern bank of Nahal Shiqma, not far from site 114, "Uyun es Sahra" (Arabic), or "the springs of the badlands" (Survey of Palestine, Sheet 11-10, Bureir, 1:20,000). The names of areas, fields, or lots on Mandatory maps were obtained from the local population, reflecting

traditions about geographical features in the area; thus we suggest that the location of site 114 may have been because of a spring there. The third site, meanwhile, is situated close to one of the southern tributaries of Nahal Shiqma (Nahal Dorot/Wadi Raml; chapter 5, site 177).

As a rule, settlement of the inner part of the southern coastal plain during the Late Bronze Age was sparse. There are more Late Bronze Age sites farther to the east, near Tell el-Hesi (Tel Hasi), the only city from this period in that region (Lamdan et al. 1977). The location of sites in the Hesi region is definitely connected to the permanent springs at Nahal Shiqma. The same is true directly east of Ashkelon. Excavations at Tel Ṣippor (Tell et-Tuyur) revealed a stratum with pottery typical of the last phase of the Late Bronze Age (Biran and Negbi 1966; Biran 1993). This small ancient mound is located near a tributary of the Nahal Lachish, not coincidentally on the same longitude (174 NIG; 124 OIG) as Tell el-Hesi, both at a distance of c. 20 km from the Mediterranean.

Israel Finkelstein (1996b) noted the relatively low number of LB sites in the region in his comparison of settlement patterns in the coastal plain during the Late Bronze and Iron I periods. Relying on multiple sources of data—survey results, excavation reports, and unpublished data from regional archaeologists—Finkelstein's settlement map of the Late Bronze II Age probably reflects the general picture in the field fairly well. At the same time, he predicted that future work would reveal more sites (1996b:226); indeed, we are able to add eight sites to his total of twelve in the territory of Ashkelon, which he determines to be somewhat broader than our study area (see table 2.1). Five of Finkelstein's twelve sites are located north of Tel Ashdod and, therefore, north of our study area. They (and two additional sites from Map 84) are mentioned here primarily because, while Finkelstein notes the importance of Ashdod in the Late Bronze Age, he suggests that this city and the surrounding sites were included in the large territory of the city-state of Ashkelon. Basing his arguments on historical data, settlement patterns, and geographical features, he drew the border between the territory of Ashkelon and the territory of the city-state of Gezer somewhere on the path of Nahal Sorek (Nahr Rubin), north of Yavneh (Finkelstein 1996b:fig. 1). He also emphasized that most large sites are restricted to the territories of Ashkelon and Tell Jemmeh (Yurza?), a phenomenon he relates to the importance of those two centers of Egyptian administration (Finkelstein 1996b:229). The suggestion that the large territory of Ashkelon was connected to Egypt is reinforced by Berman's survey finds at Rasm el Jisr, northeast of Tel Ashdod (Map 84 site

37; Berman et al. 2005:28*–29*), including imported Egyptian pottery and a stone doorjamb fragment with a title of a high Egyptian official (Kitchen 1993), as well as the fragment of an Egyptian statue bearing a hieroglyphic inscription mentioning a Ramesside queen from Tel Ashdod itself (Schulman 1993). According to Alan Schulman, such a life-size statue would be erected only in a building such as a temple or palace and indicates the importance of Ashdod's role in the Egyptian administration of Canaan (1993:114), a suggestion reinforced by the doorjamb fragment.

Besides indicating its connection with Egypt, the wealth of imported Cypriot and Mycenaean pottery in Canaan in this age of internationalism allows us to track trade relationships within the country, as these items must have arrived via one of the Mediterranean ports. It is not surprising that Tel Ashkelon has the largest collection of Cypriot and Mycenaean ceramics in the region (Stager, pers. comm.). Cypriot pottery in particular has been found at most sites in the region: not only at the tell sites of Poran, Netiv Ha-ᶜAsara, and Ashdod, but also at small sites (such as Map 96 site 114; see chapter 5). Mycenaean pottery, however, is found only at Poran. The difference between the two is, in all likelihood, simply a reflection of the relative amounts of each type of pottery imported to the region via the port at Tel Ashkelon: Pottery from Cyprus is more common than that from the Aegean, presumably because of the relative proximity of Cyprus (and perhaps its role in Levantine trade). More generally, the distribution of imported pottery in the region suggests a complex, integrated trade network where material is distributed not only to other parts of the country but throughout the Ashkelon region as well. Pottery, then, was not strictly a luxury good for the elite of the larger settlements but was also traded in the hinterland. With further exposure of smaller sites in the region, more such imported pottery will presumably be found.

Iron Age I

Identifiable remains from the Iron Age I have been discerned at three sites south of Ashkelon that underwent small-scale excavations: Dimra, near Erez, where the pottery collection contains elements already known in the northern Negev, and in two small sites defined by Gophna (1966) as *hazerim* (see discussion of *hazerim* in the northern Negev south of Tell el-Farᶜah, Gophna 1963; 1964). The ceramic assemblages discovered in part of the *hazerim* are closely related to the Philistine pottery and were therefore classified by Gophna as probably belonging to the eleventh century B.C. The pottery found in Dimra dates to the very end of the eleventh century. Dimra is located 12 km south of Tel

Ashkelon and 10 km northeast of Gaza. This small settlement could have been affiliated with either of these city-states, but we prefer Gophna's suggestion that it was a satellite of Gaza since the pottery assemblage from Dimra shows close similarities to Iron I ceramic assemblages from sites such as Mefalsim A, Mefalsim B, and Zeelim, located in the northern Negev a short distance from Gaza (Gophna 1966). At Netiv Ha-ᶜAsara (Shavit and Yasur-Landau 2005) on the second *kurkar* ridge, a stratum excavated in a small area was found to contain Iron Age I remains (Yasur-Landau and Shavit 1999; Shavit and Yasur-Landau 2005). At Khirbet Bakkita (site 430), near Yad Mordechai, an excavation was conducted by Yaᶜaqov Baumgarten in 1999. While he did not excavate any Iron I architecture, Baumgarten did find Philistine bichrome sherds; based on form and decoration, they were assigned to two distinct phases, dated respectively to the twelfth century and the eleventh century B.C. (see Berman et al. 2004:61*).

North of Ashkelon, the main Iron Age I site is Tel Ashdod along with nearby cemeteries southeast of the tell, consisting of both caves and shaft tombs (Berman and Barda 2005:46*). In addition, another burial cave located along the Nahal Evtah with clear evidence of use in the first half of the twelfth century B.C. was unearthed by Ram Gophna and Dov Meron (1970; site 146). Tel Poran (site 113), located midway between Ashkelon and Ashdod, also yielded clear Iron Age I remains, including fragments of Philistine vessels. Its long period of occupation (from the EB) suggests that some permanent water source connected to the Nahal Evtah system once existed there. Whether Tel Poran was associated with Ashdod or with Ashkelon is not clear. Three more manifestations of Iron I structural remains were documented by Berman on the coast northwest of Tel Poran (sites 49, 51, and 79). One of these sites, El ᵓAbtah, on a *kurkar* hill some 80 m from the Mediterranean coast, was (as mentioned above) identified by Berman and Barda as a possible fortress.

Allen's survey results suggested only two sites reasonably dating to the Iron Age I. At the first of these (site 451, east of Ashkelon and near Negba), however, the presence of an Iron I horizon was based on a single cooking pot rim (*Ashkelon 1*, p. 30). Repeated visits to site 451 by the author turned up no Iron I sherds, nor a spring mentioned by Allen while describing the site. The absence of the spring means that this area is not a reliable Iron Age I site. This leaves only one Iron Age I site (site 591, Tel Obed) within the entire 100 km² area of the Map of Ashkelon, the same number as is contained in the Map of Sderot directly to the south.

Thus—beyond the remains exposed during excavations at Tel Ashkelon and Tel Ashdod, both thriving

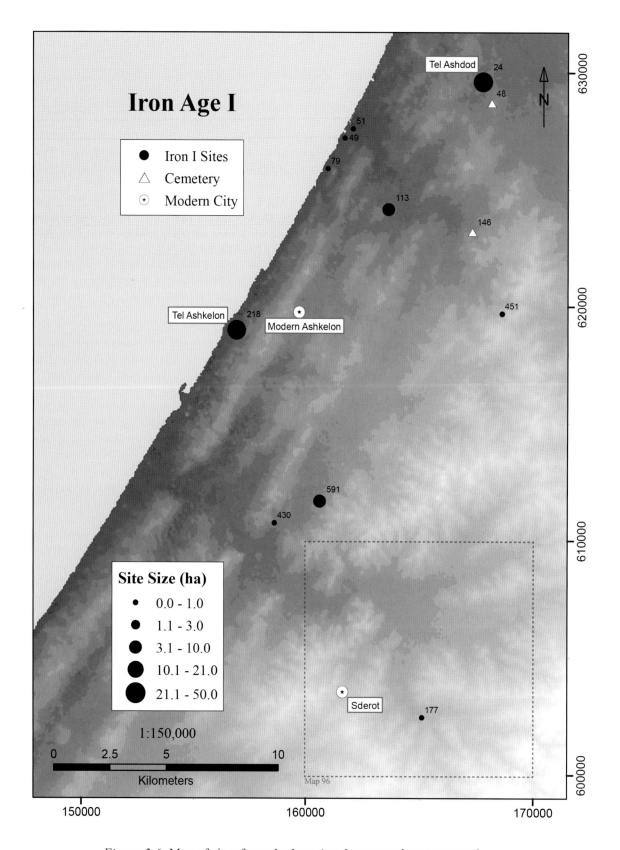

Figure 2.6: Map of sites from the Iron Age I over modern topography.

cities during the Iron I—settlement remains from this period in a wide area of c. 360 km² (Maps 87, 88, 91, 92, and 96) are scanty and summarized as follows:

1. Three sites south of Tel Ashkelon: Dimra (near Erez), Kh. Bakkita (Yad Mordechai), and Netiv Ha-ᶜAsara.

2. Two sites southeast of Ashkelon: Tel Obed (Beit Jirja) and the more distant site near Hoga (Map 96 site 177, Nahal Dorot; see chapter 5).

3. Four sites north of Ashkelon: Tel Poran and three reliable sites northwest of it (El ᶜAbtah and two other sites in the western Nahal Evtah system).

This leaves us with a total of nine settlements plus the cities of Ashkelon and Ashdod.

The most remarkable feature of the location of Iron Age I sites, both in the immediate vicinity of Tel Ashkelon and in the wider region, is that most are to be found at places founded or otherwise settled during the Late Bronze period. This fact was mentioned by Finkelstein (1996b:231) when discussing the settlement pattern in the Iron Age I in the southern coastal plain and the Shephelah. Finkelstein also suggested that there was a sharp decline in the total number of sites in the area between the LB and Iron I, from 102 to 49; he concluded that this decrease was balanced by a major shift in emphasis in the Iron I to larger central sites with few satellites, resulting in little net change in the total built-up area between the two periods (Finkelstein 1996b:231). Within a radius of 20 km of Tel Ashkelon, he identified only eight Iron Age I sites (Finkelstein 1996b:230, fig 2). Besides Tel Ashkelon itself, these include the following: Khirbet Bakkita and Telamim (Map 96 site 88, which yielded only LB finds; see chapter 5) within the Iron Age I suggested territory of Ashkelon; Hoga in the territory of Gaza; Tel Ṣippor in the territory of Gath; and Tel Ashdod, Tel Mor (Tell Murra/Tell el-Kheidar), Shafir, and Nizzanim beach 1 (Nahal Evtah) in the suggested territory of Ashdod.

Thus, according to Finkelstein, in our study area proper (and in the territory of Ashkelon) there is only one satellite site (when Telamim is omitted): Khirbet Bakkita. Dimra and Mefalsim A and B, classified as *hazerim* by Gophna (1966:44–51), were not included by Finkelstein because he considered them later than the Philistine bichrome phase (and therefore as Iron II sites; Finkelstein

1996b:228 n. 19). Philistine bichrome ware is dated by Finkelstein to the eleventh and early tenth centuries B.C. (as opposed to the conventional/high chronology of Philistine settlement, which dates Philistine bichrome from the mid-twelfth to the late eleventh century; e.g., Mazar 1985:106–7). As mentioned above, however, Gophna ascribed the sherds of the *hazerim* sites to the eleventh century B.C. The pottery from the *hazerim* may indeed represent a phase that comes after Philistine bichrome, but these assemblages seem to represent part of the material culture of the coastal entities in the Iron Age I. As Gophna (1966) pointed out, the pottery of these sites (in particular, the irregular burnishing on brown or red ground, and the bowls with atrophied horizontal handles) is not characteristic of Judah but of Philistine traditions. Furthermore, it is important to note that, in the Ashkelon region and adjacent areas, ceramics finds of bichrome ware have been found almost exclusively at excavated sites, both urban and rural, including Tel Ashkelon, Tel Ashdod, Tel Mor, Tel Ṣippor, and Kh. Bakkita. It seems that bichrome ware is rare in survey collections. Allen emphasized that within the entirety of Map 92, "[n]ot a single sherd of painted Philistine pottery was found in four years of surveying" (*Ashkelon 1*, p. 30). Nevertheless, Berman's survey of the Map of Nizzanim yielded fragments of Philistine vessels at Tel Poran, as mentioned above, as well as at site 51 (see Berman and Barda 2005:46*); his survey of Ziqim also yielded a Philistine sherd at Bakkita (Berman et al. 2004:12*). Shavit (2003:56), meanwhile, indicates only one Iron I satellite site within a radius of 10 km around Tel Ashkelon; in his dissertation, this site is included on illustration 40 c. 4 km southeast of Tel Ashkelon, at coordinates 107/115 (2003:157). Based on Shavit's survey records, it is likely a site in Holot Ziqim, coordinates (OIG) 10755/11479, an artifact scatter with pottery from every period from the EB to the Persian. The nature of this scatter, plus its location on a flat area between sand dunes, suggests it may be a "patch" rather than an ancient site; at the same time, it is worthy of note because, according to Shavit's survey records, the site yielded a Philistine bichrome sherd.

Presently, the available data permit us to suggest a new list of reliable Iron Age I sites within the Ashkelon region. For this period, we have chosen not to reproduce the borders of the presumed Ashkelon city-state from the LB, as Ashdod is generally considered (as it is by Finkelstein) a separate political entity in the Iron I; instead, we list sites

Table 2.1: Late Bronze Age and Iron Age I Sites in the Ashkelon Region, within a radius of c. 18 km

Site	Finkelstein's Site	Map reference (NIG)	Site no./Ref.	Late Bronze Age	Iron Age I
Tel Ashkelon	Tel Ashkelon	156900/619000	218	City	City
Tel Ashdod	Tel Ashdod	167750/629600	24	City	City
Holot Ashdod		163900/630950	Map 84 site 82	Settlement	
Holot Ashdod	Ashdod-Yam	163690/630890	Map 84 site 83	Occupation	
Nahal Lakhish	North of Tel Ashdod	168900/630180	Map 84 site 105	Occupation	Occupation
Holot Ashdod (SE of the tell)		168150/628700	48	Cemetery	Cemetery
Holot Ashdod	Nizzanim Beach 1	161700/627200	49	Occupation	Occupation
Nahal Evtah		162050/627600	51	Settlement	Settlement
El ꜣAbtah (NW)	Nizzanim Beach 2	160950/625900	79	Fortress?	Fortress?
Tel Poran	SE of Tel Poran	163600/624150	113	Settlement	Settlement
Nahal Evtah	SE of Nizzanim	167300/623200	146		Burial Cave
Tel Ṣippor	Tel Zippor	174800/618000	Biran and Negbi 1966; Biran 1993	Settlement	Settlement
Tel Obed		160600/611600	591	Settlement	Settlement
Khirbet Bakkita	Yad Mordekhay Junction	158600/610750	430		Settlement
Netiv Ha-ᶜAsara	Netiv Ha-ᶜAsara	156850/609300	Shavit and Yasur-Landau 2005	Settlement	Settlement
Dimra near Erez		158600/607500	Gophna 1966		Settlement
Mefalsim A		157800/600100	Gophna 1966		Settlement
Mefalsim B		159400/600900	Gophna 1966		Settlement
Nahal Shiqma		169500/607000	Chapter 5, site 88	Settlement	
Nahal Shiqma		167800/606300	Chapter 5, site 114	Settlement	
Nahal Hoga	H. Hoga	165100/602450	Chapter 5, site 177	Settlement	Settlement

within a radius of c. 18 km around Tel Ashkelon (a roughly 20 x 32 km area, east coordinates 155/175 and north coordinates 600/632 [NIG]). In table 2.1, they are presented side by side with the Late Bronze Age sites. At least for the Ashkelon region, the change between LB and Iron I is not as great as Finkelstein thought; in fact, within a radius of 18 km of Tel Ashkelon, there is no change in the number of settlements. Table 2.1 shows a total of 21 sites from one or both of these periods, including 19 settlements and two burial sites; in each period there are 15 settlements, including Ashkelon and Ashdod, along with one burial site in the LB and two in Iron I. A majority of the settlements (11) were inhabited in both periods. Thus, while four known settlements were apparently abandoned after the LB, four new ones were founded. In our study area proper, there are eight settlements plus a cemetery in the LB, and nine plus the cemetery and a burial cave in Iron I. Finkelstein, meanwhile,

claimed only five LB sites and four Iron I sites for this area. However, Finkelstein's data are superseded by the publication of the Archaeological Survey of Israel survey maps, which both add new sites to his list and clarify the periods of occupation of the other sites. Therefore, although Finkelstein claimed that sites 49 and Map 96 site 177 were inhabited only in the Iron I, they were inhabited in both periods; similarly, although he reported that sites 79 and 113 were inhabited only in the LB, they were inhabited in both. Finally, the burial cave at site 146 that Finkelstein assigned to the LB should be assigned to Iron I (though this may depend on Finkelstein's application of the low chronology and suggestion of a later starting date for Iron I).

In general, Finkelstein's suggestion that the countryside was almost completely abandoned is not visible in an extended area around Ashkelon. Despite the expansion of the urban center at

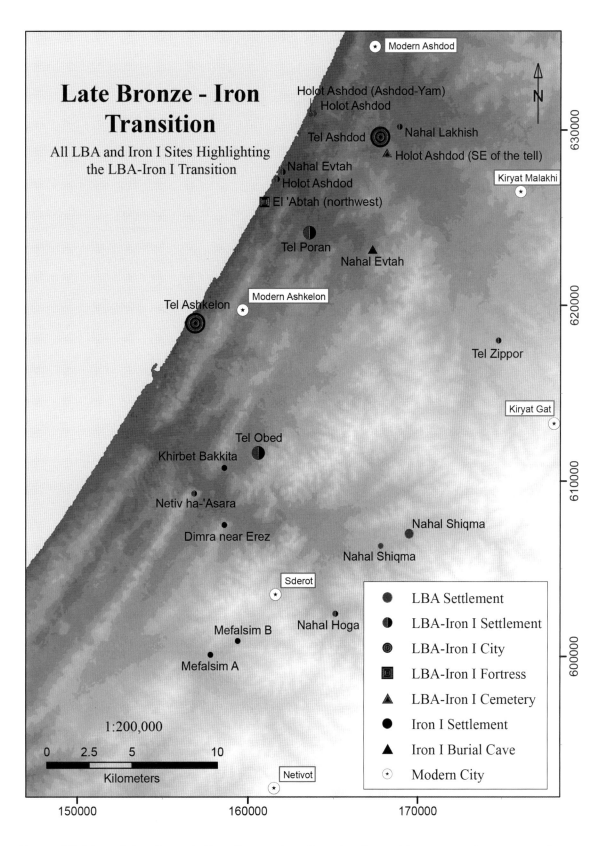

Figure 2.7: Map of sites from the Late Bronze Age–Iron Age I transition over modern topography.

Ashkelon during the Iron Age I, rural settlement remained stable to a large extent. The existence of Iron I sites at the same locations of Late Bronze Age settlements can also be attributed to environmental factors, such as the presence of water sources. While trying to delimit the border between Judah and the city-states of Gaza and Ashkelon in light of known settlements from the Late Bronze and Iron periods along the Nahal Shiqma system, Gophna (1981) pointed toward two dense concentrations of sites: an eastern concentration around Tell el-Hesi and a western one in a narrow strip near the coast close to Gaza and Ashkelon. Gophna stressed the correlation of settlement in these areas with water sources: in the eastern region, the permanent springs in Nahal Shiqma and its tributaries, and, along the coast, the high aquifer. The area between these two areas, with poor water sources and therefore less inhabited, would have served as a sort of border. Finkelstein (1996b:229) also recognized an intermediate strip between the lower Shephelah and the coast, especially sparse of sites, which helps to delineate the border between the "inner" and coastal entities, but believed it was for political reasons.

While we would suggest a total of 14 reliable Iron I settlements, this is likely to change with continued survey and excavation. Recently at Kh. Summeily, located on the northern bank of Nahal Shiqma some 300 m east of the eastern border of Map 96, an Iron Age I level was unearthed during excavation of a known Iron Age II site (Blakely, pers. comm., 2011). Furthermore, three of the sites mentioned above—Hoga, Mefalsim A, and Mefalsim B—were accidentally discovered lying under a thick layer of clay and silt because of their location near tributaries often subject to powerful floods. It is probable that additional sites like this will be revealed in the future. Regardless, Ashkelon is characterized in this period (as in the preceding Bronze Age) by the lack of a true hinterland (for further discussion, see chapter 4).

In fact, the total number of currently known sites for Ashkelon's hinterland is probably much less than 13. As noted above, the pottery of several of the *hazerim* in the south of the region was linked by Gophna to that of the northern Negev. These sites—Hoga, Mefalsim A and B, and Dimra—are all south of the Nahal Shiqma, as is Netiv Ha-ᶜAsara; the Shiqma, then, is a logical border between the territories of Ashkelon and Gaza in this period.

Iron Age II

During the Iron Age II there is a large increase, in relative terms, in the number of sites. A careful analysis of the available data, however, points toward a minimal change in settlement patterns in the first stages of this period, namely the tenth to ninth centuries B.C. Berman's survey shows an enormous increase in the number of settlements both south and north of Tel Ashkelon, 40 and 26 sites, respectively (as illustrated above in table 1.1). Most of these, however, are simply "patches," not real sites, as discussed in chapter 1. Thus, other studies of the same region and neighboring areas documented fewer settlements. Gophna (1981:49–52) identified approximately 20 sites of the Late Bronze and Iron periods in the region of the lower course of Nahal Shiqma and its central and western tributaries. A small number of these sites are located in the southern part of our study area, within the Map of Ziqim, and two others within the Map of Sderot. Gophna's map (1981:52 ill. 1) shows four Iron Age sites aligned along the northern bank of the wadi and two more south of it. In addition, he included the Beit Jirja site (Tel Obed), located within the Map of Ashkelon. Shavit's (2003) use of only secure site identifications in the region helped to identify sites and create relatively reliable site distribution maps by century.

The best example of the careful identification of definite vs. possible sites occurs outside the sand dune belt at the Beit Jirja site (Tel Obed; site 591) and involves three surveyors: Ram Gophna, Mitchell Allen, and Alon Shavit. Gophna (1965) was the first to identify the existence of an Iron II Age (plus Persian and Byzantine) site on a low hill southeast of the Arab village of Beit Jirja, revealed by deep plowing. Later, from 1986 to 1990, Allen conducted the survey of the Map of Ashkelon; the only Iron II site in his survey significant enough to merit classification as a settlement was the hill southeast of Beit Jirja, which Allen labeled "Tel Obed" (after the nearby Nahal Obed [Wadi Abd]). Allen's survey of the site revealed an important multi-period settlement, with remains of every period from MB II to modern, as well as Chalcolithic. In addition, Allen suggested that Tel Obed had Iron II satellites because of the presence of occasional Iron II sherds (site 592 and perhaps site 590, Khirbet Beit Lajus). Finally, Shavit's survey of the southern coastal plain (1994 to 1998) did not locate Iron II sherds within Map 92; however, relying on Gophna's and Allen's work, he deduced

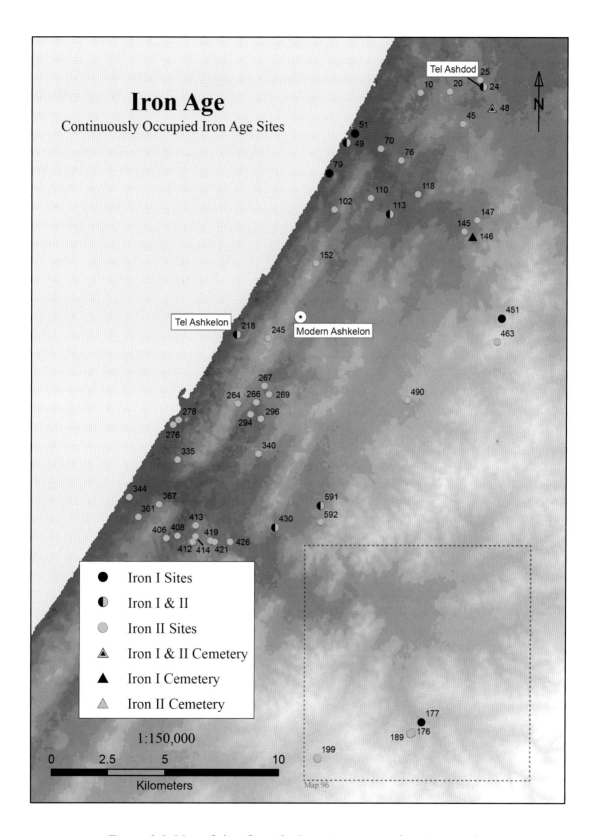

Figure 2.8: Map of sites from the Iron Age over modern topography.

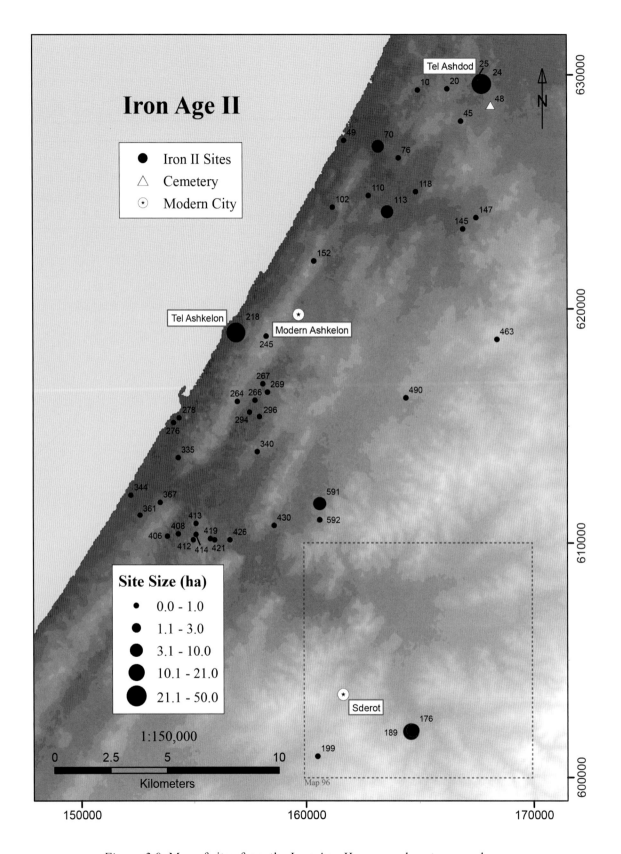

Figure 2.9: Map of sites from the Iron Age II over modern topography.

that there was one Iron II site in the area at Beit Jirja. It therefore appears that Map 92 had one settlement, Tel Obed/Beit Jirja, while a few sherds found nearby by different surveyors (Gophna; Allen) possibly indicate satellite sites. In particular, Allen's survey also suggested that Tel Obed's Iron II ceramic corpus largely dates to the eighth and seventh centuries, suggesting an increase in activity at this time.

We have more information on the economy (and other aspects) of the region during the seventh century due to the results of excavations at Tel Ashkelon. The levels from the late seventh century are well preserved (the city was destroyed by the Babylonians in 604 B.C.), with large horizontal exposure in two areas: Grid 50 Phase 7, a marketplace, and Grid 38 Phase 14, a winery (*Ashkelon 3*). The winery with four winepresses in Grid 38 reflects Tel Ashkelon's role as a wine producer in this period; most finds, however, attest to the city's other role as an international port. The imported pottery indicates connections with Egypt, Phoenicia, Cyprus, and the Aegean (both Ionia and mainland Greece). In addition, a series of finds attest to overland trade with other parts of Palestine. Some pottery points to connections with southeastern Philistia (the region of Gaza) or the northern Negev. Judahite weights (as well as Egyptian and Mesopotamian) were also found (Birney and Levine in *Ashkelon 3*, p. 483). A series of types of artifacts and botanical finds, then, point to the central role that Ashkelon played in a complex trade network as a nexus of overseas trade and an outlet for goods from the surrounding countryside.

These finds have further implications for the economic organization of the region as a whole. Noting the lack of settlement east of the sand dunes, the site of the richest farmland in the region, Allen (1997:287–88) suggests that it is unlikely that the hinterland of Tel Ashkelon and other Philistine cities could have produced enough grain to feed the urban population and that their settlement patterns do not suggest they were organized for this purpose. Similarly, Weiss, Kislev, and Maher-Slasky (*Ashkelon 3*, pp. 606–7; see also Weiss and Kislev 2004:11) concluded that the total area of the hinterland of Ashkelon was not nearly large enough to support an urban population of some 10,000–12,000 people, as estimated by Stager (e.g., *Ashkelon 3*, p. 5). Thus the city must have imported grain from outside the region. Indeed, Weiss, Kislev, and Maher-Slasky's (*Ashkelon 3*; also Weiss and Kislev 2004) analysis

of weeds in the grain piles from Grid 50 found species not native to the southern coastal plain: Some grain apparently came from farther north on the coast, while some was imported from the Judean hills.

Another way of measuring Ashkelon's hinterland is through artifact distribution. Press (2007:303–13) has used clay figurines as a means of analyzing relationships between different regions of Philistia. The seventh-century figurines of Ashkelon and Philistia are particularly well-suited for this purpose: The excavations on the tell yielded a large number (c. 150 objects), and figurines from this period typically represent local or regional variations of types of figurines (standing females and horses) found throughout much of the Levant. In particular, the use of moldmade female heads as part of a composite or mixed technique (combined with a hollow body, usually wheelmade) provides a method of tracking the spread of items from a single mold. An analysis of figurine distribution suggests that the area of the Ashkelon cultural sphere is quite small in this period. At Tel Ashdod, 15 km to the northeast, vastly different figurine types have been found. To the south, while the evidence from Netiv Ha-ᶜAsara (a mere 10 km away) is very limited, excavations yielded a horse that appears to be characteristic of southern Philistia (e.g., Tell Jemmeh).[6] Thus the north-south extent of Ashkelon's cultural sphere (if not political control) in this period appears to have been particularly restricted.[7] In fact, Ashkelon-type moldmade female heads have been found only at two other sites: Tel Ṣippor and Tel ᶜErani. At Ṣippor, three seventh-century Ashkelon-type heads were found in a favissa of the fourth century B.C. (Negbi 1966:pl. 5:15–17). Among the published finds from ᶜErani are two Ashkelon-type heads (Yeivin 1961:pl. 2, third row, third and fourth from left); however, the majority of the

---

[6] In addition, the survey of Map 91 yielded what appears to be a humped bull figurine, typical only of the Gaza region in this period, at site 421 (Berman et al. 2004:69). This site, south of the Nahal Shiqma and c. 1 km northwest of Netiv Ha-ᶜAsara, could be a satellite of the latter. Alternatively, although we have identified site 421 as a real site it is possibly a "patch," with its finds—including the figurine—brought from a nearby site, perhaps Netiv Ha-ᶜAsara.

[7] Notably, Kletter (1999) has suggested using figurines, among other types of material culture, as direct evidence for reconstructing political boundaries in the Iron IIC. While seeing some type of connection between the two, we would consider the nature of the relationship between material culture and political (or ethnic) entities to be more complex (see, e.g., discussion in Press 2007:11–21; *Ashkelon 4*, chapt. 1).

figurine corpus consists of typical Judean Pillar Figurines (JPFs), suggesting that ᶜErani is at the border of the Ashkelon sphere.

The situation contrasts greatly with that of southern Philistia, presumed to reflect the city-state or kingdom of Gaza. Gaza itself has not been extensively excavated; instead, Tell Jemmeh is the type-site for the region, with W. M. Flinders Petrie's excavations yielding more than 200 seventh-century figurines. Petrie discovered several figurine types at a number of neighboring sites: Tell el-ᶜAjjul, Tell Farᶜah (south; Tel Sharuhen), Tel Seraᶜ (Tell esh-Shariᶜa), Tel Haror (Tel Abu Hureira), Ruqeish (Tell er-Reqeish), Horvat Hoga (Khirbet Huj), Mefalsim A, Tel Milḥa (Tell el-Muleihah), and even Tell el-Hesi. Thus, unlike the Ashkelon region, the Gaza cultural sphere in this period appears to be relatively large and is well-represented at a number of sites. This figurine distribution also suggests the possibility that the Nahal Shiqma formed a sort of border between the spheres of Ashkelon and Gaza, as it appears to have done in other periods. Thus sites such as Netiv Ha-ᶜAsara and Hoga, on the southern banks of the Shiqma, would have been part of the Gazan sphere (the same would have been true for Hesi farther to the east).

It should be noted that the situation at Gaza is not paralleled at other major Philistine sites of the period—such as Ashdod and Tel Miqne (Khirbet el-Muqannaᶜ)—whose figurine types are not found over a wide area. The difference between Gaza and other Philistine sites may be due to chance of excavation (both the sites excavated and the finds at each), but without a doubt the restricted size of the Ashkelon sphere is real and contrasts with that of Gaza. As Shavit (2008:151) and Allen (*Ashkelon 1*, p. 37) have observed, the lack of a true hinterland for Ashkelon might be related to the fact that its power and influence would have come from its role as a port and therefore its maritime connections, thus supporting Stager's "port power" model (Stager 2001; cf. Finkelstein 1996b:235 for Iron I). In light of this, it is worth noting Sennacherib's mention of the cities of Ṣidqa, king of Ashkelon, that Sennacherib conquered in his campaign in 701 B.C., and which he listed in his annals: Jaffa, Bnei-Brak, Azor, and Beth-Dagon (see, e.g., Luckenbill 1924:30–31; Oppenheim 1969:287 from the Sennacherib Prism col. II, lines 60–72). All of these sites are located in the area of modern Tel Aviv, some 45 km north of Tel Ashkelon. This passage from Sennacherib's annals may therefore

be evidence of Ashkelon's maritime power: an enclave at the northern edge of Philistia.

In attempting to explain both the settlement pattern within the Ashkelon region and its lack of a hinterland, Allen (*Ashkelon 1*, pp. 23, 37) has emphasized not only Ashkelon's role as an international port but its location near the main north-south route of the country, the coastal road. At the northern end of the study area, he has noted the location of Tel Poran (site 113) close to the coastal road (1997:227, following Gophna 1963; see also Allen in *Ashkelon 1*, p. 37). He also observes that Tel Obed (site 591) in Map 92 is close to this route (1997:238, 343; the same may also be true of the possible Iron Age site at Khirbet Irza, site 490). Poran is roughly halfway between Ashdod and Ashkelon, while Tel Obed—approximately the same size—lies between Ashkelon and Gaza (as observed by Allen 1997:227). As Gophna (1963) suggested for Poran, Allen has concluded that both sites may have served as way stations along the coastal road (1997:344). We would suggest that the same may be true of Khirbet Bakkita (site 430), Netiv Ha-ᶜAsara (Shavit and Yasur-Landau 2005), perhaps Dimra (in Map 95) southeast of Ashkelon, and Tell Kursun (site 45) to the northeast. In fact, Kursun, Poran, Obed, Bakkita, and Netiv Ha-ᶜAsara are all relatively close (within c. 1 km) to the modern coastal road (Route 4) and even closer to the nineteenth-century north-south road. The locations of these sites therefore provide support for the "access resources" model of settlement in this period (Allen in *Ashkelon 1*, pp. 23, 37; 1997:330–31, 346). David Dorsey came to a similar conclusion in his discussion of the road network of ancient Israel: For him, the line of the "international coastal highway" was marked by a line of sites between Gaza and Ashdod, including Nahal Hannun, Khirbet Bakkita (his site 3), Tel Obed (site 4), Poran, and Tell Kursun (site 5; Dorsey 1991:59–60 and Map 1, route I1). In addition, the large number of jar rims found by Allen's survey at Tel Obed led him to conclude that its importance was due to its role in trade through the region (*Ashkelon 1*, p. 33; 1997:344). Allen also suggests (1997:242) that there was another north-south road farther to the east, based on the location of four large tells along the eastern part of Nahal Shiqma: Hesi, Tel Nagila (Tell en Najila), Tel Qeshet (Tell Quneitirah), and Tel Sheqef (Tell Abu esh Shuqaf). Farther to the south, Tel Milḥa (Tell el Muleiha), also along the Nahal Shiqma system, may have been situated on the same route;

to the north, Tel Ṣippor and/or Tel ᶜErani (close to the same longitude as the other sites) may also have been located near this proposed route. The situation in the Iron II, then, appears to have been similar to that observed by Gophna (1981) for the LB and Iron I. Similarly, Dorsey proposed that the sites listed by Allen were connected with interior alternates to the main coastal highway (1991:67–69 and Map 1, I15–18). This theoretical road may be the eastern branch of the coastal road, as discussed, e.g., by Aharoni (1979:49, map 3).

This analysis of sites' roles as waypoints along major trade routes has been supported by the excavations at Netiv Ha-ᶜAsara. There, Shavit and Yasur-Landau reported finds (albeit limited) of imported Aegean pottery, namely an Ionian cup and a Wild Goat-style sherd, both dated to the late seventh century (2005:80–81, fig. 14:1, 3). On the basis of the ceramics, the excavators conclude that the site's peak period of occupation stretched from the seventh century through the Persian period and note that the site takes advantage of its location on both the Nahal Shiqma and the north-south coastal road (2005:82). They reasonably suggest the imported pottery arrived through the nearby port of Ashkelon, thus showing that the hinterland sites were integrated with Ashkelon's trade network in this period.

The other Iron II sites in the study region can also be linked to roads, in this case newly developed roads. Dorsey suggested two additional north-south routes in the Ashkelon region, based on nineteenth-century roads recorded by the Survey of Western Palestine and the location of Iron Age sites: I11, running between Ashkelon and the Arab village Yasur, and I13, leaving the main coastal road at Beit Jirja (i.e., Tel Obed) and heading toward Ekron via Sawafir (1991:65–66, Map 1). In the case of I11, Dorsey noted that the two Iron II sites east of the coastal road discovered by Berman in his survey of Nizzanim East are on this route: site 140 (Kh. Khasse) and site 142 (Nahal Evtah).[8] In the case of I13, Dorsey could note only that the main junctions on this route, Beit Jirja and Sawafir, both had Iron Age remains, making the existence of an ancient route here likely; Allen's Map 92 data were not available to him. Allen's survey, in fact, appears to confirm the existence of an Iron Age route here. As in Nizzanim East, Allen's

survey of the Map of Ashkelon revealed only two sites east of the coastal road: Kh. Irza and Kh. Ijjis er Ras (site 463). While these two sites do not lie on the path of the late Ottoman road between Beit Jirja and Shawafir, they do lie almost exactly on a line between those two sites.[9]

Dorsey also proposed a set of east-west roads running through the region (1991:191, 195–96, 198–99, Maps 14, J9, 10, 14, 15, and 22). However, for the dune belt area at least, his two southern routes (J14 and J22), which he proposed connected interior sites to Tell esh Shuqaf (site 344) on the coast, could not have existed, as the sites he uses as evidence are not ancient sites but "patches."[10] Nevertheless, Dorsey's work—especially his hypothetical route between Beit Jirja and Shawafir—further confirms that Iron II settlement patterns in the region should be linked to a developing road network throughout it.

Allen (1997) noted that the Assyrians may have influenced the increase in settlement in the latter part of Iron II, and its apparent connection to an emerging road network in the region. The issue of Assyrian impact on Philistia has been a major topic of discussion (following Gitin [e.g., 1995; 2003; Gitin and Dothan 1987:216]; see also Shavit 2003). The evidence for Assyrian presence in our study area, however, is very limited. The best evidence comes from Tel Ashdod at the northern edge of Map 88, where M. Dothan's excavations uncovered a stele of Sargon (Tadmor 1971) and more recent salvage excavations by Elena Kogan-Zehavi and Pirhiya Nahshoni, which revealed an Assyrian palace of the late eighth and early seventh centuries (Kogan-Zehavi 2006; site 25). These finds can be interpreted historically as the aftermath of the revolt of Yamani, suppressed by Sargon in 712, after which Ashdod was turned into an Assyrian

---

[8] Following Berman (later published in Berman and Barda 2005:64*–65*), Dorsey erroneously named site 140 Kh. Bezze and site 142 H. Hassa. For the proper identifications of these two sites, see chapter 3.

[9] Allen, meanwhile, tried to use the existence of Iron Age sites at Tel Obed/Beit Jirja and Kh. Irza to argue for a more easterly route of the coastal road (*Ashkelon 1*, p. 37); however, he also tried to incorporate Tel Poran into the route, even though Poran does not line up well with these sites (since it lies west of the current coastal highway). Allen did propose an alternate route running southwest-northeast through Map 92 (*Ashkelon 1*, p. 37) but used a series of "possible" Iron II sites to justify it; therefore, based on the principles adopted here, this alternate route should be rejected.

[10] We must reject Allen's suggestion that these sites indicate the possibility of an alternative north-south coastal route running through Ashkelon (*Ashkelon 1*, p. 37; cf. 1997:343–44) for the same reason. In this case, it is worth observing that Allen himself recognized that some of these sites might not be real sites (1997:235).

province, *Asdudi* (as noted by Tadmor 1971:192). Possible Assyrian buildings have also been noted at the southern margins of the study region at two sites along the Nahal Shiqma system: Tell esh Shuqaf at the mouth of the Shiqma (Berman et al. 2004:45*; Gophna and Meron 1963) and Horvat Hoga in Map 96 (Porat 1976; see chapter 5, site 189). While Naʾaman (e.g., 1979:81; 1995:111) and Stern (2001:9, 21, 110), among others, have suggested that these are Assyrian forts (largely on the basis of Assyrian presence elsewhere in Philistia), the nature of these buildings is unclear as they have either been only partially excavated (Hoga) or merely surveyed (Shuqaf). For Hoga, the excavator noted only a large building with tenth-century pottery in the fill beneath and eighth-century pottery above; no floors were found in the building itself (Porat 1976:42). At Shuqaf, Gophna and Meron merely reported on Iron II pottery at the site in their original survey, suggesting the site was a coastal station between Ashkelon and (the port of) Gaza (1963). Gophna only mentioned the presence of "Assyrian" pottery and identified the site as an Assyrian fort through personal communication (as mentioned in the record files of Shavit's survey). At Tel Ashkelon, there is almost no direct evidence for Assyrian influence. It is noted only in a small amount of Assyrian-style pottery (including Assyrian Palace Ware). However, it appears that this pottery was not locally made but imported from either southeastern Philistia or the northern Negev: Petrographic analysis suggests an origin in those regions, and the corpus is paralleled particularly well at Tel Sera (*Ashkelon 3*, pp. 117–21).

Persian (539–312 B.C.) and Hellenistic (332–37 B.C.) Periods

Our analysis in chapter 1 suggested treating the Persian and Hellenistic periods together, as well as drastically reducing the number of sites in the western sandy region of the study area for each period. As presented in table 1.1, the Maps of Ashkelon (92) and Sderot (96), the area to the east chosen for comparison, the number of sites from the Persian period is ten (Map 92) and three (Map 96), while for the Hellenistic it is eight (92) and seven (96). In order to reinforce the observation that the total number of settlements from both periods was relatively small, reflecting the same settlement pattern throughout the southern coastal plain over the course of five centuries, we shall compare two additional Archaeological Survey of

Israel maps, in distinct geographical regions. The first, the Map of Urim (Gazit 1996), is located more than 30 km to the south of the Ashkelon region in the Besor basin; the second, the Map of Lakhish (Dagan 1992), is c. 25 km from Tel Ashkelon in the lower Shephelah. The Persian period in the Urim Map is represented by four sites: Tell Farᶜah (south) (including its cemeteries), two settlements, and one camp. Evidence of the Hellenistic period was observed at ten sites, two of them only tentatively ascribed to this period. Following the principles adopted in this study, we have adopted the minimal number of sites here as well: Therefore, we conclude that the Hellenistic period is represented by eight sites: Tell Farᶜah (south), six settlements, and one camp. Gazit (1996:15*) concludes that the settlement distribution in both periods was directly connected to the east-west road between Beersheba and Philistia. In both periods, the route passed near permanent water sources at Nahal Besor.

Similarly, the Lakhish area was sparsely occupied during the Persian period. Besides Tel Lachish (Tell ed-Duweir), the central city, only ten additional settlements were discerned by the survey (Dagan 1992:17*). They are arranged along and close to the wadi systems: six sites along the Nahal Lachish; two on its northern branch, Nahal Maresha; and in the south, two sites along Nahal Aduraim. The settlements along Nahal Aduraim are noteworthy in that this wadi is the main tributary of Nahal Shiqma; its origin lies in the Hebron hills, and it forms a wide drainage system where it joins the Shiqma farther to the west. The major east-west route leading from Hebron to Gaza is located along this system. During the Hellenistic period a sharp increase in the number of settlements occurs, to a total of 25. Most of them are located near Maresha. Yehuda Dagan (1992:17*–18*) ascribes the increase to the role of this city as the major administrative and religious center in the region in the Hellenistic period, superseding Lachish, which had filled the same function in the Persian period.

In our study area, Tel Ashkelon and Tel Ashdod were thriving cities during the Persian and Hellenistic periods. Tel Ashkelon, as in the Bronze and Iron Ages, was a flourishing port, as evidenced by continuing imports from Greece and Cyprus, among other places (see, e.g., *Ashkelon 1*, pp. 290, 314, 322; Barako in *Ashkelon 1*, pp. 454–56). Of particular note is a warehouse dating to the first half of the fifth century with complete and partial amphoras, both local and Greek; the excavators

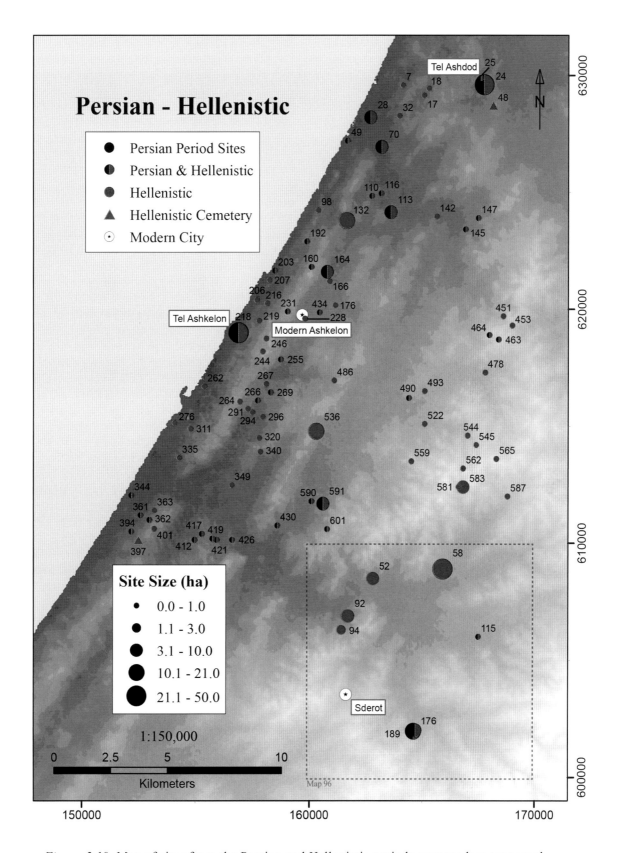

Figure 2.10: Map of sites from the Persian and Hellenistic periods over modern topography.

concluded that imported wine was transferred to smaller local storejars in this building (*Ashkelon 1*, pp. 313–14). As in the Iron Age, imported pottery is found beyond the city of Ashkelon but appears to be more widely distributed:

1. Netiv Ha-ᶜAsara (Shavit and Yasur-Landau 2005): Imports included a white-ground lekythos and possible rhyton (Shavit and Yasur-Landau 2005:80–81, fig. 14:2, 4), plus East Greek amphorae (Shavit and Yasur-Landau 2005:83).

2. El Qabu (site 262): an imported (Hellenistic?) amphora found during inspection (Berman et al. 2004:31*).

3. Ashkelon, Barnea Top (site 160): a Megarian bowl and a stamped amphora handle from Ephesus (Haimi 2008).

4. Ashkelon, Migdal (Eli Kohen St.; site 434): Persian period lekythoi (Haimi 2009).

5. Kh. Bakkita (site 430): a Persian period mortarium, whose origin was identified by petrographic analysis as southern Turkey, and a lekythos (Baumgarten, pers. comm.).

6. Ashdod (site 24): These imports could have come from the city's own port at Ashdod-Yam rather than from Tel Ashkelon.

At Netiv Ha-ᶜAsara, the excavators connected these finds both to the port of Ashkelon and to the site's position on important east-west (Nahal Shiqma) and north-south (coastal road) routes (2005:82–83).

One would perhaps expect to find some sort of network of hinterland and satellite settlements around Tel Ashkelon and Tel Ashdod due to the large number of sites for both periods documented by Berman's survey, but the results of salvage excavations point to a different picture. North of Tel Ashkelon (c. 2 km), excavations at the Early Bronze Age I site of the Ashkelon Marina revealed a Persian period cist tomb (Golani 1996). At site 434 in Migdal, a refuse pit was found at a Byzantine site containing a few pottery sherds from the Persian period (Haimi 2009); Persian-period pottery was also the earliest reported by Allen at Migdal in the Map 92 survey. East of Tel Ashkelon, at Barzilay Hospital, two amphorae were discovered dating to the Hellenistic period

(site 221, el Jura; Kogan-Zehavi 2007). North of Tel Ashdod, scanty remains were revealed over the monumental Assyrian building from the Iron II (site 25), including refuse pits from the Persian period and several potters' kilns from the Hellenistic period (Kogan-Zehavi 2006), probably representing an industrial quarter of the Hellenistic city of Tel Ashdod. The "Third Mile Estate" Byzantine-period site also yielded little from the Hellenistic period (site 164; Israel 1995a). Turning to the south of the study area, at Kh. Bakkita few remains from the Persian and Hellenistic periods were uncovered (Baumgarten, pers. comm.), and at Netiv Ha-ᶜAsara a stratum from the Persian period was excavated (Yasur-Landau and Shavit 1999; Shavit and Yasur-Landau 2005). Also of note in the Map of Ziqim is an isolated columbarium in the Shiqma basin (site 363), although it is unknown whether there was an associated settlement in the vicinity.

Despite inspection of extensive development works throughout the modern city of Ashkelon since the early 1990s, only two new settlement sites have been uncovered. In 2000, inspection works revealed remains from the Hellenistic period at the highest point of the Barnea neighborhood (c. 60 m above sea level; site 160), on the top of a thin *hamra* layer, resting on a *kurkar* ridge, and totally covered by post-Byzantine sand dunes. In 2002, a small-scale salvage excavation was conducted at the site (Sion 2008). Further large-scale salvage excavations were later carried out, revealing a sizeable village (with an estimated size of c. 20 dunams) from the Hellenistic period built of sundried mudbricks, laid out in a Hippodamian plan. Persian-period remains were exposed in a small area of the site (Haimi 2008). Remains of another settlement from the Hellenistic period were discovered during infrastructure work, c. 2 km southeast of Tel Ashkelon (site not in table, just west of site 273). Based on the local topography and the dispersal of sherds, it also appears to have been a sizeable settlement. Here, too, the remains are located on the top of a *kurkar* ridge at the same altitude above sea level (60 m) and were also covered by a shifting sand dune. Two well-preserved mudbrick walls were discerned. These are, at least for the moment, the only sizeable settlements from the Persian and Hellenistic periods between the surroundings of Tel Ashkelon and Tel Ashdod. Thus, these excavations appear to confirm our general analysis of the survey data, reducing the number of sites from Berman's surveys in the sand dunes and accepting Allen's minimal number of sites in Map 92 (and from Huster's survey of Map 96).

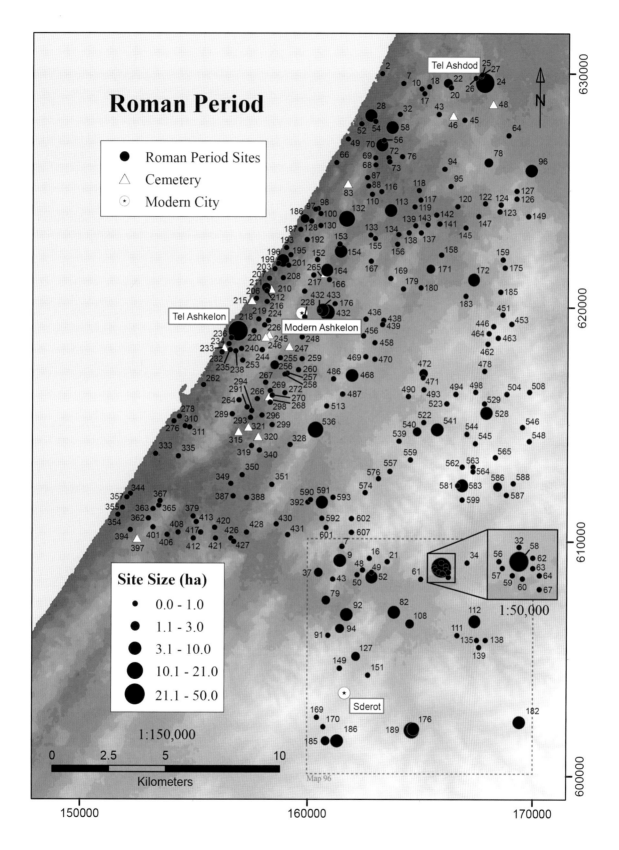

Figure 2.11: Map of sites from the Roman period over modern topography.

Meanwhile, it seems that the location of these two settlements on high points is not coincidental. Both were within sight of the city of Tel Ashkelon. Perhaps their location points toward some settlement pattern based upon lines of vision. Other sites, including Netiv Ha-ᶜAsara (Shavit and Yasur-Landau 2005), Kh. Bakkita (site 430), Tel Obed (site 591), Tel Poran (site 113), and Tell Kursun (site 45), represent continuous occupation since the earlier periods, presumably related to the location of the coastal road. The same continuity is noted at Kh. Irza (site 490) and Kh. ᶜIjjis er-Ras (site 463), again probably because of the road branching off from the coastal road at Tel Obed to the northeast. Further evidence for this road appears in the Hellenistic period: After removing Allen's "possible" sites in Map 92, we are left with eight sites east of the current coastal road. Other than ed-Dude (site 565), the other seven fall more or less in a line running northeast from Tel Obed: sites 591 (Allen's site 01/3, Obed), 490 (46/1, Irza), 522 (55/1, Beit Saman, north), 494 (66/1, Khor Breish), 498 (76/1, Qimas), 463 (88/1, ᶜIjjis er-Ras), and site 451 (89/6). Note that Allen (*Ashkelon 1*, p. 37) identified a series of three southeast-northwest lines of sites, connecting these to his access resources model, but his identification of settlement patterns was obscured by the inclusion of uncertain sites. Overall, there is an increase in the number of sites in these periods throughout the study area, although it is not as sharp an increase once the uncertain sites are removed. This increase is also paralleled by the apparent growth of previously existing sites, as at Netiv Ha-ᶜAsara (Shavit and Yasur-Landau 2005:60, 83) and (as suggested by Allen [*Ashkelon 1*, p. 37]) at Tel Obed and Kh. ᶜIjjis er-Ras with their satellite sites. In general, however, we recognize the same model as in previous periods: the lack of a rural hinterland around Tel Ashkelon.

Roman Period

As emphasized in chapter 1, the high site counts in the Maps of Ziqim and Nizzanim also extend to the Roman period. In the Ziqim map, only one-third of the 97 sites attributed to this period contained structural remains (Berman et al. 2004:13*). In the Nizzanim map, Roman-period sites at which the survey found only pottery scatters were interpreted as the remains of temporary encampments, forming part of a settlement system together with the permanent settlements and roads of the region (Berman and Barda 2005:12*). Therefore, if we are

to analyze issues such as settlement distribution or settlement patterns, we must note both the nature of the sites and, in particular, the description of sites that no longer exist. An additional problem is site size: In our view, the use of structural remains as a criterion for evaluating the area of a site is not always valid. At many small settlements and other sites, an initial Roman phase was almost completely covered and obscured by the remains of the following Byzantine and Islamic periods. In addition, the pottery collections from surveys, especially those containing types of the third to fourth centuries A.D., are often difficult to define chronologically. These factors have led surveyors to erroneous conclusions concerning the intensity and size as well as the dating of the settlements. The impressive increase reported in the number of sites during the Roman period does not reflect a paralleled growth in the number of settlements. Many of the remains have since proven to be isolated agricultural and industrial installations, while others belong to burial structures.

Prior to the archaeological surveys, part of the landscape of the surveyed area was drastically transformed due to the expansion of the modern cities of Ashkelon and Ashdod, mainly as a result of the establishment of industrial areas (but also because of the mechanization of agriculture, quarrying, and other human activities). Nevertheless, archaeological excavations and probes have taken place over substantial portions of the surveyed area.

Byzantine Period

In many respects, the Byzantine period appears to be an outgrowth of the Roman period; for this reason, we treat them together to a certain extent in this discussion. The Roman period witnesses new settlements (and other sites) in parts of the study area previously devoid of settlements—in particular throughout the area east of the coastal road. This trend intensifies in the Byzantine period. Moreover, in almost every significant excavated site of the Byzantine period, remains of the Late Roman period (second to third centuries A.D.) have also been noted. A specific example of this stratification is found in the Barnea neighborhood, c. 2 km north of Tel Ashkelon: Here a narrow passageway with structures on both sides was revealed and attributed to the Late Roman period (site 198, Oded Feder, pers. comm.). Nearby, a winepress dated to the Byzantine period was excavated on a higher elevation (site 200, Toueg 2009). The same

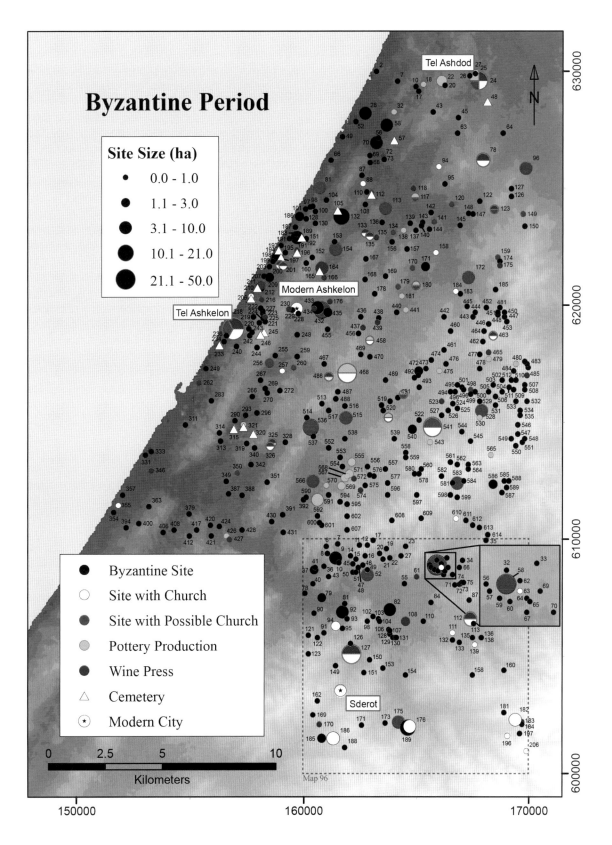

Figure 2.12: Map of sites from the Byzantine period over modern topography.

stratification is found at site 216, 0.5 km north of the tell, where two construction strata from the Roman and Byzantine periods were exposed (Varga 2002). A minority of the winepresses follow this same pattern: They were constructed in the Late Roman period but were used mainly in the Byzantine period. One exceptional case was recorded at El Qabu (site 262), c. 2 km south of Tel Ashkelon, where the winepress complex and other structural remains were ascribed to the second to third centuries A.D. without evidence of continuation into the Byzantine period (Sion 2012).

One of the outstanding features of the Roman period is the relatively large number of burial sites located outside of settlements (a phenomenon noted since the Middle Bronze Age). Generally, these consist of single or small clusters of vaulted tombs, which served the wealthy residents of cities and are therefore concentrated around urban sites. More than a dozen of these burial systems have been discovered in the vicinity of Ashdod-Yam (in Map 84, just to the north of the study area), and 30 are known around Tel Ashkelon. At the same time, burial systems are also found near rural settlements. As confirmed by excavations, they first appeared in the Late Roman period, beginning in the third century A.D., and continued into the Byzantine period (Huster and Sion 2006). In death, as in life, then, the cultural practices of the Byzantine period were an outgrowth of the preceding Roman period.

Despite the large number of small-scale salvage excavations that yielded cultural remains from the Late Roman period, we are limited in what we can say about the integration of these sites. Therefore, ancient texts dating to that period still remain the major source of our knowledge on Ashkelon and its surroundings in the Roman period (beyond the excavations at Tel Ashkelon itself). However, surveys and excavations have demonstrated that the Byzantine period witnessed the densest settlement in the history of the Ashkelon region (and of Palestine generally). In this period we see an extremely large range of sites, representing a complex hierarchy from cities and towns to large villages and small hamlets, as well as isolated industrial, agricultural, and commercial sites (and burials). Much of this hierarchy is related to the confluence of the church, the wine industry, and pilgrimage. Each of these phenomena is attested extensively in historical and inscriptional sources, and so the archaeological data confirm and elaborate this to some extent. At the same time, there

is always a danger that the textual data could lead archaeologists to unwarranted assumptions about the material remains; it is therefore best to survey the groups of data individually and then make a critical evaluation of assumptions and conclusions.

In both the Roman and Byzantine periods Ashkelon flourished and was known for its active port, serving as an international trade station for the import and export of goods. During the Byzantine period, the main product exported was wine, which was in demand as a product of the Holy Land (see, e.g., Stager and Schloen in *Ashkelon 1*, p. 9; Johnson and Stager 1995). Several researchers have focused on the topic of wine production, a subject that embraces many areas of study. The study of wine production has produced a broad literature that includes almost all aspects related to the subject: e.g., the typology and distribution of storage vessels (Johnson and Stager 1995), workshop sites (Israel 1993), and references to Ashkelon wine in ancient texts (e.g., Mayerson 1993). The wine industry involves several stages of production and distribution, from the making of the wine itself to the production of storejars, the bottling of wine, and its shipment abroad. All of these stages have to some extent been observed during surveys and revealed by excavations.

Evidence of the Wine Industry

Winepresses. We have identified 36 winepresses, winepress complexes, and clusters of winepresses over an extended area, c. 20 x 35 km (including our core study area plus Map 96, and north to Ashdod-Yam; see figure 2.13; table 2.2). Some are large, elaborate complexes (see Avshalom-Gorni et al. 2008 for a discussion of this type); others are smaller but occasionally appear in clusters suggesting large-scale production. As the survey of winepresses shows, they are associated with settlements of various sizes, from cities (e.g., Tel Ashkelon) to villages (e.g., the two winepresses at Ijjis er Ras), monasteries (e.g., the monasteries at Ashdod-Yam Quarter 11 and Tel Ashdod), and estates (e.g., site 164, the "Third Mile Estate").

The use of industrial winepresses at large farms is attested widely throughout Palestine and has been treated by Avshalom-Gorni et al. (2008). In our area, at least five such winepresses complexes have been identified (see Avshalom-Gorni et al. 2008:61, fig. 8): two at the "Third Mile Estate" (site 164), one at Ashkelon east (Hamame, site 166), and two at Ijjis er Ras (Meron, site 463 and

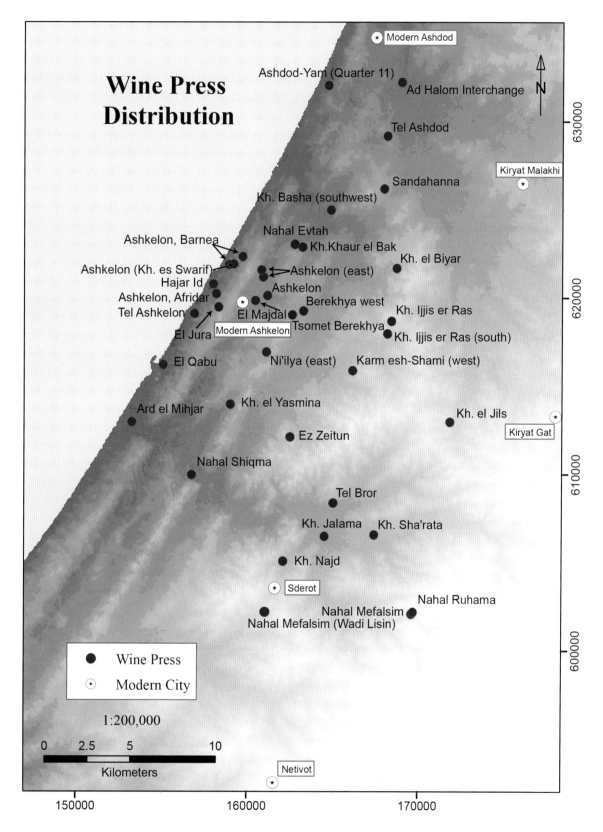

Figure 2.13: Winepress distribution during the Byzantine period over modern topography.

Table 2.2: Winepresses in the Ashkelon Region

No.	Site	Site no.	Coordinates	Details	Notes and References
1	Ad Halom Interchange		168960/632250	Winepress	Talis 2010
2	Ashdod-Yam (Quarter 11)		164690/632060	Winepress	Berman et al. 2005:30*–31*
3	Tel Ashdod	site 24	168130/629200	Founding inscription	Gudovitch 2006; Tzaferis 2006; Di Segni 2008
4	Kh. Basha (SW)	site 118	164850/625000	Winepress complex	Peretz 2011
5	Sandahanna	site 78	167950/626200	Registered winepress	Yalqut HaPirsumim 1964:1441
6	Nahal Evtah	sites 155, 133	162740/623045	Three winepresses of different plans	Varga 2010
7	Kh. el Biyar	site 175	168700/621700	Surveyed winepress	Berman and Barda 2005:70*
8	Kh. Khaur el Bak	site 135	163200/622900	Elaborate winepress; a second installation, probably a ruined winepress	Talis 2011
9	Ashkelon, Barnea	site 205	159700/622350	Three small winepresses of the same plan	Zelin 2001
10	Ashkelon (E) (Hamame)	site 166	160900/621200	Elaborate winepress	Fabian et al. 1995
11	Ashkelon (E) ("Third Mile Estate")	site 164	160800/621600	Two elaborate winepresses	Israel 1993
12	Ashkelon, Barnea (Byzantine Church) (Kh. es Sawarif [E])	site 200	158915/621900	Three plastered vats	Toueg 2009
13	Ashkelon (Kh. es Sawarif)	site 201	159180/621930	Winepress	Haiman 2011
14	Ashkelon, Afridar	site 216	158160/620250	A concrete winepress	Varga 2002
15	Ashkelon	site 176	161150/620160	Winepress	Nahshoni 1999
16	El Jura	site 225	158300/619500	Circular installation, part of a winepress	Ein Gedy 2002
17	Hajar Id	site 210	158000/620800	Treading floor, three collecting vats	Wallach 2003
18	El Majdal (Eli Kohen St.)	site 434	160450/619860	Treading floor, three fermentation cells	Nahshoni 2009a
19	Tel Ashkelon	site 218	156900/619130	Treading floor, collecting vat	Unpublished material from the Leon Levy Expedition to Ashkelon
20	Tsomet Berekhya	site 437	162600/619050	Plastered pool, probably part of a winepress	Nahshoni 2009b
21	Berekhya (W)	site 439	163250/619280	Treading floor, two collecting vats	Huster: in preparation
22	El Qabu	site 262	155075/616250	Three winepresses	Sion 2012
23	Kh. el Yasmina	site 325-326	158990/614000	Winepress	Haimi 2008
24	Ard el Mihjar (Nahal Shiqma)	site 346	153250/613000	Winepress treading floor	Nikolsky 2010

Table 2.2 (cont.): Winepresses in the Ashkelon Region

No.	Site	Site no.	Coordinates	Details	Notes and References
25	Nahal Shiqma	site 427	156750/610000	Rock-hewn winepresses from the Roman or Byzantine periods	Berman et al. 2004:60*
26	Kh. Ijjis er Ras (S)	site 465	168160/617990	Elaborate winepress	Paran 2009
27	Kh. Ijjis er Ras	site 463	168400/618700	Winepress complex	Allen in *Ashkelon 1*, p. 47, fig. 3.25
28	Ni^cilya (E)	site 486	161100/616950	In situ stone used as the base of a screw press	Inspection work by Huster
29	Karm esh-Shami (W) (Beit Tima [N])	site 523	166100/615900	Mosaic pavement (bottom part of a collecting vat)	Inspection work by Huster
30	Ez Zeitun	site 574	162480/612140	Three plastered pools	Inspection work by Huster; probably surveyed by Allen, site 22/3 (*Ashkelon 1*, p. 59)
31	Kh. el Jils		171850/613000	Weight of screw press	Inspection work by Huster. Exhibited in the open museum of Kibbutz Bror Hayl
32	Tel Bror (Tell el Mashnaga)	Ch. 5, site 61	165000/608400	Treading floor (c. 3 x 4 m)	Chapter 5, site 61
33	Kh. Jalama (H. Gluma)	Ch. 5, site 108	164500/606500	Three plastered pools	Chapter 5, site 108
34	Kh. Sha^crata (H. Se^cora)	Ch. 5, site 112	167400/606600	Two screw press weights	Chapter 5, site 112
35	Kh. Najd	Ch. 5, site 127	162100/605100	Treading floor (c. 4 x 4 m)	Chapter 5, site 127
36	Nahal Mefalsim (Wadi Lisin; Nir^cam Junction)	Ch. 5, site 170	169600/602100	Part of a collecting vat	Seriy 2010; chapter 5, site 170
37	Nahal Ruhama (Wadi Abu Rashid)	Ch. 5, site 183	169700/602200	Weight of screw press	Chapter 5, site 183

Ijjis er Ras [south], site 465 [Paran 2009]). Clearly, winemaking was an industry involving all segments of society.

Kilns. Another aspect of the wine industry is represented by sites where large quantities of ceramic containers or their fragments, mainly the so-called Gaza jars, are found together with kiln materials such as fired bricks and slag; together, these remains are clear indications of pottery workshops involved in the mass production of storage jars for storing and transporting wine. Y. Israel (1993) conducted a systematic survey of this class of sites, extending from the Nahal Lachish around Ashdod in the north down to Ḥaluza and Beersheba in the Negev. Israel identified 22 sites in this region with evidence of kilns, the majority of which were concentrated between Ashkelon and Gaza, east of the coastal road. Since Israel's survey, additional examples have been excavated.

This sort of indirect evidence for wine production should be carefully analyzed, however. The large number of pottery workshops and the enormous quantities of potsherds indicate a great demand for containers but do not necessarily indicate that wine was produced at the same site. Excavations conduced at Geva^cot Etun, near Netivot, c. 20 km southeast of Tel Ashkelon, uncovered a small settlement from the Byzantine period, whose economy was based on agriculture and especially on industrial pottery manufacture. No winepresses were found (Seriy, forthcoming).

Shipping Facilities. At the Ard el Mihjar site (Ziqim beach; site 331), located c. 6 km south of Tel Ashkelon, salvage excavations unearthed a structure attributed to the sixth century A.D. that served as a warehouse for sealed wine jars seemingly ready for shipping (Fabian and Goren 2000; 2001). The excavators also suggested the existence of an anchorage nearby. While much wine from the region would have been funneled through the markets of Tel Ashkelon, there is no reason to believe that it was the only distribution channel.

Evidence of Churches and Synagogues

Bishops from Ashkelon, as well as the bishop of Maiumas Ascalonis (a separate, neighboring quarter), are well represented in ecclesiastical documents (Hirschfeld 1990). Indeed, the spread of Christianity resulted in the establishment of a large number of churches. This prominent institution existed in almost every settlement in Byzantine times, especially toward the end of the period,[11] while towns and cities had multiple churches (both Ashdod-Yam and Barnea/Kh. es Sawarif [Maiumas Ascalonis?; so Tsafrir et al. 1994:175] had two each, while Tel Ashkelon had at least six). The large number of churches also reflects the central role that the institution of the Church played in city and rural life—both religious and secular.

At this point, some remarks about methodology are in order. Surface indications of public buildings are clearly visible. These include marble columns, capitals, bases or their fragments, marble tiles, and large amounts of colored tesserae for flooring. However, surveyors have sometimes had difficulty determining the exact nature of these finds. Allen (*Ashkelon 1*, p. 41) labeled these sites as "villas" in his survey publication. Much earlier, Petrie had employed the same terminology. In an extremely short note on the excavations at Kh. Umm Laqis he stated, "At a little distance to the north, on a rise, we cleared part of a building of concrete and small stones; which, from the large bath in it, seemed to be a Roman villa" (1891:10). We judged this to be a winepress upon

our visit to the site, but it illustrates the difficulty in determining the precise nature of these remains. Almost as a rule, the remains of elaborate rural structures from the Byzantine period do not appear to be residences but rather some sort of public building.

We used two methods to identify a church at a site. The first was the comprehensive analysis of all available data: geographical details on maps, the name of sites with clear connection to Christian personalities (i.e., in the Ashkelon region, Sandahanna [= St. Anne] and Barbara), the use of the Arabic noun "Deir" for an actual or former monastery (as perhaps was the case in the Arab village el Jiya, whose name according to Guérin [1869:173] was ed Deir, and the village of Deir Suneid, both located south of Ashkelon),[12] travelers' accounts, historical documents, and unpublished archaeological reports. The second involved repeat visits to potential sites and intensive collection of indicative finds, such as marble fragments of chancel screen panels and posts, offering tables, column fragments, revetment slabs, and stones with incised crosses. In addition, glass finds—window pane fragments, bowl rims, vertical suspension handles, and especially the thick cylindrical stems—were extremely significant. These glass finds are characteristic remains of hanging lamps in churches (Patrich 1988).

Based on these methods, we have been able to add significantly to the corpus of known churches in the Ashkelon region and thus to our knowledge of the religious life of the region in the Byzantine period. We chose an expanded area of c. 25 by 35 km that encompassed the core study area, Map 96, and the area between Ashdod and Ashdod-Yam. Within this area, Asher Ovadiah and Carlos Gomez de Silva (1981–84) were able to identify a total of nine churches from eight different settlements. Tsafrir et al., however (1994, esp. Map 5), identified a total of 14 episcopal sees and church sites (including the sees of Anthedon, Maiumas Gazae, Saraphia, and Gaza and a church at Ruhama, which are not in our list). Dauphin's list of 16 is the most expansive list of Christian communities (1998:170–73, 231, 306, figs. 51, 65, 82). In this study (see table 2.3), we present 55 churches from

---

[11] This phenomenon was emphasized by Jerome Schaefer who listed several sites with evidence of a church in the region of Tell Jemmeh, south of our study area (Schaefer 1979:Table 9, Appendix C).

[12] Cf. Elitzur and Ben-David 2007, who argue that the element "Deir" in place names has no connection to monasteries.

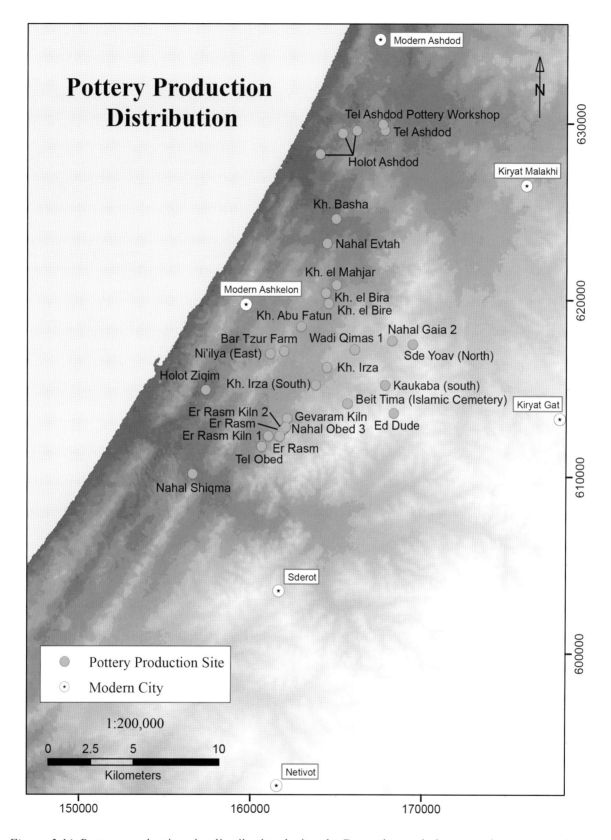

Figure 2.14: Pottery production site distribution during the Byzantine period over modern topography.

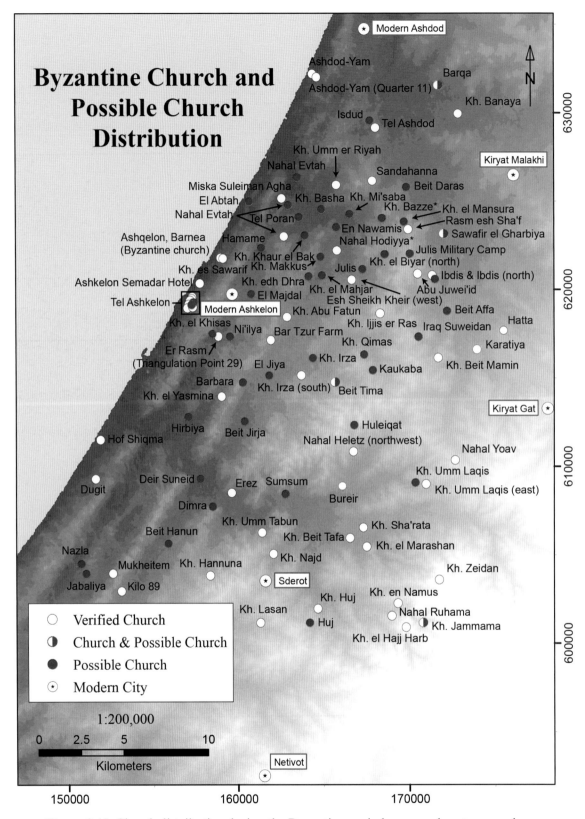

Figure 2.15: Church distribution during the Byzantine period over modern topography.

Table 2.3: Byzantine Churches in the Ashkelon Region

No.	Site	Site no.	Coordinates	Architectural Elements, Structural Remains, & Inscriptions	Notes and References
1	Ashdod-Yam		164410/632250	Columns and capitals	Piphano 1990:144
2	Ashdod-Yam (Quarter 11)		164690/632060	Segments of mosaic	Monastery. Piphano 1990:145, figure p. IV; Berman et al. 2005:30*-31*
3	Barqa		171700/631600	Basilical church; founding inscription	Sion et al. 2010
4	Kh. Banaya (Hazor Ashdod)		173000/630000	Basilical church; founding inscription	Ovadia and Silva 1981-1984, Part 2:133; Avi-Yonah et al. 1993:310-11
5	Tel Ashdod	site 24	168130/629200	Mosaic floor; winepress and monastery founding inscription	Monastery. Gudovitch 2006; Tzaferis 2006
6	Miska Suleiman Agha	site 88	162600/625200	Marble chancel; screen panels	Ovadia and Silva 1981-1984, Part 2:123
7	Kh. Umm er Riyah (Kh. el Wawiyat; Nizzanim)	site 94	165820/625970	Marble fragments; tesserae	Ovadia and Silva 1981-1984, Part 3:147
8	Sandahanna	site 78	167950/626200	Marble fragments; tesserae	Berman and Barda 2005:51*
9	Nahal Evtah	sites 155, 133	162740/623045	Basilical church	Varga 2010
10	Rasm esh Shaᵓf (Massuᵓot Yizhaq)		170048/623460	Marble chancel screen panels; mosaic sections	Segal 2006
11	Sawafir el Gharbiya		172000/623200	One capital; marble fragments	Inspection work by Huster
12	Nahal Hodiyya* (Nir Israel)	site 158	165850/622250	Marble columns and capitals	Inspection work by Huster
13	Ashkelon, Barnea (Byzantine church)	site 200	158950/621840	Mosaic pavement; two inscriptions	Tzaferis 1967
14	Kh. es Sawarif (Ashkelon, Barnea)	site 201	159100/621800	Marble columns and capitals; basilical church	Ovadia and Silva 1981-1984, Part 2:123
15	Abu Juweiᶜid		170590/620930	Marble fragments; mosaic pavement	IAA Archives (Mandatory report, J. Ory)
16	Ibdis (N)		171450/620855	Marble chancel screen posts; scattered tesserae	Inspection work by Huster
17	Esh Sheikh Kheir (W)	site 184	166720/620600	Mosaic sections	
18	Ashkelon, Semadar Hotel	site 206	157700/620400	Mosaic pavement	Meron 1976; Brand 2001; Berman and Barda 2005:26*; Map 87 site 16.
19	Tel Ashkelon	site 218	157260/619630	Cross-shaped chapel; mosaic pavement	Unpublished material from the Leon Levy Expedition to Ashkelon
20	Tel Ashkelon	site 218	157230/619530	Marble bases; basilical church	Conder and Kitchener 1881–83:240.
21	Tel Ashkelon	site 218	157140/619430	Marble chancel screen post; disturbed mosaic sections	Unpublished material from the Leon Levy Expedition to Ashkelon

Table 2.3 (cont.): Byzantine Churches in the Ashkelon Region

No.	Site	Site no.	Coordinates	Architectural Elements, Structural Remains, & Inscriptions	Notes and References
22	Tel Ashkelon	site 218	157060/619200	Small marble capital to support altar table; colored glass tesserae	Unpublished material from the Leon Levy Expedition to Ashkelon (Grid 38)
23	Tel Ashkelon	site 218	157000/619000	Basilical church	Guérin 1869:147; Garstang 1921a: 12–13
24	Tel Ashkelon	site 218	157300/619050	Granite columns; basilical church; liturgical texts	Tzaferis and Stager in *Ashkelon 1*
25	Er Rasm (Triangulation Point 29)	site 257	158800/617400	Marble fragments; tesserae	Inspection work by Huster
26	Kh. Abu Fatun (Sheikh el Kubakba)	site 458	162900/618500	Marble fragments; tesserae	Probably Map 92 site 28/4, Mashen
27	Bar Tzur Farm (Bat Hadar, Hadaryiah)	site 468	161950/617200	Marble columns; tesserae; two inscriptions	IAA Archives (reports Ram Gophna, Dov Meron); Map 92 site 17/1, Bar Tzur Farm
28	Kh. Ijjis er Ras	site 463	168400/618700	Marble capital with a cross; tesserae	Inspection work by Huster
29	Karatiya		173900/616900	Marble columns; baptistery	Yalqut Ha-Pirsumim 1964:1448; Ovadiah and Silva 1981–1984, Part 3:147
30	Kh. Irza (S) (Beit Shiqma/ Gaia modern cemetery)	site 521	163730/615200	Fragments of marble chancel screen; tesserae	Inspection work by Huster; probably same site as site 35/2, Beit Shiqma Villa, coordinates 163500-115500 (Allen in *Ashkelon 1*, p. 60)
31	Kh. el Yasmina	site 325-326	158990/614000	Fragments of marble chancel screen and altar table; six Greek letters on altar table fragment	Inspection work by Huster; for a winepress, see Haimi 2008
32	Beit Tima	site 541	165700/614800	Marble columns and capitals; tesselated pavement	Yalqut Ha-Pirsumim 1964:1447
33	Kh. Beit Mamin (Ozem)		171800/616200	Basilical church; three Greek inscriptions	Avi-Yonah et al. 1993:311
34	Hof Shiqma (Tell esh Shuqaf [S])	site 355	151770/611560	Marble column, altar table fragments; basilical church; founding inscription	Huster: in preparation; Map 91 site 128.
35	Dugit		151470/609330	Marble columns; tesserae	Naftali Aizik (pers. comm.)
36	Nahal Heletz (NW)	site 610	166800/610900	Marble pillar and base; tesserae	Near Map 92 site 70/1, Khirbet Nogga/ el Mahzuk
37	Nahal Yoav		172800/610400	Marble fragments; mosaic sections	Inspection work by Huster
38	Kh. Umm Laqis (E) (Sde David)		171070/609050	Marble fragments; tesserae	Petrie 1891:53

Table 2.3 (cont.): Byzantine Churches in the Ashkelon Region

No. Site	Site no.	Coordinates	Architectural Elements, Structural Remains, & Inscriptions	Notes and References
39 Bureir	Ch. 5, site 63	166100/608950	Marble columns and capitals; tesselated pavement, baptistery	Chapter 5, site 63
40 Erez		159600/608550	Marble fragments; mosaic pavement	Porat and Meron 1977
41 Kh. Umm Tabun	Ch. 5, site 94	161400/606300	Marble fragments; building remains	Chapter 5, site 94
42 Kh. Shaᶜrata	Ch. 5, site 112	167400/606600	Marble pillars; one with a cross, fragment of chancel screen; tesserae	Monastery. Chapter 5, site 112
43 Kh. Beit Tafa	Ch. 5, site 111	166600/606000	Marble fragments; roof tiles; small tesserae	IAA Archives; chapter 5, site 111
44 Kh. Najd	Ch. 5, site 127	162100/605100	Marble fragments; massive curved wall facing east	Chapter 5, site 127
45 Kh. el Marashan	Ch. 5, site 139	167600/605500	Marble capital; tesselated pavement; small crypt	Chapter 5, site 139
46 Mukheitem (Jabaliya)		152500/604000	Basilical church	Humbert et al. 2000; coordinates are only approximate
47 Kh. Hannuna		158300/603890	Marble base in situ; mosaic sections	Peretz 2008
48 Kilo 89 (Kh. es Sawaqi)		153000/603000	Marble base; mosaic pavement	Dauphin 1998:883, site 319; IAA archives (Mandatory report, J. Ory); coordinates are only approximate
49 Kh. Zeidan		171850/603640	Marble column, marble fragments; mosaic pavement	Monastery. Lamdan et al. 1977:188
50 Kh. Huj (En Nabi Huj)	Ch. 5, site 176	164700/602000	Marble columns; fragments of chancel screen; tesselated pavement; inscription on marble slab (unpublished, now lost)	Monastery. The inscription: IAA archives, file Hoga (report Ruth Amiran); the mosaic: Meron 1969; chapter 5, site 176
51 Kh. en Namus (H. Berekha; Kh. el Hammam, Kh. Umm Rujum)	Ch. 5, site 182	169400/602300	Marble columns, bases, capitals, and chancel screen fragments	IAA Archives (reports Ram Gophna); chapter 5, site 182
52 Kh. Lasan	Ch. 5, site 186	161300/601200	Marble columns, bases, capitals, and chancel screen fragments	Chapter 5, site 186
53 Nahal Ruhama (Wadi Abu Rashid)	Ch. 5, site 196	169050/601600	Marble fragments; tesselated pavement	Lamdan et al. 1977:184; Cohen 1993:64; chapter 5, site 196
54 Kh. Jammama		170800/601200	Marble columns; tesselated pavement	Monastery. Gophna and Feig 1993
55 Kh. el Hajj Harb (H. Herev)	Ch. 5, site 206	169900/600950	Vaulted wall, tesselated pavement	Lamdan et al. 1977:184; Cohen 1993: 62; Schuster 2000a; chapter 5, site 206

48 different sites. Of these, we believe that six are monastery sites.[13]

Apart from these 55 sites, it appears likely that there were a number of additional churches in the region, but these are difficult to identify definitively. Scanty finds of the indicative items listed above were reported at several rural sites within Berman's surveyed Maps of Ziqim (Berman et al. 2004) and Nizzanim West and East (Berman and Barda 2005). We attempted to reexamine all of them. These efforts, however, proved to be only partially successful. We are still left with a long list of possible churches. The majority of possible church sites are the sites of later Arab villages, which complicates matters. When these Arab villages were destroyed during the first years of the existence of the state of Israel, mainly between the years 1948 and 1950, enormous quantities of debris were left behind. This rubble almost completely obscures earlier levels, though surveys and probes indicate that almost every Arab village was inhabited in earlier times, at least from the Byzantine period.

The descriptions of Arab villages prior to their destruction constitute some basis for our knowledge of the ancient material remains. The most detailed descriptions of Roman and Byzantine architectural elements were made by Victor Guérin (1869). But he typically found the architectural elements in secondary use at the public wells, sheikhs' tombs, and other holy buildings. Guérin also provided information on stone robbery and the removal of building material from archaeological sites to Arab villages. At Beit Tima, some of the marble capitals, according to the testimony of inhabitants, were brought from the neighboring site of Kh. Qimas, while the rest were originally found at the village. At Kh. Qimas and Kh. Umm Lakis, Guérin discerned robber trenches (Guérin 1869:128, 299). Similarly, Petrie (1891:52–53) mentioned the transfer of marble columns from Ashkelon to Bureir (c. 15 km distant), and the dismantling of stones

from a well at Kh. el Hammam for the building of a new well at Jemmameh (c. 2 km distant). Despite this, we argue that some sites still have enough original evidence to propose that a local Byzantine church was the source of some of the architectural elements, for instance at Beit Tima and Bureir (see chapter 5, Map 96 site 63). In the end, we are confident that a Byzantine church existed in eleven of the thirty Arab villages with evidence of a church.

It should be noted that at least some of the evidence used to identify churches—e.g., marble chancel screen fragments and tesserae—are also found at Byzantine synagogues. Therefore, some of the rural structures we have identified as churches could conceivably have been synagogues; our identification of them as churches is influenced to some extent by the textual depiction of ubiquitous churches and a low Jewish population in the region. It is probably not coincidental that in our study area indicative remains of synagogues—e.g., marble chancel screen panels and a lintel decorated with Jewish symbols—have been found at two sites only: the cities of Ashkelon (Clermont-Ganneau 1884:82 no. 71, pl. IB; 1905:169–72; Dalman 1903:23–28; Dussaud 1912:71–72, no. 86) and Ashdod (Kohl and Watzinger 1916:160, 190–91; Avi-Yonah 1960; for general discussion, see Sukenik 1935:58–69; Goodenough 1953:218–21; Hachlili 2001:66–68, 304–6).

Farther to the south, the synagogue at Ma͑on is also located within the boundaries of a sizeable settlement, while evidence of synagogues has also been found in the cities of Gaza and Maiumas Gazae/el Mina.[14]

This distribution resembles the pattern suggested by Yizhar Hirschfeld (1997:81–84), in which the Jewish population of the Late Roman and Byzantine periods was concentrated in large rural settlements (and cities) for both religious (to

---

[13] These monasteries are mostly concentrated at the northern and southern edges of the survey area. The monastic life of Ashkelon appears to have been an extension of the monastic system of Gaza, an area with a heavy concentration of monasteries—one of the highest in the entire country (Hirschfeld 2004, esp. 87). Also of note is that monasteries were not found in isolated settlements only but could also occur in villages and even in cities (Ashdod, Ashdod-Yam). Monasteries, like churches, were an established and integral part of life in the southern coastal plain in the Byzantine period.

[14] Tsafrir et al. (1994:93, map 4) used textual sources to claim that a synagogue existed at Bureir (Buriron/Bror Hayil). Similarly, Dauphin (1998:231, fig. 65) used textual evidence to identify Jewish communities at Bureir, Barbara (Barbarit), Hamame (based on Clermont-Ganneau's [1897:2–3] proposed identification with Peleia/Palaia), and Diocletianopolis/Sarafia (although their identification with each other, and with Kh. esh Sheraf [site 312], is unclear), as well as at Jura (based on its erroneous identification with the supposed village of Yagur). To the south, Dauphin (1998:231–32 and fig. 67) again used textual sources to identify Jewish communities at Kh. Suq Mazin (Sycomazon), Rafah (Raphia), and Kefar Darom (Deir el Balah?).

be close to a synagogue) and security (to be part of a large Jewish community) reasons, whereas Christians were found at all levels of settlement down to isolated farmsteads.[15] Hirschfeld's observations concerned areas with large Jewish populations in these periods, specifically the Galilee and the Golan. Thus the pattern in the Ashkelon region could simply reflect the relatively low Jewish population in the southern coastal plain, with the few Jews in the region choosing to live in large, cosmopolitan cities (cf. Sharon's observations on Gaza [2009:19] relating to his discussion of the synagogues found in and around that city [2009:20–22]). Of course, this difference in population density does not disallow the application of Hirschfeld's suggestions (as in Fischer et al. 2008) to other areas of Jewish settlement.

Churches and Wine Production

The overall picture of settlement in the region is one of a developed hierarchy of settlements and sites, consisting of cities and towns, estates and farmsteads, monasteries, and isolated industrial areas. These sites are witness to an integrated economy focused especially on wine production and export, evidence of which can be seen in winepresses at monasteries, estates, and villages; pottery production at the same types of sites; and the port of Ashkelon itself (as well as the small anchorage at Ard el Mihjar), which shipped wine throughout the Mediterranaean and Europe.

In some cases, the synergy between the many churches in the region and the wine trade is more explicit. In the large-scale excavations east of Hamame (site 155), the existence of a church, an inn, and large winepresses there led the excavator to suggest that this site was part of an official government/church system, serving pilgrims traveling through the Ashkelon region. In the Barnea neighborhood, sites 198, 200 and 201 contain evidence of a large-scale settlement (Kh. es-Sawarif), dating to the Roman and especially to the Byzantine period. A church (IAA Archives,

Mandatory section, report by J. Ory) and a winepress (Haiman 2011) were located at Site 201, Kh. es-Sawarif. A winepress (Toueg 2009) was found next to a church (Tzaferis 1967) at Site 200, Ashkelon-Barnea, while site 198 (excavated by Vitto in 1995) was the location of a Byzantine hostel for Christian pilgrims (according to Berman and Barda 2005:21*).

Other sites also included a church and winepress, side by side: site 206, Semadar Hotel, a church (*HA* 59–60, 1976:40) and presumably a winepress nearby (Brand 2001); neighbor sites 325 and 326, Kh. El Yasmina, a church (surveyed by Huster) and a winepress (Haimi 2008), respectively; site 24, Tel Ashdod, an inscription describing the inauguration of a winepress at a monastery (Gudovitch 2006; Tzaferis 2006); site 218, Tel Ashkelon, a winepress (Master, pers. comm.), located c. 80 m from one of the churches. In the Map of Sderot (chapter 5) sites with a church accompanied by a winepress were found at sites 108, Kh. Jalama; 112, Kh. Shaᶜrata; 127, Kh. Najd; and 139, Kh. Marashan.

The presence of a church and winepress side by side may be merely an indication of similarly ubiquitous religious and economic inclinations during the Byzantine period, but, as with Hamame, there may be instances where the two institutions worked closely together.

Finally, the distribution of settlements of the Roman and Byzantine periods is particularly noteworthy: For the first time, we have a more or less even spread of settlements throughout the study area. This means that a number of settlements were established away from water sources—wadis, springs, and the coastal aquifer. It should not be seen as a coincidence that a large number of wells and cisterns, usually surrounding the village sites, can also be dated to this period, especially to the Byzantine. Sherds embedded in the sides of wells can often be dated to the Byzantine period, and this technique can therefore also be used to date wells without diagnostic sherds. It appears that the spread of settlements, and change in the basic pattern of settlement, is intimately connected to water exploitation. Similarly, it is worth mentioning that the vast majority of excavated wells at Tel Ashkelon itself can be dated to the Byzantine or Early Islamic periods; most of the remaining wells are from the Roman period (see Lass in *Ashkelon 1*; also Carmi et al. in *Ashkelon 1*). This observation shows how important water exploitation was from the Roman period onward.

---

[15] Note, however, the surveys of Tsafrir et al. 1994 and Dauphin 1998, who used textual evidence to identify Jewish communities at several other sites in the region. These sites, however, appear to have been towns or at least large villages, and so do not contradict our general conclusions here. In addition, Dauphin observed (1998:306–8) that the number of Jewish communities in both the Ashkelon region and the northwest Negev declined in the sixth century under pressure from Christianity.

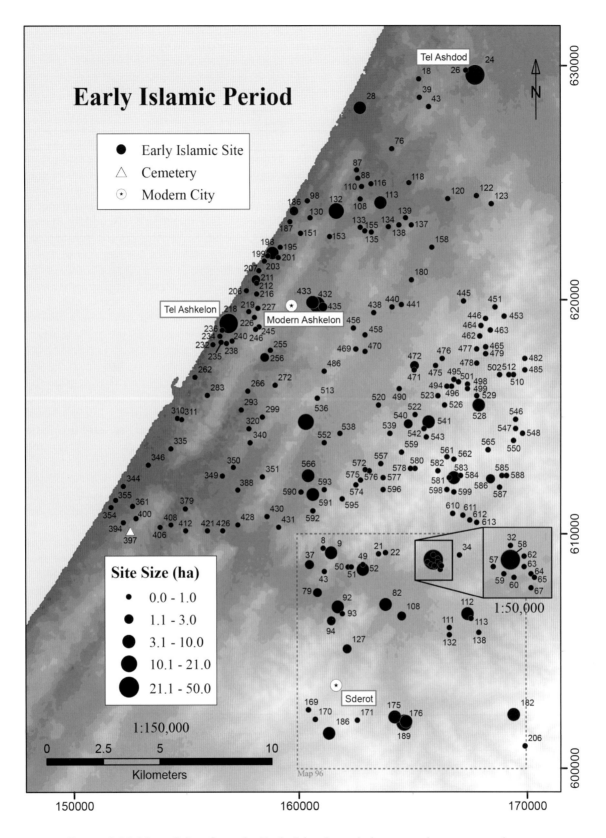

Figure 2.16: Map of sites from the Early Islamic period over modern topography.

Table 2.4: Number of Early Islamic Sites in the Surveyed Maps

Map of Ziqim (91)	*Map of Nizzanim West, East (87, 88)*	*Map of Ashkelon (92)*	*Map of Sderot (96)*
Berman et al. 2004	*Berman and Barda 2005*	*Allen (Ashkelon 1)*	*Chapter 5*
87	60	76	42

Early Islamic Period (A.D. 638–1099)

Our knowledge of the history of Ashkelon under the rule of the Umayyad, Abbasid, and Fatimid dynasties is based mainly on a broad literature written by Arab historians (for a brief summary, see Sharon *Ashkelon 1*, pp. 407–15). Early Islamic period texts describe Ashkelon as a flourishing coastal city whose hinterland was one of the most fertile in the country (as observed by Elᶜad 1982:151). In addition, there is supplementary archaeological evidence of the historical events in the city itself and in the surrounding area. This summary is based on the different surveys of the region and, to a lesser extent, on the result of salvage excavations that serve as a representative sampling of the Early Islamic settlement.

As is the case with sites from earlier periods, the relatively high number of Early Islamic sites in the Ziqim and Nizzanim maps derives from the fact that some of them are located within the sand belt, at sites suggested to be "patches." In Map 91, only about a dozen sites contained structural remains; the other 87 sites held mostly scatters of pottery and other artifacts (see Berman et al. 2004:14*). In Maps 87 and 88, some 15 sites are located on flat terrain along the Nahal Evtah, probably reflecting seasonal camps, and nine sites are located to the east of the modern Route 4, on relatively flat agricultural land. The remaining sites, as in the Ziqim map, are located along the western sandy zone, not far from the seashore. In Map 92, some Byzantine and Early Islamic findspots are clustered around a central site. These material remains were not in situ but were moved from their original point of deposition by various activities (human and natural) and, therefore, should not be classified as sites. In particular, surveyors do not appear to have been aware of the degree for potential dispersal of ancient remains by modern agricultural machinery, which can transfer large quantities of stones and sherds long distances and can therefore misleadingly present the appearance of a real site. Since remains from the Byzantine

and later periods are found on the surface, these are the first to be moved during agricultural activities. Based on this information, we emphasize the need to reduce the total number of sites from these periods within Map 92 (as in the other maps). Nevertheless, the Early Islamic is still the second most densely settled period in the survey area, after the Byzantine.

In general, the surveys of the Ashkelon hinterland reveal a continuous occupation from the Byzantine period at most Early Islamic sites but an overall decline in settlement—not only in settlement density in the region but also in site size. A comprehensive survey of several Byzantine sites within the Map of Sderot shows that the surface area of the Early Islamic remains appears to be consistently smaller than the total area of the site. This observation, however, is valid only at sites located in pasture lands, where modern agriculture has not interfered with cultural remains. The survey results also suggest that new settlements were not established during this period.

A detailed survey of the results of recent salvage excavations suggest that the usual discussion of major change between the Byzantine and Early Islamic period, encouraged by the gross nature of the survey data, is oversimplified. For instance, at site 346, Vlada Nikolsky (2010) excavated a winepress that was clearly not being used by the end of the Byzantine period; the same is true for a winepress excavated by Ilan Peretz (2011) at site 118 (Kh. Basha southwest). At the same time, there is evidence of continuity in the archaeological remains—for instance, in the use of winepresses. Nir-Shimson Paran (2009) notes that the excavated winepress at Kh. ᶜIjjis er Ras (south; site 465) continued to be used in the Early Islamic period. In other cases, the excavators do not explicitly state whether there is evidence of continuity or abandonment before the Early Islamic.[16] At site 200,

---

[16] At his excavation of the large Byzantine complex east of Hamame (site 155), Varga reported building remains as late as the ninth century; however, he does not specify the Early Islamic remains in his report (2010).

Toueg excavated collecting vats from a winepress in use at the very end of the Byzantine period; he was unsure of whether it went out of use at the end of the Byzantine or in the Early Islamic (2009). A similar situation was reported for a winepress and other installations excavated at Kh. Khaur el Bak (site 135; Talis 2011) and at site 201 (Haiman 2011); both sites yielded Early Islamic remains, but it is unclear whether they were connected to the winepresses. While these results are a small sample, they suggest that wine production in the Ashkelon region—although more limited—probably continued beyond the end of the Byzantine period.

Based on archaeological evidence, it seems that Ashdod ceased to function as a major city in this period and was reduced to the status of a village, although its decline in size and importance may have begun during the Byzantine period when Ashdod-Yam became the major settlement north of Ashkelon (Dothan 1993:102; Petersen 2005:85–86, 91; see also Sharon 1997:124–25). Thus, by the Early Islamic period, Ashkelon was the only urban center within our study area. Ashkelon, however, was a thriving city in this period, as described in the accounts of various Arab travelers and geographers (see, e.g., Le Strange 1890:400–3). The thirteenth-century geographer Yāqūt even reports that it was known as "the bride of Syria" (1866–73c:674). During the Early Islamic period, Ashkelon functioned as part of the *ribāṭ* system for coastal warning along the Levantine coast (see Khalilieh 1999; Masarwa 2006). *Ribāṭs* were established in existing cities or fortresses on small hills at fairly regular intervals along the coast (see Khalilieh 1999:215, 219); according to the tenth-century geographer Muqaddasī (or al-Maqdisī; 1906:177; 1886:62; see also Le Strange 1890:24), the closest *ribāṭ* to the south was at Mīmās (the port of Gaza, Byzantine Maiumas Gazae), while Māḥūz Azdūd (Minat el-Qalᶜa, Ashdod-Yam) was the closest to the north.

Western Palestine is rich in Arabic inscriptions, but little attention has been paid by archaeologists to this source. A number of Arabic inscriptions originated at Ashkelon and other sites in its vicinity. Of these, a small portion of them dates to the Early Islamic period. Qurᵓānic texts and epitaphs are most commonly found. These inscriptions not only confirm the great strategic importance placed on the city of Ashkelon from the time of the Islamic conquest but also serve as evidence for Islamic presence in the Ashkelon region and supplement literary sources (i.e., historians' testimonies),

providing important information concerning names of governors, rulers, commanders, judges, imams, and building projects in Ashkelon and its vicinity. We mention, here, several inscriptions, arranged in roughly chronological order, that in our opinion benefit this study:

1. Within the Map of Sderot, at Kh. Jalama (chapter 5, site 108), Muslim conquerors left graffiti inscribed on an ancient marble column that belonged to a Byzantine church. The longest inscription mentions the name of the third Caliph, Uthmān ibn Affān (644–56). The inscription was carved on the lower half of the column, suggesting that it was written when the column was still standing on its base (Sharon 2013). We believe that the church went out of use or was deserted in the second half of the seventh century A.D.

2. A marble slab discovered at Tel Ashkelon in 1883 bears an inscription that mentions the building of a mosque and a minaret, around the year 771–72 (Clermont-Ganneau 1887:485–91; for discussion of the problematic nature of this inscription, see Sharon 1997:144–47).

3. A construction text or epitaph of an official (the *qāḍi* of Ashkelon?), dated to the mid-eleventh century, refers to the city as a border fortress (Sharon 1997:151–53; reanalyzed by Sharon 2007:21–23).

4. A series of inscriptions about the shrine (*mashhad*) of Husein (Ḥusayn ibn ᶜAlī, grandson of Muhammad), describing the circumstances surrounding the discovery of Husein's head in Ashkelon and the erection or repair of the shrine in the year A.D. 1091 (see van Berchem 1915; Sharon 1997:154–61). The sanctuary was noted in the Survey of Western Palestine map (Sheet XX, Ev), as well as by Mandatory surveyors, who reported the name as En Nabi Husein or Mashhad Sidna el Husein (e.g., Survey of Palestine, 1:20,000, Sheet 10-11, Ashkelon; 1944 Schedule:1264). Guérin (1869:142) labeled the ruins of the building east of Tel Ashkelon "el-Hassan Mosque." But Guérin's description of the site as a small mosque appears to be incorrect. He saw the site only from a distance—from Tel Ashkelon. The "ruins" seen by Guérin probably belonged to the original sanctuary, an immense compound around a

large building that stood until 1950.[17] The place where the sanctuary stood is today within the grounds of Barzilay Hospital (site 245). Its remains were noted by Berman in 1972–73. It is worth mentioning that, according to Berman's description, the "ruinous sheikh's tomb" was surrounded by dozens of simple tombs (Berman et al. 2004:28*). Relying on pottery collection, Berman concluded that the latest period represented at the site is the Early Islamic. More recently, however, Ottoman-period pottery has been found, suggesting that the cemetery was active during the late Ottoman period and probably during the time of the British Mandate as well.

5. Though the year A.D. 1099 is formally considered to be the beginning of the Crusader period in Palestine (see discussion in the medieval period, below), we mention in this summary of epigraphic material from the Early Islamic period an inscription on a marble slab dated to the year A.D. 1150, just three years before Ashkelon was captured by the Crusaders for the first time. The inscription was found by the Leon Levy Expedition in the debris of the Islamic fortifications of the city and commemorates the construction of a tower by the Fatimid governor of Ashkelon (Sharon in *Ashkelon 1*). This imperial inscription indicates the great importance of the city as the last Islamic stronghold along the southern coast, which was surrounded by Frankish territories. The same slab was reused much later by the Crusaders who engraved heraldic shields over the inscription.

6. Also of note is the large group of Muslim epitaphs—both from old collections (especially the Ustinow collection) and from recent salvage excavations—coming from the cemeteries around Tel Ashkelon (see Sharon 1997:147–50, 153–54, 161–62; 2007:14–29; 2009:1–7). The epitaphs date mainly to the ninth to eleventh centuries, becoming more common over the course of that

timespan. Epitaphs from the first century and a half of Islamic rule have not been found.

As a whole, these inscriptions attest to the importance of the city of Ashkelon and its hinterland from the very beginning of, and throughout, the Early Islamic period and show that in many respects the region continued to flourish despite decline in the settlement pattern. The inscriptions also indicate that Islamization and Arabization was a gradual process, not only in the region but throughout Palestine and the Middle East as a whole (e.g., Bulliet 1979).

Medieval Period

As mentioned earlier in this chapter, and in chapter 1, we have adopted the term "medieval" for the timespan between the official beginning of the Crusader period in A.D. 1099 until the end of the Mamluk period in 1516. This usage stems not only because of the difficulty of identifying Crusader-period sites based on pottery, as discussed above, but also for historical considerations. According to the *New Encyclopedia of Archaeological Excavations in the Holy Land* (Stern 1993), the Crusader and the Ayyubid periods coincide in the years 1099–1291. The next historical archaeological period is the Late Arab period (Fatimid and Mamluk) 1291–1516 (*NEAEHL*, Vol. 4, p. 1259).

In the Ashkelon region there are two historical anomalies. The first is the continuation of Muslim (Ayyubid) rule for half a century after the initial Crusader conquest in 1099 of almost all the country until 1153, when Ashkelon fell into Crusader hands. The second is the return of Crusader sovereignty to the region twice: for a very short time, from January to September 1192, under Richard I, King of England ("the Lionheart"); and from 1241 to 1247 under Richard, Earl of Cornwall, and other Crusader leaders who rebuilt the fortifications of Ashkelon (Prawer 1956:246–47). The shields engraved over the Arabic inscription mentioned above, representing the arms of an English knight, are ascribed to the time of this last fortification (Sharon in *Ashkelon 1*, pp. 414–15). During this time, from 1099 to the mid-thirteenth century (with the Muslim recapture of Ashkelon in 1247 and its ultimate destruction by the Mamluks in 1270), the rural settlements in Ashkelon's vicinity underwent several changes (Prawer 1956:233, 239). The surrounding fortresses of Ibelin (Yavneh), Blanchegarde (Tell es-Safi), and Beit Jibrin,

---

[17] Images of the standing building are available at the Library of Congress, Print and Photograph Division, reproduction numbers LC-DIG-matpc-21683 to 21690: Moslem Celebrations at Mejdal (Wady Nemill and Sey'd Hussein Shrine at Ascalon, April 1943) (http://www.loc.gov/pictures/search/?q=%22sey%27d%20hussein%22). For information on the destruction of the building, see Meron Rapoport, "History Erased", *Haaretz*, 5/7/ 2007. http://www.haaretz.com/weekend/magazine/history-erased-1.224899.

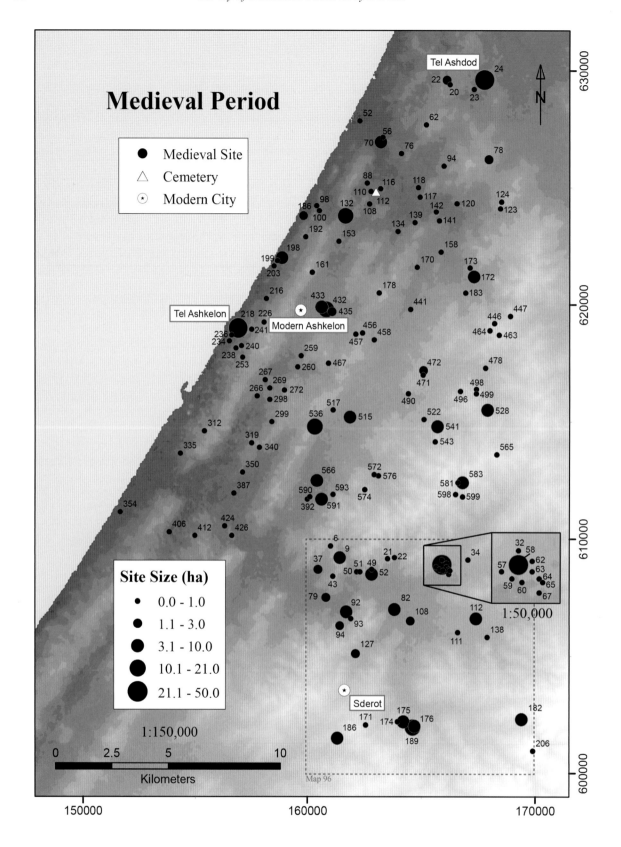

Figure 2.17: Map of sites from the medieval period over modern topography.

founded between 1134 and 1143, became administrative centers surrounded by agricultural villages (Prawer 1951, esp. 1067–69). There are also documented attempts of Frankish frontier colonization by Christian farmers.

The archaeological data from this span of time (1099–247), however, are very sparse. Berman's survey of the Map of Ziqim ascribes a mere five sites to the Crusader period: Tel Ashkelon; a site (site 240) located outside the city walls, dated because of a single coin of Amaury I (1163–74); a probable "patch" site (site 300) containing a silver coin (also Amaury I); the site of Hirbiya (site 350), known from historical sources as Forbie; and a site with Crusader pottery (site 412) at the southern edge of the survey area. In the survey of the Map of Nizzanim, only two sites from the Crusader period were noted: the first (site 198) in an excavation in the Barnea neighborhood (in 1995 by F. Vitto, not published), yielding a few items dated to the early Crusader period; the second (site 186, Bir Shuqeir) was included in the list of sites by period (under the category "Middle Ages") but lacked decisive finds in the pottery description.[18] These negligible results justify our adoption of the approach used by Allen (*Ashkelon 1*), which treats the Crusader

and the Mamluk periods as a single archaeological period, the "medieval."

The names of villages and settlements throughout the country are mentioned in Crusader documents, especially charters, deeds, and contracts between Crusader nobles and military orders. Following Edward Robinson's travels in the Holy Land, nineteenth-century scholars suggested geographical identifications for these settlements, at both inhabited Arabic villages and *khirbehs* described by Robinson and Smith (1841). Several Crusader *casals* (villages) mentioned in the various documents were located in the *Comté d'Ascalon*, meaning the Duchy (or County) of Ashkelon. Yehoshua Prawer (1958) provided the best summary of this subject, and also suggested his own identifications. In his analysis, Prawer lists almost 40 identified settlements in the Duchy's territory. Twenty-four or possibly twenty-five settlements are located within our study area and immediately beyond its borders (an area of 30 x 35 km, coordinates 150-180 east and 600-635 north, NIG; see table 2.5 and figure 2.17). Fourteen villages derive from a single document, a contract between John d'Ibelin, Count of Ascalon (and Jaffa), and the Hospital of Saint John (Paoli 1733:150–53). The geographical location of these villages has been recently reassessed by Huster and Blakely (in press).

Besides the identification of individual sites of the period, these documents provide important information on overall settlement patterns. They clearly demonstrate a continuity of settlement at Arab village and *khirbeh* sites through this period

---

[18] Note that the index of sites by period for Nizzanim West includes an additional site under the Crusader heading (Map 87 site 21; our site 216); however, the description of this site (Berman and Barda 2005:28*–29*) lists not Crusader but Mamluk pottery (which is not noted in the index by period). Meanwhile, no Crusader sites are listed for Nizzanim East (Map 88).

Table 2.5: Crusader Villages and Their Identifications with Archaeological Sites

Crusader Name	Site Name	Coordinates (NIG)
Castellum Beroardi	Minat el Qalʾa (Ashdod-Yam)	164300/632150
Azotum	Isdud (Ashdod; site 24)	167750/629600
Betheras	Beit Daras (site 96)	169850/625850
Zeophir	Es Sawafir*	172/623
Beze	Kh. Bazze (site 123)**	168450/624100
Geliadia	Kh. Jaladiya	176350/622900

* Es Sawafir is the common name shared by three (now ruined) neighboring Arab villages. They were distinguished by the addition of their geographical relative position, Shamaliya, Gharbiya, and Sharqiya, meaning the northern, western, and eastern Sawafir, respectively. Ceramic remains from the medieval period have been observed at es Sawafir el Gharbiya.

** See chapter 3 for the location of this site.

Table 2.5 (cont.): Crusader Villages and Their Identifications with Archaeological Sites

Crusader Name	Site Name	Coordinates (NIG)
Machoz	Kh. Makkus (site 170)***	164800/621600
Carcapha/Caicapha	Kh. Qarqafa	175250/621600
Hebde	Ibdis	171500/620730
Bethafe	Beit Affa	172200/618970
Semma/Casale Episcopi	Kh. Sama (site 472)	165080/617200
Galatia	Karatiya	173920/616900
Bethamamin	Kh. Beit Mamin	171360/616170
Phaluge	el Faluja	176200/614800
Coquebel	Kaukaba (site 528)	167900/615500
Algie	el Jiya (site 515)	161850/615200
Forbie	Hirbiya (site 350)	157100/612850
Amouhde	Kh. Amuda (site 576)	163100/612700
Heleiquat	el Huleiqat (site 583)	166800/612400
Semsem	Sumsum (Map 96 site 52)	162800/608500
Zeite	Kh. Zeita (Map 96 site 9)*4*	161400/609200
Camsa	Kh. Kums/Qamsa (Map 96 site 82)*5*	163800/607000
Saarethe	Kh. Shaᶜrata (Map 96 site 112)	167400/606600
Malaques	Kh. Umm Laqis (Mulaqis)	170300/609100
Phetora	Tatura (Fatura)*6*	163/616

*** See chapter 3 for the location of this site.

4 "Zeite" is a common name in Palestinian toponymy. Two archaeological sites named Zeita in Map 96 are candidates for Zeite from the Crusader period. We prefer southern Zeita, since it is located near the ruined village Sumsum, identified as Semsem in the same document (see chapter 5, Map 96 site 9; also Huster and Blakely, in press).

5 Camsa is a *casal* mentioned in the 1256/57 contract between John d'Ibelin and the Hospital of Saint John. Several researchers believe that Camsa was located at Kh. Kemas/ Qimas (site 498), east of Ashkelon (see, e.g., Prawer 1958:235; Allen in *Ashkelon 1*, p. 50). We prefer to identify it with Kh. Kums, for its location between Semsem and Saarethe (see chapter 5, Map 96 site 42; for more details see also Huster and Blakely, in press).

6 The identification of Phetora, mentioned in the contract between John d'Ibelin and the Hospital of Saint John, has been problematic. Röhricht (1887:240) and Prawer (1958:235-36), for example, suggested a possible identification with Kh. Fattata (Horvat Patot; 17940-61119, NIG). The name is also shared with Phathoura from the *Onomasticon* of Eusebius (K 168:22, L 288:99); this early Byzantine village is generally identified with Kh. Fur(u)t, hence its Hebrew name, H. Ptora (18243-61080, NIG; e.g., Clermont-Ganneau 1896:191; Abel 1938:409; Tsafrir et al.1994:203; Elitzur 2004:301). Huster and Blakely (in press) favor this identification for the Crusader village. However, the site is roughly 9 km east of the closest site from the 1256/7 deed (Phaluge/Faluja), where the other sites are tightly bunched together. It is therefore worth noting the existence of a village near Ashkelon named Fatura. This village appears in a *waqfiyya* (deed) of the Ashrafiyya madrasa in Jerusalem, from the year 1477; unfortunately the complete *waqfiyya*—including, most notably, the list of endowed properties—is unpublished (contra Burgoyne and Richards 1987:591, 605 ns. 2, 23), but the summary provided by Ibrāhim (1961:409; see also Lutfi 1985:121) suggests that there was a village called Fātūrā in the ᶜamal (subdistrict) of ᶜAsqalān, and that its lands were bordered on the west by the lands of Majdal. The first Ottoman mufassal defter (TD 427, from 1525–26) gives a similar toponym (transcribed by al-Swarieh [2009:42] as Ḥātūrā), registered not as a village but as a *mazraᶜa* (sown field, usually the lands of an abandoned village) between Sama and Beit Saman (see also icmal defter TD 131, which lists a village transcribed by al-Swarieh [2008:111] as Qābūra). The Survey of Palestine noted a field near Kh. Sama and Kh. Beit Saman named Tatura (1:20,000, Topocadastral Series, Sheet 11-11, El Majdal). Thus the evidence, while not clear, suggests that a village named Fatura (or something close to this) was located east of Majdal, around coordinates 1635-6160 (NIG)—approximately 3 km north of Kh. Amuda/Amouhde from the 1256/7 contract. The exact identification of this site is uncertain (complicated by its proximity to the major site Kh. Irza, which was inhabited in the sixteenth century and presumably earlier), but one possible candidate is site 520 (Map 92 site 35/2), which Allen designated as a questionable Crusader site (*Ashkelon 1*, p. 60; in his survey files he noted a single Crusader sherd from the site).

Table 2.6: Number of Sites from the Medieval Period

Number of Sites from the Mamluk Period		Medieval (Crusader and Mamluk periods)	
Map of Ziqim (91)	Map of Nizzanim West and East (87, 88)	Map of Ashkelon (92)	Map of Sderot (96)
Berman et al. 2004	Berman and Barda 2005	Allen (Ashkelon 1)	Chapter 5
62 (26)*	56 (28)*	29 (+ 9 possible sites)**	39

* Number of sites (in parentheses) that revealed remnants of structures. The rest consisted of pottery scatters.

** When the period was represented by one or two sherds only, or otherwise lacked clearly indicative remains, Allen suggested a possible occupation for the period. It is likely that repeated collection of ceramics would have turned up additional medieval sherds, causing the identification of the period to be secure. If this is true, then the number of sites from the medieval period in the Map of Ashkelon is almost the same as in the Map of Sderot.

and refine the picture established on a coarser chronological scale by the survey data; beyond the fact that the villages were inhabited in the Crusader period, the remarkable continuity of toponyms must reflect an overall stability in the population throughout the period from the Crusades to the end of the British Mandate. In addition, the large number of identifiable Crusader villages stands in stark contrast to the few Crusader sites identified by the archaeological surveys, further justifying the approach taken for the medieval period in this study.

Mamluk Remains

Despite the use of the term "Middle Ages" in the Archaeological Overview by period in both of Berman's surveyed maps, Ziqim and Nizzanim (Berman et al. 2004:14*; Berman and Barda 2005:13*), both surveys report Mamluk finds and sites in the site catalogues and period maps. The above-mentioned low number of Crusader sites in both maps is further accentuated by the large number of sites ascribed to the Mamluk period. As with previous periods, the real number of sites is better demonstrated in the Maps of Ashkelon and Sderot.

While noting that the majority of Berman's sites from the Mamluk period are located within the sand dune belt and are devoid of structural remains, we may accept the suggestion that some of them were probably campsites belonging to nomads (Berman et al. 2004:14*). In our opinion, however, the majority of sites without ancient structures are "patches." After the removal of the "non-sites" in the Maps of Ziqim and Nizzanim, and the plausible

count of medieval sites in the Maps of Ashkelon and Sderot, we can analyze the general settlement patterns in the study area. Many medieval sites are continuations of Early Islamic occupation, while others (according to the pottery remains) were re-founded on settlements from the Byzantine period that had been abandoned in the Early Islamic period. After the destruction of Ashkelon in 1270, the village of Majdal became the new center for the region, building on its history from the Byzantine and Early Islamic periods. Thirty years separate the destruction of Ashkelon and the inauguration of the Great Mosque of Majdal Ascalan. Unlike Ashkelon, however, Majdal was merely a secondary center, oriented toward Gaza. It is therefore striking that none of the many salvage excavations in Majdal and its satellite settlements have yielded any significant remains dating to the Mamluk period.

Fortunately, another type of archaeological evidence exists that fills in this gap in our knowledge: Several complete buildings, mostly of a religious nature, have been documented within our study area. Some of them were ruined by natural processes, others were intentionally destroyed, while the rest (or their remains) are still visible. Two of the main types of buildings attested in this period are mosques and *welis* (sheikhs' tombs). Along with these structural remains, a series of Mamluk and later Arabic inscriptions serves both to clarify various aspects of life and settlement in the region and to date the buildings. The best-preserved Muslim building in the village of Majdal (site 432)—and in the entire study area—is the Great Mosque (*al-Jāmiᶜ al-Kabīr*). A foundation inscription over the main entrance indicates that the mosque was built in 1300 by an important Mamluk official, Sayf ad-Dīn Salār (Sharon 1997:184–86), while the adjacent courtyard and the surrounding rooms appear to constitute a later phase based on structural considerations. The main entrance to the mosque is through a door on the eastern side of the courtyard; the door is set in a frame in which stones of alternating colors were used as panels. The courtyard has arcades on three sides. The southern side of the courtyard consists of a vaulted portico; the side vaults of it were constructed with the use of black ceramic jars (set vertically in mortar). This fact contradicts Moshe Sharon's description (1997:184–85), which supposes that the complex—i.e, the mosque, the courtyard with the three surrounding arcades, and the portico—all belong to the Mamluk period on the basis of the architectural features (although Sharon was probably influenced by the date of the inscription). Petersen's description of the side vaults of the portico (2001:211) mentions the use of black ceramic jars, which he had previously designated "terracotta vaulting tubes" (1994). Petersen suggests that this technique probably dated back to the eighteenth century (1994:91; 2001:33), which coincides with the beginning of the "Black Gaza Ware" industry around 1700 (Israel 2006). The architectural style of the portico and the use of an eighteenth-century technique (the vaulting tubes) suggest that features west of the main mosque building were constructed in the Ottoman period. (The eastern arcade abuts the portico and probably also represents a later phase.)

The other major group of Mamluk buildings in the region consists of the tombs of sheikhs (saints, holy men), often referred to as *welis*. As Petersen notes (2001:36), *welis* are the most common type of religious building in the country; Petersen separates these buildings into shrines and tombs but observes that in general they are both tombs and shrines. For our study area (Maps 87, 88, 91, and 92), we have compiled a list of roughly 26 sheikhs' tombs.[19] Most of these are located within or im-

mediately around villages, a pattern observed more generally by Canaan (1927:2–3, 6–7). Of the few not located close to a village inhabited in the nineteenth century, most appear to be associated with earlier Ottoman or medieval settlements: e.g., Nabi Sama (site 471; a very clear example, as it is adjacent to Kh. Sama, site 472) and Sheikh el Kubakba (site 459; at Kh. Abu Fatun, site 458). Generally, *welis* are found (or at least recorded) for the larger villages, and the largest villages often have more than one. The largest villages in our study area in the medieval and Ottoman periods contained at least two *welis*: Majdal (three *welis*, at least according to Guérin [1869:131]); Isdud (also three, although they were clustered around Khan Isdud, southwest of the village); and Hamame (two *welis*). Similarly, Beit Tima and Barbara, which at times (during the Ottoman period at least) had a population almost as high as the largest villages, had two and three shrines, respectively.

In Miriam Rosen-Ayalon's survey of Islamic art and archaeology, she notes that "numerous tombs of saints and their adjacent shrines were built in Palestine in the Middle Ages" (2006:123). We would suggest, however, a refinement of this dating. In our view, most (though not all) of these tombs likely date to the Mamluk period, though many shrines have a later addition (one or two wings to the core tomb) that can be dated to the Ottoman period (and usually to the latter half of it, the eighteenth or nineteenth century).[20] Many of these tombs cannot be dated, as they were only reported by nineteenth-century travelers (especially Guérin) and were not noted by twentieth-century surveyors (archaeological or cartographic), nor is

---

[19] The exact number of sheikhs' tombs in the region is unclear, largely due to the fact that it is not always easy to correlate monuments, inscriptions, and historical sources with individual tombs. For example, Guérin (1869) refers to several sheikhs' tombs that do not appear in other historical sources, often without names, and so it is not always clear if specific inscriptions or tombs indicated on Mandatory maps can be matched with the tombs he mentions. In addition, an exact count depends on how certain issues are resolved, such as the status of Mashhad Sidna el Husein (as it is not a typical

sheikh's tomb but a shrine reputed to have once held his head) and the complex of Salman al-Farisi and Ibrahim al-Matbuli (two tombs included in the same complex). Finally, Guérin mentioned a *weli* of Nabi Yasin at Beit Daras that we have not included in our table. If the *weli* was in the village itself, then it was not likely within our study area as the majority of the village is just east of east coordinate 170. However, Liévin de Hamme (a Franciscan monk who wrote a detailed travel guide to Palestine in the late nineteenth century) noted a "Oueli Yasine" to the west of the main north-south road where it crosses Wadi Mughraka (a branch of the Nahal Evtah; Liévin de Hamme 1887:225). If this is correct, then Sheikh Yasin (if it is the same as Guérin's *weli*) should be identical to Sheikh Abu Jaham, and the name may perhaps be related to Khirbet Yasin.

[20] Petersen (2001:36–37) similarly suggests a pattern of development over time in many sheikhs' tombs but does not attempt to demonstrate the pattern systematically or to date it precisely.

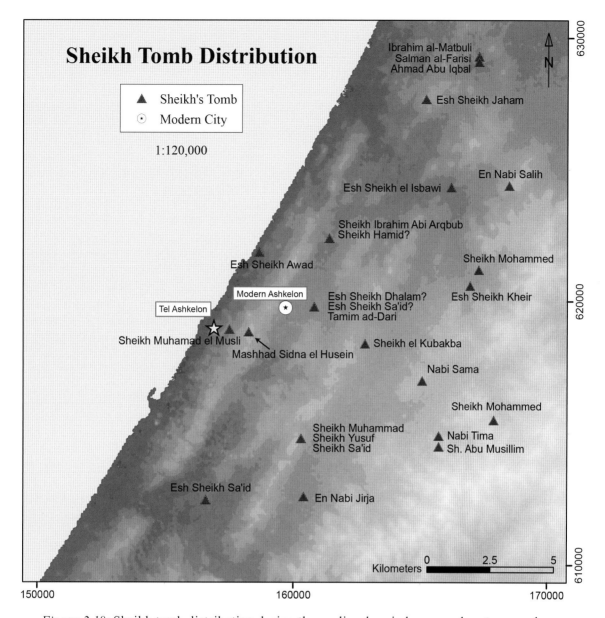

Figure 2.18: Sheikh tomb distribution during the medieval period over modern topography.

there extant inscriptional evidence. For most of those with dating evidence, however, we can suggest that it is likely—if not certain—that they date to the Mamluk period:

1. Esh Sheikh Awad (site 199), built on the *kurkar* cliff facing the sea in the Barnea neighborhood, is composed of a central domed chamber flanked by two later side chambers. In this case, as with other structural remains in our study area, the architectural features, similar to those of the Great Mosque of Majdal, help us to date it. The two side chambers of Sheikh Awad likely

date to the late eighteenth or nineteenth century on the basis of various architectural elements (Petersen 2001:98). For the central chamber, Petersen suggested a pre-eighteenth-century date. In our opinion, the central room of Maqam Sheikh Awad can be dated to the Mamluk period based on the parallel pattern of two building phases at similarly structured sheikhs' tombs along or near the coast.

2. Sheikh Muhammad el Musli (site 241): The same pattern, i.e., a structure with an older core (probably Mamluk) constructed of well-dressed

Table 2.7: Sheikh Tombs in the Ashkelon Region

No.	Site	Village	Site no.	Coordinates	Notes and References
1	Salman al-Farisi	Isdud	site 23	167300/629300	Map 88 site 23; Petersen 2001:156–57; Sharon. Dated by inscription to the Mamluk period; in same complex as no. 2; destroyed.
2	Ibrahim al-Matbuli	Isdud	site 23	167300/629300	Map 88 site 23; Petersen 2001:156–57; Sharon; Survey of Palestine, Sheet 11-12, Hamame. Dated by inscription to the Mamluk period; in same complex as no. 1; destroyed.
3	Ahmad Abu Iqbal	Isdud	site 23	167300/629100	Map 88 site 23; Petersen 2001:156; Survey of Palestine, Sheet 11-12, Hamame.
4	Esh Sheikh Jaham		site 62	165200/627680	Map 88 site 59; SWP, Sheet XVI, Fu; Survey of Palestine, Sheet 11-12, Hamame. Mamluk coin hoard found nearby (Berman and Barda 2005: 48–49*).
5	Esh Sheikh el Isbawi	Kh. el Mic ṣaba?	site 121	166180/624340	Map 88 site 117; Survey of Palestine, Sheet 11-12, Hamame. Berman and Barda with no diagnostic finds; Yaakov with Ottoman in our table.
6	En Nabi Salih		site 124	168500/624400	Map 88 site 120; Survey of Palestine, Sheet 11-12, Hamame. Berman and Barda noted LR, Mamluk, and Ottoman pottery (2005:60*).
7	Sheikh Ibrahim Abi Arqbub	Hamame	site 154	161400/622400	Petersen 2001:146 (based on Mandatory inspectors); al-Nabulsi (17th c). Mosque; earliest attestation is al-Nabulsi, who notes the *qabr* (tomb) of this sheikh.
8	Sheikh Hamid?	Hamame	site 154	161400/622400	Petersen 2001:146 (based on Mandatory inspectors); Dauphin 1998:869. Mosque only?
9	Sheikh Mohammed	Julis	site 172	167300/621200	Map 88 site 165 (as *maqam* in Julis; photo p. 79); Guérin 1869:127; Khalidi? Named by Guérin; otherwise nameless *maqam*.
10	Esh Sheikh Kheir	Julis (or site 100 m to south?)	site 182	166950/620600	Map 88 site 175; SWP, Sheet XVI, Fu; Survey of Palestine, Sheet 11-12, Hamame (as "Ruin"); Khalidi 1992.
11	Esh Sheikh Awad		site 199	158650/621880	Map 87 site 8; Survey of Palestine, Sheet 10-10, Ashkelon; Petersen 2001:98. Two phases recognizable: later 18th/19th c, earlier pre-18th c.
12	Sheikh Muhamad el Musli	SE of Tel Ashkelon	site 241	157500/618950	Map 91 site 19; Survey of Palestine, Sheet 10-11, Ashkelon (unnamed); Petersen? Two phases: Huster (inspection work) suggests medieval and Ottoman (but only based on architecture and not pottery)
13	Mashhad Sidna el Husein	Tel Ashkelon	site 245	158250/618850	Map 91 site 23; Survey of Palestine, Sheet 10-11, Ashkelon; Sharon; Petersen 2001:98; etc. Dated by historical sources and inscriptions to Early Islamic (11th c).

Table 2.7 (cont.): Sheikh Tombs in the Ashkelon Region

No. Site	Village	Site no.	Coordinates	Notes and References
14 Esh Sheikh Saᶜid	Hirbiya	site 349	156600/612480	Map 91 site 123; Survey of Palestine, Sheet 10-11, Ashkelon. Only Hell–EI pottery at site (Berman, Stark, and Barda 2004:46*).
15 Tamim ad-Dari	Majdal	site 432	160800/619800	Guérin 1869:131 (unnamed); Sharon 1997:186–89; Petersen 2001:212–13. One of three *welis* noted by Guérin; inscription dates construction to mid-16th c.
16 Esh Sheikh Saᶜid?	Majdal	site 432	160800/619800	Guérin 1869:131 (unnamed); Survey of Palestine, Sheet 11-11, El Majdal. One of three *welis* noted by Guérin; possibly just a mosque.
17 Esh Sheikh Dhalam?	Majdal	site 432	160800/619800	Guérin 1869:131 (unnamed); El Majdal Index (1:5000; to 1:625 town survey, Survey of Palestine, 1931). One of three *welis* noted by Guérin; name from El Majdal Index, but of a girls' school.
18 Sheikh el Kubakba	Kh. Abu Fatun	site 459	162800/618400	SWP, Sheet XX, Fv; Petersen 2001:66, pl. 3.
19 Nabi Sama	Kh. Sama	site 471	165060/617000	Survey of Palestine, Sheet 11-11, El Majdal. Huster (inspection work) notes Rom–Ott pottery.
20 Sheikh Mohammed	Kaukaba	site 528	167900/615500	Guérin 1869:127; SWP, Sheet XX, Fv.
21 Sheikh Yusuf	Barbara	site 536	160300/614800	Guérin 1869:172–73; Lievin de Hamme 1887 part 2:208; Khalidi 1992:81 (with refs); Dauphin 1998:876; List of Mandatory Records Files 1976:133 (three unnamed *maqams*). Only noted by Guérin and Lievin de Hamme (latter calls it a mosque), but Khalidi notes it (supposedly ultimately based on Mujir ad-Din). Yusuf died in 14th c, but mosque built by Murad III (second half of 16th c).
22 Sheikh Saᶜid	Barbara	site 536	160300/614800	Dauphin 1998:876; List of Mandatory Records Files 1976:133 (one of three unnamed *maqams*).
23 Sheikh Muhammad	Barbara	site 536	160300/614800	Dauphin 1998:876; List of Mandatory Records Files 1976:133 (one of three unnamed *maqams*).
24 Nabi Tima	Beit Tima	site 541	165700/614900	Guérin 1869:127–28; SWP, Sheet XX, Fv (unnamed holy place?); Petersen 2001:126; Sharon 1999:158–60. Mosque; two phases, dated by inscription to 14th and 19th c.
25 Sh. Abu Musillim	Beit Tima	site 541	165700/614500	SWP, Sheet XX, Fv.
26 En Nabi Jirja	Beit Jirja	site 566	160400/612600	Guérin 1869:173 (unnamed); Survey of Palestine, Sheet 11-11, El Majdal; Sharon 1999:143. 19th c inscription in building, recording rebuilding of entire village.

stones supplemented by a later wing, also occurs at this shrine or tomb just east of Tel Ashkelon.

3. Ibrahim al-Matbuli and Salman al-Farisi (site 23): A complex (now destroyed) containing shrines of these two holy men stood near Isdud (Tel Ashdod), adjacent to the now destroyed Khan Isdud. Both tombs are known to have been built during the Mamluk period: An inscription commemorates the building of a mosque at the sanctuary of Salmān al-Fārisī in 1269 (Sharon 1997:126–28), while a second inscription mentions the death of Ibrāhīm al-Matbulī in 1472 (Sharon 1997:128; see also Petersen 2001:156–57).

4. Ahmad Abu Iqbal (also site 23): Unlike the complex of Ibrahim al-Matbuli and Salman al-Farisi, this tomb is still standing. Petersen identified two building phases, the domed tomb chamber and a later wing, but did not suggest a date (2001:156). Berman and Barda (2005:40*) surveyed the standing sheikh's tomb (although they did not provide the name) and also identified two building phases, suggesting that the earlier phase (the tomb itself) dated to the Mamluk period (but they did not provide evidence to justify this dating).

5. Esh Sheikh Jaham (site 62): Berman and Barda suggested that the tomb might have been built during the Mamluk period and noted the discovery of a Mamluk coin hoard in the vicinity (2005:48*–49*).

6. En Nabi Salih (site 124): Other than Late Roman, the earliest pottery reported by the survey of the Map of Nizzanim was Mamluk, suggesting that the tomb might have been built in this period.

7. Esh Sheikh Kheir (site 182): At the site of the tomb itself, Berman and Barda (2005:72*) noted only Ottoman pottery. However, a settlement site 100 m to the south yielded Late Roman, Byzantine, Mamluk, and Ottoman pottery. In addition, Khalidi recorded that, according to local tradition, Sheikh Kheir had died fighting the Crusaders (1992:115). Together, this evidence suggests the Mamluk period as a likely date for the erection of the *weli*.

8. Nabi Tima (in Beit Tima, site 541): At the ruined Arab village Beit Tima, located some 12

km east-southeast of Tel Ashkelon, remnants of a large building (a mosque or a *maqam*) of the late Ottoman period, dedicated to a certain Nabi Tima, were recorded by several researchers, including Guérin (1869:127–28) and Allen (*Ashkelon 1*, fig. 3.35). The name of this "prophet" or sheikh, Nabi Tima, is clearly related to that of the village. Many Arab villages boasted supposed tombs or mosques of eponymous "prophets" that in fact were named ex post facto after their village (noted by Guérin 1869:70; Conder 1877:101; Sharon 1999:98; cf. the extended discussion by Canaan 1927:284–88). In our study area we have three such cases: En Nabi Jirja, at Beit Jirja (Sharon 1999:143; see also Survey of Palestine, Sheet 11-11, El Majdal); Nabi Sama (at the site of Kh. Sama, abandoned between the sixteenth and nineteenth centuries); and Nabi Tima (cf. also Nabi Huj in Map 96, site 176). The Ottoman remains of the Nabi Tima shrine were found over an earlier structure, whose foundations are also visible at the site (Sharon 1999:158). Two Arabic inscriptions were recorded in the twentieth century, when the building was still standing. The first dates to the Mamluk period; it commemorates the establishment of a mosque in the year A.D. 1390. The second inscription is from the Late Ottoman period and mentions the reconstruction of the mosque in 1836 (Sharon 1999:158–60). It is worth mentioning that the older Mamluk inscription was recorded and photographed while embedded in an ordinary wall that was probably built in the late Ottoman phase of the mosque, apparently out of its original context (see Petersen 2001:126, pl. 82). (Similarly, in the Arab village Bureir, a fragment of a Mamluk inscription dated to the second half of the fifteenth century A.D., recording either the digging or the repair of a well or cistern, was found in the ruins of the modern village mosque [see chapter 5, sites 63 and 65; Sharon 2004:xlvi–l].) Therefore, the mosque structure of Beit Tima, with its two architectural phases (Mamluk and Ottoman) supported by textual evidence, further demonstrates the pattern suggested above.

The only clear cases that contradict this dating of tombs to the Mamluk period are Mashhad Sidna el Husein, site of the most elaborate *mawsim* (festival) in our study area, which is known from inscriptional and historical evidence to have been

Table 2.8: Location of Coastal *Welis* and Umayyad/Abbasid *Ribāṭs*

Ribāṭ *According to Muqaddasī* (1906:177; translation 1886:62)	*Coastal* Weli
Mīmās (el Mina)	Sheikh Hassan (at the site); also Sheikh Ridwan (c. 2 km inland)
ᶜAsqalān	Sheikh Awad (c. 2 km north)
Māḥūz Azdūd (Ashdod-Yam; Minat el-Qalᶜa)	Nabi Yunis (c. 4.5 km north, at the Nahal Lachish)
Māḥūz Yibnā (Yavneh-Yam)	Nabi Rubin (c. 4 km inland)
Yāfah	Sheikh Abd en Nabi (c. 4.5 km north)
Arsūf	Haram Sidna ᶜAli (ᶜAli ibn ᶜAleim; c. 500 m south)

built in the eleventh century (see above),[21] and Tamim ad-Dari, where an inscription appears to date the founding of the structure to the mid-sixteenth century (Sharon 1997:186–89; Petersen 2001:212–13).[22]

The suggestion that the majority of sheikhs' tombs date to the Mamluk period is bolstered by a survey of the detailed information on the shrines in and immediately around Gaza—*mazārs*, *maqāms*, and mosques, as well as *zāwiyas*—founded at the tombs of, or otherwise commemorating, holy men. Sharon (2009) provides inscriptions relating to the founding of eight such shrines, and the establishment of all of these shrines can be dated to the Mamluk period; in fact, all were likely built between the mid-thirteenth and late fourteenth centuries.[23] In Gaza, however, there are very few extant inscriptions prior to the Mamluk period, as observed by Sharon (2009:26) and earlier by Max van Berchem (quoted in Meyer 1907:149–50, and Sharon 2009:26). However, as van Berchem noted (in his handwritten notes, quoted in Sharon 2009:27), the Gaza inscriptions mainly date to the fourteenth and fifteenth centuries, whereas we have no datable shrines founded after the fourteenth century—including none in the early

Ottoman period, for which we have a significant number of inscriptions.

The conclusion that most of these buildings date to the Mamluk period suggests a significant program, however loosely organized, for the construction of religious buildings in this period—similar to that of the Byzantine period, although on a smaller scale. This building program would have permeated all levels of settlement and society, from the major shrines of the Gaza district (founded by the sultans or by important officials) to those of the villages of varying size in the region (founded by officials of different ranks). It also raises the question of the purpose of such widespread building activities. Petersen, himself noting that the majority of sheikhs' tombs in Palestine as a whole were founded after the Crusader period, suggests that many were associated with soldiers under Salah al-Din and were founded as "a way of spiritually reclaiming the land for Islam" (2001:36). Canaan, partly following the suggestions of Ahmad Zaki Pasha, asserted that the early Mamluk rulers (especially Baybars) instituted a policy of building and restoring shrines and establishing festivals to bring out large numbers of pilgrims in order to protect the country (1927:299). In his view, the clustering of festivals in the weeks around Easter was a planned competition with Christian pilgrims during what was considered to be the most dangerous time of the year (1927:299; cf. Yazbak 2011:172, 174). Sharon argued against such "quasi-historical observations" (2009:120). However, his attempt to dismiss this origin for festivals and argue instead for a more ancient origin in pagan or Christian festivals—by pointing to the fact that one Gazan festival falls on Easter Sunday—is not convincing; this observation no more supports his argument than it does Canaan's. Nevertheless, while some shrines may have been built by Baybars and other Mamluk sultans to

---

[21] On this festival and its importance, see Canaan (1927:213, 215); see also the set of photographs from the Library of Congress collection noted above.

[22] Note also the mosque/shrine of Sheikh Yusuf al-Barbarawi in Barbara: The mosque containing his tomb was apparently built by Sultan Murad III in the second half of the sixteenth century; however, Yusuf died in the fourteenth century, and it is not clear whether there was some shrine prior to the mosque (see Khalidi 1992:81; al-Dabbāgh 1975:255).

[23] Sharon (2009:40) refers to an additional shrine, the *weli* of al-Kharrubah, noted by L. A. Mayer in 1923 but no longer extant, with an inscription that dates it to 688 A.H./A.D. 1289. See also the information provided by Sadek in his detailed survey of Mamluk architecture in Gaza (1991).

re-establish the Muslim nature of the land and establish their role as its spiritual guardians or patrons (see Meri 2002:259–60, who suggests that Baybars carried out this campaign throughout the sultanate), it is difficult to see how the presence of hundreds or even thousands of pilgrims at a shrine at a certain time of the year would have served as an effective defense, or why the country would have been at risk of attack during Easter week (as implied by Canaan 1927:299).

At the same time, we believe that at least some of the shrines had a defensive role. Mahmoud Yazbak (2011:174) noted that several were strategically positioned along the Cairo-Damascus highway, i.e., the main north-south road.[24] In order to make this point, he emphasizes the number of shrines built or renovated by the early Mamluk sultans, especially by the Baybars: Salman al-Farisi (Isdud), Abu Hureirah (Yibna), and Haram Sidna ᶜAli (Arsuf). However, contrary to Yazbak's implication, Sidna ᶜAli is not located on the Cairo-Damascus highway but on the coast. This brings up what we would identify as a special class of shrines, the coastal *welis*. As noted above, almost every *weli* in our study area appears to be within or connected to a specific village. The one definite exception to this is Sheikh Awad, which is also the one *weli* in the region located on the coast: Apparently, there were no medieval or Ottoman villages on or near the coast north of Tel Ashkelon (most or all of the sites recorded here appear to be "patches"). Instead, Sheikh Awad seems to belong to the coastal *welis*. From Gaza north, these include Sheikh Hassan (and nearby Sheikh Ridwan), Sheikh Awad, Nabi Yunis, Nabi Rubin, Sheikh Abd en Nabi (now in Tel Aviv), and Haram Sidna ᶜAli (ᶜAli ibn ᶜAleim, now in Herzliya). Haram Sidna ᶜAli deserves special attention (on the shrine, see Mayer and Pinkerfeld 1950:36–39; Petersen 2001:146–48). As Rosen-Ayalon (2006: 123–24) notes, the fifteenth-century historian Mujīr al-Dīn considered it one of the most famous pilgrimage sites on the coast of Palestine; thus Petersen (2001:146) names it, Nabi Rubin, and Nabi Musa as the three most important religious sites in Palestine, apart from Jerusalem and Hebron (cf. Canaan 1927:213–15). Although ᶜAli himself died in 1081, the earliest traditions reported by Mujīr al-Dīn are Mamluk (relating

specifically to the Baybars), and the complex itself dates to the 1480s, by which time the *mawsim* was established (see Mujīr al-Dīn 1876:212–13). These facts suggest that the sultans could conceivably have both begun construction on the complex and established the festival. Rosen-Ayalon calls the complex "a true *ribat*, a seaside fortress, a rallying point, a pilgrimage site, and the starting point for the jihad" (2006:124).

The coastal *welis* listed above are located at or near the locations of former Umayyad/Abbasid *ribāṭs* (see table 2.8).

This pattern is especially noteworthy in the area between Ashdod and Jaffa, as this coastline was largely abandoned in the medieval and Ottoman periods; Nabi Yunis and Nabi Rubin are the only two shrines in this stretch, and they are relatively close to Ashdod-Yam and Yavneh-Yam—the two *ribāṭs* between Ashkelon and Jaffa.[25] Thus it is conceivable, although far from proven, that the coastal shrines may have played some role in replacing the defunct *ribāṭs* of the Early Islamic period. While it is difficult to imagine that an annual festival at a coastal shrine could provide defense, staff at such shrines may conceivably have served as watchmen. It is also possible that there was simply a general rise in interest in saints' tombs in this period, a more bottom-up approach to this phenomenon, but these explanations, of course, are not mutually exclusive.[26]

---

[24] Yazbak cites Meri (2002:259–60) for this idea, but Meri does not make this claim.

[25] In the List of Mandatory Records Files, Nabi Yunis is called a "late maqâm" (1976:123); there is little information from any source on its date. On the other hand, Nabi Rubin, which was a much more substantial shrine, is attested in the medieval period: The tomb was being noted by the late twelfth century, and was described by the traveler Abu al-Ḥasan ᶜAlī al-Harawī; however, an inscription over the entrance dates the construction of the shrine to 1431, and in the late fifteenth century Mujīr al-Dīn reported that there was an annual *mawsim* (see Yazbak 2011, esp. 175–76; Mujīr al-Dīn 1876:211). Note that Yazbak elsewhere claims (2011:174) that the building over the tomb was first erected in the late thirteenth century, but this seems to be an error. Petersen also suggests (2001:232) that the remainder of the Nabi Rubin complex was built in the Ottoman period, paralleling the pattern we have seen elsewhere. Petersen concludes, mostly for structural reasons, that the *maqam* of Abd en Nabi was likely built in the fifteenth or sixteenth century (2001:299).

[26] On a broader geographical scale, Meri (2002:257–62) cites the significant growth in pilgrimage shrines in the medieval Middle East within the context of both the role of the Baybars as patrons of holy places and the rise of Sufism.

Table 2.9: Table of All Survey Sites

No.	Site	Coordinates	Area (m²)	Excavated	Periods (patch sites noted by [p])
1	Holot Ashdod	162900/629360	5,000		Epi, Neo, Rom(p), Byz(p)
2	Holot Ashdod	163200/629990	200		Epi, Rom, Byz
3	Holot Ashdod	163880/629750	2,500		Rom(p), Byz(p)
4	Holot Ashdod	163550/629220	4,000		Rom(p), Byz(p)
5	Holot Ashdod	163320/629120	500		Rom(p), Byz(p)
6	Holot Ashdod	164200/629900	2,500		Rom(p), Byz(p)
7	Holot Ashdod	164130/629580	1,400		Hell, Rom, Byz, Ott
8	Holot Ashdod	164400/629480	20,000		Rom(p), Byz(p)
9	Holot Ashdod	164750/629360	1,000		Rom(p), Byz(p)
10	Holot Ashdod	164950/629350	200		Iron2, Pers, Rom, Byz
11	Holot Ashdod	164850/629100	2,500		Rom(p), Byz(p), EI(p), Med(p), Ott(p)
12	Holot Ashdod	164300/629010	2,000		Hell(p), Rom(p), Byz(p)
13	Holot Ashdod	165700/629550	2,000		Rom(p), Byz(p), EI(p), Ott(p)
14	Holot Ashdod	165900/629700	30,000		Iron2(p), Rom(p), Med(p)
15	Holot Ashdod	165400/629780	1,500		Iron2(p), Pers(p), Hell(p), Rom(p), Byz(p)
16	Holot Ashdod	165300/629900	1,000		Rom(p), Byz(p)
17	Holot Ashdod	165070/629150	200		Hell, Rom, Byz
18	Holot Ashdod	165290/629440	100		Hell, Rom, Byz, EI
19	Holot Ashdod	165410/629460	500		Rom(p), Byz(p)
20	Holot Ashdod	166240/629400	1,000		Iron2, Pers, Rom, Byz, Med
21	Holot Ashdod	166100/629510	500		EB(p), LB(p), Iron2(p), Pers(p), Hell(p), Rom(p)
22	Holot Ashdod	166110/629590	30,000		Pers, Rom, Med
23	Khan Isdud	167300/629200	200		Med, Ott
24	Tel Ashdod	167750/629600	360,000	x	Chalco, EB, MB, LB, Iron1, Iron2, Pers, Hell, Rom, Byz, EI, Med, Ott

Mayer 1934; Dothan and Freedman 1967; Dothan 1971; 1973; 1993; Dothan and Porath 1982; 1993; Tsafrir, Di Segni, and Green 1994:62 (Azotos Hippenos); Naᵓaman 1998; Finkelstein and Singer-Avitz 2001; 2004; Ben Shlomo 2003; Dothan and Ben Shlomo 2005.

No.	Site	Coordinates	Area (m²)	Excavated	Periods (patch sites noted by [p])
25	Tel Ashdod "Assyrian Palace" Varga 2005; Kogan-Zehavi 2006.	167600/629900	1,000	x	Iron2, Pers, Hell, Rom, Byz
26	Tel Ashdod Well and pool Baumgarten 1999.	167350/629800	150	x	Rom, Byz, EI
27	Tel Ashdod Pottery workshop Baumgarten 2000.	167630/629950	150	x	Rom, Byz
28	Holot Ashdod	162700/628200	100,000		Pers, Hell, Rom, Byz, EI
29	Holot Ashdod	163720/628480	4,800		Rom(p), Byz(p), EI(p)
30	Holot Ashdod	163650/628980	2,000		Rom(p), Byz(p)
31	Holot Ashdod	163640/628100	600		Rom(p), EI(p)
32	Holot Ashdod	163980/628260	900		Hell, Rom, Byz
33	Holot Ashdod	164980/628300	1,500		Iron2(p), Byz(p), EI(p)
34	Holot Ashdod	164900/628500	2,000		Iron2(p), Rom(p), Byz(p)
35	Holot Ashdod	164700/628380	1,000		Pers(p), Rom(p), EI(p)
36	Holot Ashdod	164680/628700	2,000		Rom(p)
37	Holot Ashdod	164010/628620	400		Rom(p), Byz(p)
38	Holot Ashdod Non-indicative pottery.	164210/628700	8,000		

Table 2.9 (cont.): Table of All Survey Sites

No.	Site	Coordinates	Area (m²)	Excavated	Periods (patch sites noted by [p])
39	Holot Ashdod	165320/628650	500		EI
40	Holot Ashdod	165300/628770	1,000		EI(p)
41	Holot Ashdod	165800/628780	1,500		Iron2(p), Rom(p)
42	Holot Ashdod	165130/628360	2,000		Iron2(p), Rom(p), Byz(p)
43	Holot Ashdod	165720/628250	2,500		Pers, Rom, Byz, EI
44	Holot Ashdod	166070/628780	3,000		Iron2(p), Pers(p), Rom(p)
45	Tell Kursun	166840/628010	1,500		LB, Iron2, Pers, Rom, Byz
46	Holot Ashdod	166340/628200	100		Rom(cem)
47	Holot Ashdod	166000/628000	5,000		Rom(p), Byz(p), EI(p)
48	Holot Ashdod Cemetery	168150/628700	1,000		LB(cem), Iron1(cem), Iron2(cem), Hell(cem), Rom (cem), Byz(cem), Ott
49	Holot Ashdod	161700/627200	1,200		Epi, LB, Iron1, Iron2, Pers, Hell, Rom, Byz
50	Holot Ashdod	161790/627420	100		Rom(p), Byz(p), Med(p)
51	Nahal Evtah	162050/627600	5,000		LB, Iron1
52	Nahal Evtah	162280/627850	400		Rom, Byz, Med
53	Nahal Evtah	162700/627220	30,000	x	PtryNeo
	Yeivin and Olami 1979; 1980.				
54	Nahal Evtah	162900/627950	100		MB, Rom
55	Holot Ashdod	163680/627900	1,000		Iron2(p), Pers(p), Hell(p), Rom(p), Byz(p)
56	Nahal Evtah	163280/627150	1,000		Rom, Byz, Med
57	Holot Ashdod	163990/627050	200		Byz(cem)
58	Holot Ashdod	163650/627700	40,000	x	Chalco, EB, Rom, Byz
	The Nizzanim Area [in Hebrew], *HA* 69–71 (1979):84; Yekutiely and Gophna 1994.				
59	Holot Ashdod	163850/627000	400		Rom(p), Byz(p), Med(p)
60	Holot Ashdod	164180/627680	1,500		Rom(p), EI(p)
61	Holot Ashdod	164480/627850	2,400		Rom(p), Byz(p), EI(p)
62	Esh Sheikh Jaham	165200/627680	200	x	Med
	A Coin Hoard from Nizzanim, *HA* 50 (1974):28.				
63	Kh. Yasin	166800/627350	200		Byz
64	Kh. Ghaiyada	168840/627350	2,000		Rom, Byz
65	Holot Ashdod	161400/626700	1,500		Ott
66	Holot Ashdod	161200/626200	100		Rom, Byz
67	Holot Ashdod	161920/626160	1,500		Rom(p), Byz(p)
68	Nahal Evtah	162920/626100	1,500		Rom, Byz
69	Nahal Evtah	162900/626400	1,000		MB, Pers, Rom, Byz
70	Nahal Evtah	163200/626950	60,000		Iron2, Pers, Hell, Rom, Byz, Med
71	Nahal Evtah	163360/626750	5,000		Pers(p), Rom(p), Byz(p), EI(p), Med(p)
72	Nahal Evtah	163500/626400	8,000		Pers, Rom, Byz
73	Nahal Evtah	163540/626240	2,000		Rom, Byz
74	Nahal Evtah	164380/626600	1,500		Byz(p), Med(p), Ott(p)
75	Holot Ashdod	164200/626900	1,000		Med(p), Ott(p)
76	Holot Ashdod	164100/626450	3,000		Iron2, Pers, Rom, EI, Med
77	Tell Abu Haraze Non-indicative pottery	166950/626010	500		
78	Sandahanna	167950/626200	12,000		Rom, Byz, Med, Ott
79	El ᶜAbtah (NW)	160950/625900	2,500		LB, Iron1
80	Holot Ashdod	160960/625580	2,500		Rom(p), Byz(p), EI(p), Ott(p)
81	El ᶜAbtah	160690/625040	60,000		Epi, Byz
82	Holot Ashdod	161150/625700	400		Epi

Table 2.9 (cont.): Table of All Survey Sites

No.	Site	Coordinates	Area (m²)	Excavated	Periods (patch sites noted by [p])
83	Holot Ashdod	161700/625300	100		Rom(cem)
84	Holot Ashdod	161400/625680	1,000		EI(p), Med(p), Ott(p)
85	Holot Ashdod	162540/625800	5,000		Rom(p), Byz(p), EI(p)
86	Holot Ashdod	162300/625800	2,000		Pers(p), Rom(p), Byz(p), EI(p)
87	Holot Ashdod	162550/625550	2,000		Rom, Byz, EI
88	Miska Suleiman Agha	162600/625200	5,000		Rom, Byz, EI, Med
	Warren 1871:89.				
89	Holot Ashdod	162300/625050	3,200		Rom(p), Byz(p), Med(p)
90	Holot Ashdod	162770/625050	1,000		Iron2(p), Pers(p), Rom(p), Byz(p), EI(p), Med(p)
91	Nahal Evtah	163300/625280	1,000		Rom(p), EI(p), Med(p)
92	Nahal Evtah	163340/625550	500		Rom(p), Byz(p), EI(p)
93	Nahal Evtah	163040/625400	2,000		Iron2(p), Pers(p), Hell(p), Rom(p), Med(p), Ott(p)
94	Kh. Umm er Riyah	165980/625920	500		Rom, Byz, Med
95	Nizzanim (E)	166240/625180	400		Rom, Byz
96	Beit Daras	169850/625850	60,000		Rom, Byz, Ott
97	Ashkelon (N)	160280/624210	100		Rom, Byz
98	Ashkelon (N)	160390/624230	1,000		Hell, Rom, Byz, EI, Med
99	Ashkelon (N)	160510/624520	3,000		Iron2(p), Hell(p), Rom(p), Byz(p), EI(p), Med(p)
100	Ashkelon (N)	160500/624020	1,500		Rom, Byz, Med
101	Ashkelon (N)	160070/624110	200		Byz, Ott
102	Ashkelon (N)	161180/624350	200		Iron2, Pers
103	Nahal Evtah	161800/624380	2,500		Rom(p), Byz(p), EI(p), Med(p), Ott(p)
104	Ashkelon (N)	161000/624500	100		Byz
105	Ashkelon (N)	161500/624050	200		Byz(cem)
106	Nahal Evtah	162300/624100	100,000		Rom(p), Byz(p), EI(p), Med(p), Ott(p)
107	Nahal Evtah	162100/624600	1,000		Rom(p), Byz(p), Med(p)
108	Tell el Farahand	162700/624300	2,000		Byz, EI, Med
109	Holot Ashdod	162100/624950	3,200		Iron2(p), Rom(p), Byz(p), Med(p), Ott(p)
110	Nahal Evtah	162770/624840	5,000		Iron2, Pers, Hell, Rom, Byz, EI, Med
111	Nahal Evtah	162700/624500	25,000		Pers(p), Hell(p), Rom(p), Byz(p), EI(p), Med(p)
112	Nahal Evtah	162980/624830	1,000		Byz(cem), Med(cem)
	Berman and Barda 2005:57*, site 109; Huster and Sion 2006 (mentioning two tombs).				
113	Tel Poran	163600/624150	100,000	x	EB, MB, LB, Iron1, Iron2, Pers, Hell, Rom, Byz, EI
	Ram Gophna and Joseph Naveh, Tel Poran [in Hebrew], *HA* 43 (1972):21; Gophna 1977; 1992.				
114	Nahal Evtah	163020/624650	3,500		Pers(p), Rom(p), Med(p)
115	Nahal Evtah	163280/624600	500		Rom(p), Byz(p)
116	Nahal Evtah	163180/624950	2,000		Pers, Hell, Rom, EI, Med, Ott
117	Kh. Basha	164920/624600	1,000		Rom, Byz, Med, Ott
118	Kh. Basha (SW)	164850/625000	3,600	x	Iron2, Rom, Byz, EI, Med
	Peretz 2011.				
119	Nizzanim (SW)	164650/624300	500		MB, Rom
120	Kh. Micṣaba	166550/624320	4,000		Rom, Byz, EI, Med, Ott
121	Esh Sheikh el Isbawi	166180/624340	3,000		Ott(cem)
	Surveyed by Huster.				
122	Nahal Evtah	167800/624450	500		EB, Rom, Byz, EI
123	Nahal Hodiyya,	168450/624100	5,000		Rom, Byz, EI, Med, Ott
	Kh. Bezzeh				
	Map 88 site 119; Berman and Barda 2005:60*; Huster and Blakely, in press.				
124	En Nabi Salih	168500/624400	100		Rom, Med, Ott

Table 2.9 (cont.): Table of All Survey Sites

No.	Site	Coordinates	Area (m²)	Excavated	Periods (patch sites noted by [p])
125	Nahal Hodiyya	168250/624950	100		
	Non-indicative pottery				
126	Kh. Auda (S)	169200/624650	1,000		Rom, Byz, Ott
127	Kh. Auda, Kh. Ode. Bir en Nebah	169200/624980	1,000		Rom, Byz
128	Ashkelon (N)	160100/623700	100		Rom, Byz
129	Ashkelon (N)	160300/623850	100		Ott
	Berman and Barda 2005:61*				
130	Ashkelon (N)	160500/623500	1,000		Rom, Byz, EI
131	Ashkelon (N)	161200/623900	100		
	Probably from the Ottoman period, due to the use of mud and straw as bonding materials.				
132	Nahal Evtah	161650/623800	210,000		Hell, Rom, Byz, EI, Med
133	Nahal Evtah	162700/623100	1,000	x	Rom, Byz, EI
	Map 88 site 129; Varga 2010.				
134	Kh. Khaur el Bak	163940/623120	1,500		Rom, Byz, EI, Med, Ott
135	Kh. Khaur el Bak	163200/622900	1,000		Byz, EI
	Talis 2011.				
136	Nahal Evtah	163450/623550	1,000		Byz
137	Kh. el Msalle, Kh el Mussalla	164950/623200	1,500		EB, Rom, Byz, EI, Ott
	Resurveyed by Huster; Huster and Sion 2006 (nos. 28, 29).				
138	Nahal Evtah	164400/623200	3,000		Rom, Byz, EI, Ott
139	Nahal Evtah	164700/623500	2,000		Rom, Byz, EI, Med
140	Nahal Evtah	165200/623400	100		Byz
141	En Nawamis	165780/623580	2,500		Rom, Byz, Med, Ott
	Berman and Barda 2005:63*, site 136.				
142	Kh. Balas	165630/623960	2,000		EB, Hell, Rom, Byz, Med, Ott
143	Nahal Evtah	165250/623550	500		Rom, Byz
144	Nahal Evtah	165560/623250	1,000		Byz
145	Kh. Khasse	166920/623420	2,000		Iron2, Pers, Hell, Rom, Byz
	Berman and Barda 2005:64*, site 140. Erroneously identified as Kh. Bazza due to a mistake in Israeli maps. Huster and Blakely, in press.				
146	Nahal Evtah	167300/623200	100	x	Iron1(cem)
	Gophna and Meron 1970.				
147	Nahal Evtah	167500/623900	1,000		Iron2, Pers, Hell, Rom, Byz
	Berman and Barda 2005:65*, site 142. Erroneously identified as Kh. Khassa.				
148	Nahal Evtah	167300/623920	100		Byz
149	Kh. Mansura	169720/623900	1,500		Rom, Byz
150	Nahal Evtah	169800/623380	100		Byz
151	Ashkelon, Barnea	160100/622850	1,000		Byz, EI
152	Ashkelon (NE)	160360/622040	100		Iron2, Rom, Byz
153	Hamame (NW)	161350/622700	5,000		Rom, Byz, EI, Med
154	Hamame	161400/622400	90,000		Rom, Ott
155	Nahal Evtah	162900/622950	2,000		Rom, Byz, EI
	Map 88 site 155; Varga 2010.				
156	Nahal Evtah	163900/622700	2,000		MB, Rom, Byz
157	Nahal Evtah	164550/622400	100		Byz
158	Nahal Hodiyya	165850/622250	2,000		Rom, Byz, EI, Med
159	Kh. el Biyar (N)	168600/622050	2,500		Rom, Byz

Table 2.9 (cont.): Table of All Survey Sites

No.	Site	Coordinates	Area (m²)	Excavated	Periods (patch sites noted by [p])
160	Ashkelon, Barnea Top	160100/621800	10,000	x	Pers, Hell, Byz
	Sion 2008; Haimi 2008.				
161	Ashkelon (NE)	160200/621380	2,000		Rom, Med, Ott
162	Ashkelon (NE)	160350/621600	3,000		Rom(p), Byz(p), Med(p), Ott(p)
163	Ashkelon (NE)	160400/621800	6,000		Rom(p), Byz(p), Med(p)
164	Ashkelon (E)	160800/621600	40,000	x	MB(cem), MB(cem), Pers, Hell, Rom, Byz
	Israel 1995a; 1995b; Zelin 2002.				
165	Ashkelon (E)	160690/621460	100	x	Rom(cem), Byz(cem)
	Israel 1995a; Huster and Sion 2006 (nos. 36, 37, 38).				
166	Ashkelon (E)	160900/621200	200	x	Hell, Rom, Byz
	Fabian, Nahshoni, and Ein Gedy 1995.				
167	Ashkelon (E)	162730/621980	1,000		Rom, Byz, Ott
168	Ashkelon (E)	162690/621110	7,000		Byz
169	Nahal Evtah	163600/621250	90		MB, Rom, Byz
170	Kh. Makkus	164800/621600	7,800		Byz, Med, Ott
	Gibson, Vitto, and Di Segni 1998.				
171	Nahal Evtah	165380/621650	11,000		Rom, Byz
172	Julis	167300/621200	50,000		Rom, Byz, Med, Ott
173	Nahal Hodiyya	167120/621580	100		Med, Ott
174	Nahal Hodiyya	168700/621880	100		Byz
175	Kh. el Biyar	168700/621700	2,000		Rom, Byz, Ott
176	Ashkelon	161150/620160	200	x	Chalco, MB(cem), MB(cem), Hell, Rom, Byz
	Gershuni 1996; 1997; Nahshoni 1999.				
177	Miskat el Jummeize	162980/620420	100		Ott
	Berman and Barda 2005:75, site 170, suggested an Ottoman burial monument. We suggest that the structure represents the Miska itself (and see above, site 88, Miskat Suleiman Agha).				
178	Jummeizet el Qaᵓa	163120/620500	500		Byz, Med, Ott
179	Kh. Umm esh Shuqaf, Kh. Edh Dhira,	164160/620800	2,000		Rom, Byz, Ott
180	Kh. el Mahjar	164950/620850	2,000		Rom, Byz, EI
	Berman and Barda 2005:71*–72*, site 173.				
181	Kh. el Bira	164330/620400	1,000		Byz
	Resurveyed by Huster. Among finds: potter's wheel and waste of potter's workshop.				
182	Esh Sheikh Kheir	166950/620600	100		Ott
183	Esh Sheikh Kheir (S)	166930/620500	1,000		Rom, Byz, Med, Ott
184	Esh Sheikh Kheir (W)	166720/620600	200		Byz
185	El Farsh	168500/620680	500		Rom, Byz
186	Bir Shuqeir	159800/623800	18,000		Rom, Byz, EI, Med
	Map 87 site 1.				
187	Ashkelon, Barnea B	159630/623340	500		Rom, Byz, EI
	Map 87 site 2.				
188	Ashkelon, Barnea B	159650/623050	2,000		Byz
	Surveyed by Huster 2003. Concentration of marble architectonic elements under a thin layer of sand. Disturbed by mechanical equipment.				
189	Ashkelon, Barnea B	159700/622900	55,000	x	EB, Byz
	Golani 2005; 2007.				
190	Ashkelon Barnea B	159750/622800	1,000	x	Byz
	Milevski and Krokhmalnik 2010.				

Table 2.9 (cont.): Table of All Survey Sites

No.	Site	Coordinates	Area (m²)	Excavated	Periods (patch sites noted by [p])
191	Ashkelon Barnea B	159370/622850	500	x	Byz
	Milevski and Krokhmalnik 2010.				
192	Ashkelon, Barnea	159900/622900	450		Pers, Hell, Rom, Byz(cem), Med
	Map 87 site 4; Berman and Barda 2005:22*.				
193	Ashkelon, Barnea	159000/622560	2,000		Rom, Byz
	Map 87 site 5. Resurveyed by Huster, further collapsed structures.				
194	Ashkelon, Barnea	158900/622350	100		Byz(cem)
	Surveyed by Huster; Huster and Sion 2006 (nos. 30, 31).				
195	Ashkelon, Barnea	159200/622250	3,000		Rom, Byz, EI
	Map 87 site 6.				
196	Ashkelon, Barnea	159700/622350	100	x	Byz(cem)
	Meron 1983; Huster and Sion 2006 (no. 34).				
197	Ashkelon, Barnea	159000/622050	100	x	Byz(cem)
	Huster and Sion 2006 (nos. 30, 31); Varga 2007.				
198	Ashkelon, Barnea	158850/622010	60,000	x	Rom, Byz, EI, Med
	Map 87 site 3; Vitto (not published). Nearby Feder (not published).				
199	Esh Sheikh Awad	158650/621880	150		EB, Rom, Byz, EI, Med, Ott
	Map 87 site 8.				
200	Ashkelon, Barnea (Byzantine Church)	158950/621840	150	x	Byz
	Tzaferis 1971; Map 87 site 9.				
201	Kh. es Sawarif	159100/621800	200	x	Rom, Byz, EI
	Map 87 site 15; Haiman 2011.				
202	Ashkelon, Barnea	159950/622250	60,000		Rom(p), Byz(p)
	Map 87 site 7.				
203	Ashkelon	158500/621650	300		Pers, Hell, Rom, Byz, EI, Med
	Map 87 site 10.				
204	Ashkelon, Afridar	158980/621440	2,000		Rom(p), Byz(p), Med(p)
	Map 87 site 11.				
205	Ashkelon, Barnea	159700/622350	100	x	Byz
	Zelin 2001.				
206	Ashkelon, Semadar Hotel	157700/620400	200	x	Hell, Rom, Byz(cem), EI
	Map 87 site 16; Berman and Barda 2005:26*.				
207	Ashkelon, Afridar	158250/621250	2,000	x	Neo, PtryNeo, EB, Hell, Rom, Byz, EI
	Map 87 site 12; Perrot 1955; Perrot and Gopher 1996; Garfinkel 1999; Varga 2002a; Huster and Sion 2006.				
208	Ashkelon, Afridar	158860/621270		x	Rom
	Map 87 site 14; Avi-Yonah 1976.				
209	Ashkelon, Afridar	158500/621200	20,000	x	Neo, Chalco, EB, Byz
	Map 87 site 13; Brandl and Gophna 1993.				
210	Hajar Id	158130/620800	2,000	x	Rom(cem), Byz(cem)
	Ory 1939; Golani 2004; Huster and Sion 2006. The exact location of the "Peacock" tomb (Michaeli 2001) is unknown.				
211	Hajar Id	158120/620870	12,000	x	EB, Rom, Byz, EI
	Map 87 site 17; Israeli 1997; Wallach 2003; Golani 2004.				
212	Hajar Id	158160/620710	10,000	x	EB, Pers, Rom, Byz, EI
	Map 87 site 18; Golani 1996; 1997; 2004; Golani and Milevski 1999.				

Table 2.9 (cont.): Table of All Survey Sites

No.	Site	Coordinates	Area (m²)	Excavated	Periods (patch sites noted by [p])
213	Ashkelon, Afridar	158350/620500	200	x	Chalco, EB
	Map 87 site 19; Khalaily and Wallach 1998; Khalaily 2004.				
214	Ashkelon, Afridar	158400/620600	200	x	Chalco, EB
	Map 87 site 20; Baumgarten 1996; 2004.				
215	Ashkelon, Hof Ha-Dayyagim	157500/620300	100	x	Rom(cem)
	Huster and Sion 2006 (no. 44); Varga 1999.				
216	Ashkelon, Afridar	158160/620250	100	x	Hell, Rom, Byz, EI, Med
	Map 87 site 21; Varga 2002b.				
217	Ashkelon, Afridar	159800/620700	100	x	Rom
	Map 87 site 22; Barel 1999.				
218	Tel Ashkelon	156900/619000	500,000	x	Chalco, EB, MB, LB, Iron1, Iron2, Pers, Hell, Rom, Byz, EI, Med, Ott
	See *NEAEHL* and *Ashkelon 1*.				
219	El Jura, Arab village	157800/619500	10,000		Hell, Rom, Byz, EI, Ott
	Map 91 site 2; Berman, Stark, and Barda 2004:23*, site 2.				
220	El Jura	157600/619000	50	x	Rom, Byz
	Masarwah 2000; Huster 2007.				
221	El Jura	158300/619300	100	x	EB, Byz, Ott
	Kogan-Zehavi 2006b.				
222	El Jura	158120/619870	100	x	Byz
	Map 91 site 3; Nahshoni 1999.				
223	El Jura	158200/619750	120	x	Byz
	Map 91 site 4; Nahshoni 1998.				
224	El Jura	158220/619440	150	x	Rom, Byz
	Map 91 site 5; Wallach 2000.				
225	El Jura	158300/619500	100	x	Byz
	Map 91 site 5, NE section; Ein Gedy 2002.				
226	El Jura	158050/619250	5,000	x	Rom, Byz, EI, Med
	Recent excavation; Seriy 2012.				
227	El Jura	158200/619650	1,000	x	Byz, EI
	Map 91 site 5, north section, and in the area of Map 91 site 6 (El Jura east); Varga 1999c.				
228	Bir Ali el Madhun	159750/619650	100	x	Hell, Rom, Byz
	Map 91 site 7; Kogan-Zehavi 1997; 1999b.				
229	Ashkelon (College)	159500/619800	200	x	Byz
	Map 91 site 8; Paran 2007.				
230	Ashkelon (College)	159350/619830	100	x	Byz
	Varga 1999a.				
231	Ashkelon	159050/619900	20		Pers, Hell
	Map 91 site 9.				
232	Holot Ashkelon	156200/618100	600		Rom, EI
	Map 91 site 10.				
233	Holot Ashkelon	156300/618300	300		Rom(cem), Byz(cem)
	Map 91 site 11.				
234	Tel Ashkelon (S)	156500/618450	200		Rom, Byz, EI, Med
	Map 91 site 12.				
235	Holot Ashkelon	156550/618200	100		Rom, EI
	Map 91 site 13.				

Table 2.9 (cont.): Table of All Survey Sites

No.	Site	Coordinates	Area (m²)	Excavated	Periods (patch sites noted by [p])
236	Tel Ashkelon (S) Map 91 site 14.	156600/618700	1,000		Rom, Byz, EI, Med
237	Holot Ashkelon Map 91 site 15.	156750/618400	1,000		Rom(p), EI(p)
238	Holot Ashkelon (91/16)	156800/618150	2,000		Rom, EI, Med
239	Holot Ashkelon (91/17)	156950/618450	600		Rom(p), Byz(p), EI(p), Med(p)
240	Tel Ashkelon (S) (91/18)	157050/618250	7,500		Rom, Byz, EI, Med
241	Sheikh Muhammad el Musli (91/19) Resurveyed by Huster.	157500/618950	1,000		Med, Ott
242	Ashkelon (91/20) Varga 2001.	157630/618700	100	x	Byz
243	Ashkelon (91/21) Varga 2003.	157730/618850	100	x	Byz
244	Ashkelon (91/22)	157950/618200	100		Hell, Rom, Byz
245	Mashhad Sidna el Husein (91/23) Map 91 site 23; Kogan-Zehavi 2007. Vaulted tombs (Baumgarten, pers. comm.).	158250/618850	2,000	x	Iron2, Rom(cem), Byz(cem), EI, Ott
246	Ashkelon (91/24) Kol-Yaᶜaqov and Shor 1999; Kol-Yaᶜakov and Farhi 2012.	158100/618750	400	x	Hell, Rom(cem), Byz(cem), EI
247	Ashkelon (91/25)	159150/618350	100		Rom(cem)
248	Ashkelon Declaration by P. Nahshoni, registered as site 17529/0 in IAA system.	159700/618750	5,000		Rom, Byz
249	Holot Ashkelon (91/26)	155700/617300	100		Byz
250	Dureibat Abu Qutuf (91/27)	156480/617600	3,000		Rom(p), EI(p), Med(p)
251	Holot Ashkelon (91/28)	156850/617700	2,500		Rom(p), Byz(p), EI(p)
252	Holot Ashkelon (91/29)	156900/617500	2,000		Rom(p), EI(p), Med(p)
253	Holot Ashkelon (91/30)	157100/617750	120		Rom, Med
254	Holot Ashkelon (91/31)	157700/617500	1,000		MB
255	Kh. el Khisas (NE) (91/32) Nahshoni 2001.	158750/617850	1,000	x	Pers, Hell, Rom, Byz, EI
256	Kh. el Khisas Resurveyed by Huster.	158500/617550	15,000		Rom, Byz, EI, Ott
257	Er Rasm (near triangulation point 29); surveyed by Huster.	159050/617200	2,000		Rom, Byz
258	Er Rasm (91/33)	158950/617150	100		Rom
259	Ashkelon Givᶜat Ziyyon Gershuny 1999.	159700/617820	200	x	MB(cem), MB(cem), Rom, Byz, Med, Ott

Table 2.9 (cont.): Table of All Survey Sites

No.	Site	Coordinates	Area (m²)	Excavated	Periods (patch sites noted by [p])
260	Niᶜilya	159550/617350	5,000		Rom, Byz, Med, Ott
261	Holot Ashkelon	159300/617400	150		Chalco, EB, MB(p), MB(p), Iron1(p), Iron2(p), Rom(p), Byz(p)
262	El Qabu	155400/616700	2,000	x	Hell, Rom, Byz, EI
	Haimi 2007; Sion 2009.				
263	Holot Ashkelon	156700/616150	2,000		Neo, Chalco
264	Holot Ashkelon	156950/616050	1,500		Iron2, Hell, Rom
265	Holot Ashkelon	157200/616200	450		Rom(p), Byz(p), Ott(p)
266	Holot Ashkelon	157750/616100	1,000		Iron2, Pers, Hell, Rom, Byz, EI, Med
267	Holot Ashkelon	158100/616800	1,500		Iron2, Hell, Rom, Byz, Med
268	Holot Ashkelon	158250/616200	100		Rom(cem)
	Berman, Stark, and Barda 2004:32*, site 43.				
269	Holot Ashkelon	158300/616450	2,000		Iron2, Pers, Hell, Rom, Byz, Med, Ott
270	Holot Ashkelon	158400/616250	1,500		Pers, Rom, Byz
271	Holot Ashkelon	158500/616090	1,000		Pers(p), Rom(p)
272	Holot Ashkelon	158950/616350	300		Rom, Byz, EI, Med
273	Holot Ashkelon	159400/616600	2,000		Pers(p), Rom(p), Med(p)
274	Niᶜilya (S)	159400/616900	200		Ott
275	Holot Ashkelon	159700/616150	2,000		Rom(p), Med(p)
276	Saknat Muhammad Mahmud (SW)	154100/615150	3,000		Chalco, EB, Iron2, Hell, Rom
277	Saknat Muhammad Mahmud	154200/615300	2,000		Iron2(p), Pers(p), Hell(p), Rom(p)
278	Holot Ashkelon	154350/615350	100		Iron2, Rom
279	Holot Ashkelon	154400/615150	50,000		Rom(p), Byz(p), EI(p), Ott(p)
280	Holot Ashkelon	154850/615600	1,500		Rom(p), EI(p)
281	Holot Ashkelon	154940/615850	500	x	Neo, Chalco, Rom(p), EI(p)
	Noy and Berman 1974.				
282	Holot Ashkelon	155200/615850	1,000		Iron2(p), Rom(p), Med(p)
283	Holot Ashkelon	155950/615920	100		Byz, EI
284	Holot Ashkelon	155200/615100	1,000		Chalco, Rom(p), EI(p)
285	Holot Ashkelon	155450/615400	1,000		Rom(p), Med(p)
286	Holot Ashkelon	156200/615300	500		Rom(p), EI(p)
287	Holot Ashkelon	156450/615600	2,000		Iron2(p), Rom(p)
288	Holot Ashkelon	156500/615450	1,000		Iron2(p), Byz(p)
289	Holot Ashkelon	156650/615450	1,500		Rom
290	Holot Ashkelon	156990/615070	200		Byz
291	Holot Ashkelon	157300/615750	1,500		Hell, Rom
292	Holot Ziqim	157400/615100	500		Rom(p)
293	Holot Ziqim	157450/615300	2,000		Rom, Byz, EI
294	Holot Ziqim	157500/615600	1,500		Iron2, Hell, Rom
295	Holot Ashkelon	157800/615500	200		Chalco, Iron2(p), Rom(p)
296	Holot Ashkelon	157950/615400	100		Iron2, Hell, Rom, Byz
297	Holot Ashkelon	158200/615350	2,000		Hell(p), Rom(p), Byz(p), EI(p), Ott
298	Holot Ashkelon	158300/615950	100		Pers, Rom, Med
299	Holot Ashkelon	158400/615000	5,000		Pers, Rom, EI, Med, Ott
300	Holot Ashkelon	158450/615300	500		Pers(p), Hell(p), Rom(p), EI(p), Med(p)
301	Holot Ashkelon	158700/615100	2,000		Rom(p), Byz(p), EI(p), Med(p), Ott(p)
302	Holot Ashkelon	158950/615700	5,000		Rom(p), EI(p), Med(p), Ott(p)

Table 2.9 (cont.): Table of All Survey Sites

No.	Site	Coordinates	Area (m²)	Excavated	Periods (patch sites noted by [p])
303	Holot Ashkelon	159550/615650	5,000		Rom(p), Med(p), Ott(p)
304	Holot Ashkelon	159600/615300	1,000		Iron2(p), Pers(p), Rom(p), EI(p), Med(p)
305	Holot Ashkelon	159750/615600	1,000		Chalco, Byz(p), Med(p), Ott(p)
306	Ard el Mihjar	153600/614150	70,000		Chalco, Rom(p), Byz(p), EI(p), Ott(p)
307	Ard el Mihjar	153900/614000	40,000		EI(p), Med(p)
308	Holot Ashkelon	153950/614550	1,000		Neo, EI(p), Med(p)
309	Holot Ashkelon	154500/614600	1,000		Neo, EI(p), Med(p)
310	Holot Ashkelon	154600/614950	3,000		Rom, EI
311	Holot Ashkelon	154800/614900	3,000		Chalco, Hell, Rom, Byz, EI
312	Kh. esh Sheraf	155400/614600	1,500		Med, Ott
313	Holot Ziqim	156350/614200	2,000		Byz, Ott
314	Holot Ziqim	156300/614550	100		Byz
315	Holot Ziqim	156930/614720	200		Rom(cem), Byz(cem)
316	Holot Ziqim	157200/614300	1,000		Rom(p), Byz(p)
317	Holot Ziqim	157400/614250	1,000		Iron2(p), Rom(p), Byz(p)
318	Holot Ziqim	157450/614600	1,000		Rom(p), Med(p)
319	Holot ziqim	157500/614100	1,500		Rom, Byz, Med, Ott
320	Holot Ziqim	157800/614500	10,000		Hell, Rom(cem), Byz(cem), EI
321	Holot Ziqim	157370/614910	200		Rom(cem), Byz(cem)
322	Holot Ziqim	157900/614950	2,500		Rom(p), Byz(p), EI(p)
323	Holot Ziqim	157950/614700	2,800		Rom(p), Byz(p)
324	Holot Ziqim	157990/614250	2,500		Iron2(p), Pers(p), Rom(p), Byz(p), EI(p), Med(p), Ott(p)
325	Kh. el Yasmina	158620/614120	2,000		Byz
326	Kh. el Yasmina	158530/613980	200	x	Byz
	Haimi (pers. comm.).				
327	Holot Ziqim	158400/614700	1,500		Rom(p), Byz(p), EI(p), Med(p), Ott(p)
328	Mavqiᶜim (SW)	159200/614150	2,800		Rom, Byz
329	Mavqiᶜim (SW)	159500/614100	200		Byz(p)
330	Nahal Shiqma	152750/613100	1,000		EI(p), Med(p), Ott(p)
331	Ard el Mihjar	153050/613600	200	x	Byz
	Fabian and Goren 2001.				
332	Ard el Mihjar	153350/613450	1,000		EI(p), Med(p)
333	Ard el Mihjar	153300/613750	100		Rom, Byz
334	Ard el Mihjar	153600/613800	2,000		EI(p), Med(p)
335	Holot Ziqim	154300/613650	2,500		Chalco, Iron2, Hell, Rom, EI, Med
336	Holot Ziqim	154650/613900	3,000		Chalco, Pers(p), Rom(p), EI(p)
337	Holot Ziqim	154850/613750	3,000		Rom(p), Byz(p), EI(p), Med(p), Ott(p)
338	Holot Ziqim	155100/613750	1,000		Rom(p), Byz(p)
339	Holot Ziqim	156950/613650	500		Byz(p)
340	Holot Ziqim	157850/613900	4,000		Iron2, Hell, Rom, Byz, EI, Med, Ott
341	Holot Ziqim	157750/613650	200		Iron2(p), Rom(p), Byz(p), Ott
342	Holot Ziqim	157700/613200	200		Byz, Ott
343	Holot Ziqim	157400/613200	100		Rom(p), Byz(p)
344	Tell esh Shuqaf	152200/612050	2,250		Iron2, Pers, Hell, Rom, EI
345	Tell esh Shuqaf	152300/612050	2,000		EI(p), Med(p)
346	Ard el Mihjar	153300/612950	200	x	Rom(p), Byz, EI
	Nikolsky 2010.				

Table 2.9 (cont.): Table of All Survey Sites

No.	Site	Coordinates	Area (m²)	Excavated	Periods (patch sites noted by [p])
347	Nahal Shiqma	153400/612200	200	x	PtryNeo, Chalco
	Noy 1976; 1977.				
348	Nahal Shiqma	154300/612600	100		EB(p)
349	Esh Sheikh Saᶜid	156600/612480	1,000	x	Hell, Rom, Byz, EI
	Porat and Meron 1977.				
350	Hirbiya	157100/612850	10,000		Rom, Byz, EI, Med, Ott
351	Kh. er Rasm,	158400/612450	500		Rom, Byz, EI
	Kh. El Hajar				
352	Nahal Oved (NW)	158550/612800	100		Ott
353	Hof Shiqma	151500/611100	500		EI(p), Med(p), Ott
354	Hof Shiqma	151650/611150	10,000		Neo, Chalco, Rom, Byz, EI, Med
355	Hof Shiqma	151850/611450	2,000	x	Rom, Byz, EI
	Huster: in preparation.				
356	Hof Shiqma	151950/611750	100		Neo, Chalco
357	Tell esh Shuqaf (SE)	152050/611900	200		Rom, Byz
358	Nahal Shiqma (SW)	152100/611150	2,000		Pers(p), Rom(p), EI(p), Med(p)
359	Nahal Shiqma (SW)	152200/611600	2,000		Chalco, Rom(p), EI(p)
360	Tell esh Shuqaf (SE)	152280/611850	5,000		Neo, Chalco, Rom(p), Byz(p), EI(p), Med(p), Ott(p)
361	Nahal Shiqma (S)	152600/611200	1,000		MB, Iron2, Pers, Hell, EI, Ott
362	Nahal Shiqma (S)	153000/611000	100		MB, Pers, Hell, Rom, Ott
363	Nahal Shiqma (S)	153200/611400	600	x	Hell, Rom, Byz
	Zissu 1996.				
364	Nahal Shiqma (S)	153300/611400	4,000		Neo, Chalco, Rom(p), Byz(p), Ott(p)
365	Nahal Shiqma (S)	153450/611550	2,000		Neo, Chalco, Rom
366	Nahal Shiqma (S)	153320/611540	300		Paleo
367	Nahal Shiqma (S)	153500/611750	500		Neo, Chalco, Iron2, Rom, Ott
368	Nahal Shiqma	153520/611950	500		Neo, Chalco
369	Nahal Shiqma (S)	153600/611200	4,000		Neo, Chalco, Byz(p), EI(p), Med(p)
370	Nahal Shiqma (S)	153650/611420	5,000		Neo, Chalco, Rom(p), EI(p), Med(p), Ott(p)
371	Maᵓagar Shiqma (S)	153860/611900	500		Neo, Chalco, Rom(p)
372	Maᵓagar Shiqma (S)	153950/611750	1,000		Neo, Chalco
373	Maᵓagar Shiqma (S)	153950/611400	100		Neo, Chalco
	Non-indicative flint and pottery.				
374	Maᵓagar Shiqma (S)	153600/611680	600		Neo, Chalco
	Non-indicative flint and pottery.				
375	Maᵓagar Shiqma (S)	154100/611080	10,000		Neo, Chalco, Rom(p), Byz(p), EI(p)
376	Maᵓagar Shiqma (S)	154160/611300	1,000		Neo, Chalco, Hell(p), Rom(p)
377	Maᵓagar Shiqma (S)	154550/611400	2,500		Neo, Chalco, Hell(p), Rom(p), Byz(p)
378	Maᵓagar Shiqma (S)	154580/611600	12,000		Neo, Chalco, Iron2(p), Hell(p), Rom(p), Byz(p), EI(p), Med(p)
379	Maᵓagar Shiqma (S)	154970/611080	100		Neo, Chalco, Rom, Byz, EI
380	Maᵓagar Shiqma (S)	155080/611700	15,000		Chalco, Rom(p), Byz(p)
381	Maᵓagar Shiqma (S)	155200/611450	20,000		Chalco, Iron2(p), Pers(p), Rom(p), Byz(p), Med(p)
382	Maᵓagar Shiqma (S)	155440/611600	1,000		Pers(p), Rom(p), Med(p)
383	Nahal Shiqma (SW)	155750/611400	10,000		Iron2(p), Pers(p), Hell(p), Rom(p), Byz(p), Med(p)
384	Nahal Shiqma (SW)	155770/611100	8,000		Hell(p), Rom(p), Byz(p)
385	Nahal Shiqma (SW)	155980/611150	10,000		Hell(p), Rom(p), Byz(p)
386	Holot Karmiyya	156670/611650	1,000		Iron2(p), Byz(p), EI(p), Med(p), Ott
387	Holot Karmiyya	156700/611950	1,200		Chalco, EB, Rom, Byz, Med, Ott

Table 2.9 (cont.): Table of All Survey Sites

No.	Site	Coordinates	Area (m²)	Excavated	Periods (patch sites noted by [p])
388	Karmiyya (SE)	157300/611880	1,000		Rom, Byz, EI
389	Yad Mordekhai (NW)	157780/611300	500		Rom(p), Byz(p)
390	Nahal Oved (NW)	158450/611850	200		Paleo
391	Nahal Oved (NW)	159080/611050	500		Byz
	Map 91 site 162; plus Huster inspection work.				
392	Kh. Beit Lajus	159980/611700	3,000		Rom, Byz, Med, Ott
393	Hof Shiqma (S)	151180/610620	1,000		EI(p)
394	Ele Sinai (NW)	152200/610500	1,000		Pers, Hell, Rom, Byz, EI
395	Ele Sinai (NW)	152300/610380	100		Pers(p), Hell(p)
396	Ele Sinai (NW)	152300/610620	500		Neo, Chalco
397	Ele Sinai (SW)	152500/610150	1,000		Hell(cem), Rom(cem), EI(cem)
398	Ele Sinai	152700/610200	1,000		Neo, Chalco, EI(p), Med(p)
399	Ele Sinai (S)	152720/610000	500		Neo, Chalco, Byz(p), EI(p)
400	Ele Sinai (N)	152750/610680	300		Byz, EI
401	Ele Sinai (NE)	153200/610620	200		Hell, Rom
	Map 91 site 172.				
402	Ele Sinai (E)	153280/610250	500		Chalco, MB(p), MB(p), Rom(p), Med(p)
403	Ele Sinai (NE)	153340/610680	500		Chalco
404	Ele Sinai (E)	153480/610110	60		Med(p)
405	Maʾagar Shiqma (S)	153740/610850	500		Neo, Chalco, Rom(p), Byz(p), EI(p)
	Map 91 site 176.				
406	Maʾagar Shiqma (S)	153820/610300	1,500		Neo, Chalco, Iron2, Pers, Rom, Byz, EI, Med
407	Netiv Ha-ᶜAsara (NW)	154250/610080	500		Chalco, Rom(p), Byz(p)
408	Netiv Ha-ᶜAsara (NW)	154300/610400	500		Chalco, Iron2, Rom, Byz, EI
409	Netiv Ha-ᶜAsara (NW)	154650/610600	5,000		Iron2(p), Rom(p), Byz(p), EI(p)
410	Netiv Ha-ᶜAsara (NW)	154680/610750	100		Chalco
411	Netiv Ha-ᶜAsara (NW)	154950/610600	500		Iron2(p), Pers(p), Byz(p)
412	Netiv Ha-ᶜAsara (NW)	154980/610150	3,000		Iron2, Pers, Hell, Rom, Byz, EI, Med
413	Netiv Ha-ᶜAsara (N)	155100/610850	1,000		Iron2, Rom
414	Netiv Ha-ᶜAsara (N)	155110/610380	300		Iron2, Pers
415	Netiv Ha-ᶜAsara (N)	155220/610150	1,000		Iron2(p), Pers(p), EI(p)
416	Netiv Ha-ᶜAsara (N)	155250/610300	2,000		Rom(p), Byz(p), Med(p)
417	Netiv Ha-ᶜAsara (N)	155300/610400	150		Pers, Hell, Rom, Byz
418	Netiv Ha-ᶜAsara (N)	155450/610000	30,000		Hell(p), Rom(p), EI(p), Med(p), Ott(p)
419	Netiv Ha-ᶜAsara (N)	155750/610200	1,200		Iron2, Pers, Hell
420	Nahal Shiqma (W)	155900/610600	150		Rom, Byz
421	Nahal Shiqma (W)	155950/610150	4,000		Iron2, Pers, Hell, Rom, Byz, EI, Ott
422	Nahal Shiqma (W)	156100/610420	1,500		Rom(p), EI(p)
423	Nahal Shiqma (W)	156300/610150	4,000		Iron2(p), Pers(p), Hell(p), Rom(p), Byz(p), Ott(p)
424	Nahal Shiqma	156300/610550	2,000		Byz, Med, Ott
425	Nahal Shiqma	156450/610300	7,000		Pers(p), Hell(p), Rom(p), Byz(p), EI(p), Med(p), Ott(p)
426	Nahal Shiqma	156620/610150	1,500		Iron2, Pers, Hell, Rom, Byz, EI, Med

Table 2.9 (cont.): Table of All Survey Sites

No.	Site	Coordinates	Area (m²)	Excavated	Periods (patch sites noted by [p])
427	Nahal Shiqma	156750/610000	500		Chalco, EB, Rom, Byz
428	Kh. Macraba	157300/610400	500		Rom, Byz, EI
429	Kh. Macraba	157300/610500	100	x	MB(cem), MB(cem)
	Kh. Macraba [in Hebrew], *HA* 67–68 (1978):76.				
430	Kh. Bakkita (Yad Mordekhai)	158600/610750	1,000	x	Iron1, Iron2, Pers, Hell, Rom, Byz, EI
	Baumgarten (pers. comm., 2011); A Byzantine Burial Cave in Qibutz Yad Mordekhai [in Hebrew], *HA* 13 (1965):4.				
431	Nahal Oved	159100/610300	5,000		Rom, Byz, EI
432	El Mejdel (Mosque and center)	160800/619800	150,000		Rom, Byz, EI, Med, Ott
	Surveyed by Huster.				
433	El Mejdel (Islamic cemetery)	160600/619900	40,000		EB, MB, Rom, Byz, EI, Med, Ott(cem)
	Surveyed by Huster.				
434	El Mejdel (Eli Kohen St.)	160450/619860	600	x	Pers, Hell, Rom, Byz
	Kogan-Zehavi 1999a; Haimi 2009; Nahshoni 2009a.				
435	El Mejdel	161050/619700	30,000		Byz, EI, Med, Ott
	Ottoman-Mandatory (Map 92 site 19/1); Allen in *Ashkelon 1*, p. 59; also resurveyed by Huster.				
436	Tsomet Berekhya 1	162500/619500	100		Rom, Byz
	Map 92 site 29/1.				
437	Tsomet Berekhya	162600/619050	2,000	x	Byz
	Nahshoni 2009b.				
438	Kh. er Rasm	163300/619450	1,500		Rom, Byz, EI
	Map 92 site 39/1; Allen in *Ashkelon 1*, p. 60.				
439	Berekhya (W)	163250/619280	1,000	x	Rom, Byz
	Huster, forthcoming.				
440	Kh. el Bire (S)	164100/619700	500		Byz, EI
	Map 92 site 49/1.				
441	Kh. el Bire	164500/619800	1,000		Byz, EI, Med
	Map 92 site 49/2.				
442	Batan el Qarad 2	166200/619500	100		Byz
	Map 92 site 69/1.				
443	Abu Anabe 1	167500/619500	200		Byz
	Map 92 site 79/1.				
444	Abu Anabe 2	167600/619700	200		Byz
	Map 92 site 79/2.				
445	Nahal Hodiyya	167230/619950	1,500		Byz, EI
	Surveyed by Huster.				
446	Kh. Ijjis er Ras (N)	168200/619200	500		Pers, Rom, Byz, EI, Med, Ott
	Map 92 site 89/1.				
447	Nahal Hodiyya 1	168900/619500	1,000		Byz, Med
	Map 92 site 89/2.				
448	Nahal Hodiyya 2	168600/619600	500		Byz
	Map 92 site 89/5.				
449	El Farsh 1	168700/619900	200		Byz
	Map 92 site 89/3.				
450	El Farsh 2	168900/619700	200		Byz
	Map 92 site 89/4.				

Table 2.9 (cont.): Table of All Survey Sites

No.	Site	Coordinates	Area (m²)	Excavated	Periods (patch sites noted by [p])
451	El Farsh 3	168600/619700	200		Chalco, Iron1, Hell, Rom, Byz, EI
	Map 92 site 89/6.				
452	Nahal Hodiyya 3	168100/619900	100		Byz
	Map 92 site 89/7.				
453	El Farsh 4	169000/619300	200		Hell, Rom, Byz, EI
	Map 92 site 99/1.				
454	Givᶜat Ziyyon	160800/618300	100		
	Map 92 site 08/1; non-indicative pottery.				
455	El Mejdel	161050/618970	400		Byz
	(HaNahal St.)				
	Surveyed by Huster.				
456	Tsomet Ashkelon 1	162400/618800	200		Rom, Byz, EI, Med
	Map 92 site 28/1.				
457	Tsomet Ashkelon 2	162100/618740	100		Med
	Map 92 site 28/2.				
458	Kh. Abu Fatun	162900/618500	2,000		Rom, Byz, EI, Med, Ott
	Includes site 28/4 (*Ashkelon 1*, p. 60); resurveyed by Huster; site 28/3 was eliminated.				
459	Sheikh el Kubakba	162800/618400	100		Ott
	PEF map-1880, sheet XX; Petersen 2001:66. Surveyed by Huster.				
460	Batan el Qarad 1	166500/618900	200		Byz
	Map 92 site 68/2.				
461	Karsane	166200/618100	200		Byz
	Map 92 site 68/1.				
462	Kh. Ijjis er Ras (W)	167950/618450	500		Rom, Byz, EI
	Surveyed by Huster.				
463	Kh. Ijjis er Ras	168400/618700	200	x	Iron2, Pers, Hell, Rom, Byz, EI, Med, Ott
	Map 92 site 88/1; Meron, not published; Huster and Sion 2006.				
464	Kh. Ijjis er Ras (W)	168000/618900	100		Paleo, Pers, Hell, Rom, Byz, EI, Med
	Map 92 site 88/2.				
465	Kh. Ijjis er Ras (S)	168200/618000	2,000	x	Byz, EI
	Paran 2009; Haiman 2010.				
466	Negba	169900/618900	100		MB(cem), MB(cem)
	Map 92 site 98/1.				
467	Givᶜat Ziyyon	160900/617500	100		Byz, Med
	Orchards				
	Map 92 site 07/1.				
468	Bar Tzur Farm	161900/617100	60,000		Rom, Byz
	Map 92 site 17/1.				
469	Kh. Abu Fatun ?	162500/617900	100		Rom, Byz, EI
	Map 92 site 27/1.				
470	Kh. Abu Fatun (E)	162900/617800	500		Rom, Byz, EI
	Map 92 site 27/2.				
471	Kh. Sama (tomb)	165060/617000	1,000		Rom, Byz, EI, Med, Ott
	Surveyed by Huster.				
472	Kh. Sama Nabi Sama	165080/617200	20,000		Pers, Rom, Byz, EI, Med, Ott
	Map 92 site 57/1; correction of coordinates.				
473	Kh. Sama , (NE)	165400/617300	200		Byz
	Surveyed by Huster.				

Table 2.9 (cont.): Table of All Survey Sites

No.	Site	Coordinates	Area (m²)	Excavated	Periods (patch sites noted by [p])
474	Kh. Sama (NE)	165650/617670	200		Byz
	Surveyed by Huster.				
475	Wadi Qimas 1	166000/617200	200		Byz, EI
	Map 92 site 67/1.				
476	Wadi Qimas 2	166300/617500	500		Paleo, Byz, EI
	Map 92 site 67/2.				
477	Kh. Ijjis er Ras (SW)	167800/617900	1,000		Byz, EI
	Map 92 site 77/1.				
478	Nahal Gaia 1	167800/617300	200		Hell, Rom, Byz, EI, Med
	Map 92 site 77/2.				
479	Nahal Gaia 2	168200/617700	200		Byz, EI
	Map 92 site 87/1.				
480	Sde Yoav (N)	169400/617500	100		Byz
	Map 92 site 97/3.				
481	Mezudat Yoav (N)	169800/617600	100		Byz
	Map 92 site 97/4.				
482	Mezudat Yoav (Ay Sidim)	169900/617500	1,000		Byz, EI
	Map 92 site 97/5.				
483	Shaᶜafat el Biyar	169950/617350	10,000	x	Byz
	Shaᶜafat el Biyar Mandatory file (IAA), Ory Yaakov. Excavation Licences W-10/1933, W-7/1944.				
484	Sde Yoav (W)	119300/117200	4,000		Byz
	Map 92 site 97/2.				
485	Sde Yoav (E)	169900/617000	1,500	x	Byz, EI
	Map 92 site 97/1; Rina Avner (pers. comm.).				
486	Niᶜilya (E)	161100/616950	10,000		Hell, Rom, Byz, EI
	Map 92 site 16/3.				
487	el Qasali	161500/616300	100		Rom, Byz
	Map 92 site 16/2.				
488	Sabahiya	161400/616000	1,500		Paleo, Byz
	Map 92 site 16/1.				
489	Beit Shiqma North	163600/616800	100		Byz
	Map 92 site 36/1.				
490	Kh. Irza	164400/616200	10,000	x	Iron2, Pers, Hell, Rom, Byz, EI, Med, Ott
	Map 92 site 46/1; Allen in *Ashkelon 1*, p. 61; Israel 1995b; Huster and Sion 2006.				
491	Kh. Irza	164150/616050	200		Byz
	Surveyed by Huster.				
492	Kh. Sama (SW)	164880/616900	100		Byz
	Resurveyed by Huster (Byzantine cistern).				
493	Kh. Irza (E)	165100/616500	200		Hell, Rom, Byz
	Map 92 site 56/1.				
494	Khor Breish	166500/616300	200		Rom, Byz, EI
	Map 92 site 66/1.				
495	Kh. Qimas West 1	166800/616600	1,500		Paleo, Byz, EI
	Map 92 site 66/2.				
496	Kh. Qimas West 2	166700/616300	500		Byz, EI, Med
	Map 92 site 66/3.				
497	Kh. Qimas West	167080/616400	200		Byz
	Not in Allen's list; surveyed by Huster.				

Table 2.9 (cont.): Table of All Survey Sites

No.	Site	Coordinates	Area (m²)	Excavated	Periods (patch sites noted by [p])
498	Kh. Qimas	167400/616400	10,000		Rom, Byz, EI, Med, Ott
	Map 92 site 76/1.				
499	Kh. Qimas (S)	167400/616200	500		Byz, EI, Med
	Map 92 site 76/2; Allen in *Ashkelon 1*, p. 63. Wrongly named Abu Fatun?				
500	Kh. Qimas East	167600/616300	100		Byz
	Map 92 site 76/3.				
501	Kh. Qimas West 3	167000/616500	1,000		Byz, EI
	Map 92 site 76/4.				
502	el Hdeibe 5	168800/616800	50		Byz, EI
	Map 92 site 86/5.				
503	el Hdeibe 2	168400/616600	100		Byz
	Map 92 site 86/2.				
504	el Hdeibe 4	168800/616300	100		Rom, Byz
	Map 92 site 86/4.				
505	el Hdeibe 1	168200/616300	100		Byz
	Map 92 site 86/1.				
506	el Hdeibe 3	168500/616100	100		Byz
	Map 92 site 86/3.				
507	Sde Yoav Quarry	169800/616600	100		Byz
	Map 92 site 96/1.				
508	Wad el Gharbi 1	169800/616400	100		Rom, Byz
	Map 92 site 96/2.				
509	Wad el Gharbi 2	169300/616400	100		Byz
	Map 92 site 96/3.				
510	Wad el Gharbi 3	169400/616800	100		Byz, EI
	Map 92 site 96/4.				
511	Wad el Gharbi 4	169100/616500	100		Byz
	Map 92 site 96/5.				
512	Wad el Gharbi 5	169200/616800	100		Byz, EI
	Map 92 site 96/6.				
513	Barbara (N)	160800/615800	100		Rom, Byz, EI
	Map 92 site 05/1.				
514	Barbara (N)	160120/615200	1,000		Byz
	Surveyed by Huster.				
515	El Jiya	161850/615200	60,000		Med, Ott
	Map 92 site 15/1.				
516	El Jiya (N)	161800/615700	500		Byz
	Map 92 site 15/2.				
517	El Jiya (W)	161100/615500	100		Byz, Med
	Map 92 site 15/3.				
518	Kh. Irza (S)	163800/615900	200		Byz
	Map 92 site 35/1.				
519	Kh. Irza (S)	163430/615740	1,000		Byz
	Surveyed by Huster.				
520	Beit Shiqma Villa	163500/615500	200		Byz, EI
	Map 92 site 35/2.				
521	Kh. Irza (S)	163730/615200	2,000		Byz
	Surveyed by Huster.				

Table 2.9 (cont.): Table of All Survey Sites

No.	Site	Coordinates	Area (m²)	Excavated	Periods (patch sites noted by [p])
522	Kh. Beit Saman (N) Map 92 site 55/1.	165100/615100	100		Hell, Rom, Byz, EI, Med, Ott
523	Karm esh-Shami (W) Map 92 site 65/4.	166100/615900	500		Rom, Byz, EI
524	Karm esh-Shami Map 92 site 65/1.	166600/615800	500		Byz
525	Karm esh-Shami (E) Map 92 site 65/2.	166800/615600	500		Byz
526	Karm esh-Shami (S) Map 92 site 65/3.	166400/615500	100		Byz, EI
527	Beit Tima (N) Surveyed by Huster.	166100/615300	100		Byz
528	Kaukaba Map 92 site 75/1.	167900/615500	100,000		Rom, Byz, EI, Med, Ott
529	Kaukaba (N) Map 92 site 75/2.	167800/615900	5,000		Rom, Byz, EI
530	Kaukaba (S) Map 92 site 75/3.	167800/615200	1,000		Byz
531	Kaukaba (Islamic cemetery) Surveyed by Huster (Site 28613/0, IAA system).	168500/615730	1,500		Byz, Ott(cem)
532	Wad es-Sahra 1 Map 92 site 95/1.	169900/615900	200		Byz
533	Kaukaba Quarry Map 92 site 95/4.	169400/615900	100		Byz
534	Wad es-Sahra 3 Map 92 site 95/3.	169600/615500	2,000		Byz
535	Wad es-Sahra 2 Map 92 site 95/2.	169600/615300	1,000		Byz
536	Barbara Map 92 site 04/1.	160300/614800	160,000		Hell, Rom, Byz, EI, Med, Ott
537	Barbara (SE) Surveyed by Huster.	160420/614400	1,000		Byz
538	El Jiya (S) (Gaia Villa) Map 92 site 14/1.	161800/614300	200		Byz, EI
539	Talmei Yafeh Orchard Map 92 site 44/1.	164000/614300	500		Rom, Byz, EI, Ott
540	Kh. Beit Saman Map 92 site 44/2.	164800/614700	30,000		Rom, Byz, EI
541	Beit Tima Map 92 site 54/1.	165700/614800	100,000		Rom, Byz, EI, Med, Ott
542	Beit Tima (S) Map 92 site 54/2.	165500/614500	100		EI
543	Beit Tima (Islamic cemetery) Surveyed by Huster.	165600/614150	2,000		Byz, EI, Med, Ott(cem)
544	Wadi Tima 2 Map 92 site 74/2.	167000/614600	500		Hell, Rom, Byz

Table 2.9 (cont.): Table of All Survey Sites

No.	Site	Coordinates	Area (m²)	Excavated	Periods (patch sites noted by [p])
545	Wadi Tima 1	167400/614200	100		Hell, Rom, Byz
	Map 92 site 74/1.				
546	Kochav (S) cemetery	169500/614900	100		Rom, Byz, EI
	Map 92 site 94/4; modern cemetery of Kochav settlement. The nearby site Kh. Melita was mistakenly identified as an Arab village due to cement waste dumping; also a Byzantine cistern.				
547	Kochav (S) 2	169500/614500	100		Byz, EI
	Map 92 site 94/3				
548	Kochav (S) 3	169800/614300	100		Rom, Byz, EI
	Map 92 site 94/5.				
549	Kochav cistern	169200/614300	100		Byz
	Map 92 site 94/1.				
550	Kochav (S) 1	169400/614000	100		Byz, EI
	Map 92 site 94/2.				
551	Kochav (S) cisterns	169700/614150	200		Byz
	Surveyed by Varga (pers. comm.).				
552	Barbara (E)	161100/613900	100		Byz, EI
	Map 92 site 13/3.				
553	Nahal Obed 2	161600/613500	200		Byz
	Map 92 site 13/2.				
554	Nahal Obed 1	161700/613100	500		Byz
	Map 92 site 13/1.				
555	Gevaram Kiln	162100/613300	10,000		Byz
	Map 92 site 23/1; also resurveyed by Huster.				
556	Nahal Obed 4	162800/613100	500		Byz
	Map 92 site 23/2.				
557	Kh. Amuda East	163600/613000	1,000		Rom, Byz, EI
	Map 92 site 33/1.				
558	Kh. Beit Saman (SW)	164500/613700	2,000		Byz
	Surveyed by Huster.				
559	Talmei Yafeh Coop	164500/613500	500		Hell, Rom, Byz, EI
	Map 92 site 43/1.				
560	Wadi Umm et Tire 2	165200/613000	200		Paleo, Byz
	Map 92 site 53/1.				
561	Kh. Daldum	166500/613300	2,000		Byz, EI
	Surveyed by Huster.				
562	Kh. Daldum	166800/613200	500		Paleo, Hell, Rom, Byz, EI
	Map 92 site 63/1; Allen in *Ashkelon 1*, p. 62.				
563	Karm el-Kharrub 3	167300/613200	100		Paleo, Rom, Byz
	Map 92 site 73/2.				
564	Karm el-Kharrub 2	167300/613000	100		Paleo, Rom, Byz
	Map 92 site 73/1.				
565	Ed Dude	168300/613600	2,000		Hell, Rom, Byz, EI, Med
	Map 92 site 83/1.				
566	Beit Jirja	160400/612500	100,000		Byz, EI, Med, Ott
	Map 92 site 02/1.				
567	Er Rasm	161800/612620	5,000		Byz
	Site 27358/0, IAA system; surveyed by Huster.				
568	Er Rasm Kiln 2	161900/612700	2,000		Byz
	Map 92 site 12/2.				

Table 2.9 (cont.): Table of All Survey Sites

No.	Site	Coordinates	Area (m²)	Excavated	Periods (patch sites noted by [p])
569	Er Rasm	161650/612280	5,000		Byz
	Site 30413/0, IAA system; surveyed by Huster.				
570	Er Rasm Kiln 1	161000/612300	2,000		Byz
	Map 92 site 12/1.				
571	Nahal Obed 3	162000/612800	10,000		Byz
	Map 92 site 12/3.				
572	Kh. Amuda	162900/612750	5,000		Byz, EI, Med, Ott
	Map 92 site 22/1; Allen in *Ashkelon 1*, p. 59. Western edges of Kh. Amuda. Not Arab village. Now, sites 26160/0 and 26260/0, IAA system.				
573	Nahal Obed (cisterns)	162200/612600	2,000		Byz
	Map 92 site 22/2.				
574	Ez Zeitun	162500/612100	3,000		Rom, Byz, EI, Med
	Map 92 site 22/3.				
575	Kh. Amuda (S)	162700/612300	1,000		Byz, EI
	Map 92 site 22/4.				
576	Kh. Amuda (center)	163100/612700	10,000		Rom, Byz, EI, Med
	Surveyed by Huster.				
577	Kh. Amuda cisterns	163700/612400	1,000		Byz, EI
	Map 92 site 32/1; Petrie 1890.				
578	Wadi Umm et Tire (cistern)	164900/612800	100		Paleo, Byz, EI
	Map 92 site 42/1.				
579	Tell el Hawa	165700/612600	100		Paleo
	Map 92 site 52/1; Antl-Weiser 2007:155, fig 4.				
580	Wadi Umm et Tire 1	165100/612800	200		Paleo, Byz, EI
	Map 92 site 52/2.				
581	Tariq Beit Tima	166600/612400	1,000		Hell, Rom, Byz, EI, Med, Ott
	Map 92 site 62/1.				
582	Tell el Hawa (N)	166100/612700	500		Paleo, Byz, EI
	Map 92 site 62/2.				
583	Huleiqat (center)	166800/612400	40,000		Hell, Rom, Byz, EI, Med, Ott
	Surveyed by Huster and Blakely (in press).				
584	Karm el Kharrub 1	167100/612500	500		Paleo, Byz, EI
	Map 92 site 72/1.				
585	Kh. Simbis (N)	168900/612500	10,000		Byz, EI
	Map 92 site 82/2; Allen in *Ashkelon 1*, p. 63.				
586	Kh. Simbis	168400/612350	12,000		Rom, Byz, EI
	Surveyed by Huster.				
587	Kh. Simbis	168800/612000	10,000		Hell, Rom, Byz, EI
	Map 92 site 82/1; Allen in *Ashkelon 1*, p. 63.				
588	Kh. Simbis 4	169100/612500	1,000		Rom, Byz, EI
	Map 92 site 92/2; Allen in *Ashkelon 1*, p. 64.				
589	Kh. Simbis 3	169000/612220	1,000		Byz
	Map 92 site 92/1; Allen in *Ashkelon 1*, p. 64.				
590	Kh. Beit Lejus	160100/611800	500		Pers, Hell, Rom, Byz, EI, Med, Ott
	Map 92 site 01/2.				
591	Tel Obed	160600/611700	50,000		Chalco, MB, LB, Iron1, Iron2, Pers, Hell, Rom, Byz, EI, Med, Ott
	Map 92 site 01/3.				

Table 2.9 (cont.): Table of All Survey Sites

No.	Site	Coordinates	Area (m²)	Excavated	Periods (patch sites noted by [p])
592	Beit Jirja Quarry	160600/611000	1,000		Iron2, Pers, Rom, Byz, EI
	Map 92 site 01/1.				
593	Er Rasm	161100/611900	10,000		Rom, Byz, EI, Med
	Map 92 site 11/1.				
594	Er Rasm well 1	161600/611600	2,000		Byz
	Map 92 site 11/2.				
595	Er Rasm well 2	161900/611500	100		Byz, EI
	Map 92 site 11/3.				
596	Wadi Amuda 1	163700/611900	500		Byz, EI
	Map 92 site 31/1.				
597	Wadi Amuda 2	165000/611900	300		Paleo, Byz
	Map 92 site 51/1.				
598	Huleiqat (W)	166500/611900	200		Byz, EI, Med, Ott
	Map 92 site 61/1.				
599	Huleiqat (E)	166800/611800	1,000		Rom, Byz, EI, Med, Ott(cem)
	Map 92 site 61/2; at the northeast edge, village's cemetery; at the southeast edge, village's well.				
600	Beit Jirja Tumulus 1	160700/610700	200		Byz
	Map 92 site 00/1.				
601	Beit Jirja Tumulus 2	160800/610600	300		Pers, Hell, Rom, Byz
	Map 92 site 00/2.				
602	Beit Jirja (S)	161900/610980	300		Paleo, Rom, Byz
	Surveyed by Huster; site 13395/0, IAA system.				
603	Beit Jirja (S)	161150/610700	500		Paleo
	Surveyed by Huster; site 13393/0, IAA system.				
604	Beit Jirja (S)	161100/610600	600		Paleo
	Surveyed by Huster; site 13390/0, IAA system.				
605	Beit Jirja (S)	161000/610250	500		Paleo
	Surveyed by Huster; sites 13392/0 and 16060/0, IAA system.				
606	Beit Jirja (S)	161800/610460	300		Paleo
	Surveyed by Huster; site 13394/0, IAA system.				
607	Beit Jirja (S)	161900/610400	1,000		Paleo, Rom, Byz
	Surveyed by Huster; site 13391/0, IAA system.				
608	Gevaram (S)	163900/610800	500		Paleo, Byz
	Map 92 site 30/1.				
609	Lapidot	165200/610900	500		Byz
	Map 92 site 50/1.				
610	Nahal Heletz (NW)	166750/610880	3,000		Byz, EI
	Surveyed by Huster; site 27361/0, IAA system.				
611	Kh. Nogga el Mahzuk	167200/610800	500		Byz, EI
	Map 92 site 70/1.				
612	Nahal Heletz Site	167500/610600	2,000		Byz, EI
	Map 92 site 70/2.				
613	Heletz	167800/610500	2,000		Byz, EI
	Map 92 site 70/3.				
614	Nahal Heletz (E)	168180/610200	1,500		Byz
	Surveyed by Huster.				

3. Identification of Ottoman Sites

by Michael D. Press

THE Ottoman period is unique for the wealth and variety of data at our disposal to understand settlement in the Ashkelon region. In addition to the survey (and excavation) data that serve as the backbone of this study, and the textual sources that add to this picture, there are several sets of Ottoman land and tax registers, village lists, and censuses that provide detailed information for each village.[1] As a result, for this period we are able to check the conclusions reached on the basis of the survey data and come to a new and more powerful synthesis.

The survey data suggest a continuing decline in the number of villages in the Ottoman period. However, this decline may be exaggerated. From late Ottoman and Mandatory censuses, village lists, and travelers' accounts, we know that there were 15 villages inhabited at the end of the Ottoman period: Isdud, Beit Daras, Hamama, Julis, El Jura, Khisas, Hirbiya, Niꜥilya, Majdal, Barbara, El Jiya, Beit Jirja, Beit Tima, Huleiqat, and Kaukaba. (There were an additional four villages within Map 96: Sumsum, Bureir, Najd, and Huj.) It is therefore noteworthy that the surveys of Map 87, 88, 91, and 92 were able to identify Ottoman occupation at only eight of these sites (53 percent). Allen, in his survey of Map 92, was able to identify Ottoman remains at five of the seven villages in his area. (Plus, we would note that one of the two missing sites, Kaukaba, is difficult to access.) The Berman surveys, however, were much less successful, identifying only three of eight late Ottoman villages. This problem reflects a more general difficulty in identifying Ottoman remains in the surveys: Thus Huster and Paran, in their survey of site 123 (Kh. Bazze), noted a large amount of Ottoman pottery, while the latest period noted by Berman and Barda was Mamluk (2005:60*). In general, Allen's survey pays close attention to recent periods, even noting modern (i.e., post-Ottoman) remains at sites. However, the lack of attention to Ottoman-period remains in the Berman surveys is remarkable and could have several explanations. According to the Israeli antiquities law, inherited from the British Mandate, only remains up to the

year 1700 are considered antiquities; thus over half of the Ottoman period, including the time of the late Ottoman period, is not covered by this law. It is possible that surveyors pay less attention to recent finds as a result. This problem may also reflect an ingrained belief in the idea of "Ottoman decline," the idea that settlement and general standards of living in the country were in continuous decline until the late nineteenth century when large-scale Jewish immigration to Palestine began. In addition, we would note that the Ottoman and Mandatory remains were generally bulldozed, with few if any in situ foundations of these structures. As most structures were built of mudbrick, they are often difficult to detect in survey.

Nevertheless, that there was some decline in the number of villages is a clear reality. The 1596–97 Ottoman *defter* lists at least 27 villages that fall within our study area: Amuda, Beit Tima, Hamama, Bazza, Basha, Akhsas Asqalan, Sama, Irza, Isdud, Majdal, Niꜥilya, Huleiqat, Beit Jirja, Hirbiya, Kaukaba, Miꜥṣaba, Beit Daras, Maqqus, Sandahanna, Julis, Ashraf, Bira, Beit Saman, Auda, Jura, Ijjiz ar-Ras, and Barbara.[2] However, as we have seen, the late Ottoman data indicate a total of only 15 villages. The 1871 Ottoman *Salname* indicates a total of 16 settlements: those listed above, plus Ashraf. However, Ashraf (Kh. esh Sheraf, site 312) as well as Khisas (Kh. el Khisas, site 256) were noted by Gatt (1884:296) to be merely seasonal settlements related to the agricultural cycle. Thus nearly 50 percent of the villages inhabited toward the end of the sixteenth century were abandoned by the late nineteenth century. A similar pattern can be found in the subdistrict (*nahiye*) of Gaza as a whole. Thus, at least on one level, the Ottoman period reflects the culmination of the decline in settlement we have noted since the Byzantine period.

The existence of demographic records also allows us to calibrate the evidence from surveys and understand the settlement complex on the ground in greater detail than in earlier periods. The first category of sites are villages inhabited for most or all of the period: these consist of the 15 villages noted above (Isdud, Beit Daras, Hamama, Julis, El Jura, Khisas, Hirbiya, Niꜥilya, Majdal, Barbara, El Jiya, Beit Jirja, Beit Tima,

---

[1] In this chapter, our analysis will focus on two datasets: the final Ottoman tax register, or *tahrir defter*, dated to 1596–97 (data published in Hütteroth and Abdulfattah 1977); and the 1871–72 Ottoman *Salname-i Vilayet-i Suriye*, or Yearbook of the Province of Syria (available in Turkish, with publication of data for southern Palestine in Hartmann 1883 in German).

[2] Some of the remaining unidentifiable villages may also fall within this area. In addition, El Jiya, known as a village in the late Ottoman and Mandatory periods (as well as apparently in the Crusader period) is surprisingly missing from this and the other Ottoman *defters*.

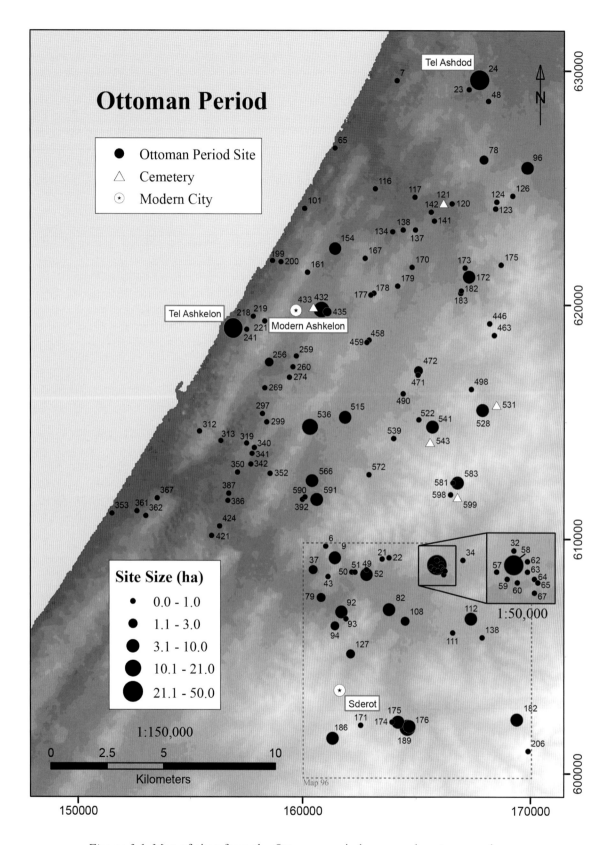

Figure 3.1: Map of sites from the Ottoman period over modern topography.

Huleiqat, and Kaukaba). The next category consists of *khirbehs*. This category can be broken down further into sites that were inhabited villages for a portion of the period—the 13 sites of Kh. Amuda, Kh. Bazza, Kh. Basha, Kh. Sama, Kh. Irza, Kh. Miᶜṣaba, Kh. Maqqus, Sandahanna, Kh. Sheraf, Kh. Bira, Kh. Beit Saman, Kh. Auda, and Kh. Ijjis er Ras—and other *khirbehs* that do not appear to have attained the status of village in the Ottoman period but which still show some signs of occupation or human activity. At least some of the latter sites were classified (in the Ottoman *defters*) as *mazraᶜas*, i.e., farms (or, more properly, sown fields) that generally represent the fields of abandoned villages farmed by neighboring villages (İnalcik 1991). In our study area, Kh. Balas (site 142) and Kh. Fatun (site 458) are clear examples, as each is noted as such in Ottoman *evkaf defters* (İpşirli and al-Tamīmī 1982:9 no. 25, 6 no. 13; also Kh. Beit Tafa in Map 96, for which see chapter 5, site 111). In some instances, these *mazraᶜas* may have served as seasonal settlements during the harvest, as was the case in the late Ottoman period for Kh. el Khisas and Kh. esh Sheraf. Finally, there are a series of features (wells, cisterns, pools, etc.) that cluster in and immediately around villages and should be associated with them.

Thus we can see that the total of 87 sites for the Ottoman period should be reduced to a much smaller number of villages (between 15 and 30, fluctuating over the course of the period; see table 2.9). In many cases, separate registered sites noted by survey, or opened up in small windows by excavation, should be considered sections of a single larger site. This conclusion is reinforced by maps, aerial photographs, and other records from the late Ottoman and Mandatory, which show not only the large built-up area of these villages but also document that their fields extended far beyond the built-up area. We can then use this reconstruction as a model to interpret earlier periods. (Compare the conclusions under the Early Islamic period in chapter 5 that findspots clustered around a central site often reflect the movement of archaeological remains by modern agricultural activity—and that they are not separate sites.) At the same time, some caution is needed in this approach. There is no reason to assume that village size remained constant over the course of several centuries; in fact, the Ottoman population data clearly demonstrate that village size or population density (or both) were very fluid even within the Ottoman period.

As they are primarily tax documents, the Ottoman *tahrir defters* also indicate the economic activity of the villages. The villages of the region were engaged almost exclusively in agricultural production, with wheat and barley as the major crops. Fruit trees, goats, and bees were also a focus, and smaller amounts of sesame and cotton were grown. This agricultural activity matches the relatively even distribution of villages throughout the study area, which we would expect for a model of agricultural production (as opposed to Allen's "access resources" model, with sites clustered along major routes). Again, we can use the combined information from the *defters* and surveys to model land use in earlier periods—at least back to the Roman and Byzantine periods, when we first meet this pattern of site distribution.

One of the outstanding features of the Ottoman-period landscape—not covered by the model of fewer nucleated settlements described above, since they are located beyond the built-up areas of the villages—are public water fountains. As discussed by Sasson (2002), these installations are of two main types, *sabils* and *misqas*. A *sabil* has a storage tank, with a well (or cistern) attached as the source of its water, and is usually more elaborate (Sasson 2002:116); a *misqa* has no connected water source but is simply a pitcher of water placed by local residents (Sasson 2002:122). These installations can be urban, with major *sabils* constructed by rulers or important officials (e.g., Sabil Sulayman in Jaffa, Sabil Qāytbāy [Mamluk?] in Jerusalem), or rural; in the latter case, they are not located within villages but, as Sasson points out (2002; see also Petersen 2001:50), along major roads. (Thus the word "*sabil*" is cognate with, and perhaps derived from, the Aramaic and Hebrew *šĕbîl*, "way" or "path," also the original meaning of the Arabic term; see Bosworth 1995). These installations first appear in the Mamluk period but generally date to the Ottoman period, especially toward the end of it (see Sasson 2002).

In our study area, there are at least ten (nine on the map and in chapter 5, plus another whose location is unclear on the road between Niᶜilya and El Jiya). Unfortunately, it is difficult to compile a complete list of *sabils* and *misqas* in the area, as these were not often recorded by travelers and surveyors. The best source is the Survey of Western Palestine map, but this includes only six within the limits of our study area. For modern Ashkelon itself, Sasson gives a more complete survey; of the four he lists, only two are on the Survey of Western Palestine map. Comparing the locations of the known fountains with the major roads of the area (from the Survey of Western Palestine and Mandatory maps), we see that all are indeed found along major roads or paths between villages—and especially at important junctions (cf. Sasson 2002:123): note three examples on junctions of roads heading east from Majdal with the Cairo-Damascus highway and one on the junction of the road north from Hamame with the Cairo-Damascus highway. Some, meanwhile, are located just outside of villages, along roads or paths.

A handful of inscriptions provide an additional category of evidence about the character of settlement in the region in the Ottoman period. Most relate to continuing building activity, albeit on a smaller scale than in the Mamluk period. An inscription from the sanctuary of Tamim ad-Dari in Majdal appears to date the construction of this shrine to the middle of the sixteenth century (Sharon 1997:186–89). This shrine also served as a second mosque in the village, reinforcing Majdal's status as a major village in the region by the presence of multiple mosques; this status is confirmed by the sixteenth-century Ottoman *defters*, which indicate that Majdal is the only village in *nahiya* Gaza to have more than two imams or other religious personnel exempt from taxes (3; see al-Swarieh 2008:91; Yalçinkaya 2006). An inscription from Beit Tima, dated to 1836, indicates the reconstruction of the village mosque and shrine of Nabi Tima in that year (Sharon 1999:160); as with most sheikhs' tombs and associated shrines, it was originally built in the Mamluk period. Of special note is an inscription from the shrine of En Nabi Jirja in Beit Jirja, dated 1825–26, that commemorates the rebuilding of the village, which had been previously "wiped out" (Sharon 1999:143–44). This rebuilding was conducted by Muhammad Shahin Agha, the local governor, representing Abdallah Pasha (the *vali* of Sidon—i.e., the governor of the *vilayet* or province). The nature and date of the event recorded in the inscription, however, are problematic, as we have several sources indicating the existence of the village of Beit Jirja in the years immediately preceding the inscription: Johann Scholz's list, dating to c. 1820 (as "Dscherdcha," Scholz 1822:255); Robert Richardson's travels in 1818 (Richardson 1822:200, as "Bedigga"); and the Jacotin map (Sheet 43, Gaza) surveyed in 1799 (as "Gergîéh"; for discussion see Karmon 1960:173). Finally, an inscription from the general area of Ashkelon records the epitaph of an artillery officer, from the year 1721 (Sharon 2004:xix–xx).

The overall picture of settlement in the Ottoman period is continuing decline, with fewer settlements, and decreased building activity.

Corrections to Earlier Surveys

The suggested identifications in this chapter serve especially to correct errors by Berman and Barda in the Map 88 (Nizzanim East) publication (2005) and to provide additions and corrections to the set of identifications made by Wolf-Dieter Hütteroth and Kamal Abdulfattah (1977) for the villages of *nahiye* Gaza in TD 546 (1596–97). Hütteroth and Abdulfattah noted (1977:13) that the identification of place names was the most difficult task involved in their work—and therefore the most time-consuming. Given this fact, it is surprising to find that Hütteroth and Abdulfattah did not provide any detailed discussion in support of their identifications. In fact, they did not provide exact identifications at all: They noted only the rough coordinates of the identified site (within a single square kilometer) and the source of their identification. As a result, it is sometimes difficult to be certain of the identification they suggested, especially when their coordinates are incorrect (as they appear to be in several cases). Similarly, Etkes (2012:fig. 7.2) provides only a map that largely adopts the identifications (and romanizations, also sometimes in error) of Hütteroth and Abdulfattah while suggesting a few additional localizations—localizations that can only be guessed at roughly since no exact coordinates or identifications were provided.

We therefore believe that it is essential to indicate exact sites for all of our suggested identifications—in terms of both names of sites and coordinates. The exact coordinates and site names are indicated in Appendix A. However, we believe that providing justifications for these identifications is also essential, so that—in combination with the coordinates and site names—other scholars will be able to check our work. As a result, for several cases for which a more detailed justification was necessary than could be given in Appendix A, we have provided an extended discussion in Appendix B, in which the sites are arranged alphabetically.

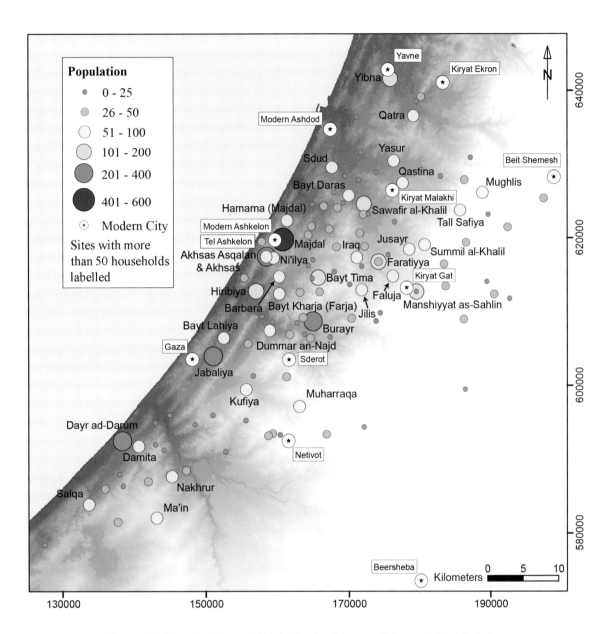

Figure 3.2: Sites in Hütteroth/Abdulfattah with over 50 households labeled
from the Ottoman period over modern topography.

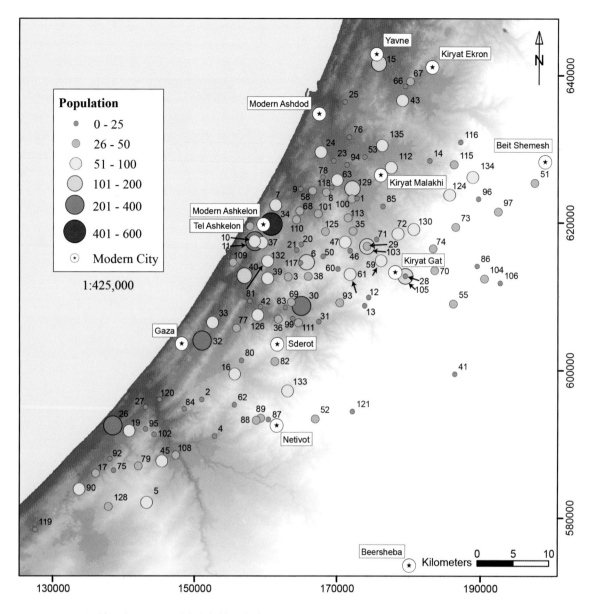

Figure 3.3: Sites in Hütteroth/Abdulfattah from the Ottoman period over modern topography.

APPENDIX A: IDENTIFICATION OF OTTOMAN SITES IN HÜTTEROTH/ABDULFATTAH

No.	Name in Hütteroth/Abdulfattah	Coordinates
1	Ṣawāfīr ash-Sharqī	172750/623300

Taxable Households: 0

| 2 | Ḥawādī | 151000/596000 |

Taxable Households: 25

New Identification: Survey of Western Palestine:Sheet XIX, 252 (Kh. el Hawady) and name list (Kh. Hawadi)

| 3 | ꜥĀmūdat (Banī Kināna) | 163170/612650 |

Taxable Households: 30

Name in the Crusader Period: Amouhde, 1256 (Röhricht 1983:327; Prawer 1958:224–37; Rey 1883:415)

| 4 | ꜥUṣayfiriyya | 152800/591050 |

Taxable Households: 0

New Identification: Survey of Western Palestine:Sheet 23, Dx, 389

| 5 | Maꜥīn | 143200/582100 |

Taxable Households: 80

| 6 | Beit Ṭīma | 165700/164650 |

Taxable Households: 126

| 7 | Ḥamāma (Majdal) | 161400/622400 |

Taxable Households: 84

| 8 | Bazzā | 168400/624100 |

Taxable Households: 50

Name in the Crusader Period: Beze, 1256 (Röhricht 1983:327; Prawer 1958:224–37; Rey 1883:406)

| 9 | Bashā | 164920/624600 |

Taxable Households: 0

| 10 | Akhṣāṣ ꜣAsqalān | 158450/617500 |

Taxable Households: 55

| 11 | Akhṣāṣ | 158500/617500 |

Taxable Households: 201

| 12 | Jadīda | 174400/609850 |

Taxable Households: 12

Name in the Crusader Period: Elgedeide, 1256 (Röhricht 1983:327; Prawer 1958:224–37; Rey 1883:407)

| 13 | ꜥAjlān | 173800/608750 |

Taxable Households: 10

Name in the Crusader Period: Agelen el Hayet, 1256 (Röhricht 1983:327; Prawer 1958:224–37; Rey 1883:404)

| 14 | Tīnā | 182900/628400 |

Taxable Households: 10

| 15 | Yibnā | 175800/641600 |

Taxable Households: 129

Name in the Crusader Period: Ibelin (Rey 1883:409)

| 16 | Kūfiya | 155650/599500 (correction of coordinates) |

Taxable Households: 55

| 17 | Saṭar | 136000/586000 |

Taxable Households: 45

New Identification: Two tracts of land, Es Satar and Wadi es Satar, on 1:20,000 map

| 18 | Zāwiya | |

Taxable Households: 5

| 19 | Damīṭa | 140700/591800 |

Taxable Households: 62

New Identification: Guérin 1869:252

| 20 | Sāma | 165000/617050 |

Taxable Households: 6

Name in the Crusader Period: Semma (Casale Episcopi) (Prawer 1958)

No.	Name in Hütteroth/Abdulfattah	Coordinates
21	Arza (better "Irza")	164350/616300
	Taxable Households: 3	
22	Beit Mīrīn	
	Taxable Households: 0	
23	Khārijat as-Sdūd	169500/628400
	Taxable Households: 18	
24	Sdūd	167700/629600
	Taxable Households: 75	
	Name in the Crusader Period: Azot (Rey 1883:404)	
25	Sukrīr (better "Sukrayr")	171100/636370
	Taxable Households: 10	
26	Dayr ad-Dārūm	138400/592500
	Taxable Households: 300	
	Name in the Crusader Period: Darum	
27	Farāsha	143000/595000
	Taxable Households: 6	
	New Identification: Tract of land, Farahsa, on 1:20,000 map	
28	Manshiyyat as-Saḥlīn (better "Manshiyyat as-Saḥalīn")	179500/612750
	Taxable Households: 130	
29	Farātiyya (better "Qarātiyya")	174150/616800
	Taxable Households: 121	
30	Burayr	165000/608700
	Taxable Households: 210	
31	Shaᶜāriyya al-Kubrā (Tābiᶜ Burayr) (better "Shaᶜārta al-Kubrā [Tābiᶜ Burayr]")	167400/606600
	Taxable Households: 6	
	Name in the Crusader Period: Saarethe, 1256 (Röhricht 1983:327; Prawer 1958:224–37)	
32	Jabāliya	151050/604000
	Taxable Households: 331	
33	Beit Lāhiyā	152500/606500
	Taxable Households: 70	
34	Majdal	160800/619800
	Taxable Households: 559	
35	Beit ᶜAffā	172200/618850
	Taxable Households: 26	
36	Najd al-Gharbī	161750/606900
	Taxable Households: 39	
37	Niᶜilyā	159500/617300
	Taxable Households: 80	
38	Khalīfāt (better "Hulayqāt")	165950/612700
	Taxable Households: 35	
39	Beit Kharja (Farja) (better "Beit Jirja")	160300/612450
	Taxable Households: 85	
40	Hiribiya (better "Hirbiya")	157000/612800
	Taxable Households: 175	
	Name in the Crusader Period: Forbie (Rey 1883:408)	
41	Barriyat al-Ḥarādīn	186400/599500
	Taxable Households: 22	
42	Beit Darās aṣ-Ṣughrā	159300/608600
	Taxable Households: 0	
	New Identification: Schedule of Historical Sites and Monuments. *Official Gazette* No. 1091, 18 May 1964:1451	
	Name in the Crusader Period: Beitderas secunda, 1256 (Röhricht 1983:327; Prawer 1958:224–37)	

No.	Name in Hütteroth/Abdulfattah	Coordinates

No. Name in Hütteroth/Abdulfattah   *Coordinates*

43 Qaṭrā   179100/636600
      Taxable Households: 61
      Name in the Crusader Period: Cathara

44 Mashhad
      Taxable Households: 95

45 Nakhrūr   145300/587700 (correction of coordinates)
      Taxable Households: 69

46 Beit Māmīn   171800/616200
      Taxable Households: 10
      Name in the Crusader Period: Beth-Amamin; Bethaman, 1155 (Prawer 1958:224–37)

47 ᶜIrāq   171100/617400
      Taxable Households: 61

48 Beit Zaytūn
      Taxable Households: 23

49 Miyūsīḥ
      Taxable Households: 50

50 Kawkab   168000/615450
      Taxable Households: 16
      Name in the Crusader Period: Coquebel (Prawer 1958:224–37)

51 Beit Jimāl   197500/625400
      Taxable Households: 37

52 Juhaytīn   166900/593400
      Taxable Households: 43

53 Baṭān ash-Sharqī   173800/628900
      Taxable Households: 7

54 Munayᶜir
      Taxable Households: 30

55 Qubayba   186200/609000
      Taxable Households: 33

56 Furātiyya
      Taxable Households: 22

57 Qūrtān
      Taxable Households: 26

58 Muᶜayṣiba (better "Miᶜ(i)ṣaba")   166550/624320
      Taxable Households: 44

59 Fālūja   176150/614850
      Taxable Households: 75
      Name in the Crusader Period: Phaluge, 1155 (Prawer 1958:224–37)

60 Balīṭā (Malīṭā) (better "Malīṭā")   170100/613700
      Taxable Households: 16
      Name in the Crusader Period: Melius, 1110 (Prawer 1958:224–37)

61 Jilis   171800/613000
      Taxable Households: 64

62 Ṣīḥān   155600/595300
      Taxable Households: 11

63 Beit Darās   170000/625800
      Taxable Households: 58
      Name in the Crusader Period: Betheras, 1173 (Röhricht 1983:132; Prawer 1958:224–37)

64 ᶜIdrā
      Taxable Households: 59

65 Sawāmiriyya aṣ-Ṣughrā (better "Shaᶜārta aṣ-Ṣughrā")
      Taxable Households: 7

No.	Name in Hütteroth/Abdulfattah	Coordinates

66   Imghār   179500/638500
     Taxable Households: 22
67   Ṣummīl al-Mughār (better "Ṣummayl al-Mughār")   180200/639150
     Taxable Households: 31
     New Identification: Schedule of Historical Sites and Monuments. *Official Gazette* No. 1091, 18 May 1964:1439
68   Maqqūs   164800/621600
     Taxable Households: 36
     Name in the Crusader Period: Machoz, before 1110 (Prawer 1958:224–37)
69   Bābilliya (better "Bābliya")   163600/609200
     Taxable Households: 27
     New Identification: Schedule of Historical Sites and Monuments. *Official Gazette* No. 1091, 18 May 1964:1451
70   Manṣūra   183600/613500
     Taxable Households: 33
71   Ḥattā ash-Shajara   175500/617750
     Taxable Households: 15
72   Jusayr   178500/618500
     Taxable Households: 60
73   Zikrīn   186500/619400
     Taxable Households: 40
74   Zaytā   183400/616500
     Taxable Households: 30
     Crusader Period: (Röhricht 1983:327; Prawer 1958:224–37)
75   Sūq Māzīn   138500/586400
     Taxable Households: 19
     New Identification: Avi-Yonah 1940
76   Barqā   171700/631600
     Taxable Households: 12
77   Beit Ḥānūn   155900/605700
     Taxable Households: 36
78   Ṣandaḥana (better "Ṣandaḥanna")   167950/626200
     Taxable Households: 12
     New Identification: Schedule of Historical Sites and Monuments. *Official Gazette* No. 1091, 18 May 1964:1441
79   Ḥarsa (better "Kharsa")   142000/587000
     Taxable Households: 50
     New Identification: Guérin 1869:262; Musil 1908:325; Musil 1907c
80   Beit Durdis   156600/601350 (correction of coordinates)
     Taxable Households: 21
81   Dayr Sunayd   157800/609350
     Taxable Households: 12
82   Lasun   161300/601200
     Taxable Households: 49
     New Identification: Schedule of Historical Sites and Monuments. *Official Gazette* No. 1091, 18 May 1964:1452
83   Sumsum   162750/608500
     Taxable Households: 20
     Name in the Crusader Period: Semsem, 1256 (Röhricht 1983:327; Prawer 1958:224–37)
84   Barjaliyya   148500/594750 (correction of coordinates)
     Taxable Households: 12
85   Jaladiyya   176400/622200
     Taxable Households: 16
     Name in the Crusader Period: Geladia; Galiadia, 1160 (Prawer 1958:224–37)
86   ꜥIrāq Ḥālā   189500/614100
     Taxable Households: 7

No.	Name in Hütteroth/Abdulfattah	Coordinates

87 al-Bahā — 160400/693300
Taxable Households: 15

88 Rasm al-Gharbī — 158700/593200
Taxable Households: 35

89 Rasm ash-Sharqī — 159300/593500
Taxable Households: 43

90 Salqā — 133700/583900
Taxable Households: 63

91 Shamsiyyāt
Taxable Households: 48

92 Naḥāsa — 138000/588000
Taxable Households: 17
New Identification: Musil 1907b; 1907c

93 Mulāqis — 170350/609150
Taxable Households: 44
Name in the Crusader Period: Malaques, 1256 (Röhricht 1983:327; Prawer 1958:224–37)

94 Bardāgha — 171350/627850
Taxable Households: 11
New Identification: Schedule of Historical Sites and Monuments. *Official Gazette* No. 1091, 18 May 1964:1443

95 Taḥāw (Taḥād) (better "Takhāw") — 143000/592000
Taxable Households: 18
New Identification: Musil 1907a:220, 301 n.3; 1907b:54; 1907c; Yāqūt 1866–73a:827–28; Le Strange 1890:542

96 Aṭraba — 189700/623200
Taxable Households: 23

97 ᶜAjjūr — 192400/621500
Taxable Households: 35

98 Kafr Ghār
Taxable Households: 65

99 Qamṣā — 163800/607000
Taxable Households: 8
New Identification: Schedule of Historical Mouments and Sites. Supplement No. 2 to the *Gazette Extraordinary* No. 1375, 24 November 1944:1297; Warren 1871:95
Name in the Crusader Period: Camsa, 1256 (Röhricht 1983:327; Prawer 1958:224–37)

100 Ṣawāfīr al-Gharbī — 172000/623200
Taxable Households: 43
Name in the Crusader Period: Zeophir, 1109–1110 (Rey 1883:415)

101 Jūlis — 167300/621200
Taxable Households: 37

102 Nāmīra (Nāṣira) (better "Nāṣira") — 144200/591300 (correction of coordinates)
Taxable Households: 16

103 Kartā (better "Kudnā") — 174150/616800
Taxable Households: 46
Name in the Crusader Period: Galatia (Prawer 1958:224–37)

104 Beit Jibrīn — 190500/612400
Taxable Households: 50

105 ᶜIrāq Ḥātim — 179500/612750
Taxable Households: 11

106 Dayr Shāṭir — 192700/611800
Taxable Households: 4
New Identification: Survey of Western Palestine:Sheet XX, 275

107 Umm an-Nuᶜūr (an-Nuṣūr)
Taxable Households: 46

No. Name in Hütteroth/Abdulfattah	Coordinates
108 Tall Jamma	147300/588500

Taxable Households: 32

New Identification: Schedule of Historical Sites and Monuments. *Official Gazette* No. 1091, 18 May 1964:1478

109 Asrāf (better "Ashrāf")	155400/614600

Taxable Households: 29

110 Bīra	164330/620400

Taxable Households: 44

New Identification: Schedule of Historical Sites and Monuments. *Official Gazette* No. 1091, 18 May 1964:1442

111 Jalama	164600/606450

Taxable Households: 30

112 Qasṭīna	177550/627500

Taxable Households: 70

113 ᶜIbdīs	171500/620650

Taxable Households: 35

Name in the Crusader Period: Hebde (Prawer 1958:224–37)

114 Mirfaqa (better "Qarqafa")

Taxable Households: 8

115 Dinba (better "Dhinba")	186300/627900

Taxable Households: 36

116 Jilya	187200/630900

Taxable Households: 17

117 Beit Samᶜān	164900/614550

Taxable Households: 8

118 ᶜAwda	169200/624800

Taxable Households: 15

119 Rafāḥ	127500/578400

Taxable Households: 15

120 Manshiyyat al-ᶜUjūl	145000/596000

Taxable Households: 17

New Identification: Mandatory 1:20,000; van de Velde 1858:53

121 ᶜAmmūdiyya	172120/594400

Taxable Households: 16

122 Jawrit al-Ḥajja (better "Jūrat al-Ḥajja")	157800/619500

Taxable Households: 46

123 Līna

Taxable Households: 20

124 Tall Ṣāfiya	185700/623800

Taxable Households: 88

125 ᶜAjiz ar-Rās (better "ᶜIjjiz ar-Rās")	168300/618800

Taxable Households: 46

126 Dummar an-Najd	158900/607500 (correction of coordinates)

Taxable Households: 60

Name in the Crusader Period: Dimra?

127 ᶜĀmūdat Banī ᶜĀmir

Taxable Households: 38

128 ᶜAbasān	137800/581500

Taxable Households: 28

129 Ṣawāfīr al-Khalīl	172100/624650

Taxable Households: 112

130 Ṣummīl al-Khalīl (better "Ṣummayl al-Khalīl")	180700/619100

Taxable Households: 66

No.	Name in Hütteroth/Abdulfattah	Coordinates
131	Rashīra (Rashīda)	
	Taxable Households: Not Given	
132	Barbarā	160300/614800
	Taxable Households: 73	
133	Muḥarraqa	163100/597200
	Taxable Households: 83	
134	Mughlis	188900/626200
	Taxable Households: 77	
135	Yāsūr	176300/630500
	Taxable Households: 55	
136	Ramādāt	
	Taxable Households: 93	

Ashrāf

Asrāf (Hütteroth and Abdulfattah) = **Kh. esh Sheraf** (Kh. Ashraf), OIG 105-114 (site 109)

The only difference in spelling is *sīn* vs. *shīn*; both letters have the same form but different dotting. El Ashrāf appears in Socin's list of villages and population from the late 1860s—Socin, in Gaza district (1879:144); the list is organized in some geographical order, and el Ashrāf occurs between Hirbiya and Beit Jirja. In the 1931 census Ashraf is a subheading under Hirbiya (Mills 1932:3). The site should be identified with Kh. esh Sheraf, also known as Kh. Ashraf (an alternate form with prosthetic ᶜ*alif*, appearing in the List of Mandatory Records Files [1976:132]). Note also the tract of land marked "Ashraf" on the 1:20,000 Survey of Palestine topocadastral map (Sheet 10-11, Ashkelon), northeast of Hirbiya. Finally, note that the Map 91 survey identified Mamluk and Ottoman pottery at Kh. esh Sheraf, making it a good fit.

As the Socin list shows, Ashraf can be spelled with or without long *ā*.

Barriyat al-Ḥarādīn (site 41)

We doubt that the identification suggested by Hütteroth and Abdulfattah, with Kh. Umm Ḥaratain (OIG 136.099), is correct. This site is distant from the other villages of the 1596–97 *defter*. The name Haratain, *Ḥ-ā-r-t-y-n*, is close to Ḥarādīn, *Ḥ-r-ā-d-y-n*, but the switch between *dāl* and *tā*ᵓ is not easy to explain, as these are not the same letter and not close in form; also, the loss of Umm would be unusual. In addition, based on the pattern of other village names, we would expect that the basic name of the village is Barriya/Barriyat and that (al-)Ḥarādīn is a qualifier of that name (either the name of a nearby village, or something else; see Manshiyyat al-ᶜUjūl below). This is confirmed by the occurrence of a village named Zayt al-Ḥarādīn in other sources. Unfortunately, we do not have a good suggestion for an identification.

Bazzā

Kh. Bazze/Bezzeh/Beze, OIG 118-124 (site 8)

Kh. Bezzeh was marked on the Survey of Western Palestine map (Sheet XVI, Fu) at c. 2.5 km southwest of Beit Daras. The Mandatory Survey of Palestine 1:20,000 map, however, indicated the site (as Kh. Bazze) roughly at coordinates 117-123 (OIG), 1 km farther to the southwest than the Survey of Western Palestine site—and at a distance of c. 3.5 km west-southwest from Beit Daras (Sheet 11-12, Hamame). On the 1:100,000 scale Survey of Palestine map (Sheet 9, Gaza), meanwhile, there are two ruins marked Bazze, one at each of the above locations. Both locations were resurveyed by Huster in June 2012. The results of this survey lead us to conclude with a high degree of certainty that the original location of Kh. Bezzeh/Bazze on the Survey of Western Palestine map is the correct one. There is no clear ancient site near coordinates 117-123, other than site 146 (an Iron I tomb); on the other hand, the Survey of Western Palestine Bezzeh is located at the site of a sizeable village, yielding Roman to Ottoman period pottery (site 123). The actual central location of the site is at coordinates 118400-124100 (OIG), 168400-624100 (NIG). This determination results in the removal of the name Kh. Bezzeh/Bazza for site 145, used mistakenly by Berman and Barda (2005:64*, site 140) for the ruins of an ancient settlement that was occupied from the Iron II period until the Byzantine period—but not later. The real name of site 145 is Kh. Khasse, whose location was marked correctly on both the Survey of Western Palestine and Mandatory maps but incorrectly on later Israeli maps. As noted by Berman and Barda (2005:65*, site 142; see our site 147), the location marked Ḥ. Ḥassa (Kh. Khasse) on Israeli maps has no visible archaeological remains.

Beit Jirja

Beit Kharja (Hütteroth and Abdulfattah) = **Beit Jirja**, OIG 110-112 (site 39)

The letters *khā*ᵓ and *jīm* have the same form, differing only in their dotting. This identification was previously suggested by Khalidi (1992:88). Note that Yāqūt has an entry for a village in the territory of ᶜAsqalān named Jarha (1866–73b:56; see also Le Strange 1890:462), which Clermont-Ganneau (1896:379) already suggested was to be identified with (Beit) Jirja (thereby implicitly suggesting the same type of error).

Dimra

Dummar **an-Najd** = **Dimra**, OIG 108-107 (site 126)

Hütteroth and Abdulfattah appear to have identified the sixteenth-century village with Kh. Najd (OIG 112-105). We imagine that Hütteroth and Abdulfattah might have suggested this identification on the meaning of the word "*dummar*," from the root "to destroy" or "to ruin," thus equating *dummar* with *khirbeh*. However, the name *d-m-r* from the *defter* is almost identical to Dimra *d-m-r-ā*, the only difference being the omission of the *tā*ᵓ *marbūṭa*. It is worth noting a peculiar pattern in this list and the other *defters*, where in some cases the final ᶜ*alif* or *tā*ᵓ *marbūṭa* is not written. Thus Kawkaba (alternatively Kawkabā) is always written as Kawkab, and the place name Takhāwa is probably the same as the Takhāw of the 1596–97 *defter*. There is also some indication that the names Zayt/Zaytā and Bayt/Baytā are interchangeable in different *defters*. We would therefore argue that this name, which appears in the same form (Dmr an-Najd) in all *defters*, is simply Dimra without the final letter. (Note that this identification was already suggested by Zadok [1995–97:137].)

Farasha (OIG 093-095, approx.) (site 27)
The Survey of Palestine 1:20,000 topocadastral map (Sheet 9-9, Wadi Ghazza) has a tract of land called Farasha (093-095).

Ḥawādī = Kh. el Ḥawādī (Kh. Hawadi), OIG 101-096 (site 2)
The site appears in the Survey of Western Palestine name lists and map (Palmer 1881:361; Sheet XIX, Dx) and the List of Mandatory Records Files (1976:198); it is also mentioned by van de Velde (1858:53) as el-Hawadeh, a site in the general Gaza-Hesi area (which he did not visit, however). There is also a tract of land (on the Survey of Palestine 1:20,000 topoca-dastral map, Sheet 10-9, Khirbet el Mashrafa) called Daribet el Hawadi at 101-097.

Ḥulayqāt
Khalīfāt (Hütteroth and Abdulfattah) = **Ḥulayqāt (Huleiqat)**, OIG 115-112 (site 38)
Again, the difference is between *fāʾ* and *qāf*, which have the same form but with different dottings. This name is often con-fused in the sources; thus Socin's list has it as Ḥalāfāt (1879:149). In the 1871 list the name was read as Ṭīfān (Hartmann 1883:133). This reading results from multiple errors in writing or reading the script: *qāf/fāʾ*, *tāʾ/nūn*, and the misreading of *ḥāʾ + lām* as *ṭāʾ*. (They could look similar, especially in bad handwriting.)

ʿIdrā (site 64)
It appears that the Hütteroth and Abdulfattah identification, at OIG 113-088, is supposed to be with Kh. Umm ʿAdra (109-089). If so, there are two problems with this identification: 1) This area has few, if any, villages in 1596–97; and 2) there is the unexplained absence of "Umm." Would Kh. al ʿAdāra (Kh. el Adar; 096-093) be a better candidate? This area was fairly densely settled in the late sixteenth century, as we have seen. In this case there is the missing *ʾalif* in the *defter*, but this dif-ference is not insurmountable as we have seen other cases where the same name can be spelled with or without a long vowel.

ʿIrāq Ḥātim (site 105)
Unknown; see Manshiyyat al-ʿUjūl.

Juhaytīn (site 52)
We are skeptical that Hütteroth and Abdulfattah's identification, Kh. el Juʿethini (Juʿaythinī), OIG 116-093, is correct. For one thing, it is in an area where few if any villages were inhabited in 1596–97. Also—and we believe that this is very signifi-cant—in almost every case the form of the names in the fifteenth- and sixteenth-century records are identical, or nearly so, with their nineteenth- and twentieth-century forms. Juʿethini presents a problem: It is spelled *J-ʿ-y-th-n-y* vs. Juhaytin as *J-h-y-t-y-n*. While *tāʾ* and *thāʾ* are the same letter with different dottings, *ʿayn* and *hāʾ* are not similar forms, and the difference in endings (-*nī* vs. -*īn*) is also problematic.

Meanwhile, in the *waqf defter* 522, the *waqf* for a building in Gaza (İpşirli and al-Tamīmī 1982:6, no. 13) includes the *mazraʿa* Fātūn (= Kh. Abu Fatun?), which is said to be near Niʿilyā and Juhaytīn. (The village of Juhaytīn itself also appears in the *waqf*; the editors of the volume suggest an identification with Kh. Jahalīn, said to be between al-Akhṣāṣ and Hirbiya [İpşirli and al-Tamīmī 1982:6], but we are not aware of any such site in this area, and the name is always spelled in the *defters* with *tāʾ* and not *lām*.) In any case, this information strongly suggests that Juhaytin should be in the area south or southeast of Majdal, but we have not been able to locate any similar toponym in this area in any source.

Kafr Ghār, OIG 119-100 (approx.) (site 98)
The Survey of Western Palestine (Sheet XX, Fx) and 1:20,000 Survey of Palestine (Sheets 11-10, Bureir, and 11-9, Kaufakha) maps have a Wadi el Ghar, located on the Mandatory map between 118-101 and 120-99.

Khārijat as-Sdūd (site 23)
We do not know what this site is—or what Hütteroth and Abdulfattah identify it as.

Kharsa
Ḥarsa (Hütteroth and Abdulfattah) = **Kh. el Kharsa**, OIG 092-088 (approx.) (site 79)
Again, *ḥāʾ* and *khāʾ* have the same form but different dotting. Unfortunately, the exact location of this *khirbeh* is now lost; we have only a general area. Guérin (1869:262) visited the site between Umm el-Jerar and Tell Jemma. Alois Musil (1908:325) is the only other person we know of to have visited the site; he called it *ḥ. el-ḥarsi* and located it south of Umm el-Jerar. The Karte von Arabia Petraea (1907a; 1907b), based on Musil's travels, has the site as el-Ḥursi, southeast of ed-Dejr (Deir el-Balah), southwest of Tell Ǧemma, and northeast of Sûḳ Mâzen. Based on this map, we can locate the site at approximately 092-088.

Note that the List of Mandatory Records Files (1976) included Kh. el Kharsa but stated that it was not found in 1942 and that its coordinates were unknown, and that it could be in paragraph nos. 110, 111, or several others in the vicinity.

Khassa, Kh.
See Bazzā.

Kudnā
Kartā (Hütteroth and Abdulfattah) = **Kudnā**
See Qarātiyya.

Makkus/Maqqus (site 170)
There are two possible locations for this site. Kh. Makkus was marked on the Survey of Western Palestine map (Sheet XVI, Fu) between Wady el Bireh and an eastern tributary of that wadi, at a bend on the road leading from Majdal to Beit Daras. On the Survey of Palestine 1:20,000 map (Sheet 11-12, Hamame), the name Kh. Makkus is marked at a different site, on the western side of Wadi el Bire, at approximate coordinates 114800-121650 (OIG; site 170). The Survey of Western Palestine Makkus, meanwhile, between the two branches of Wadi el Bire and at the bend of the Majdal-Beit Daras road, is also indicated on Sheet 11-12—but simply marked "Ruin"; it is at approximate coordinates 115800-122250 (site 158), c. 1.5 km northeast of the previous site. Unfortunately, it is not currently possible to decide between these two candidates. A village named Maqqus in *nahiya* Gaza appears in all of the sixteenth-century Ottoman *tahrir defters*, and so we would expect the site to have both medieval and Ottoman pottery. Berman and Barda identified both periods at site 170 (2005:69*–70*, site 163). They noted only medieval at site 158 (2005:67*, site 153), but as noted above they often failed to identify Ottoman-period pottery.

Note that in the sixteenth-century *defters* the name of the site appears as Maqqus—suggesting a parallel case to Qarātiyya/Karātiyya with the replacement of *qāf* with *kāf* by the late Ottoman period.

Manshiyyat al-ʿUjūl = (Kh.) Manshiyya, OIG 095-096 (approx.) (site 120)
Manshiyyat as-Saḥ(a)līn = ʿIrāq al Manshiyya, OIG 130-112 (site 28)
ʿIrāq Ḥātim = unknown (site 105)
These identifications involve a reassessment of the three places named ʿIrāq (Arak) and the two places named Manshiyya (Menshiye) in the 1596–97 *defter*. The three ʿIrāqs are: ʿIrāq, ʿIraq Ḥātim, and ʿIrāq Ḥālā. Iraq Hala is a known site (OIG 139-114), so its identification is clear. Logically, the other two would be Iraq Suweidan and Iraq el-Menshiyeh, although how Hütteroth and Abdulfattah determined which should be which is unclear. However, we know that there are several other places called Iraq (although these are mostly caves). We also know that there are two places called Manshiyya: Manshiyyat al-ʿUjūl and Manshiyyat as-Saḥlīn.

As we know from many other examples (Akhṣāṣ ʿAsqalān vs. Akhṣāṣ ʿAjlān, Ṣummayl al-Mughār vs. Ṣummayl al-Khalīl, etc.), village names were often qualified in Mamluk and Ottoman records by the name of a nearby village or town to distinguish them from other villages of the same name. That appears to be the case with the two Manshiyyas. Thus Manshiyyat al-ʿUjūl appears in other sources as Manshiyyat Tall ʿUjūl, that is, Manshiyah near Tell el-ʿAjjul (the correct spelling is actually ʿUjūl and not ʿAjjûl, as noted by Schumacher [1886:176–77, 194]; it is the plural of ʿijl [= Hebrew ʿegel], "calf"). In fact, just southeast of Tell el-Ajjul on the 1:20,000 Mandatory topocadastral map (Sheet 9-9, Wadi Ghazza) are two tracts of land called El Menshiya (OIG 094-096 and 096-096). While the location of the site itself was apparently lost, the name of the village lands was thus preserved into the Mandatory period. Van de Velde (1858:53) noted a ruin named el Menshiyeh in the general area of Gaza-Hesi, although he did not visit the site; we are not aware that anyone else ever noted the site.

Thus, Manshiyyat as-Saḥlīn should be a village called Manshiyya near another village named (as-)Saḥlīn. Saḥlīn is a toponym that appears in other sources, and there is much discussion as to its location. Sahalin appears in a Crusader charter (dated 1136; with Fectata, Zeita, and Courcoza) relating to Beit Jibrin (Röhricht 1893:40). Yāqūt mentions it, as Siḥillīn (or Sijillīn), in the territory of ʿAsqalān (1866–73c:46, 49–50). Eusebius (K. 160:11) mentions a Saaleim seven miles west of Eleutheropolis. While it is clearly somewhere west or northwest of Beit Jibrin, Saḥlīn's exact location is unclear, and there is not space here to discuss the problem in detail. It is worth noting Elitzur (2004:381–82), using the data known at the time, including the 1596–97 *defter*, identified Saaleim/Sahalin with Manshiyyat as-Saḥlīn—and both with Iraq el-Menshiyeh. The *waqfiyya* of the Sultan Qāytbāy for his madrasa in Jerusalem (al-Ashrafiyya, 1477), however, provides important additional information; according to the summary of Ibrāhim (1961:409), Manshiyyat Saḥlīn and Saḥlīn are listed as two separate villages in the district of Qaratiyya, and the lands of Manshiyyat Saḥlīn are bordered on the west by the lands of al-Fālūja. This means that Manshiyyat (as-)Saḥlīn is almost certainly ʿIraq el-Menshiyeh—or is at least extremely close to it. (Note that Hütteroth and Abdulfattah transliterated the name as Saḥlīn, while—based on the earlier forms of the name—it is likely to be Sahalīn, a name that would be written the same way in Arabic script.)

This leaves us again with the names ʿIrāq and ʿIraq Ḥātim. One should still be Iraq el-Suweidan, and we would suggest ʿIrāq. It is a much larger place in the 1596–97 *defter* and, therefore, more likely to still be inhabited in the nineteenth century. Also, the 1525–26 *defter* lists the following villages as part of the administrative unit of Qaratiyya (al-Swarieh 2008:91–96): ʿIjjis ar-Rās, ʿIrāq, Fālūja, and Judayda (or Jadīra). This grouping again suggests that ʿIrāq = Iraq el-Suweidan. This also means that the identity of ʿIrāq Ḥātim is uncertain.

Manṣūra (site 70)
Hütteroth and Abdulfattah would identify it with Kh. el Manṣura (OIG 133-113). However, Kh. (el) Manṣura at OIG 099-096 might be a better candidate. While the area of the northeastern Kh. el Mansura was certainly inhabited in this period, so was the area of the southwestern Kh. Mansura, and a number of other identifications have turned out to be located in its general area. We would note in connection with this the 1525–26 *defter*, which has two places named Manṣūriya or Manṣūra: One is a

village, the other is a *mazraᶜa*. The *mazraᶜa* appears in a group of *mazraᶜas* in the area of Iraq el-Menshiyeh. Meanwhile, the village is said to be part of the administrative unit of Gaza, suggesting it is (as with the majority—but not all—of the villages in this subdistrict) in the general area of Gaza and not farther to the northeast. If it were the northeastern Mansura, it might be more likely to be part of the subdistrict of Qaratiyya. This suggests that the village in 1526–27 is the southwestern Mansura and the *mazraᶜa* is the northeastern one. (Of course, this is not conclusive proof that the southwestern Mansura is the village of 1596–97; it is possible that one Mansura was settled and the other abandoned over the course of the sixteenth century.)

Maqqus
See Makkus.

Miᶜṣaba
Muᶜayṣiba (Hütteroth and Abdulfattah) = **Kh. Miᶜṣaba** (OIG 116-124) (site 58)
The difference in spelling is between *M-ᶜ-y-ṣ-b-a* and *M-ᶜ-ṣ-b-a*—that is, one additional letter (*yāʾ*). The name appears in the other two *defters*, transcribed by al-Swarieh (2008:94; 2009:40) in the first as *M-ᶜ-ṣ-y-a* (or *M-q-ṣ-y-a*) and transliterated into Turkish by Yalçinkaya (2006) as Maᶜasaba in the second. Based on these spellings, it is pretty clear that there should not be a *yāʾ* after the *ᶜayn*—and that this is simply a mistake either by Hütteroth and Abdulfattah or by the scribe of the 1596–97 *defter*. The only other discrepancy is the appearance of *yāʾ* in place of *bāʾ* in the first *defter*; again, these are the same letter form with different dotting.

Al-Swarieh (2008:91–96) also records information on the administrative units within *nahiya* Gaza in the 1525–26 *defter*. One of these units, as mentioned above, is ᶜAsqalān. While a couple of the villages of ᶜAsqalān are outliers (Ibdis, Jusayr), most are in the immediate vicinity of Tel Ashkelon and correspond well to our core study area (Maps 87, 88, 91, and 92). The inclusion of Miᶜṣaya/Miᶜṣaba in this group means it is likely (though not certain) that this place was close to ᶜAsqalān and Majdal, making Kh. Miᶜṣaba an excellent candidate. Note also that the Map 88 survey found Mamluk and Ottoman pottery at the site.

Naḥāsa = **Kh. an Naḥāsa**, OIG 088-088 (approx.) (site 92)
Musil (1908:56) mentioned a site called *ḥ. an-Nhâse*. The Karte von Arabia Palaestina (1907c) locates *en-Nhâse* north-northwest of Sûk Mâzen and Weli eš-Šeiḥ Ḥmûdi, south of Wadi es-Selḳi and Weli abu Abîde, and south-southeast of ed-Dejr (Deir el-Balah) on the road to Khan Yunis before it turns to the southwest.

Qarātiyya
Farātiyya (Hütteroth and Abdulfattah) = **Qarātiyya** (**Karātiyya**) (site 29)
Correction: **Kartā** (Hütteroth and Abdulfattah) = **Kudnā** (site 103)
We are skeptical of Hütteroth and Abdulfattah's identification of the site Kartā (*K-r-t-ā*) as Karātiyya. The spelling does not appear correct: Not only is it missing the *yāʾ*, which always appears in spellings of the name, but also the name usually (though not always) has a long *ā* after the *rāʾ*. As an alternative, we would suggest Farātiyya, a large site (121 adult males) which we should be able to identify in some way—given the pattern that the larger the village in the sixteenth century, the greater the likelihood that it continued to be inhabited into the nineteenth century. Karātiyya was a subdistrict center in the Mamluk administration (and in the 1525–26 *defter*; see Ibrāhim 1961:409; al-Swarieh 2008:89) and is mentioned by the medieval geographer Dimashqī (1866:213), suggesting it was of some importance in the period.

We believe that the explanation is the confusion of *fāʾ* and *qāf*: They are the same form, merely with different dotting. Not only is Qarātiyya (with *qāf*) an acceptable variant of Karātiyya (with *kāf*), but it appears that the original spelling was in fact Qarātiyya—and that Karātiyya is a much later development. It appears with initial *qāf* in Yāqūt (1866–73d:53), Dimashqī, the 1477 *waqfiyya* of al-Ashrafiyya madrasa in Jerusalem (Ibrāhim 1961:409), as a district center in 1520s Gaza (al-Swarieh 2008:89), and in the lists of Scholz (c. 1820; Scholz 1822:254), Eli Smith (1841:118), and Socin (the late 1860s village list; Socin 1879:155). The earliest appearance with *kāf* that we can find is the Survey of Western Palestine (Palmer 1881:368); it then appears as Karatiyya in all later Ottoman and Mandatory sources that we have seen (such as Gatt 1884 and the 1931 census). This change may have occurred because in Palestinian Arabic *qāf* is pronounced as *kāf* (see, e.g., Talmon 2004:216). This leaves the identification of Kartā. We believe that *K-r-t-ā* is a mistake for or misreading of *K-d-n-ā*, Kudna. Each has the same number of letters but with two differences. As mentioned above, *nūn* and *tāʾ* have the same form but with different dottings. *Rāʾ* and *dāl* are different forms, but depending on the handwriting could possibly be confused; note that Hütteroth and Abdulfattah (1977:151) could not decide whether one village should be Rashīra or Rashīda, supporting our idea of the confusion of these letters. Note that Kudna is roughly on the border of the Gaza, Hebron, and Jerusalem *nahiyes*. There are no villages with similar names in the 1596–97 *defter* in the other two *nahiyes*; this means that either it must be "Karta," or else it appears under another name. Meanwhile, Kudna appears in the two other *defters*, spelled as Kudnā, in *nahiye* Gaza.

Zadok (1995–97:140) already mentioned the possibility of these two identifications (of Qarātiyya and Kudnā), while noting the interchange of *kāf* and *qāf* in Palestinian Arabic, although he suggested that the form Qarātiyya is a "mistake," while it in fact appears to be the original form. Etkes (2012:fig. 7.2) appears to have reached the same conclusion concerning Farātiyya but still repeats Hütteroth and Abdulfattah's location of "Kartā" at the same site.

Qarqafa

Mirfaqa (Hütteroth and Abdulfattah) = **Kh. Qarqafa** (125.121)? **125260-121570** (site 114)

The difference in spelling is between *M-r-f-q-a* and *Q-r-q-f-a*. As apparent elsewhere, *fāʾ* and *qāf* are commonly mistaken for each other. This name appears in the other *tahrir defters*, transliterated into Turkish as Mirfeka from one (Yalçinkaya 2006) and transcribed as Mirqafa/Mirfaqa in the other (al-Swarieh 2009:42). Thus, other scholars have had a problem distinguishing the two. The mistake of *qāf* for *mīm* would be more difficult to explain, as these are not the same form, but it might still be possible. (In the 1525–26 *defter*, al-Swarieh [2009:43] transcribes the name of a *mazraᶜa* as Qarṭ as-Sabl, almost certainly a mistake for Marṭ as-Sayl.) It is likely that the different scholars may have been influenced to render this name Mirfaqa in order to fit it to the Arabic word "*mirfaqa.*"

Ramādāt (site 136)

Perhaps this is a mistake for Ramāḍān. Musil (1908:29–30) recorded a *bîr Ramaḍân* serving as a water source for En-Nṣêrât, in the area of Deir el-Balaḥ and Wadi es-Selḳi. Note that *nūn* and *tāʾ* share the same form, with different dottings; the consonant *ḍād* is not a similar sign to *dāl*, however. Meanwhile, the Turkish transliteration of villages from the 1548–49 *defter* (Yalçinkaya 2006) has a village Remadan of similar size to Ramadat of the 1596–97 *defter*.

Salqā = Khan Yunis, OIG 083-083 (site 90)

This identification is not based on an error—but on information from medieval Arab sources. Salqa was a Mamluk postal station on the Cairo-Damascus highway between Rafah and Gaza, as reported by al-ᶜUmayrī, Khalīl al-Ẓāhirī, and Qalqashandī; Qalqashandī records that it was specifically between Rafah and Darum, i.e., Deir el-Balaḥ (see Hartmann 1910:689). Later the station between Rafah and Darum appears as Khan Yunis (Hartmann 1910:696). Meanwhile, the fourteenth-century historian Ibn al-Furāt and the fifteenth-century historian Badr al-Dīn al-ᶜAynī both stated that Yūnis al-Nawrūzī built his khan at the postal station of "Salfa" or Salqa near Gaza in the late fourteenth century (see Tamari 1987:136, 141; see also Abu Khalaf 1983:183). This identification also helps to explain why Khan Yunis is mysteriously missing from all of the sixteenth-century *defters*.

　　Note that Etkes (2012:fig. 7.2) locates Salqā just southeast of Deir el-Balaḥ, presumably identifying it with the modern town of Wadi as-Salqa in this area. However, this town is a recent founding, receiving its name from the nearby wadi; the historical sources clearly indicate that medieval Salqa should be placed southwest of Deir el-Balaḥ at the site of Khan Yunis.

Ṣandaḥanna (site 78)

We have chosen to mark Ṣandaḥanna near Majdal, though we cannot be sure that this is not Kh. Sandahannah near Beit Guvrin.

Saṭar, OIG 086-086 (approx.) (site 17)

The Survey of Palestine 1:20,000 topocadstral map (Sheet 8-8, Khan Yunis) has two tracts of land named Es Satar (one between 084-086 and 085-086, the other around 087-086) and a Wadi es Satar (between 086-087 and 087-085).

　　Al-Dabbāgh (1972:492, cited in Grossman 1992:107) noted a former village Saṭar in the Qalaᶜiya area around Khan Yunis, whose residents are said to have founded a seminomadic village. He notes that the inhabitants next appear in Sautariya, near Ramla—but does not give a date for the desertion of Saṭar.

　　In addition, Abel (1940:70) noted a cultivated area north of Khan Yunis called Saṭar, along the Wadi es-Saṭar, and that in this area there are a few sycamores which are the remnants of a large group of trees lining "la grande allée ou *saṭar*" (*saṭar* in Arabic means "line"), mentioned by al-Muhallabī (end of tenth century) and Yāqūt (early thirteenth century) between Rafah and Darum, apparently referring to the main coastal road (see Hartmann 1910:685; 1916:488).

　　Etkes (2012:fig. 7.2) appears to have located Saṭar in the same area.

Shaᶜārta aṣ-Ṣughrā

Sawāmiriyya aṣ-Ṣughrā (Hütteroth and Abdulfattah) = **Kh. Shaᶜartā** (south)?, OIG 098-090 (site 65)

In the 1596–97 *defter*, let us consider two names: Shaᶜāriyya al-Kubrā and Sawāmiriyya aṣ-Ṣughrā. First, Shaᶜāriyya al-Kubrā is clearly the northern Shaᶜarta (as indicated by the notation *tābiᶜ*, "dependent of", Burayr). Since *tāʾ* and *yāʾ* are the same form, merely with different pointings, the name in the list was probably misread as "Shaᶜāriyya" by Hütteroth and Abdulfattah and should be transliterated as Shaᶜārta.

　　The qualifications *kubrā* and *ṣughrā* = *kabīr* and *ṣaghīr*, that is, major and minor or large and small (*ṣughrā/ṣaghīr* is a cognate of Hebrew *ṣaᶜir*, "young"). This means there should be a second Sawāmiriyya (al-Kubrā) and a second Shaᶜārta (aṣ-Ṣughrā), but neither appears. It is possible that they were uninhabited at this time. However, there is an interesting situation when we try to track these names in the other *defters*. First, Sawāmiriyya never occurs in any other *defter* or any other source; since there should in fact be two of them, this suggests that the reading "Sawāmiriyya" is an error. In the 1548–49 *defter* we have the names Ṣaᶜāriyye el-Kübra and Sefertâ el-Kübra, as transliterated into Turkish (Yalçinkaya 2006). In the 1525–26 *defter*, we have neither form, but we do have a *S-q-r-t-ā* aṣ-Ṣughrā transcribed by al-Swarieh (2008:95; 2009:40). In the *waqf defter* 522, we have one *waqf* (İpşirli and al-Tamīmī 1982:14, no. 44) with a village transcribed as Sāfiriyya in Gaza subdistrict and another with two villages transcribed as Safiriyyā al-Kabīrā and aṣ-Ṣaghīrā in Gaza subdistrict (İpşirli and al-Tamīmī

1982:10, no. 29). In the various late Ottoman and Mandatory records and maps, the only known village or ruin Safiriyya in the southern coastal plain is near Lud (which is not part of Gaza subdistrict). There is a tract of land called Safiriyyā north of Mughallis and east of Idhnibba, but this is on the border of the subdistrict and is the only instance of the name that we have found within the subdistrict (and we need two). We would therefore suggest, though we are not certain, that Sawāmiriyya, Safiriyya, Seferta, Ṣaᶜāriyye, and Shaᶜāriyya are all mistakes for a single name, Shaᶜārta, which we know was applied to two separate *khirbeh*s (a northern one at OIG 117-106 and a southern one at OIG 098-90). To us, the variety in these names suggests the possibility of confusing the different letters: *S-w-ā-m-r-y-a*, *S-f-r-y-a*, *S-f-r-t-ā*, *S-q-r-t-ā*, *Sh-ᶜ-ā-r-y-a*, and *Sh-ᶜ-ā-r-t-a*. Other than Sawāmiriyya, which is an outlier, each has five letters (besides optional long *ā* after the *ᶜayn*). The letters *yāʾ* and *tāʾ* are the same form with different dottings, as are *sīn* and *shīn*. *Fāʾ* (or *qāf*) and *ᶜayn* are not the same letter, but in their medial forms they are similar and could certainly be confused, as has happened in transcriptions of the *defters*: For instance, in listing the villages of the 1525–26 *defter*, al-Swarieh (2008:94; 2009:40) could not decide between *M-ᶜ-ṣ-y-a* and *M-q-ṣ-y-a* for the entry we have interpreted as Miᶜṣaba (see above). The only difficult entry is *S-w-ā-m-r-y-a*, which is more difficult to explain. Also, according to Yalçinkaya the 1548–49 *defter* has both Seferta and Ṣaᶜāriyye qualified as "al-Kubrā"; our guess is that this is simply a mistake—either by the original scribe or by Yalçinkaya—and that it should be aṣ-Ṣughrā.

We would suggest that this name has been repeatedly misinterpreted due to lack of familiarity with sites in the region and with this name, derived ultimately from a non-Arabic source (Seᶜarta); it was probably misread as Safiriyya under the influence of a known village or villages of this name, such as the one near Lud.

Takhāw

Taḥāw/Taḥād (Hütteroth and Abdulfattah) = **Takhāw(a)**, 093-092 (approx.) (site 95)
Musil (1907:220) mentioned a site *ḫ. Taḥāwa* and cited Yāqūt for a reference to a medieval village Taḥāwa near Darum (Musil 1907:301 n.3; see Yāqūt 1866–73a:827–28). Elsewhere, Musil (1908:54) mentioned that *at-Thāwa* is the old name for a *khirbeh* now generally called abu Meddên. The Karte von Arabia Palaestina (1907c) locates Taḥāwa east of Deir el-Balah on the road to Sheikh Nebhan.

Note (as mentioned above) that this appears to be one of several cases where the final *ʾalif* or *tāʾ marbūṭa* is omitted in the *defters*.

Umm an-Nuṣūr (or Nuᶜūr) (site 107)

On the Survey of Palestine 1:20,000 topocadastral map sheets, there are two tracts of land called Umm an-Nuṣur: One is just south of Suq Mazin (OIG 088-084; Sheet 8-8, Khan Yunis), and the other is at 104-107 (Sheet 10-10, Beit Hanun).

4. ASHKELON AS MARITIME GATEWAY AND CENTRAL PLACE

by George A. Pierce and Daniel M. Master

THIS study seeks to offer a first glimpse at the significance of local settlement patterns for the history of Tel Ashkelon based upon the information assembled in the previous chapters. In many ways, this is an addendum to Huster's fundamental work, but we have tried to address some new synthetic ideas. No archaeological site is an island (even island sites), and hence the necessity of regional syntheses for archaeology cannot be overstated. Even the "empty space" between sites attests to land use—or lack thereof—and contributes to the knowledge of a region (Smith and Parsons 1989:179). In this chapter, the focus will be on the diachronic relationship between Tel Ashkelon and the land behind it.

Settlement Theories

Archaeologically visible settlement patterns imposed on the landscape of the southern coastal plain of Israel reflect conscious choices made by their inhabitants regarding availability of natural resources, safety, and proximity to pathways. Several descriptive models have been used to explain the distribution of sites, but—with some modifications—Walter Christaller's Central Place Theory (1933) remains the most widely applied theoretical framework used to explain settlement patterns in the southern Levant (e.g., Levy 1995:229; Dever 1987:150; Jasmin 2006). A. F. Burghardt (1971) famously modified Christaller's work by focusing on gateway cities, larger urban centers at the end of a transportation network. Burghardt's model provided a diachronic model whereby an initial settlement at the terminus of a transportation route could develop into a stable central place surrounded by a new frontier.

For this study, Levantine ports in antiquity can be considered nodes in a network of ports across the eastern Mediterranean basin. The port connected the maritime system to a set of roadways to various consumption and production centers. In this sense, the port was similar to the gateway cities that Burghardt envisioned. Functioning at the junction between land and water, ports present a unique challenge for analysis of settlement patterns and hierarchies since a port does not typically occupy a node in the traditional, optimally hexagonal settlement pattern for market centers

simply by virtue of its "excentric coastal position" (Bird 1973:110). Christaller (1966:16) acknowledged the difference between central places, areally bound places, and point-bound places in his original work, describing the last as "those settlements the inhabitants of which make their living from resources found at specific locations . . . especially harbors."[1] As a point-bound place, the port—obviously situated at the land-water nexus—often attracts central functions such as administration or markets toward the waterfront, although the port is not usually the only "center" of an urban environment.[2]

The hinterland of a port widens inland with boundaries formed by hinterlands of competing ports (Bird 1973:110). For coastal gateways, the "core area" would be overseas markets (Bird 1973:112, quoting pers. comm. with Burghardt). The gateway model together with considerations of port-hinterland dynamics results in dendritic patterns of settlement locations with various "branches" spreading from the gateway. A settlement pattern for the "access resources" model proposed by Mitchell Allen (*Ashkelon 1*) would be linear, or dendritic, with sites positioned along trade routes, connecting inland centers to a coastal outlet and a few rural sites. Dendritic models place emphasis on highest order sites, or attachment points, and lower order settlements to map communication or commercial lines (Haselgrove 1986:7). Based on the models developed by B. Bronson (1977) and S. Hall (1985), Lawrence E. Stager proposed such a model for coastal Levantine sites in the Bronze and Iron Ages in which merchants leveraged economic "port power" to connect hinterland resources to wider markets such as dynastic Egypt, reaping the profits of this trade

---

[1] While central places exist as markets and service their surrounding region, areally bound places are settlements in which the inhabitants depend on agricultural activities determined by the neighboring countryside (Christaller 1966:16). J. H. Bird (1973:111) observed that Christaller then noted that harbors become central places, making the unique situation of ports subservient to the overarching Central Place Theory.

[2] Within a city, the process of centro-symmetric ordering occurs as several centers of commerce or administration may develop in an urban environment, each of which could potentially offer specialized goods or services (Bird 1973:108).

(Stager 2001; 2002; see adaptation for MB IIA by Cohen 2002). Stager's model makes two assumptions about coastal commercial sites and the control wielded by the merchants. First, the site was tied to inland polities via east-west networks of drainage or transport systems (Stager 2001:625). Second, power was exercised via economic measures external to the political or military power of the state (Stager 2001:628–29). Power exerted by the state as punitive measures against hinterland polities could actually be counterproductive and costly.

The Rise of the Gateway (Early Bronze–Iron I)

While these theories use analogies and economic logic to sketch out Asheklon's history, the data assembled by Huster force the theoretical models to confront a robust data set which prompts some re-evaluations (or at least nuancing) of Tel Ashkelon's role in its landscape. However, the one element that is not changed by Huster's regional survey is the core orientation of Tel Ashkelon toward the sea and its links with overseas markets. This is abundantly clear from the numerous imported transport amphorae (see Barako in *Ashkelon 1*) to the numerous anchors and pottery off the coast ranging in date from the Late Bronze Age to the Islamic period (see Raban and Tur-Caspa in *Ashkelon 1*; Wachsmann in *Ashkelon 1*). From the perspective of Tel Ashkelon, Mediterranean connections are justifiably emphasized. Yet, within this framework, Huster's results indicate Tel Ashkelon appears to be part of two different settlement regimes: a first from the Early Bronze Age through the end of the second millennium B.C. and a second from the late Iron II period through the end of the Crusades.[3] This is not a new observation, originating at least with Allen (*Ashkelon 1*), but in the following pages, we will address how Huster's collection modifies our understanding of Tel Ashkelon and its hinterland.

Prehistoric Periods

Huster's collation of the data from the Ashkelon region reveals an era before Tel Ashkelon played any role in the region at all. He observes that Epipaleolithic sites were located on or nearby the first *kurkar* ridge inland from the Mediterranean. During the Neolithic, settlements were located predominantly along the Shiqma drainage basin southeast of Tel Ashkelon rather than near the coastal zone, indicating that Mediterranean trade was not a major aspect of subsistence. Even close to the Mediterranean, the PPNC pastoral camp in Afridar (Site 207; Garfinkel and Dag 2008) was not commercially oriented. The inhabitants did utilize the fishing resources of the near shore, as evinced by fish bones among the faunal remains (Perrot and Gopher 1996:165; *Ashkelon 1*, p. 57), but commerce along the Mediterranean littoral (Stager 1993:105) was not substantive enough to shape settlement.

At some point in the Chalcolithic period, a series of poorly understood encampments were founded in and around Tel Ashkelon and in the Afridar region immediately to the north. For Tel Ashkelon, the Chalcolithic period is represented by Chalcolithic pottery, particularly cornet bases, in secondary deposition in alluvium (see Rosen in *Ashkelon 1*, p. 101; see also Stager 1993:105). The secondary presence of these sherds in the alluvium may suggest that the primary Chalcolithic period settlement was located on higher ground, on *kurkar* bedrock of Ashkelon's central tel, perhaps due to swampy conditions indicated by increased wadi alluviation during the Chalcolithic and nascent Early Bronze Age (see Carmi et al in *Ashkelon 1*, p. 127; Rosen in *Ashkelon 1*, p. 103). Another encampment on the north side of Ashkelon's north tell was indicated by the residual Chalcolithic pottery recovered in the fills of the MB II fortifications on the North Slope (see *Ashkelon 1*, p. 215). This same pattern of secondary discoveries of Chalcolithic material, most easily distinguished by the presence of cornets, is found in the settlements north of Ashkelon in the Afridar region (Gophna 2004:3; compare figures 2.2 and 2.3). All of these sites have Early Bronze Age I habitation as well, leading to some thought that the Chalcolithic material may be from the portion of that period immediately preceding Early Bronze Age I.

Early Bronze Age

EB IA and EB IB settlements in the Afridar region just north of Tel Ashkelon represent a new way of conceiving the landscape. Gophna (2004) summarizes the situation well when he notes

---

[3] A third "null" pattern is also visible in the moments when Tel Ashkelon appears to be entirely abandoned (Prehistoric–Neolithic, Intermediate Bronze Age, early to mid-sixth century B.C., after the Crusades). These periods are characterized by an absence of Mediterranean trade within the Ashkelon region. In that sense, this pattern highlights Mediterranean trade as Tel Ashkelon's sine qua non.

that these sites were entrepôts connecting the lo-cal agricultural products (cereals, olives, grapes, products of animal husbandry), goods transported overland from long distances (bitumen, copper), and the products of Levantine coastal shipping. Archaeobotanical analysis of wood fragments revealed *Cedrus libani* and *Quercus cerris* from Lebanon and Turkey (Gophna and Liphschitz 1996:143). Other finds included freshwater Nilotic mollusk shells, Egyptian or Egyptianized drop-shaped vessels, and enigmatic ceramic "Clayton rings" (Gophna 2004:6). The core rationale for these sites was proximity to the Mediterranean transportation networks (Gophna 2004:4). The (ad-mittedly sparse) EB I pottery from Tel Ashkelon marks the site as just another small site at the southern border of the Afridar cluster (Stager 1993:105–6). There is no sense that Tel Ashkelon, or any site, was of a higher rank within a settle-ment hierarchy. Further, the lack of additional lo-cal settlement within the region highlights the role of the Afridar cluster as a regional rather than lo-cal gateway, serving sites such as Tell el-Hesi, Tel ᶜErani, and points east (Gophna 2004:7).[4]

---

[4] The nature of the terrestrial and maritime trade networks in relation to the Egyptian presence in southern Palestine during the EB I and the settlements in the Ashkelon region warrants further consideration. While a limited Egyptian presence in southern Palestine is attested during the EB IA, Egyptian involvement in the area increased in the late EB IB after a brief hiatus (Wilkinson 1999:128 and references there). In the interval between those phases, Wilkinson observes a de-cline in Egyptian material culture in southern Palestine but an increase in imports from the Levant at Abydos Tomb U-j (1999:129). The increase in Egyptian activity in the region during the EB IB was concomitant with the rise of the state in Egypt. State-sponsored trade is demonstrated by Egyptian or Egyptianized material culture found at more than twen-ty sites in southern Palestine (Moorey 1987:43; Oren and Yekutieli 1992:381; Brandl 1992). This includes clear in-dications of an Egyptian presence at Tel ᶜErani (Weinstein 1984) and En Besor (Gophna and Gazit 1985; Gophna 1990; 1992a; 1992c), which functioned as way stations or administrative centers on the terrestrial route. The title of "overseer of foreign lands" bestowed upon an official dur-ing the reign of Khasekhemwy may indicate a shift from non-bellicose trading colonies to diplomatic contacts with local merchants or officials at the end of the Second Dynasty (Wilkinson 1999:133). Tel ᶜErani has even greater indica-tions of Egyptian presence than Afridar-Ashkelon. This pat-tern complicates our understanding of Ashkelon as a gate-way—at least for Egyptian goods. It could be that Tel ᶜErani was part of a different (or additional) overland network with Egypt, or it is equally possible that Tel ᶜErani was a more central place than Afridar-Ashkelon and that Ashkelon was a dependent port of more powerful inland polities.

This pattern changed markedly in the EB III though this difference is not transparent in Huster's summative survey maps. All of the Afridar EB I sites north of Tel Ashkelon disappeared; Tel Poran arose as a fortified settlement, and Tel Ashkelon became a site of 8–9 hectares.[5] Locally, Tel Ashkelon likely took over all of the functions (and the population) of the earlier, smaller sites to the north. These sites share Tel Ashkelon's proximity to the Mediterranean as well as its access to the fresh water of the coastal aquifer. The most ob-vious difference, however, is that Tel Ashkelon's northern mound is a *kurkar* ridge that rises some 20 m above the sea below. This locale offers an unparalleled view of the coastal waterways along with a degree of protection that is not found in the Afridar settlements. In situ EB III remains on Tel Ashkelon's north mound include a single room delimited by mudbrick walls containing olive oil separator jars and metallic-combed ware storage jars for that product. This small window does not provide much insight into the period though it is likely that the range of maritime and terrestrial connections uncovered in the Afridar EB I settle-ments continued at Tel Ashkelon into the EB III.

In his discussion of "port power" in the Early Bronze Age, Stager (2001) argues that Ashkelon became a preeminent city in the region by using its economic advantages as a port to shape the choices of inland producers. Of course Tel Ashkelon, by its very location, was surely a port, but the ex-cavations have yet to establish Tel Ashkelon as a city as large as Tel ᶜErani or Tel Yarmuth. From the surveys at least, it is apparent that EB III Tel Ashkelon had no satellite agricultural towns and villages.[6] This gap emphasizes that Ashkelon was

---

[5] If one connects the dots of clean EB III primary and sec-ondary archaeological deposits uncovered by the Leon Levy Expedition, the EB III site would be limited to Ashkelon's northern tell (c. 8–9 hectares). If the scattered single sherds occasionally found in later Middle Bronze through Iron Age deposits on Ashkelon's south tell are included as a marker of the original size of a single settlement, the site grows con-siderably. Stager (2001) originally used the latter measure, but in the last few years, every excavation area or probe on Ashkelon's south tell to reach bedrock has failed to find EBIII deposits immediately below immediately below the Middle Bronze Age remains, leading Stager to modify his position.

[6] This null result has greater weight because of Huster's use of salvage excavation to fill out earlier surface surveys. In the last twenty years, the modern city of Ashkelon has expanded rapidly covering the area east of Ashkelon with a carpet of multistory residential buildings. In the construction process, innumerable IAA test pits have been excavated down to bed-rock. Because these test pits follow the variables of modern

not a typical agrarian center with an emphasis on maximally exploiting the surrounding agricultural fields. Instead, Ashkelon was a commercial outlet with an economic reach beyond its immediate hinterland. The question remains, however, whether Ashkelon was a true "port power" or merely Tel ᶜErani's port.

Middle Bronze Age

Following a gap in occupation during the MB I, Tel Ashkelon was enlarged and fortified in the MB IIA with renewed emphasis on maritime commercial ties. The city and its ruler, *Mwri*, were deemed enough of a threat to warrant its inclusion in an Execration Text where the port city's commercial nature is reflected in the name of the site, *Isk3i*, an Egyptian rendering of the city name *ᵓAṯqalānu* derived from the Semitic (i.e., Canaanite) root **ṯql* "to weigh" (Posener 1940:65 [E2]; see Sethe 1926:e23 for an earlier rendering and different ruler). Susan Cohen (2002) suggests that initial settlement was made on the coast and settlements began to be established on routes into the highlands possibly to obtain natural resources there. Luxury items and imported pottery appear in higher concentrations closer to the coastal trade centers such as Akko, Ashkelon, and Dor, in addition to "gateway" cities to inland settlements such as Megiddo and Gezer (Cohen 2002:129–30). She attributes this dendritic exchange system and "cultural renaissance" of the MB IIA to contact with Middle Kingdom Egypt and the powerful trade cities such as Byblos (Cohen 2002:131).

In the Middle Bronze Age, Tel Ashkelon was closely connected with the rest of the eastern Mediterranean. Ceramic evidence from various contexts related to Ashkelon's fortifications and gate illustrate renewed seaborne trade connections in the Middle Bronze Age (see *Ashkelon 1*, pp. 24–36). Additional ceramic evidence for Ashkelon's maritime connections comes from a cemetery containing more than 200 individuals in sixteen chambers in Grid 50, Phase 11 dated from the MB IIB to LB I–II transition (Baker 2006; 2010; *Ashkelon 1*, pp. 300–3). The pottery includes imported wares from outside the Levant that were preferred as grave goods for the deceased.

Middle Bronze Age Ashkelon was more than ten times the size of any other site in Huster's survey

region. Once again, as in the Early Bronze Age, the inhabitants of Ashkelon did not view the immediate terrestrial hinterland as a region to be developed or exploited for agriculture despite a complete lack of competition for these resources. A few sites were uncovered in the survey area, but, two of the largest—Tel Obed and Tel Poran—have no published non-Levantine material culture; the ceramics are thoroughly local. This emphasis on local production is such a contrast with the diverse assemblage at Ashkelon that it is difficult to see how these sites might be closely related. It seems more likely that these sites were related to the coastal highway routes (see chapter 2, Iron II road discussion, pp. 34–36). In such a setting, the idea of Ashkelon as a territorial, agrarian kingdom seems difficult to support (contra Burke 2008:130). Ashkelon's closest peers in the interior of the country are as far east as Tell el-Hesi, Gezer, Lachish, Tel ᶜErani, or Tell Beit Mirsim. These sites do contain imports, and Tel Ashkelon is the most likely conduit for them. Between the two sets of sites, there are few settlements that contain any material evidence indicating that they were way stations. There is no down-the-line trail of imported objects which might mark the routes.

In this period, for the first time, Ashkelon has all the elements that Stager described as belonging to a "port power." Both from the standpoint of site size and market hierarchy, Tel Ashkelon was dominant, but its power was not expressed through the accumulation of more land, direct political control, or a slowly expanding set of routes to the interior. The unwillingness of Tel Ashkelon's inhabitants to settle and exploit even its immediate hinterland highlight an economy fully supported by the commercial gains that came from its role as a node in Mediterranean commerce, with a secondary role as a regional gateway between the coast and large agrarian cities 25 km to the west.[7] There is no sense that it had any interest in controlling those interior cities politically. Rather, it was the power of Ashkelon's commerce that shaped inland production for export.

---

construction, they serve as an independent control to the design of the archaeological surface surveys.

---

[7] Given the importance of pastoral populations to the history of the Middle Bronze Age, it is possible that these groups played a substantive role in Ashkelon's hinterland. See the discussion by Huster (p. 22) of the MB II cemeteries in the region. Hence, the above observations on the exploitation of the hinterland should be linked primarily to permanent agricultural settlements which were designed to exploit the grain, wine, and oil production capacities of the region.

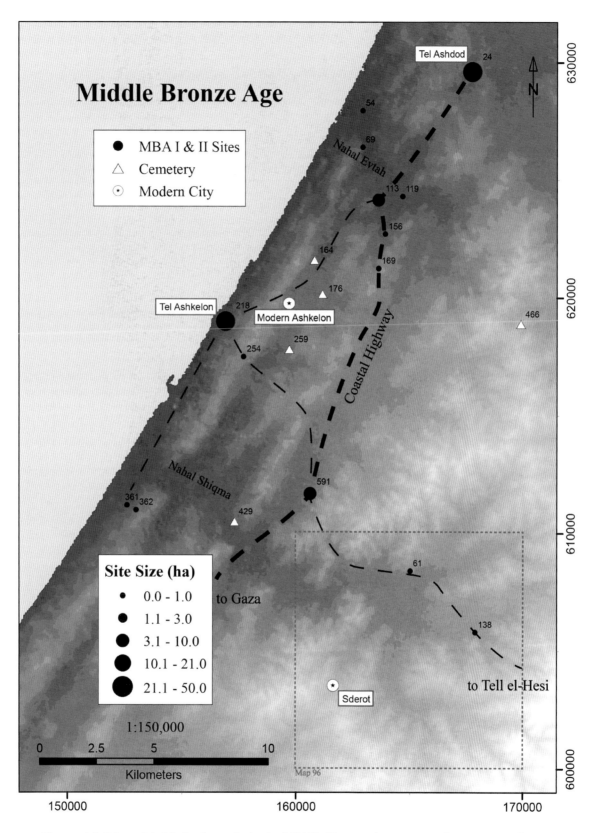

Figure 4.1: Map of Ashkelon's roads in the Middle Bronze Age over modern topography.

Late Bronze Age–Iron I

The Late Bronze and Iron I periods represent two of the most different cultural epochs in the history of Tel Ashkelon. In the early twelfth century B.C., Ashkelon changed from an international port in the Egyptian empire to a member of the Philistine Pentapolis. Nevertheless, from the standpoint of regional settlement, the patterns are virtually the same, and Ashkelon stands alone in the midst of an underdeveloped hinterland.

The Late Bronze Age presents both archaeological and textual data to build a comprehensive picture of items imported into Tel Ashkelon's tributary area and commodities exported from the region or acquired by the ruler for tribute to the Egyptian court. The status of Ashkelon as a vassal under Egyptian control in the LB II is clearly attested in the Amarna Letters. Yidya of Ashkelon repeatedly asserts his loyalty to the Egyptian king (EA 320) and his willingness to hearken to the orders of the king's envoys, Irimayašša and Reanapa (EA 321, 322, 326; cf. EA 370).[8] The range of commodities available to Yidya—and requested of him—illuminate the potential of Ashkelon: thirty ingots of glass, bread, beer, oil, grain, straw, horses, cattle, sheep, and goats (EA 324, 325).

From the excavations at Tell Ashkelon, it is clear the site was part of the Eastern Mediterranean commercial world. A central-courtyard house dated to the LB IIB contained Cypriot, Mycenaean, and Minoan wares (see *Ashkelon 1*, p. 304). In addition to these finds, scribal training at Ashkelon in the international tradition is attested by a cuneiform lexical tablet bearing Sumerian and Canaanite terms (Huehnergard and van Soldt 1999; Stager 2008:1580). In another area, courtyard surfaces yielded Cypriot and Mycenaean imports (see *Ashkelon 1*, p. 251). Toward the end of the LB II, Egyptianized bowls and beer jugs mark an Egyptian presence at Ashkelon while imported amphorae and handled cups from Egypt contained products for the Canaanite market (Martin 2008:265; 2011:195–201).

Unlike the pattern in the Middle Bronze Age, Huster argues that Late Bronze Age cities in Ashkelon's immediate vicinity did receive imports. Indeed the penetration of imported Mycenaean and Cypriot wares into the smallest hamlets of the interior is a distinctive feature of the Late Bronze Age in the southern Levant. Ashkelon was surely the conduit for many inland cities, but, given the ubiquity of these forms, determining which Levantine port served as the gateway for these containers and their contents proves difficult. Within a dendritic system, each port should have a unique hinterland located directly behind it, but Ashkelon's depopulated hinterland makes it quite challenging to trace a unique dendritic system eastward. The most likely route ran southeast of Tel Ashkelon through Tel Obed and from there to Tell el-Hesi and beyond. However, Tell el-Hesi is equidistant from the Gaza gateway. Thus, Ashkelon's unique connections to the east are unclear.

As Huster notes, Israel Finkelstein relates the importance of Ashkelon as an Egyptian administrative center and reconstructs a sparsely settled territory for Ashkelon that bordered territories of Gezer and Gath, citing the Amarna Letters for justification (1996a:225, 233). Whether or not territory in the ancient Near East was ever sketched out in the post-Westphalian blobs that he describes remains unclear (see Smith 2005 for another approach), but in the Amarna Letters themselves, Ashkelon is never pictured as territorially expansionist nor is there evidence that it was defending a core territory outside the city itself.

Allen (*Ashkelon 1*, p. 33) submits that shortage of Bronze and Iron Age remains east of Ashkelon indicate that the north-south trade routes were more important connections than east-west ties. Similarly, Michaël Jasmin's study (2006) of city-state territories in the LB IIB clearly shows a dichotomy between coastal sites and sites located in the Shephelah, or hill country, giving further evidence of the difference between ports and their tributary areas and inland central places with a hierarchy of secondary centers and lower-tier villages or hamlets. In observing the lack of settlements in the hinterland of Ashkelon, Jasmin attributes this absence to the area necessary for agricultural work by the urban populace (2006:166). While the settlement patterns in the territory of Ashkelon do not fit within his "ideal" organization as seen in the Shephelah, he proffers that Ashkelon's strength may have come from control of the north-south trade route, noting that the lack of rural sites and organization contrary to a classic central place hierarchy "may have been determined by [Ashkelon's] very different economic basis" (Jasmin 2006:172, 176). The economy of Tel Ashkelon did have a

---

[8] While Yidya's loyalty to the Egyptian pharaoh may have been steadfast, his actions toward fellow Canaanite rulers may have not been as trustworthy, for Ashkelon was implicated together with Gazru (Gezer) and Lakisi (Lachish) in an attempt to overthrow Abdi-Hepa of Jerusalem (EA 287).

different basis, but it is the maritime route that allowed it to bypass normal agrarian conventions and perhaps even control the coastal highway.

Life at Tel Ashkelon was dramatically different in the Iron I period, and the work of the Leon Levy Expedition has done much to enrich our understanding of this transition (see *Ashkelon 1*, pp. 257–72). The Canaanite city, having been first destroyed by the Egyptians at the end of the thirteenth century, received Sea Peoples from the west and became a city of the Philistines. This transition included fundamental shifts in all aspects of material culture, from ceramics (Stager 1995) and foodways (Master 2009) to architecture (Aja 2009). The ceramic distinctions with the preceding Late Bronze Age are so clear that they form the basis for the attribution of sites within the survey area to the Iron I. That is, all the Iron I sites in the survey area have the Philistine pottery forms that are found at Tel Ashkelon in the same period. In that sense, the relationship between Tel Ashkelon and the sites in its immediate hinterland was culturally close.

In this period, the evidence for Tel Ashkelon's connections with overseas centers is not as widely understood. In his treatment of Egyptian and Egyptianized pottery at Tel Ashkelon, Mario Martin (2011:201) mentions five Egyptian ovoid to globular jar rims from Philistine contexts with no exemplars found in LB IIB units. While not ruling out residual vessels, he suggests that the absence of these from LB contexts supports a contemporaneity with the earliest Philistine levels and a continued relationship with Egypt. Clearer Iron I imports include amphorae from the southern Lebanese coast, some bearing Cypro-Minoan signs, alongside imported Mycenaean IIIC pottery (Cross and Stager 2006; Master 2009). Ashkelon was still a port, even though the Mediterranean networks had changed.

In addition, some goods from inland centers were brought to Ashkelon and Ashdod during the Iron I (Ben Shlomo 2006:Fig 5.2). Between this trade from the hinterland and Ashkelon's continued role as a port, one can imagine a relationship between Ashkelon and its hinterland that is similar to the Late Bronze Age pattern: Maritime trade was still Tel Ashkelon's raison d'être, supplemented by its function as a regional gateway. Radical cultural changes within sites did not alter this underlying pattern visible in the wider landscape. Instead, Tel Ashkelon and its hinterland had a consistent relationship for the third, second, and

early first millennia. Ashkelon's maritime focus, even to the extent that the immediate hinterland was ignored, was a fundamental feature of the site over the *longue durée*.

The Dynamic Gateway (Iron II–Byzantine)

Iron II

In the eighth and seventh century, Tel Ashkelon's international trade flourished. As during the Middle Bronze Age, objects were imported from the entirety of the Eastern Mediterranean. The full scope of these discoveries has been extensively discussed in *Ashkelon 3*. Further, as during the Late Bronze Age, objects from Ashkelon's Mediterranean commerce made their way inland, perhaps most vividly illustrated by the discovery of distinctive late seventh-century Aegean pottery at inland sites (see chapter 2, p. 33; also Stern 2001:216). The connections are identical to relationships forged in earlier periods and are not indicators of newly established links. Ashkelon had been a Mediterranean port, a large urban center, even a gateway city, for some time. During the late Iron Age, however, something changed such that Ashkelon's immediate hinterland took on new significance.

The fundamental shift in settlement was recognized by Allen (*Ashkelon 1*, p. 23) who saw a contrast between an "access resources" model in the Bronze and Iron Ages and an "organic" model in the millennia that followed. In short, the "access resources" model builds on his dissertation (1997) where he argued that the value of Ashkelon lay in its ability to use transportation networks to collect goods from other places rather than in its ability to produce resources locally. As long as Ashkelon relied on its maritime network, it could access the coastal goods from the entire Levantine littoral and did not need to develop its own hinterland. In some cases, it could draw on other hinterlands in other places, either through trade or through direct control. As Huster notes, in the eighth century, the records of Sennacherib's campaign record that Sidqa, king of Ashkelon, maintained direct control of an agricultural hinterland in the modern Tel Aviv region accessible only via a maritime network (Oppenheim 1969:287). The breadth and flexibility of the maritime network was a key asset.

In the seventh century, the settlement pattern changed. Huster has removed the distortion of false "patch" sites from our survey maps, but he

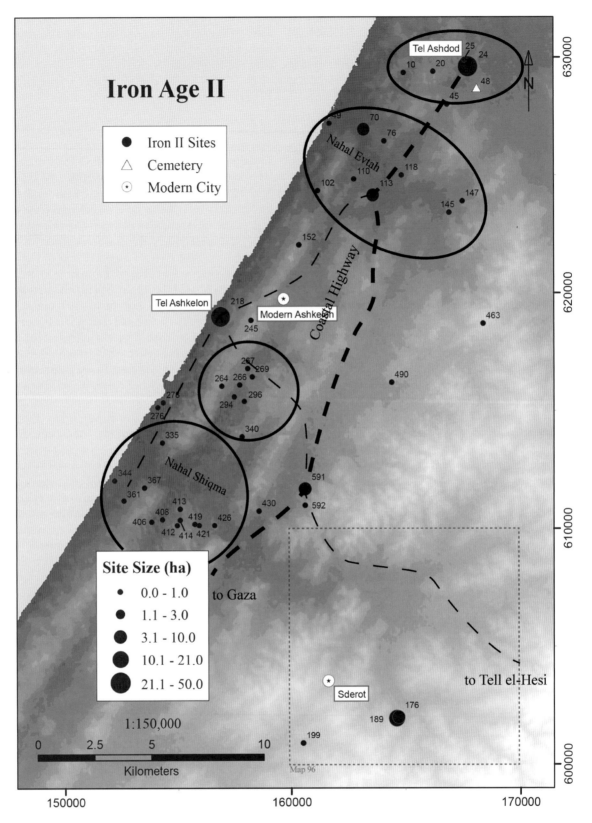

Figure 4.2: Map of Ashkelon in the Iron II with Middle Bronze Age road system over modern topography. Circles emphasize clusters of agricultural settlements.

still outlines a proliferation of small agricultural settlements around Ashdod, Tel Poran, just east of Ashkelon, and on the south side of the Nahal Shiqma (see figure 4.2). These are precisely the type of agricultural satellite villages which had been missing in the earlier periods and represent a fundamental shift in settlement strategy. From Huster's results, it appears that these settlements cluster in some of the wetter areas of the region such as the Nahal Shiqma, Nahal Evtah, and the low areas between the dunes east of Ashkelon, showing a preference for low-lying areas.

Explaining the agricultural exploitation of the hinterland behind Tel Ashkelon, after such a period of disinterest, is not easy. As Huster comments, Allen (1997) and many others have looked to Assyria for an explanation since this empire was dominant at the time. Perhaps new tax pressures led to a renewed emphasis on increased local production (after Gitin). Perhaps the local fields around Ashkelon were to replace fields lost to Assyria as Israel Finkelstein argued for the seventh-century Negev (1994). These explanations, however, fail to convince because they are chronologically narrow. If the move to the hinterland was just the result of a temporary pressure or setback, one might imagine that Tel Ashkelon's patterns would revert once the Assyrian pressure was removed. However, the seventh-century change that took place in Tel Ashkelon's relationship with its hinterland endured through the medieval period. Whether the inhabitants were Philistines, Phoenicians, Greeks, Romans, Fatimids, or Mamluks, the agricultural potential of the region was never again ignored.

Several studies show that the late Iron Age was somewhat wetter than preceding centuries, perhaps increasing the viability of the area around Ashkelon:

1. Aharon Horowitz suggests that pollen analyzed from two bore holes in Haifa Bay showed an increase in arboreal pollen of oak (*Quercus* sp.) and olive (*Olea europa*) from c. 700–600 B.C. The peak suggests that more vegetation was present following a period of drier climate (Horowitz 1979:214).

2. Tony Wilkinson cites studies of pollen cores from the Sea of Galilee that point to an abatement of oak woodlands during the second millennium B.C. with a substantial decline in oak starting c. 1000 B.C. and "a dramatic increase in olives in the eighth and seventh centuries B.C.E.

and fourth and fifth centuries C.E." (Wilkinson 2003:144).

3. Thomas Litt argues that around twenty-six hundred years ago, evergreen and deciduous oak as well as olive values increase and grapes appear in the pollen record from the Dead Sea, signaling a more moist period (Litt et al. 2012:102).

4. Recent studies by Frank H. Neumann show a rise in the level of the Dead Sea at the end of the Iron Age that indicates more precipitation; however, some sand layers in the Zeᵓelim core attest to arid fluctuations (Neumann et al. 2010:760–61).

5. In conjunction with these findings, the climate proxy data of Arie Issar and Mattanyah Zohar show that, following a cool, humid period around 1000 B.C., a warm and dry period occurred with a nadir at 850 B.C. Following this, conditions were increasingly favorable to agriculture with a peak between the third century B.C. and the third century A.D. (Issar and Zohar 2007:193).

Often, such changes in the landscape result not merely from a change in climate but from a new geographical potential which is unlocked by a new technology. One thinks of transformations such as the Neolithic revolution or the Roman advances in water management which transformed how land was used or how its economic potential was viewed. Obviously, what happened in the seventh century was not on that scale, but it was a unilinear change of that type. We are not sure of the particulars, but we would note that it is during the discussion of the Iron II that Huster's summary starts to include the term "winepress," a theme which will dominate the next millennia. The use of the land around Ashkelon changed. Some new method, new technology, or new condition allowed the vineyards to grow, unlocking long latent agricultural potential in Tel Ashkelon's hinterland.

Persian–Hellenistic Periods

Following the devastation of Tel Ashkelon in 604 B.C., the site lay abandoned until it was refounded under the political sway of Tyre. Likewise, other regional sites, such as Netiv Ha-ᶜAsara, reveal occupational gaps that suggest abandonment following this event, signaling that the destruction of Tel

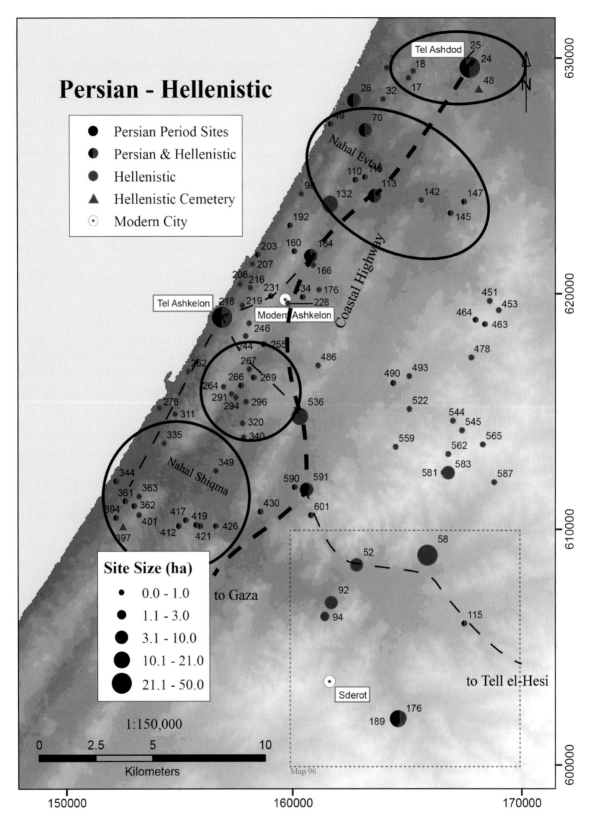

Figure 4.3: Map of Ashkelon in the Persian/Hellenistic period with road system over modern topography. Circles mark clusters of Iron IIC agricultural intensification for comparison.

Ashkelon was part of wider devastation (Shavit and Yasur-Landau 2005:83). Regional recovery from the destruction event and subsequent growth are indicated by the settlement density which shows continuity between the Iron II and Persian periods. More than this, the settlements of the Persian period follow the patterns of the late Iron II.

Tel Ashkelon, as would befit a Tyrian foundation, was once again a port with a strong interest in Mediterranean commerce. The excavations have uncovered a district of import/export warehouses which emphasize the commercial capacities of the city. Abundant imported Greek amphorae were decanted into smaller storage jars leaving mounds of imported containers (see *Ashkelon 1*, p. 314). The presence of a camel scapula, used for making bone implements, suggests long-distance trade from remote regions to the east (Stager 1993:108). The late Persian–Early Hellenistic period included Phoenician silver coins (Stager 1993:107) alongside facilities for producing wine for export (see *Ashkelon 1*, pp. 317, 322). By the Hellenistic period, the Letter of (Pseudo-)Aristeas lists Ashkelon, Joppa, Gaza, and Ptolemais (Acco) as harbors for maritime trade, and excavations at Ashkelon have found imported Rhodian and Italic transport amphorae and fine wares from Chios, Greece, and Italy (see *Ashkelon 1*, pp. 290, 293).

Huster's work has substantially lowered the number of Persian period sites in the Ashkelon region, and it is justifiably described as sparse. In many ways, this reshaping of the settlement pattern is one of his great contributions, but the Persian patterns still show a use of the landscape that differs from Ashkelon's Bronze and early Iron Age patterns. Specifically, beyond the framework of substantial sites along the roads, tiny agricultural sites exist near wadi channels or as satellites of regional centers (see figure 5.3). This is true even after the many "patch" sites have been removed. As in the Iron IIC, the immediate hinterland of Tel Ashkelon included agricultural villages.

Perhaps the most significant site founded in the Persian period is Majdal, 3 km east of Tel Ashkelon (Site 164). This site is emblematic of all the inland interests of the region. It is close enough to the coastal highway to be a way station between Tel Obed and Tel Poran, while being able to stand as an intermediary between all of the east-west routes and Tel Ashkelon. The remainder of the regional history can be summarized as the rise of Majdal. In the Hellenistic period, the appearance of sites farther inland such as Horvat Hoga, Bureir,

Huleiqat (center), Barbara, and Nahal Evtah (site 132)—together with the increased settlement density of smaller sites—not only indicate regional growth and in-filling of previously unsettled territory but also the development of another tier of larger settlements that supported satellite villages, hamlets, and farmsteads while acting as intermediaries between those sites and the gateway of Tel Ashkelon.

Roman and Byzantine Periods

By far, the densest settlement patterns in all regions of Palestine occurred during the Roman and Byzantine (Late Roman) periods. In the region of Ashkelon, more sites were founded in marginal areas away from permanent water sources, continuing a trend from the Hellenistic period, and many wells and cisterns at Tel Ashkelon and numerous other sites dated to the Byzantine period attest to the exploitation of the coastal aquifer in that and succeeding periods. During the Roman period, the port city of Ashkelon itself was noted as a center for wheat trade and also produced, inter alia, henna, dates, and onions (such as *caepa Ascalonia*; Stager 1993:105). The city's affluence is marked not only by a mint that produced silver coins proclaiming the free status of the city but also by monumental public architecture, such as the Severan forum and nearby basilica (Stager 1993:111).

The imported pottery of the Roman and Later Roman periods detailed by Barbara Johnson (*Ashkelon 2*) illuminates the wide trade network in which Ashkelon participated during those periods. Even utilitarian items such as lamps were imported from Italy, Asia Minor, Egypt, and North Africa (*Ashkelon 2*, p. 127). Although no large marketplace or port facilities have been found at the site of Tel Ashkelon, the recovered fragments of transport amphorae demonstrate the wide trade connections between the city and various Mediterranean maritime outlets, arriving at the exchange gateway with the three staples of the ancient world: wine, oil, and grain (*Ashkelon 2*, p. 135).

During these periods, the Ashkelon region as a whole became a major center for wine export. Coupled with a plethora of winepresses in the hinterland, imported ceramics and local pottery production facilities testify to the importance of this commodity, especially from the fourth century A.D. forward. Both the *Gazition* and *Ashkalónion* have been found in far-flung locales such as London, Trier, and the Crimea as markers of the

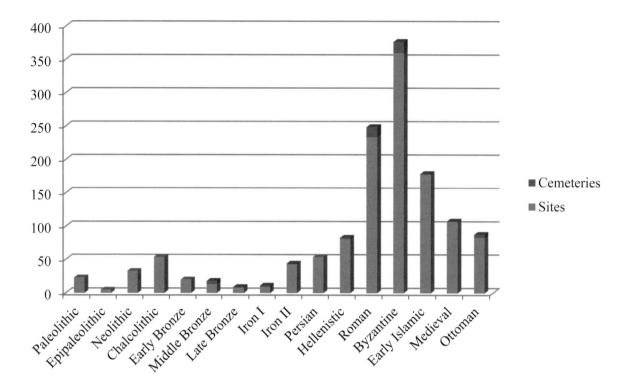

Figure 4.4: Graph of Settlement Density in the Ashkelon region
based upon the number of recorded sites.

wine exported from the Ashkelon region to the Byzantine Christian world (Johnson and Stager 1995:103–4; see also Mayerson 1993).

The Roman and Byzantine periods witnessed dense settlement within the region, in many cases into previously vacant areas, which can be categorized into a complex hierarchy that included cities and towns, villages and hamlets, and single installations or burial sites. The coverage of the landscape with agricultural plots appears to be comprehensive. Connections between farmsteads and villages and larger sites presented opportunities for the larger sites to support the smaller entities with a more diverse array of goods and services. These larger sites functioned as central places within the classical definitions of the term, providing outlets for the wine produced by satellites such as the Byzantine agricultural estate in Barnea with its associated oil and winepresses, storehouses, and pottery kilns (Israel 1993; 1995a; see also Fabian, Nahshoni, and Ein Gedy 1995; Nahshoni 1999; and Varga 1999 for other sites with winepresses). Ashkelon enjoyed prosperity as the dominant regional exchange gateway mediating the wine trade between the growing region and the consumers across the Mediterranean. The

Roman and Byzantine settlement is an elaboration of an attitude toward the landscape that began in the Iron IIC. Once the land behind Ashkelon was seen as agriculturally viable, the succeeding millennium witnessed the intensified exploitation of this resource.

The Demise of the Gateway (Early Islamic–Mamluk)

Following the Byzantine period, the overall settlement density exhibits in the Ashkelon region declined from 360 sites in the Byzantine period to 177 sites in the Early Islamic. Despite the regression in number of sites and site size, some continuity between Byzantine and Early Islamic periods existed. As Huster observes, the persistent use of winepresses indicates that the wine industry continued, albeit decreased, after the Islamic conquest. The settlement patterns during the Early Islamic and Crusader periods reveal inland centers at sites on the coastal highway with occupational histories from the Hellenistic period or earlier such as Tel Poran, Nahal Evtah (site 132), El Mejdel (site 433), Barbara, and Bureir with smaller sites remaining from the Byzantine period widely distributed in the region, many of which were satellites of larger

Figure 4.5: British Aerial Photograph, January 5, 1945, showing the agricultural potential of the region from the nineteenth-century field system around Ashkelon; linear landscape features south of the Majdal road marked from high-resolution analysis.

towns. While diminished, the wider region continued the agricultural trajectory that began in the late Iron Age.

Tel Ashkelon remained as the only major "urban center" in the region following the decline of Ashdod. Tel Ashkelon, the port city that textual sources describe as a thriving city with fertile hinterland and hail as "the bride of Syria" continued its millennia-old function as the region's premier seaport and as a *ribāṭ*, part of the coastal warning system. The Umayyad caliph ʿAbd al-Malik fortified the city and established a mint that issued coins with the *šahādah* and the phrase "Struck in Filasṭīn ʿAsqalān" (Sharon in *Ashkelon 1*, p. 408). During the Abbasid caliphate, Mahdī built a mosque and minaret (Clermont-Ganneau 1887:485). The site was clearly prosperous in the Fatimid period as indicated by massive fortifications and illustrated by a cache of gold jewelry recovered in excavations (Stager 1993:112).

In many ways, the late first millennium A.D. appears as a slightly diminished version of the Byzantine settlement patterns. The very smallest Byzantine sites are missing from the map, and it is likely that many of the villages were somewhat smaller—though this is beyond the resolution of survey data. Tel Ashkelon, however, does not seem to be diminished at all. The fortifications of the period show that the entire 60-hectare settlement was still protected, and within the city, every area of the site shows substantive occupation in this period (Hoffman 2003).

After the fall of Jerusalem in A.D. 1099, Tel Ashkelon remained in Fatimid control and, together with Tyre, remained a stronghold against the Franks (Sharon in *Ashkelon 1*, p. 409). Muslim efforts to thwart the Crusaders' governance of Palestine originated from Ashkelon with the assistance of supplies shipped from Egypt. The construction of three Crusader castles—Beth Gibelin (Beth Guvrin), Ibelin (Yavneh), and Blanchgard (Tell es-Safi)—were designed to restrict Ashkelon inland influence. Yet the city, as it had since its founding, was able to ignore the hinterland and maintain itself using maritime networks. In the end, it took an additional seven months of siege for Baldwin III to capture the city in 1153. Saladin retook the city in 1187, but it was recaptured by the armies of the Third Crusade in 1191 after its defenses were systematically demolished by Saladin's forces. The Crusaders' interest in the site as a beachhead resulted in fortification efforts by

Richard the Lionheart in 1192 and Richard, Earl of Cornwall, in 1241.

After Tel Ashkelon's final destruction in the late thirteenth century, the land behind Ashkelon was now just one more landlocked region of the southern Levant, wholly dependent on local conditions. Majdal became the new locus of administration, and, in a complete inversion of the Bronze Age settlement model, Tel Ashkelon was incorporated into the agricultural hinterland of inland villages.

Conclusion

Bruce Trigger's observation that "Settlement Archaeology forces us to think through problems from a new angle—that of social relations" (1967:158) also resonates on an economic level for this consideration of the connectivity of the sites in the Ashkelon region. While Central Place Theory examines economic behavior among many centers at a regional scale, the role of Ashkelon in international trade almost from its inception requires a broader model of settlement that accounts for such anomalous sites.

From the settlement data, it appears that Tel Ashkelon was so integrated into the Mediterranean world that its local terrestrial connections never substantially influenced its economic trajectory. In some moments, a single phenomenon influenced both Tel Ashkelon and its hinterland, such as the collapse of the Early Bronze Age or the destruction of the Babylonians, but these are rare. For more than a thousand years, Tel Ashkelon was a flourishing port surrounded by virtually empty land. Even when Tel Ashkelon traded inland, there is no evidence that it directly controlled the routes. Whether the inhabitants of Tel Ashkelon were unable or simply unwilling to exploit the region next door, this did not seem to be to their detriment. Stager's model of "port power" highlights that Ashkelon did not control the hinterland because it was not necessary. The distant hinterland brought goods to the port of its own accord.

When the Ashkelon hinterland was finally settled, it was done in a way that established a parallel agricultural world. The intense settlement throughout the region and subsequent development of central places in this hinterland signal a change in settlement patterns from somewhat "static" in the Bronze and Iron Ages to "dynamic" in the Persian and subsequent periods. Secondary markets (classic central places) and smaller satellites were established in those periods, from which the larger centers seemed to persist through the medieval period. Tel Ashkelon undoubtedly benefited from the increased prosperity of the surrounding villages, but it is not clear that the grapes or wine from 2 km away were preferred to those from 25 km away. Tel Ashkelon itself was surrounded by a network of agricultural fields that completely filled the landscape (see figure 4.5). Still, Tel Ashkelon was independent enough that when the agricultural fortunes of the region declined after the Byzantine period, the seaport continued to thrive.

In the end, however, Tel Ashkelon's unique networks were its downfall. Because the site had the ability to maintain maritime connections in the face of local opposition and because it sat just a few kilometers from the major coastal road, it was a tempting beachhead for Europeans. The threat of a city able to exist outside of the terrestrial caliphates of the day was too great, so Tel Ashkelon was intentionally left in ruins. The irony, of course, is that just as Tel Ashkelon ignored its hinterland, so the hinterland ignored the destruction of Ashkelon. The agricultural settlement pattern did not change. Crops were still harvested. Life went on without maritime trade.

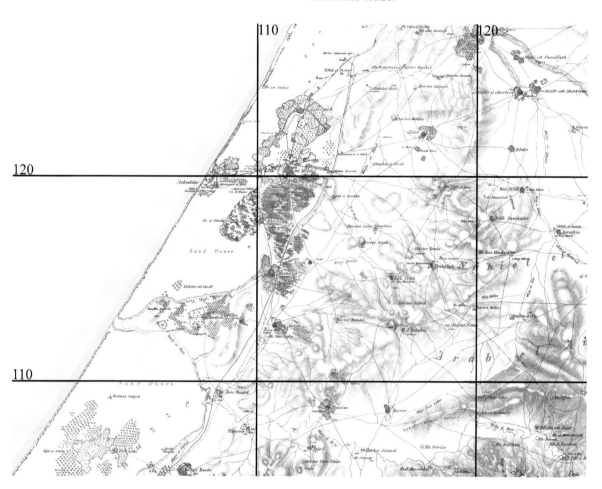

Figure 4.6: The Ashkelon Region in the late nineteenth century A.D. (from Conder and Kitchener 1882: sheet 16; 1883: sheets 19 and 20). Scan courtesy of Todd Bolen.

5. Regional Archaeological Survey: Map of Sderot (96)

by Yaakov Huster

The archaeological survey of the Map of Sderot (96) was conducted as part of the Archaeological Survey of Israel (ASI), a project initiated in 1964 by the state of Israel to undertake a systematic survey of the entire country by dividing it into 10 x 10 km squares (see Dagan n.d.). These surveys followed the 1:20,000 map sheets first published by the Survey of Palestine in 1931, based on survey work in the 1920s; the Map of Sderot corresponds to map sheet 11-10, Bureir (map ref. 110-120/100-110, OIG). The division of the survey is reflected in the division of sites by paragraph in the 1964 Schedule of Monuments and Sites, in Hebrew *Reshumot—Yalqut HaPirsumim*, No. 1091 (Yalqut HaPirsumim 1964). In that publication, the Map of Sderot is recorded in paragraph 96.

As the survey of Map 96 was undertaken as part of the Archaeological Survey of Israel, the format of the publication of its results largely follows that in the Archaeological Survey of Israel publications. This is a particularly important point to note, given that the publication of M. Allen's survey of the Map of Ashkelon (92; *Ashkelon 1*)—which serves as an important comparative dataset for the current survey—does not follow this format in many respects. As a result, it is important to introduce the format of the ASI publications and to note where Allen differs from that format.

In the catalogue of sites, the entries are presented in the order of 1 km² squares, starting in the northwest corner of the map and working in rows across before ending in the southeast corner of the map. (By contrast, while Allen also presents his sites in 1 km² squares, he begins in the southwest corner of the map and proceeds by columns, ending in the northeast corner.) The first row of the entry heading includes the site number, its serial number, its coordinates in the Old Israel Grid (OIG), and its corresponding coordinates in the New Israel Grid (NIG). The serial number reflects the Mandatory 1:20,000 scale map sheet (11/10) followed by the specific square kilometer on the map and the number of the site within that square kilometer. The numbering of the square kilometers for this purpose begins in the southwest corner of the map and proceeds in columns upward (i.e., the order used by Allen to arrange his sites; note that Allen uses his serial numbers as site numbers).

The site numbers and coordinates are followed in the heading by the name or names of the sites. If the site has a declared name (e.g., a tell or a *khirbeh*), that name is given; in other cases, the name of an adjacent city/town/moshav/kibbutz or other geographical feature is given. Thus multiple sites may have the same name (sometimes qualified by direction), indicating the portion of the settlement or geographical feature. As a result, the site numbers and coordinates are generally better used as site references, since they are unique. The basic sources of the names are the Schedules of Monuments and Sites, starting with No. 1091 (Yalqut HaPirsumim 1964) with periodic updates; and the Map of Ashqelon, scale 1:50,000, published by the Survey of Israel (1995). Other important data used come from sources relating to the Survey of Western Palestine and those concerning the Mandatory surveys and records files. These sources are marked either "S" or "M" in the heading. The Survey of Western Palestine sources include the *Memoirs* of the survey (Conder and Kitchener 1881–83); map sheet XX of the survey, scale 1:63,360; and the Arabic and English name lists (Palmer 1881). The Mandatory sources include the 1929 and 1944 Schedules of Historical Monuments and Sites; Survey of Palestine map sheet 11-10, Bureir (Jaffa, 1931); and the Department of Antiquities Geographical List of the Mandatory Records Files (Jerusalem 1976). The specific issue of the Map of Bureir in use was updated on November 11 and November 17, 1959, probably by L. Y. Rahmani from the Israeli Department of Antiquities. The updating consisted of the annotation of non-printed site names and their supposed locations on the map.

The heading is followed by the description of the site itself: its geographical and geological setting, observed architectural remains, and artifacts noted and collected. Where relevant, dating of collected ceramic and/or lithic finds is noted. (The periodization used here follows that discussed in chapter 1 above; see also the discussion under Roman and Byzantine Periods and medieval period below.) For some sites, we have included a discussion of their identification in cases where the site can be matched to settlements known from historical sources or where previous site identifications (including in some cases the official, declared name of the site) are erroneous.

Geological and Geographical Overview

The area of the Map of Sderot extends over the central portion of the southern coastal plain of Israel. This specific area comprises several landscape units formed by deposits originating from three sources: the sea, responsible for the deposition of sand dunes from the west; the wadi system, depositing alluvium from the elevated regions to the east; and the wind, bringing dust primarily from the south and southwest (Horowitz 1979:109). All these deposits have undergone and are still undergoing pedogenic processes, which occur in situ, modifying the deposits. It is well accepted by various investigators that ingressions of the Mediterranean during the *Quaternary* pushed dunes forward (Nir and Bar-Yosef 1976:27–39; Horowitz 1979:96–97). The sand dunes later solidified into calcareous sandstone, comprising several *kurkar* ridges that run parallel to one another along the coast of the Mediterranean Sea. The nomenclature employed for the various ridges follows the outcrops of these sediments and their localities, running from west to east: Ziqim Ridge, Yad Mordekhay Ridge, Erez Ridge, Nirᶜam Ridge, Yakhini Ridge, and Hirbet Herev Ridge. Three of these ridges are present within the surveyed area. The Hirbet Herev Ridge (+180 m), one of the few outcrops of an earlier phase of the *Gaza Formation* that can presently be seen, lies along the southeastern edge of the map area. It comprises several meters of calcareous sandstone and is associated with other sediments overlying the *Ahuzam Conglomerate* in other localities. Here, the *kurkar* phase is overlaid by a younger sediment, a layer of *hamra* that consists of a red paleosol, roughly 2–3 m thick, called the *Dorot Hamra Member* (Horowitz 1979:111). The top of this *hamra* layer yielded Late Acheulean artifacts. The next *kurkar* ridge, the Nirᶜam Ridge, runs roughly southwest to northeast through the survey area. It is not a typical *kurkar* ridge and comprises a series of thick cross-bedded aeolian calcareous sandstone hills extended over a width of 2 km, almost touching the next western ridge. Its highest elevations in the survey area vary between 90–120 m (topographic Map of Bureir; Horowitz 1979:Table 5.1). Here, too, the *kurkar* is overlain by a *hamra* layer, although it is mostly eroded due to post-depositional processes. In certain locations the *hamra* is sandwiched between two *kurkar* layers. The Erez Ridge crosses the northwestern edge of the surveyed area. The *hamra* layer exists here as well, yielding flint artifacts ascribed to the Lower Paleolithic period, as well as the *hamra* layers of the previous *kurkar* ridge. In between the hilly zones, in the east and in the west of the surveyed region, is the low terrain of the area. It is an alluvial plain, limited by low hills situated in the north and in the south of it. The soil here contains a mixture of all the components of the lands around: sand, clay, silt, and loess. The last component covers wide areas in the region. Between Dorot and Ruhama loess is between 25–30 m deep in places and at present is still being deposited during dust storms. On the other hand, it has

been seriously eroded by the recent drainage system. On the top of the loessic accumulations several archaeological sites were surveyed.

The main geographical feature in the region is Nahal Shiqma (Wadi Hesi), one of the largest and oldest wadis in the southern coastal plain. This wadi crosses the central section of the map from east to west. In the past, as indicated by the existence of archaeological sites, perennial or seasonal water sources were available in the western part of map 96, probably due to a wetter climate. This assumption is reinforced and illustrated by the existence of a tract of land located just to the south of the wadi, the so-called Uyun es Sahra, meaning "the springs of the Badlands" in Arabic. Farther to the east the sources were and still are available permanently. Several early period sites are therefore located near the banks and tributaries of the wadi. In the surveyed area the annual precipitation average is c. 400 mm. Measurements carried out in four modern settlements over a number of years have yielded the following results: Erez (on the northwestern edge, beyond the map), 25 years—436 mm; Bror Hayil, 22 years—396 mm: Nirᶜam, 23 years—390 mm; Dorot, 32 years—344 mm (Cohen 2010:20). The large drainage basin of c. 750 km² and the enormous quantities of water flowing almost every winter enrich the aquifer, which provides ample water. The utilization of these sources, the aquifer and the precipitation, is recognizable through the presence of many wells and almost one hundred cisterns from the Byzantine period in the surveyed area. Nahal Shiqma also provided flint as a raw material for tool production. Pebbles dislocated from the exposed *Ahuzam Conglomerate* and from Eocene limestone outcrops in the eastern section of the wadi were carried to the west by major floods and became available for knappers. At prehistoric period sites, crude pebbles form part of the stone inventory. More recent floods in the wadi are responsible for the partial clay deposits at sites located near the banks.

History of Research

Research in the surveyed area began in the nineteenth century, mainly conducted by travelers and explorers attempting to identify biblical sites (Robinson and Smith 1841; Guérin 1869; Warren 1871). Systematic surveys were conducted by Conder and Kitchener (1881–83), who described 12 sizeable sites within Map 96. Petrie's later work at Tell el-Hesi established a pottery sequence (1891:40–50) that enabled him to determine the occupational history of dozens of sites in southern Palestine (1891:51–62), 10 of which are located in the Map of Sderot. Charles Clermont-Ganneau (1896:437–38) described several sites that he visited during his journey from Gaza to Jerusalem, providing comprehensive historical, geographical, and linguistic surveys. Generally, this research covered almost all the area of Map 96, but focused mainly on the remains along the traditional routes that crossed its northern portion from west to east, i.e., the road leading from Gaza to Beit Guvrin and on to Hebron.

More recently, Ram Gophna (1963; 1966; 1970) conducted studies in the area of Map 96, as part of his investigations of the southern part of the country. In the 1970s, the author participated in a formal prehistoric archaeological survey of the central part of Nahal Shiqma (Wadi Hesi), carried out over an extensive area of 140 km² (Lamdan et al. 1977), including large portions of the Map of Sderot. The data obtained from this survey concerning the Late Bronze and Iron I period sites, together with his own previous studies, enabled Ram Gophna (1981) to suggest a historical and geopolitical framework for the relationship between the Judahite and Philistine entities. Later, a comprehensive study of the transitional area between arable country and the desert (Cohen 1993) summarized the settlement patterns during selected periods in a region of 1200 km², including all of Map 96; the study mentioned 50 archaeological sites in the map area, all of them described previously in the Nahal Shiqma survey publication. A less extensive regional analysis involving geographical, geological, and archaeological issues was carried out on the city and immediate vicinity of Sderot, the only city situated within Map 96 (Sasson 2010).

Excavations

In 1941 Jacob Ory directed the first excavation undertaken within the map area, near Umm Tabun (site 94). Some 500 m east (site 95) of the settlement, Ory excavated a painted tomb that he had discovered in 1922. Later, the site was rediscovered by Tsafrir, who subsequently published his findings (1968). The paintings were later analyzed by Talila Michaeli (1990). Two other burial systems were probed, the first at the southern edge of Hurvat Hoga (site 176; Meron and Ginat 1963), the second at the Arab village Bureir (site 64; Meron 1975). At the center of Hurvat Hoga (site 189), Yosef Porat (1976) excavated an extensive structure of the Iron II. Nearby, remains of a settlement from the Byzantine period and a pottery workshop from the Umayyad period were unearthed (Varga 1999a, wrong coordinates). At H. Herev (site 206) scanty remains from the Byzantine period were discovered (Schuster 2000a). Following accelerated development of the area that consisted mainly of road-paving work, several excavations were conducted, most of them at Khirbet

Lasan (site 186) and its vicinity. Ofer Katz (2012) excavated a Byzantine winepress and a structure from the Ottoman period. Pirhiya Nahshoni and Yossi Nagar (2002) excavated pit graves and Ilan Peretz (2011) exposed cist tombs, all part of an extensive cemetery from the Byzantine period. Nearby, at site 170, Nir°am Junction, Yishai Schuster (2000b) excavated remains of an industrial area dated also to the Byzantine period. Most recently, Gregory Seriy conducted salvage excavations before the construction of a railroad track (Seriy 2010).

Archaeological Overview

The Lower Paleolithic Period

The Map of Sderot is characterized by interrupted settlement during the prehistoric periods. The Middle and Upper Paleolithic periods as well as the Epipaleolithic are absent. The last stage of the Lower Paleolithic period, however, is represented by the typical element of the Upper Acheulean culture, the handaxe. Lower Paleolithic remains were recorded at 61 sites and findspots that are concentrated in two parts of the surveyed area: along the southeastern edge, on hills related to the Hirbet Herev *kurkar* ridge; and in the west, on *hamra* paleosols overlying calcareous sandstone. Predominant finds at these sites are handaxes accompanied by elements created during the industrial process, mainly primary flakes and tools trimmed from them. Other elements related to the flint industry are pebbles, exhausted cores, and waste, all of them reinforcing the conclusion that knapping activities occurred in situ. The typology and technology of the lithic industry all over the survey area are homogeneous. Despite the intensive use of the Levallois technique and, in some cases, the appearance of tools of Mousterian type, features such as the high percentage of handaxes preclude the attribution of sites to the Middle Paleolithic, instead dating the industry to the last stages of the Lower Paleolithic period. The same picture was observed in the Kissufim area (Ronen et al. 1972); on the other hand, south of Kissufim, in the central portion of the lower Besor region in the northwestern Negev, the Middle Paleolithic was the most significant of the Paleolithic eras in the region (Gazit 1996:11*).

The Neolithic Period

No clearly identifiable Neolithic sites were found. Only three findspots were recorded, all near wadis—Nahal Shiqma, Nahal Hoga, and Nahal Ruhama—yielding four arrowheads. The paucity of sites and finds related to this period corresponds to that of the area directly to the north, Map 92 (*Ashkelon 1*, p. 27).

The Chalcolithic Period

Chalcolithic remains were recorded at eight sites, all near wadis. All of the settlements are located on loessic soils. A cluster of four sites was found along a length of 2 km of Nahal Ruhama. Here, the relatively small sites occupy areas varying from 500 m² to 2500 m² and contain few building remains. The other sites are located near Nahal Hoga (two sites), Nahal Shiqma, and Wadi Abu Ali.

The Bronze Age

The Bronze Age is sparsely represented in the survey area. No traces of the Early Bronze Age were found within the area of the map. The complete absence of Early Bronze Age sites corresponds to the results in the area surveyed by Allen (*Ashkelon 1*, pp. 30–33) directly to the north of our survey region. In that 100 km² area (Map 92—Ashkelon), no Early Bronze Age remains were found. Within the Map of Sderot, the Middle Bronze Age I is represented by two sites (61 and 138), both cemeteries. While no traces of the Middle Bronze II Age were found, Late Bronze Age remains were documented at three sites (88, 114, and 177). Apparently, security conditions were favorable during the Late Bronze Age, allowing settlement in areas distant from the major cities.

The Iron Age I

Settlement remains of Iron Age I were found at one site in the south of the surveyed area. This site (177) also yielded Late Bronze finds (figure 5.47). The small quantity of sites from this period is consistent with the results of other surveys over a wide region. In Map 92, the Iron I period is represented by a total of two sherds. Furthermore, not a single sherd of painted Philistine pottery was found in four years of surveying (Allen in *Ashkelon 1*, p. 30). In Map 97 (Ruhama), directly to the east of Map 96, excavations at Tell el-Hesi have yielded a small amount of Philistine pottery: The American excavations found a few sherds of what may be tenth-century Philistine bowls, in fills (Jeffrey Blakely, pers. comm.). At Tell Keshet (also in Map 97), one white-slipped Philistine sherd decorated with a preening bird was seen by Jeffrey Blakely (pers. comm.). Additional Philistine sherds from this site had been reported previously (Lamdan at al. 1977:76). Farther to the east, within the area of Map 98 (Lakhish), no traces of Iron I were found (Dagan 1992:17*). Directly to the

southwest of our survey area, along the banks of Nahal Mefalsim, a southern tributary of Nahal Shiqma (Wadi Hesi), Gophna surveyed two small Iron I sites (along with a third just to the west of our region; Gophna 1966:44–51).

The Iron Age II

Only three sites in the surveyed area yielded Iron II remains. Sites 176 and 189 are probably two sections of the large site of Hurvat Hoga (Nabi Huj), where a monumental mudbrick structure dated to Iron II was unearthed. H. Hoga is a well-established settlement overlaid by Persian, Hellenistic, Roman, Byzantine, Early Islamic, medieval, and Ottoman remains. Its true extent is obscured by the debris of later periods. Site 199 is merely a findspot of a round clay tablet, bearing an inscription attributed to the seventh century B.C. The paucity of Bronze and Iron Ages remains in the surveyed area is consistent with the area Allen surveyed directly to the north. In that map his survey team found good evidence of Iron Age II occupation at only four sites. Toward the east, the number of Iron Age II settlements increases. However, Gophna (1981), following his own surveys, claims an increase in the number of Iron II period settlements in the west, mainly on the coastal plain and explains this phenomenon in light of the distribution of the water sources: In the east, along the Wadi Hesi and its principal tributaries, several permanent springs exist. On the coastal plain ground water is available. Gophna (1981) has suggested that apart from the lack of permanent water sources within the territory of map 96, the paucity of settlements from the Late Bronze and Iron Ages in the central basin of Nahal Shiqma (Wadi Hesi) was also for geopolitical reasons. Gophna assumed that this wide area was a marginal region between the eastern kingdom of Lachish and the western cities of Gaza and Ashkelon during the Late Bronze period, and that in the Iron Age the same region constituted a geographical, ethnic, and political triple border between Judah in the east and the kingdoms of Gaza and Ashkelon in the west and was therefore almost empty of settlements.

The Persian Period

The Persian period is represented at three sites. Site 115, north of Nahal Shiqma, is located at a distance from other Iron and Persian period sites, while sites 176 and 189 were found overlaying Iron II remains. At the latter sites, the pottery collection includes jars produced from a local greenish clay that can be seen in nearby wadis. The rural settlement in our survey area was sparse, probably due to the absence of important roads. On the map to the north (Map 92—Ashkelon), there is evidence of occupation at nine sites and slight evidence for five more. They are arranged mainly along longitudinal and latitudinal roads.

The Hellenistic Period

The number of sites increases to seven in this period. Three are located on multiperiod settlements containing remains from previous periods (sites 115, 176 and 189). Four others are located within or close to Arab villages (sites 52, 58, 92, and 94), and probably represent one of the first occupations of these places. The main obstacle concerning the identification of pottery from the Hellenistic period was the rarity of sherds belonging to imported vessels, the best chronological indicator for this period. Where severe identification difficulties arose because of the lack of indicative elements, the site was not incorporated into the period list. This fact may have diminished the total number of Hellenistic sites within the surveyed area. The opposite approach was implemented by Allen in the area located north of ours, in Map 92. There, the period list and the map of the Hellenistic period contain 38 sites, although the identification of 28 of them is questionable. In the Map of Urim (125), 10 Hellenistic sites were surveyed within the 100 km² area (Gazit 1996:15*); since two of them are questionable, only eight sites should be incorporated in the period list. Indeed, the Nahal Besor region is a semiarid area, although there are many springs along the Besor wadi (where most of these sites are concentrated). It seems, therefore, that the lower numbers are preferable, since they demonstrate a consistent range of 7–10 sites for 100 km² units.

The Roman and Byzantine Periods

The survey of Map 96 yielded a large number of sites attributed to these periods. While the first century B.C. and the seventh century A.D. clearly mark the beginning and end points of these periods, there is a certain controversy concerning the terminology used in their subdivision. The usual nomenclature in Israel defines the period from the first century B.C. until the middle of the second century A.D. as the Early Roman period, with the Late Roman period extending from this point until the early fourth century (A.D. 330). The Byzantine period is dated A.D. 330–638. Western scholars employ the terms "Late Roman" or "Late Roman/Byzantine" (e.g., *Ashkelon 2*, esp. 463) in order to cover the period from the third through the seventh centuries A.D. Allen (*Ashkelon 1*, esp. fig. 3.21) defines the Byzantine ("Late Roman") period somewhat differently, from c.

A.D. 400 to 640. In the survey of Map 96, the "classic" Israeli nomenclature is employed.

The Roman Period (63 B.C.–A.D. 330)

Remains of this period were generally defined broadly, since in most cases the findings did not allow the assignment of specific subphases. Sites where identification was questionable were revisited until indicative sherds were found. Forty-three sites were attributed to the Roman period. The majority of them, 36 sites, consists of settlements, occupations, and installations established during this timespan. A collapsed structure that may have been a mausoleum was found at site 137. Pottery scatters, large white tesserae, small colored tesserae, building remains, building stones, structural foundations, pieces of plaster, pieces of bonding material composed of lime, cement, ash, and crushed or entire sherds are the characteristic remains at these sites. The sites are located in all the environmental zones of the surveyed area, yet maintain close relationships to agricultural land. All the sites of the Roman period continued to exist in the Byzantine period.

The Byzantine Period (A.D. 330–638)

Byzantine remains were recorded at c. 120 sites. They are located throughout most of the surveyed area. The remains include the same elements described regarding the Roman period, and also contain many buildings and structures, some of them well preserved. Several of the sites represent large settlements. Others are connected to agricultural and industrial activities. Wells and cisterns are located inside the limits of villages as well as in outlying areas. Most of the wells were also used in later periods. Cisterns were found both in settlements and in the rural zone. In three cases additional installations accompanied the cisterns: clay pipes at site 47, a channel at site 70, and a bath at site 75. The number of cisterns in the surveyed area is c. 70. Marble architectural remains, including complete or fragmentary columns, bases, and capitals, were found at many sites. In every case they were accompanied by typical church remains such as marble chancel posts and screens, enabling us to determine that 20 Byzantine churches had stood within the surveyed area. At seven sites, the exact location of mosaic paved floors is known. The picture is similar in the Ashkelon Map (92) to the north. Allen (*Ashkelon 1*, p. 41) noted the existence of elaborate rural domestic establishments, which he labeled "villas." He also states the possibility that some of these sites were monastic settlements or churches. In Map 96, as well as in a wide region in the hinterland of Ashkelon and Gaza, many villages, estates, farmsteads, and monasteries were established in Byzantine times, mainly for the production of wine. The associated demand for containers resulted in the establishment of an enormous ceramic industrial system. Within Map 96 at least 25 sites contain remains of pottery workshops; an enormous mound of misfired Gaza jars was recorded at site 61. Two large cemeteries (sites 16 and 185) were observed next to settlements. Fifteen burial systems were also found. These vaulted tombs were first used by wealthy inhabitants of the southern coastal plain in the Late Roman period. In the Byzantine period they were adapted by the Christian population (Huster and Sion 2006).

The Early Islamic Period (A.D. 638–1099)

Remains of the Early Islamic period were recorded at 42 sites, all of them previously settled during the Byzantine period; other Byzantine settlements were abandoned, and new settlements were not established. The amount of Islamic sherds is far lower than the large quantity of ceramics of the previous Byzantine period. Based on the distribution of the Islamic pottery scatters over the sites, it appears that the occupation area was much smaller than in Byzantine times. This observation is valid at least for sites located in current pasture lands, where modern agricultural activity has not removed the surface finds. Regardless, the remains indicate a sharp decline in settlement patterns. One site reveals, in addition to the pottery sequence, direct evidence of the early Islamic occupation: At Kh. Jalama (site 108), an Arabic inscription was found on a fragment of a marble column that belonged to a Byzantine church. The name of the caliph (Uthman b. Affan, A.D. 644–56) mentioned in the inscription allows the inscription to be dated to the second half of the seventh century A.D. (Moshe Sharon, pers. comm.). Almost all of the Early Islamic settlements were inhabited in later periods.

The Medieval Period
(Crusader and Mamluk periods, A.D. 1099–1516)

We suggest use of the terminology employed by Mitchell Allen in Map 92 (Ashkelon), namely medieval. Its parallel term, the Middle Ages, was used by Berman in survey map 91 (Ziqim) and in Maps 87–88 (Nizzanim West and Nizzanim East, respectively). The main reason to unite or combine the Crusader and the Mamluk periods (in the archaeological sense, and solely in regard to surveys) is the difficulty in dating the pottery assemblages of these periods, due to geographical, political, and commercial dynamics (Avissar and

Stern 2005:1). Allen (*Ashkelon 1*, p. 57) states that "we cannot easily identify Crusader in medieval assemblages." His period map presents sites of the Crusader and Mamluk periods without further differentiation, except for five sites identified as known Crusader villages. In Map 96 the pottery identification problem is identical or even more severe. During the second half of the thirteenth century, the southern border of the Kingdom of Jerusalem crossed the area of Map 96 from west to east (Prawer 1958:236). Here, intensive commercial relations probably took place, and transfer of wares from side to side would have been a common occurrence. Thirty-nine medieval sites were identified by the presence of twelfth- and thirteenth-century glazed wares and typical Mamluk painted pottery. The identification of certain sites containing identifiable remains of the twelfth and thirteenth centuries as Crusader villages is supported by complementary historical data and includes Zeita (site 9), Sumsum (52), Camsa (82), Shaᶜrata (112), and probably Kh. Hirbiya (37), if its identification with the Crusader village Elroeiheb is correct (Huster and Blakely, in press).

The Ottoman Period (A.D. 1516–1917) and the
British Mandate Period (A.D. 1917–1948)

Forty sites of the Ottoman period were recorded. Some of them were significant, sizeable settled villages. (The names of the villages in the taxpayers list from 1596 [Hütteroth and Abdulfattah 1977] are illustrated in italics below.) Four are destroyed Arab villages settled until 1948: Sumsum (site 52; *Sumsum*); Bureir (58; *Burayr*); Najd (92; *Najd al-Gharbi*); and Huj (175). The adjacent cemeteries also include ancient tombs, as indicated by the pottery sequence. The large areas of these villages, as marked on Mandatory maps and observed in aerial photographs, are not always consistent with the scattering of building materials, since the houses were built mainly of unfired mudbricks, not always recognizable in the terrain during survey. Other sites are well-known ruins: Kh. Zeita (site 9); Kh. Babliya (21; *Babilliya*); Kh. Ghayada (34); Kh. Hirbiya (37); Kh. Umm Qallum (79); Camsa (82; *Qamsa*); Kh. Umm Tabun (94); Kh. el Jalama (108; *Jalama*); Kh. Beit Tafa (111); Kh. Shaᶜrata (112; *Shaᶜarta al-Kubra, Tabi Burayr*); Kh. Najd (127);[1] Kh. Marashan (138); Kh. en Namus (182); Kh. Lasan (186; *Lisin*); and Kh. el Haj Harb (206). The remaining sites

---

[1] Based on the coordinates they give, Hütteroth and Abdulfattah (1977:150) appear to identify Kh. Najd with Dummar en-Najd, which appears throughout the sixteenth-century *defters*. Instead, Dummar en-Najd should probably be identified with Dimra (in Map 95; for more information on this identification, see Appendix B on p. 102).

consist of eighteen wells (sites 7, 22, 36, 50, 52, 53, 65, 68, 83, 92, 105, 109, 117, 119, 127, 138, 175, 191), two of them in use since the Byzantine period; three stone quarries (17, 43, 93); one lime kiln (80); and three sheikh's tombs—Esh Sheikh Mansur (174), Nabi Huj (site 176), and Sheikha Fatma (site 189). The rest are groups of dwellings or isolated structures from the late Ottoman period or from the British Mandate. In the nineteenth and early twentieth centuries, the area of Map 96, as with other regions east of Gaza, underwent a process of sedentarization under the control and encouragement of the authorities. The best example of this process in our area is the establishment of Huj by the Egyptian ruler or the governor of Palestine. Huj was visited by Robinson in 1838 shortly after it was built (Robinson and Smith 1841, II:384–86). Two additional settlements were founded, to the east of our survey area, during Egyptian rule in the 1830s: Sukkariyeh and Qubeibeh, both visited by Robinson in 1838 (Robinson and Smith 1841, II:392–94; see also Amiran 1953:253). In the 1890s, additional settlements were founded in the south, either as part of forced sedentarization (most famously, Beersheba) or as an act against Bedouin encroachment. In the latter case, three such villages were founded south of Map 96, on lands of Sultan Abdulhamid II: Kaufakha, Muharraqa, and Jaladiya (Levin, Kark, and Galilee 2009:13–14; Braslavi 1956:360; Amiran 1953:253–54). Petrie, who visited Kaufakha (south of our survey area) in 1890, related that "it is now being mined out for a new village settled from Gaza" (1891:52). Within the borders of Map 96, two younger small settlements were discerned: Kh. Marashan, a cluster of c. 20 houses arranged along a street, built sometime after Petrie (1891:52) visited it; and the most recent (site 105), informally named Mansura (meaning "victory"), built after the Second World War by Palestinian soldiers dismissed from the British army. The latter is the only settlement built in a location without ancient remains. It is mentioned here primarily because it was wrongly identified as the Mansura from the sixteenth-century Ottoman tax lists (Grossman 2010:76).

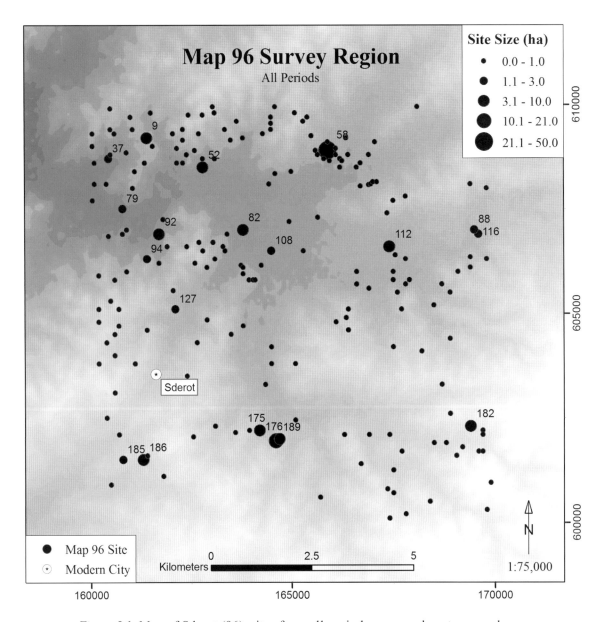

Figure 5.1: Map of Sderot (96), sites from all periods over modern topography.

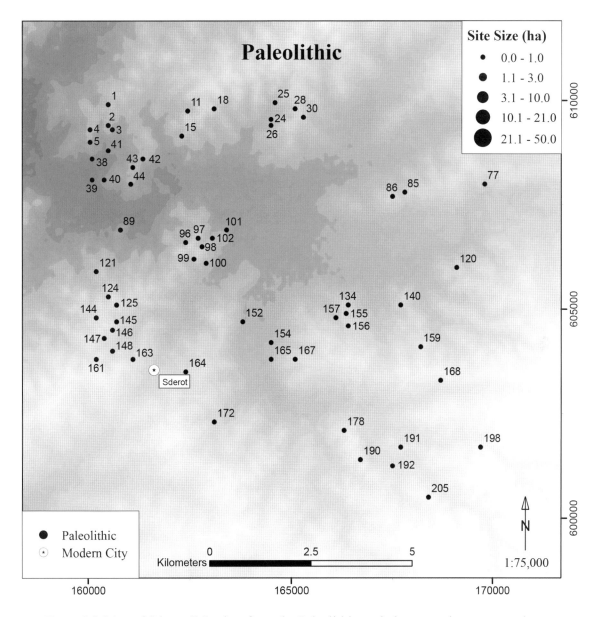

Figure 5.2: Map of Sderot (96), sites from the Paleolithic period over modern topography.

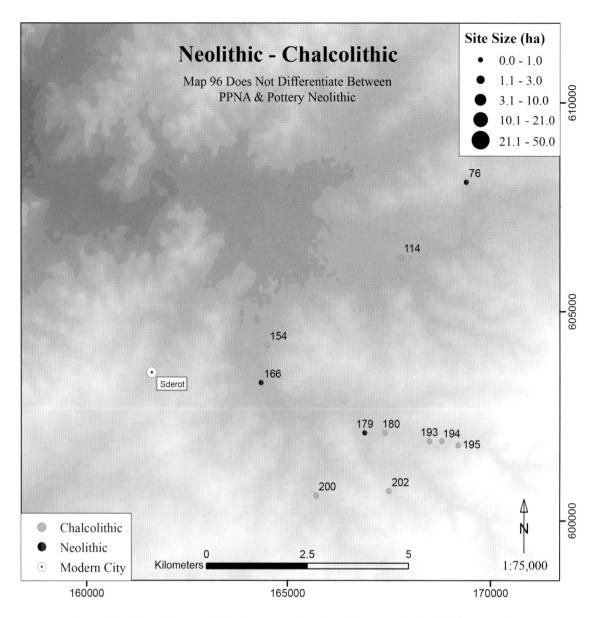

Figure 5.3: Map of Sderot (96), sites from the Neolithic and Chalcolithic periods
over modern topography.

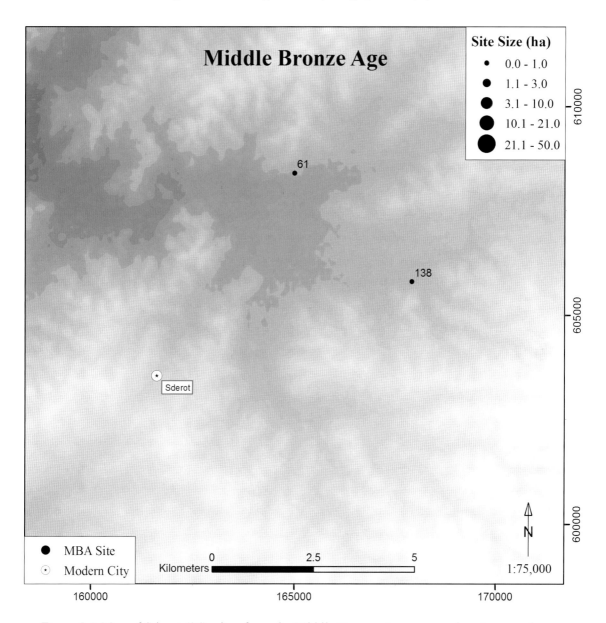

Figure 5.4: Map of Sderot (96), sites from the Middle Bronze Age over modern topography.

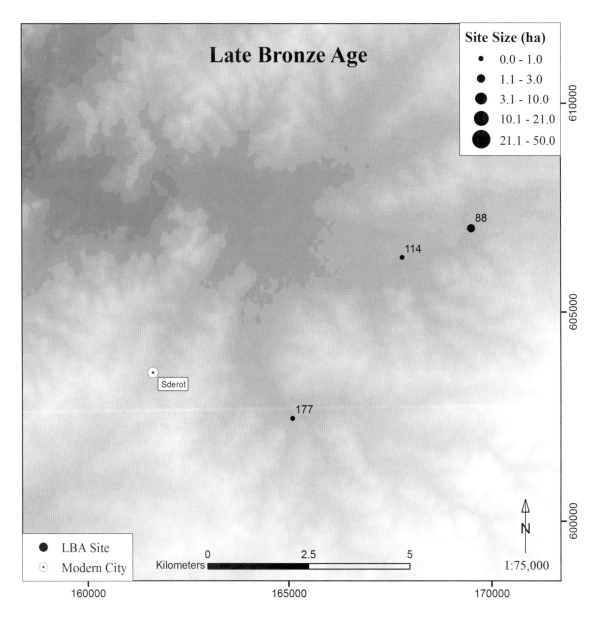

Figure 5.5: Map of Sderot (96), sites from the Late Bronze Age over modern topography.

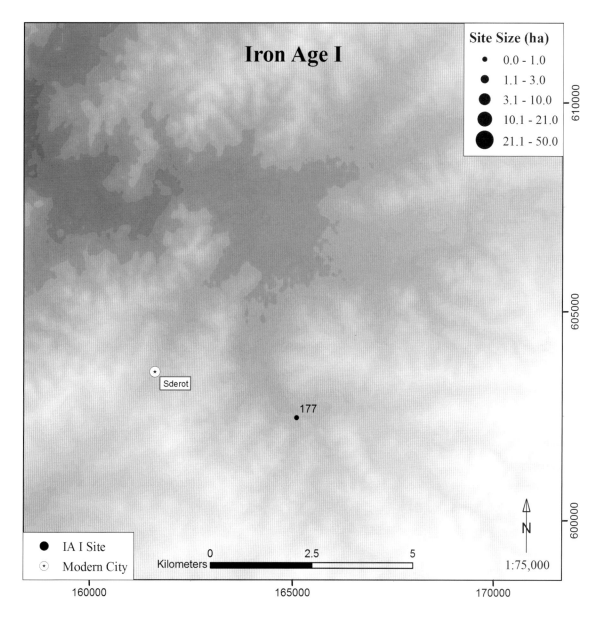

Figure 5.6: Map of Sderot (96), sites from the Iron Age I over modern topography.

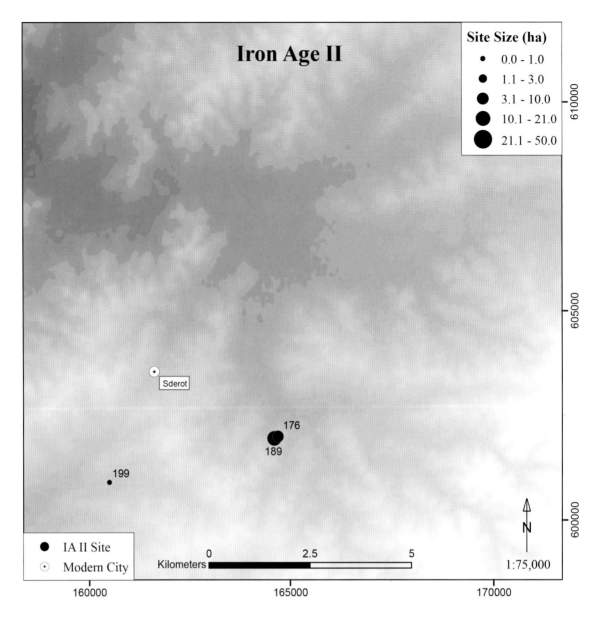

Figure 5.7: Map of Sderot (96), sites from the Iron Age II over modern topography.

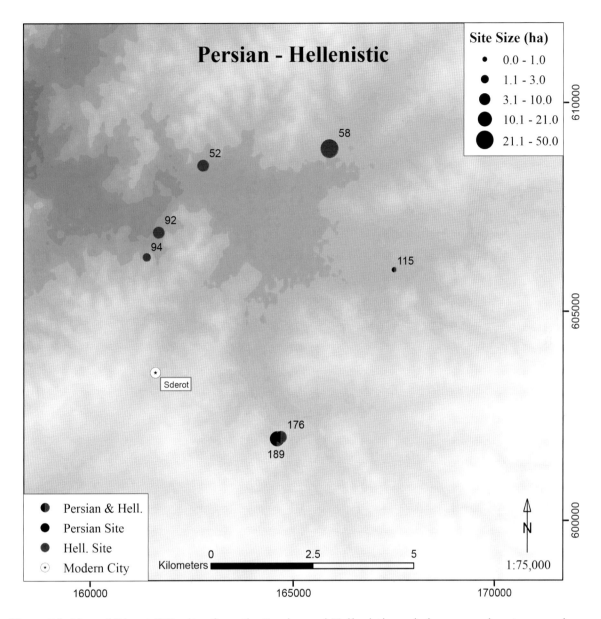

Figure 5.8: Map of Sderot (96), sites from the Persian and Hellenistic periods over modern topography.

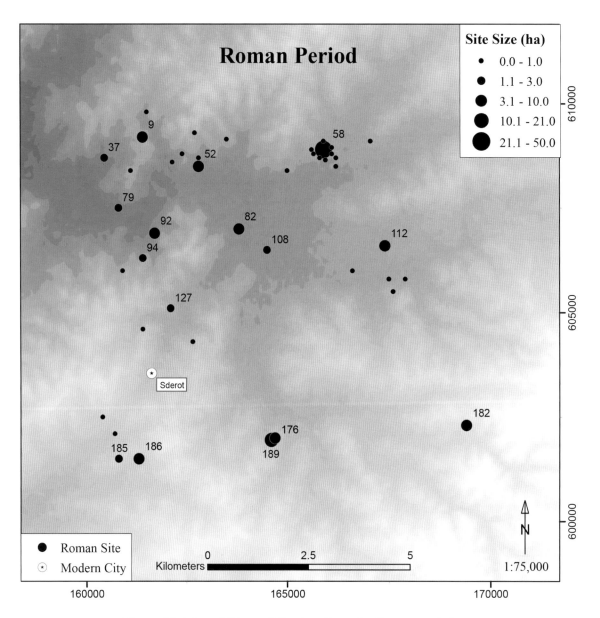

Figure 5.9: Map of Sderot (96), sites from the Roman period
larger than 3.1 hectares over modern topography

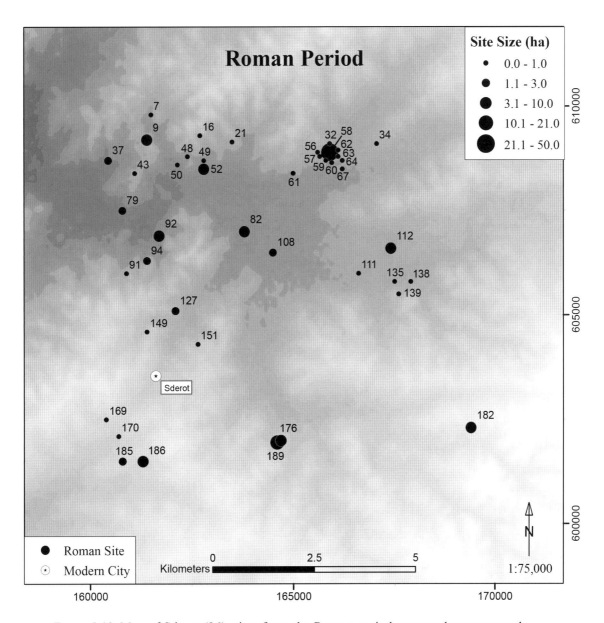

Figure 5.10: Map of Sderot (96), sites from the Roman period over modern topography.

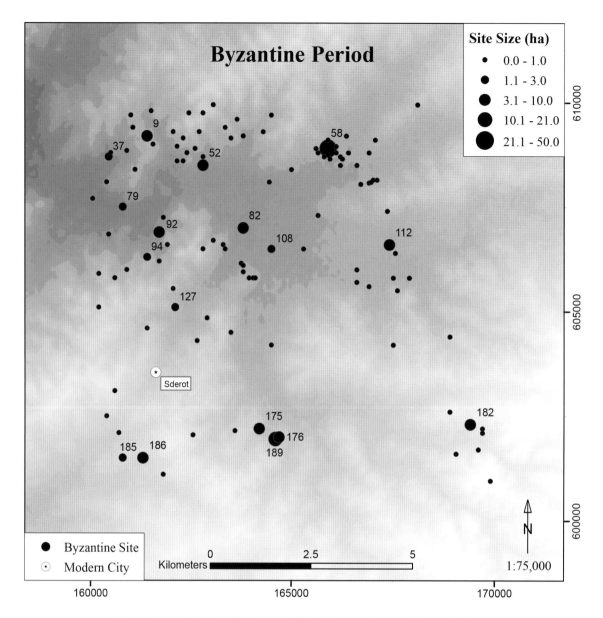

Figure 5.11: Map of Sderot (96), sites from the Byzantine period
larger than 3.1 hectares over modern topography.

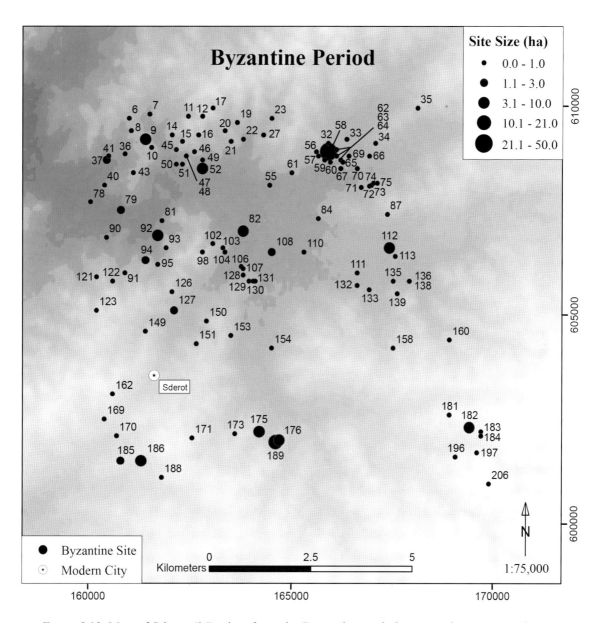

Figure 5.12: Map of Sderot (96), sites from the Byzantine period over modern topography.

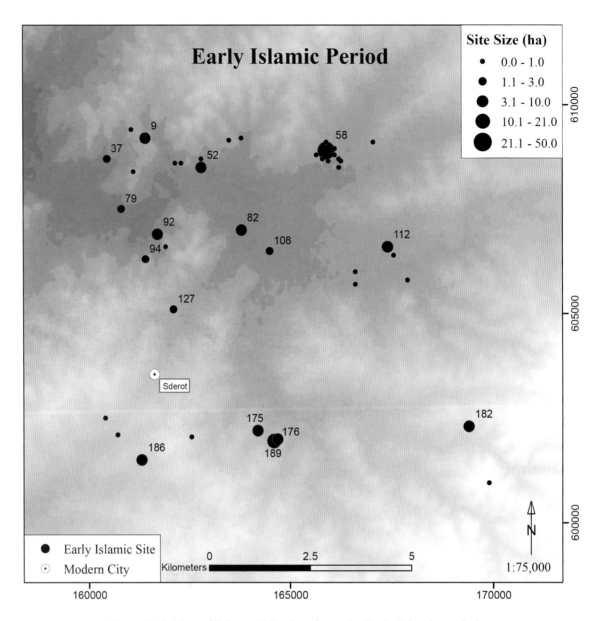

Figure 5.13: Map of Sderot (96), sites from the Early Islamic period
larger than 3.1 hectares over modern topography.

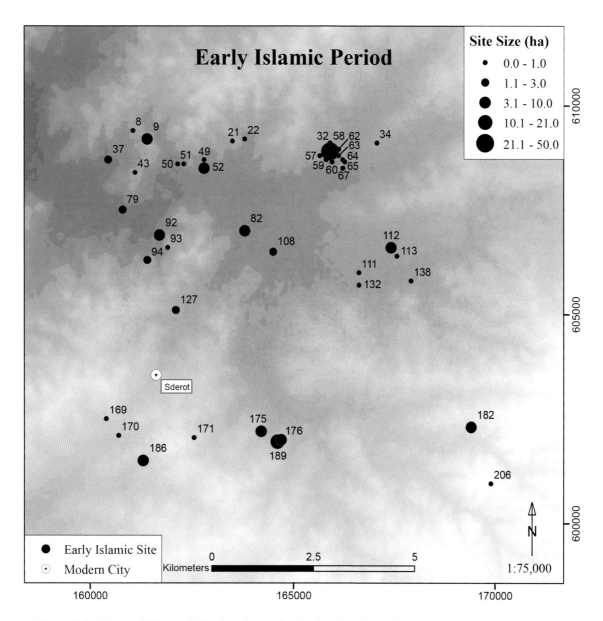

Figure 5.14: Map of Sderot (96), sites from the Early Islamic period over modern topography.

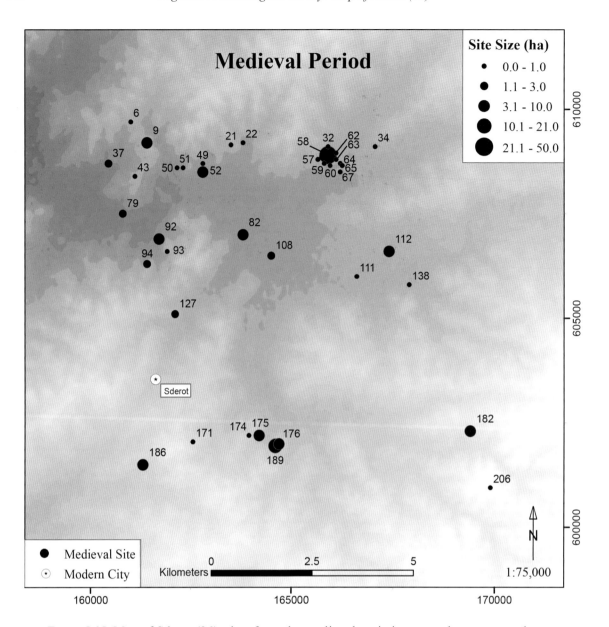

Figure 5.15: Map of Sderot (96), sites from the medieval period over modern topography.

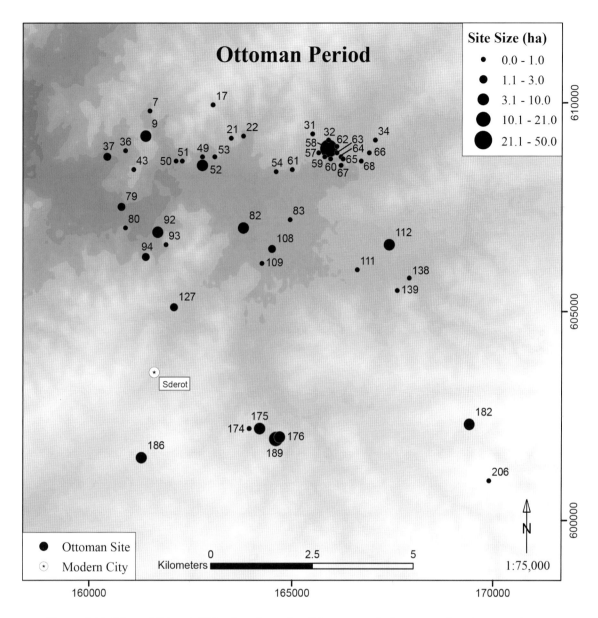

Figure 5.16: Map of Sderot (96), sites from the Ottoman period over modern topography.

APPENDIX C: INDEX OF SITE NAMES

Site	*Site No.*
Babliya, Kh. el	21, 22
Beʾer Gluma (Bir Jalama)	109
Beit Tafa, Kh.	111
Berekha, H.	181, 182
Bror, Tel	61
Bureir	31, 32, 33, 56–60, 62–65, 67–69
Buta, H.	207
Gevarᶜam Kurkar Ridge	17–20
Ghayada, Kh. el	34
Gluma, H.	108, 112
Haj Harb, Kh. el	206
Herev, H.	206
Hirbiya, Kh.	37
Hoga, H.	176, 189
Huj	175, 176
Huj, Kh.	189
Jalama, Kh.	108
Kefar Seᶜora, H.	112
Lasan Kh.	185–87
Magharat Ghazza, Tell	89
Majnuna, Tell el	191
Marashan, Kh. el	137–39
Mashnaga, Tell el	61
Nabi Huj, en	176, 189
Nahal Azur	171, 172
Nahal Bror	23–27, 54–55, 66, 70–75
Nahal Dorot	178, 190, 192, 205
Nahal Dov	168
Nahal Hatzav	116, 117
Nahal Heletz	28–30, 35
Nahal Hoga	106, 107, 128–31, 152–54, 165–67, 177, 200–4
Nahal Kosses	123, 144
Nahal Marashan	158
Nahal Mardim	91, 121, 122, 124, 125
Nahal Mefalsim	169, 170, 188, 199
Nahal Nigraf	155–57
Nahal Nirᶜam	99, 100, 102–5, 126, 150, 151, 164
Nahal Revaiya	1–6, 36, 38
Nahal Ruhama	179, 180, 183, 184, 193–98
Nahal Shiqma	39–44, 76–78, 80–88, 90, 96–98, 101, 110, 113–15, 118–19, 132–36
Nahal Sumsum	7, 8, 11–15, 45
Nahal Tal	145–49, 161–63
Nahal Zedim	140–43, 159, 160
Najd	92, 93
Najd, Kh.	127
Namus, Kh. en	181, 182
Sawabta, Kh.	137–39
Sderot	149
Shaᶜfat el Mughr	16
Shaᶜfat Umm ez-Zamilia	16
Shaᶜrata, Kh.	112
Shega, Tell	191
Sheikh Mansur, esh	174
Sumsum	46–53
Tell edh Dhahab, Kh.	173
Umm Buteih, Kh.	207

Site	*Site No.*
Umm Qallum, Kh.	79
Umm Tabun, Kh.	94, 95
Wadi Abd el Aziz	200
Wadi Abu Ali	201–4
Wadi Abu Rashid	179, 180, 183, 184, 193–98
Wadi el Badawiya	7, 8, 11–15, 45
Wadi el Bi	161–63
Wadi el Ghazawiya	171, 172
Wadi el Hadd	154
Wadi el Hesi	39–43, 76–78, 80–88, 90, 96–98, 101, 110, 113–15, 118, 119, 132–36
Wadi Hirbiya	1–5, 36, 38
Wadi Iweida	158
Wadi el Jabali	149
Wadi el Jurf	155–57
Wadi el Khanazar	116, 117
Wadi Lisin	169, 170, 188, 199
Wadi el Mahawir	106, 107, 128–31, 152–54, 165–67, 177
Wadi el Majnuna	190, 192, 205
Wadi el Makkus	123, 144
Wadi el Manyasa	140–43, 159, 160
Wadi Mardin	91, 121, 122, 124, 125
Wadi en Nada	145–49, 161–63
Wadi Najd	99, 100, 102–5, 126, 150, 151, 164,
Wadi en Namus	168
Wadi el Qaᵓa	28–30, 35
Wadi er Raml	106, 107, 128–31, 152–54, 165–67, 177, 178, 190, 192, 200–5
Wadi Shaqafat	23–27, 54, 55, 66, 70–75
Zeita, Kh.	9, 10

APPENDIX D: INDEX OF SITES LISTED BY PERIOD

Period	Site Nos.	Total No. of Sites
Paleolithic	1–3, 5, 11, 13–15, 18, 24–26, 28, 30, 38–44, 54, 77, 85, 86, 89, 96–102, 120, 121, 123–25, 134, 140, 144–48, 152, 154–57, 159, 161, 163–65, 167, 168, 172, 178, 190–92, 198, 205	64
Neolithic	76, 166, 179	3
Chalcolithic	114, 154, 180, 193–95, 200, 202	8
Middle Bronze	61, 138	2
Late Bronze	88, 114, 177	3
Iron I	177	1
Iron II	176, 189, 199	3
Persian	115, 176, 189	3
Hellenistic	52, 58, 92, 94, 115, 176, 189	7
Roman	7, 9, 16, 21, 32, 34, 37, 43, 48–50, 52, 56–64, 67, 79, 82, 91, 92, 94, 108, 111, 112, 127, 135, 137–39, 149, 151, 169, 170, 176, 182, 185, 186, 189	44
Byzantine	4–10, 12–17, 19–23, 27, 29, 32–37, 40, 41, 43, 45–52, 55–67, 69–75, 78, 79, 81, 82, 84, 87, 90–95, 98, 103, 104, 106–8, 110–13, 121–23, 126–33, 135–39, 149–51, 153, 154, 158, 160, 162, 169–71, 173, 175, 176, 181–83, 185–89, 196, 197, 206, 207	121
Early Islamic	8, 9, 21, 22, 32, 34, 37, 43, 49–52, 57–60, 62–65, 67, 79, 82, 92–94, 108, 111–13, 127, 132, 138, 169–71, 175, 176, 182, 186, 187, 189, 206	43
Medieval (Crusader and Mamluk periods)	6, 9, 21, 22, 32, 34, 37, 43, 49–52, 57–60, 62–65, 67, 79, 82, 92–94, 108, 111, 112, 127, 138, 170, 171, 174–76, 182, 186, 187, 189, 206	41
Ottoman	7, 9, 17, 21, 22, 31, 32, 34, 36, 37, 43, 49, 50–54, 57–68, 79, 80, 82, 83, 92–94, 108, 109, 111, 112, 116–18, 127, 138, 139, 174–76, 182, 186, 189, 203, 204, 206, 291; sites 49–53 are sections of one site; sites 58–60 and 62–67 are sections of one site.	44

APPENDIX E: INDEX OF MAP OF SDEROT (96) SITES

No.	Site	Coordinates	Area (m²)	Periods
1	Nahal Revaiya (W. Hirbiya)	160500/609900	1,200	Paleo
2	Nahal Revaiya (W. Hirbiya)	160500/609400	600	Paleo
3	Nahal Revaiya (W. Hirbiya)	160600/609300	500	Paleo
4	Nahal Revaiya (W. Hirbiya)	160050/609300	200	Byz
5	Nahal Revaiya (W. Hirbiya)	160050/609000	2,000	Paleo, Byz
6	Nahal Revaiya (W. Hirbiya)	161000/609700	50	Byz, Med, Mod
7	Nahal Sumsum (W. el Badawiya)	161500/609800	2,000	Rom, Byz, Ott
8	Nahal Sumsum (W. el Badawiya)	161050/609400	500	Byz, EI
9	Khirbat Zeita	161400/609200	40,000	Rom, Byz, EI, Med, Ott
	7 cisterns			
10	Khirbat Zeita	161550/609000	100	Byz
11	Nahal Sumsum (W. el Badawiya)	162450/609750	100	Paleo
12	Nahal Sumsum (W. el Badawiya)	162800/609750	150	Byz
13	Nahal Sumsum (W. el Badawiya)	162300/609400	200	Paleo, Byz
14	Nahal Sumsum (W. el Badawiya)	162050/ 609300	150	Paleo, Byz
15	Nahal Sumsum (W. el Badawiya)	162300/609150	100	Paleo, Byz
16	Shaᶜfat el-Mughr, Shaᶜfat Umm ez-Zamilia	162700/609300	10,000	Rom, Byz
17	Gevarᶜam Kurkar Ridge Reserve	163050/609950	400	Byz, Ott
18	Gevarᶜam Kurkar Ridge Reserve	163100/609800	1,000	Paleo
19	Gevarᶜam Kurkar Ridge Reserve	163650/609600	100	Byz
	Cistern			
20	Gevarᶜam Kurkar Ridge Reserve	163350/609400	100	Byz
	Cistern			
21	Khirbat el Babliya	163500/609150	3,000	Rom, Byz, EI, Med, Ott, Mod
	3 cisterns			
22	Khirbat el Babliya	163800/609200	100	Byz, EI, Med, Ott, Mod
23	Nahal Bror (W. Shaqafat)	164500/609700	200	Byz
24	Nahal Bror (W. Shaqafat)	164500/609550	400	Paleo
25	Nahal Bror (W. Shaqafat)	164600/609950	200	Paleo
26	Nahal Bror (W. Shaqafat)	164500/609400	1,200	Paleo
27	Nahal Bror (W. Shaqafat)	164300/609300	100	Byz
28	Nahal Heletz (W. el Qaᵓa)	165100/609800	300	Paleo
29	Nahal Heletz (W. el Qaᵓa)	165400/609700	100	Byz
30	Nahal Heletz (W. el Qaᵓa)	165300/609600	200	Paleo
31	Bureir	165500/609250	800	Ott, Mod
32	Bureir	165900/609100	1,000	Rom, Byz, EI, Med, Ott, Mod
33	Nahal Heletz	166350/609200	100	Byz
34	Khirbat el Ghayada	167050/609100	3,000	Rom, Byz, EI, Med, Ott, Mod
	2 cisterns			
35	Nahal Heletz (W. el Qaᵓa)	168100/609950	1,000	Byz
36	Nahal Revaiya (W. Hirbiya)	160900/608850	500	Byz, Ott, Mod
37	Khirbat Hirbiya	160450/608700	20,000	Rom, Byz, EI, Med, Ott
38	Nahal Revaiya (W. Hirbiya)	160100/608600	800	Paleo
39	Nahal Shiqma (W. el Hesi)	160100/608100	100	Paleo
40	Nahal Shiqma (W. el Hesi)	160400/608100	400	Paleo, Byz
41	Nahal Shiqma (W. el Hesi)	160500/608800	100	Paleo, Byz
42	Nahal Shiqma (W. el Hesi)	161350/608600	250	Paleo
43	Nahal Shiqma (W. el Hesi)	161100/608400	400	Paleo, Rom, Byz, EI, Med, Ott, Mod
44	Nahal Shiqma (W. el Hesi)	161050/608000	200	Paleo

No.	Site	Coordinates	Area (m²)	Periods
45	Nahal Sumsum (W. el Badawiya) Cistern	162150/608950	100	Byz
46	Sumsum Cistern	162600/608900	100	Byz
47	Sumsum Cistern	162400/608800	100	Byz
48	Sumsum	162400/608800	100	Rom, Byz
49	Sumsum	162800/608700	2,000	Rom, Byz, EI, Med, Ott, Mod
50	Sumsum	162150/608600	200	Rom, Byz, EI, Med, Ott, Mod
51	Sumsum Cistern	162300/608600	200	Byz, EI, Med, Ott, Mod
52	Sumsum Possible Byzantine church; 2 cisterns	162800/608500	60,000	Hell, Rom, Byz, EI, Med, Ott, Mod
53	Sumsum	163100/608700	500	Paleo, Ott, Mod
54	Nahal Bror (W. Shaqafat)	164600/608350	100	Ott, Mod
55	Nahal Bror (W. Shaqafat)	164450/608100	50	Byz
56	Bureir	165600/608900	2,000	Rom, Byz
57	Bureir Pottery workshop	165650/608800	500	Rom, Byz, EI, Med, Ott, Mod
58	Bureir Possible Byzantine church	165900/608900	250,000	Hell, Rom, Byz, EI, Med, Ott, Mod
59	Bureir	165800/608700	400	Rom, Byz, EI, Med, Ott, Mod
60	Bureir	165950/608650	100	Rom, Byz, EI, Med, Ott
61	Tel Bror, Tell el Mashnaga Winepress; pottery workshop	165000/608400	10,000	MB, Rom, Byz, Ott
62	Bureir Pottery workshop	166100/608950	1,500	Rom, Byz, EI, Med, Ott, Mod
63	Bureir Byzantine church	166100/608800	200	Rom, Byz, EI, Med, Ott, Mod
64	Bureir	166200/608700	100	Rom, Byz, EI, Med, Ott, Mod
65	Bureir	166250/608650	100	Byz, EI, Med, Ott, Mod
66	Nahal Bror (W. Shaqafat)	166900/608800	200	Byz, Ott
67	Bureir	166200/608500	3,000	Rom, Byz, EI, Med, Ott, Mod
68	Bureir	166700/608600	100	Ott, Mod
69	Bureir	166400/608800	100	Byz
70	Nahal Bror (W. Shaqafat)	166600/608500	60	Byz
71	Nahal Bror (W. Shaqafat) Cistern	166700/608050	100	Byz
72	Nahal Bror (W. Shaqafat) Cistern	166900/608080	100	Byz
73	Nahal Bror (W. Shaqafat) Cistern	166950/608100	100	Byz
74	Nahal Bror (W. Shaqafat) Cistern	167000/608150	100	Byz
75	Nahal Bror (W. Shaqafat)	167100/608150	100	Byz
76	Nahal Shiqma (W. el Hesi)	169400/608100	100	Neo
77	Nahal Shiqma (W. el Hesi)	169800/608000	200	Paleo
78	Nahal Shiqma (W. el Hesi) Cistern	160050/607700	100	Byz
79	Khirbet Umm Qallum Pottery workshop	160800/607500	20,000	Rom, Byz, EI, Med, Ott

No.	Site	Coordinates	Area (m²)	Periods
80	Nahal Shiqma (W. el Hesi)	160900/607000	100	Ott
81	Nahal Shiqma (W. el Hesi) Cistern	161800/607250	100	Byz
82	Nahal Shiqma (W. el Hesi) Pottery workshop	163800/607000	40,000	Rom, Byz, EI, Med, Ott
83	Nahal Shiqma (W. el Hesi)	164950/607200	100	Ott, Mod
84	Nahal Shiqma (W. el Hesi)	165650/607300	400	Byz
85	Nahal Shiqma (W. el Hesi)	167800/607800	1,000	Paleo
86	Nahal Shiqma (W. el Hesi)	167500/607700	200	Paleo
87	Nahal Shiqma (W. el Hesi)	167350/607400	50	Byz
88	Nahal Shiqma (W. el Hesi)	169500/607000	12,000	LB
89	Tell Magharat Ghazza	160800/606900	400	Paleo
90	Nahal Shiqma (W. el Hesi) Cistern	160450/606850	200	Byz
91	Nahal Mardim (W. Mardin)	160900/606000	400	Rom, Byz
92	Najd	161700/606900	40,000	Hell, Rom, Byz, EI, Med, Ott, Mod
93	Najd	161900/606600	200	Byz, EI, Med, Ott, Mod
94	Khirbet Umm Tabun Byzantine church; 4 cisterns	161400/606300	30,000	Hell, Rom, Byz, EI, Med, Ott, Mod
95	Khirbet Umm Tabun	161700/606200	100	Byz
96	Nahal Shiqma (W. el Hesi)	162400/606600	100	Paleo
97	Nahal Shiqma (W. el Hesi)	162700/606700	200	Paleo
98	Nahal Shiqma (W. el Hesi)	162800/606500	100	Paleo, Byz
99	Nahal Nirᶜam (W. Najd)	162600/606200	100	Paleo
100	Nahal Nirᶜam (W. Najd)	162900/606100	500	Paleo
101	Nahal Shiqma (W. el Hesi)	163400/606900	100	Paleo
102	Nahal Nirᶜam (W. Najd)	163050/606700	100	Paleo
103	Nahal Nirᶜam (W. Najd)	163300/606600	50	Byz
104	Nahal Nirᶜam (W. Najd)	163350/606500	50	Byz
105	Nahal Nirᶜam (W. Najd)	163100/606300	10,000	Mod
106	Nahal Hoga (W. er Raml, W. el Mahawir) Cistern	163750/606150	400	Byz
107	Nahal Hoga (W. er Raml, W. el Mahawir) Cistern	163800/606100	100	Byz
108	Hurvat Gluma, Khirbet Jalama Winepress; 2 cisterns	164500/606500	20,000	Rom, Byz, EI, Med, Ott
109	Beᵓer Gluma, Bir Jalama	164250/606150	50	Ott
110	Nahal Shiqma (W. el Hesi)	165300/606500	200	Byz
111	Khirbet Beit Tafa Byzantine church	166600/606000	10,000	Rom, Byz, EI, Med, Ott
112	Hurvat Gluma, Khirbet Shaᶜrata Byzantine church; winepress; 2 cisterns	167400/606600	40,000	Rom, Byz, EI, Med, Ott
113	Nahal Shiqma (W. el Hesi) Cistern	167550/606400	100	Byz, EI
114	Nahal Shiqma (W. el Hesi)	167800/606300	10,000	Chalco, LB
115	Nahal Shiqma (W. el Hesi)	167500/606000	4,000	Pers, Hell
116	Nahal Hatzav (W. el Khanazir)	169600/606900	15,000	Ott, Mod
117	Nahal Hatzav (W. el Khanazir)	169800/606300	100	Ott, Mod
118	Nahal Shiqma (W. el Hesi)	169400/606350	200	Ott, Mod
119	Nahal Shiqma (W. el Hesi)	169400/606100	100	Mod
120	Nahal Shiqma (W. el Hesi)	169100/606000	400	Paleo

No.	Site	Coordinates	Area (m²)	Periods
121	Nahal Mardim (W. Mardin)	160200/605900	100	Paleo, Byz
	Cistern			
122	Nahal Mardim (W. Mardin)	160600/605800	400	Byz
123	Nahal Kosses (W. el Makkus)	160200/605100	200	Paleo, Byz
124	Nahal Mardim (W. Mardin)	160500/605300	500	Paleo
125	Nahal Mardim (W. Mardin)	160700/605100	400	Paleo
126	Nahal Nirᶜam (W. Najd)	162050/605550	100	Byz
	Cistern			
127	Khirbet Najd	162100/605100	20,000	Rom, Byz, EI, Med, Ott
	Byzantine church; winepress; 5 cisterns			
128	Nahal Hoga (W. er Raml, W. el Mahawir)	163800/605950	200	Byz
	2 cisterns			
129	Nahal Hoga (W. er Raml, W. el Mahawir)	163950/605800	100	Byz
	Cistern			
130	Nahal Hoga (W. er Raml, W. el Mahawir)	164050/605800	100	Byz
	Cistern			
131	Nahal Hoga (W. er Raml, W. el Mahawir)	164100/605800	100	Byz
132	Nahal Shiqma (W. el Hesi)	166600/605700	2,000	Byz, EI
133	Nahal Shiqma (W. el Hesi)	166900/605600	800	Byz
134	Nahal Shiqma (W. el Hesi)	166400/605100	400	Paleo
135	Nahal Shiqma (W. el Hesi)	167500/605800	1,000	Rom, Byz
136	Nahal Shiqma (W. el Hesi)	167900/605800	100	Byz
	Pottery workshop			
137	Khirbet el Marashan, Khirbet Sawabta	167800/605700	100	Rom, Byz
138	Khirbet el Marashan, Khirbet Sawabta	167900/605800	10,000	MB, Rom, Byz, EI, Med, Ott, Mod
	Cistern			
139	Khirbet el Marashan, Khirbet Sawabta	167600/605500	500	Rom, Byz, Ott, Mod
	Byzantine church; cistern			
140	Nahal Zedim (W. el Manyasa)	167700/605100	200	Paleo, Mod
141	Nahal Zedim (W. el Manyasa)	168700/605700	600	Mod
142	Nahal Zedim (W. el Manyasa)	168900/605500	400	Mod
143	Nahal Zedim (W. el Manyasa)	168500/605200	400	Mod
144	Nahal Kosses (W. el Makkus)	160200/604800	100	Paleo
145	Nahal Tal (W. en Nada)	160700/604700	200	Paleo
146	Nahal Tal (W. en Nada)	160600/604500	600	Paleo
147	Nahal Tal (W. en Nada)	160400/604300	100	Paleo
148	Nahal Tal (W. en Nada)	160600/604000	100	Paleo
149	Sderot (W. el Jabali)	161400/604600	5,000	Rom, Byz
	2 cisterns			
150	Nahal Nirᶜam (W. Najd)	162900/604850	500	Byz
151	Nahal Nirᶜam (W. Najd)	162650/604300	200	Rom, Byz
152	Nahal Hoga (W. er Raml, W. el Mahawir)	163800/604700	100	Paleo
153	Nahal Hoga (W. er Raml, W. el Mahawir)	163500/604500	300	Byz
154	Nahal Hoga (W. er Raml, W. el Mahawir)	164500/604200	400	Paleo, Chalco, Byz
155	Nahal Nigraf (W. el Jurf)	166350/604900	200	Paleo
156	Nahal Nigraf (W. el Jurf)	166400/604600	100	Paleo
157	Nahal Nigraf (W. el Jurf)	166100/604800	200	Paleo
158	Nahal Marashan (W. Iweida)	167500/604200	200	Byz
159	Nahal Zedim (W. el Manyasa)	168200/604100	100	Paleo
160	Nahal Zedim (W. el Manyasa)	168900/604400	600	Byz
161	Nahal Tal (W. el Bi, W. en Nada)	160200/603800	200	Paleo

No.	Site	Coordinates	Area (m²)	Periods
162	Nahal Tal (W. el Bi, W. en Nada)	160600/603100	1,000	Byz
163	Nahal Tal (W. el Bi, W. en Nada)	161100/603800	100	Paleo
164	Nahal Nirᶜam (W. Najd)	162400/603500	200	Paleo
165	Nahal Hoga (W. er Raml, W. el Mahawir)	164500/603800	200	Paleo
166	Nahal Hoga (W. er Raml, W. el Mahawir)	164350/603300	10	Neo
167	Nahal Hoga (W. er Raml, W. el Mahawir)	165100/603800	100	Paleo
168	Nahal Dov (W. en Namus)	168700/603300	200	Paleo
169	Nahal Mefalsim (W. Lisin)	160400/602500	5,000	Rom, Byz, EI
	2 cisterns			
170	Nahal Mefalsim (W. Lisin)	160700/602100	10,000	Rom, Byz, EI, Med
	Winepress; pottery workshop; 2 cisterns			
171	Nahal Azur (W. el Ghazawiya)	162550/602050	3,000	Byz, EI, Med
172	Nahal Azur (W. el Ghazawiya)	163100/602300	200	Paleo
173	Khirbet Tell edh Dhahab	163600/602150	100	Byz
174	Esh Sheikh Mansur	163950/602200	100	Med, Ott, Mod
175	Huj	164200/602200	45,000	Byz, EI, Med, Ott, Mod
	Possible Byzantine church			
176	Hurvat Hoga ,Kh. Huj, en Nabi Huj	164700/602000	40,000	Iron2, Pers, Hell, Rom, Byz, EI, Med, Ott, Mod
	Byzantine church; pottery workshop; 5 cisterns			
177	Nahal Hoga (W. er Raml, W. el Mahawir)	165100/602450	200	LB, Iron1
178	Nahal Dorot (W. er Raml)	166300/602100	1,000	Paleo
179	Nahal Ruhama (W. Abu Rashid)	166900/602100	10	Neo
180	Nahal Ruhama (W. Abu Rashid)	167400/602100	500	Chalco
181	Hurvat Berekha, Khirbet en Namus	168900/602600	100	Byz, Mod
182	Hurvat Berekha, Khirbet en Namus	169400/602300	60,000	Rom, Byz, EI, Med, Ott
	Byzantine church; pottery workshop			
183	Nahal Ruhama (W. Abu Rashid)	169700/602200	200	Byz
	Winepress			
184	Nahal Ruhama (W. Abu Rashid)	169700/602100	100	Mod
185	Khirbet Lasan	160800/601500	20,000	Rom, Byz
186	Khirbet Lasan	161300/601500	60,000	Rom, Byz, EI, Med, Ott
	Byzantine church; pottery workshop; 4 cisterns			
187	Khirbet Lasan	161400/601600	800	Byz, EI, Med
	5 cisterns			
188	Nahal Mefalsim (W. Lisin)	161800/601100	200	Byz
	2 cisterns			
189	Hurvat Hoga, Kh. Huj, en Nabi Huj	164600/601950	120,000	Iron2, Pers, Hell, Rom, Byz, EI, Med, Ott, Mod
	5 cisterns			
190	Nahal Dorot (W. er Raml, W. el Majnuna)	166700/601400	200	Paleo
191	Tel Shega, Tell el Majnuna	167700/601700	200	Paleo
192	Nahal Dorot (W. er Raml, W. el Majnuna)	167500/601250	100	Paleo
193	Nahal Ruhama (W. Abu Rashid)	168500/601900	1,200	Chalco
194	Nahal Ruhama (W. Abu Rashid)	168800/601900	500	Chalco
195	Nahal Ruhama (W. Abu Rashid)	169200/601800	2,500	Chalco
196	Nahal Ruhama (W. Abu Rashid)	169050/601600	200	Byz
	Byzantine church; 3 cisterns			
197	Nahal Ruhama (W. Abu Rashid)	169600/601700	800	Byz, Mod
	4 cisterns			
198	Nahal Ruhama (W. Abu Rashid)	169700/601700	200	Paleo
199	Nahal Mefalsim (W. Lisin)	160500/600900	10	Iron2
200	Nahal Hoga (W. er Raml, W. Abd el Aziz)	165700/600600	1,000	Chalco
201	Nahal Hoga (W. er Raml, W. Abu Ali)	167350/600800	100	Ott, Mod

No.	Site	Coordinates	Area (m²)	Periods
202	Nahal Hoga (W. er Raml, W. Abu Ali)	167500/600700	400	Chalco
203	Nahal Hoga (W. er Raml, W. Abu Ali)	167800/600200	100	Ott, Mod
204	Nahal Hoga (W. er Raml, W. Abu Ali)	167400/600100	100	Ott, Mod
205	Nahal Dorot (W. er Raml, W. el Majnuna)	168400/600500	300	Paleo
206	Hurvat Herev, Khirbet el Haj Harb Byzantine church; 2 cisterns	169900/600950	10,000	Byz, EI, Med, Ott
207	Hurvat Buta, Khirbet Umm Buteih Cistern	169800/600300	100	Byz, Mod

APPENDIX F: CATALOGUE OF MAP OF SDEROT (96) SITES

1. 11-10/09-1 11050 10990 16050 60990
Nahal Revaiya (Wadi Hirbiya), triangulation point 823, spot height 86 m.
Scatter of flint implements (including handaxes, choppers, cores, and flakes), on top and S slope of a sandy *kurkar* hill (c. 1.2 dunams).
Lithic finds: Lower Paleolithic.

2. 11-10/09-2 11050 10940 16050 60940
Nahal Revaiya
Scatter of flint implements (c. 600 m²) on N moderate slope of a *kurkar* hill, covered with a thin layer of red soil (*hamra*). High percentage of flint tool industry waste.
Lithic finds: Lower Paleolithic.

3. 11-10/09-3 11060 10930 16060 60930
Nahal Revaiya
Scatter of flint tool industry on E slope of a *kurkar* hill, west of dry bed of Nahal Revaiya. The implements were collected from the top of a thin *hamra* layer over an area of c. 500 m².
Lithic finds: Lower Paleolithic.

4. 11-10/09-4 11005 10930 16005 60930
Nahal Revaiya
Remains of a structure (3 x 3.2 m); fieldstone walls (0.60 m wide) preserved 1–2 courses high. Segments of a coarse tiled mosaic floor. Tesserae of white color (2 x 2 cm). Around the structure, a dense scatter of pottery sherds (c. 200 m²).
Pottery: Byzantine.

5. 11-10/09-5 11005 10900 16005 60900
Nahal Revaiya
Scatter of flint implements (c. 2 dunams), including handaxes and choppers, on *kurkar* ridge and N slope W of Nahal Revaiya. Some tools were produced using the Levallois technique. Remains of structures (c. 500 m²); unhewn *kurkar* building stones, coarse tesserae (mostly 3 x 3 cm), fragments of glass vessels and many potsherds.
Lithic finds: Lower and Middle Paleolithic.
Pottery: Byzantine.

6. 11-10/19-1 11100 10970 16100 60970
Nahal Revaiya
Dense scatter of pottery sherds and broken fieldstones (c. 50 m²) on W slope of a *kurkar* hill, E of Nahal Revaiya.
Pottery: Byzantine and medieval.

7. 11-10/19-1 11150 10980 16150 60980
Nahal Sumsum (Wadi el Badawiya)
Group of five abandoned and ruined recent dwellings on moderate slope of a *kurkar* hill covered with a thin layer of loess soil, overlooking Nahal Sumsum from N. In the walls of two structures, built of mortared rough unhewn stones and preserved 1–2.5 m high, fragments of marble architectural elements and basalt vessels were embedded. Three structures are built of unfired mudbricks. Nearby, a well, partly blocked, 2.5 m diameter, built of dressed *kurkar* stones. Close to the well, a cement base of a pumping engine. The water was conducted to a square pool (3 x 3 m, 1.3 m high) situated 150 m E of the well, on a higher point. From the pool, water was brought by conduits, built of cement or flat *kurkar* stones, to lower elevations, in order to water a citrus orchard (c. 15,000 m²), now abandoned.
Pottery: Roman, Byzantine, Ottoman, and Mandatory.

8. 11-10/19-3 11105 10940 16105 60940
Nahal Sumsum
Foundations of structures (c. 500 m²) built of *kurkar* fieldstones laid with mortar on a *kurkar* hill, W of Nahal Sumsum. Scatter of pottery sherds.
Pottery: Byzantine and Early Islamic.

9.   11-10/19-4   11140 10920   16140 60920
Kh. Zeita (M)
Remains of settlement (c. 40 dunams) on top and slopes of a *kurkar* hill. Foundations of structures. Strewn amidst ruins: fragments of lintels, thresholds, marble architectural elements, basalt grinding stones, building stones, pottery sherds, and tesserae. Five plastered cisterns (4–5 m deep), currently partly blocked or ruinous. To N of settlement (100 m), on flat area, foundations of structures, two cisterns (presently blocked). Dense coverage of pottery sherds (mainly Gaza jars), fired bricks, slag, and kiln waste.
Pottery: Roman, Byzantine, Early Islamic, medieval, and Ottoman.
Identification: Zeite, a village from the Crusader period (see also site 82 below).

10.   11-10/19-5   11155 10900   16155 60900
Kh. Zeita (M)
Collapsed structure (3.2 x 1.8 m) on SW slope of a *kurkar* hill, some 200 m SW of the settlement. Built of small cemented fieldstones. The vaulted roof has collapsed inward. The remains indicate that the structure is a vaulted tomb. Nearby, light scatter of pottery and human bones.
Pottery: Byzantine.
Reference: Huster and Sion 2006:61–64, Table 1 no. 66

11.   11-10/29-1   11245 10975   16245 60975
Nahal Sumsum
Light scatter of eroded flint implements (c. 100 m²) on moderate slope of a *kurkar* hill.
Lithic finds: Lower Paleolithic.

12.   11-10/29-2   11280 10975   16280 60975
Nahal Sumsum
Light scatter of flint implements and potsherds (c. 150 m²) on a *kurkar* hill overlaid by a thin layer of *hamra* soil.
Lithic finds: Lower Paleolithic.
Pottery: Byzantine.

13.   11-10/29-3   11230 10940   16230 60940
Nahal Sumsum
Fragmentary foundation of structure (3 x 3 m) built of unhewn cemented *kurkar* stones, on S slope of a *kurkar* hill covered by *hamra* soil. Moderate scatter (c. 200 m²) of pottery and white color tesserae (2 x 2 cm). Light scatter of flint implements.
Lithic finds: Lower Paleolithic.
Pottery: Byzantine.

14.   11-10/29-4   11205 10930   16205 60930
Nahal Sumsum
Light scatter of flint implements and three concentrations of pottery sherds (c. 50 m² each) on top and W slope of a *kurkar* hill.
Lithic finds: Lower Paleolithic.
Pottery: Byzantine.

15.   11-10/29-5   11230 10930   16230 60915
Nahal Sumsum
Ruinous structure (2 x 2 m) on top of a *kurkar* hill, fieldstone walls (0.4 m wide) preserved 1–3 courses high, remains of plaster on interior walls. Dense scatter of pottery sherds around the structure (c. 100 m²). At this spot, water erosion has created a natural section. The geological layers from top to bottom are: *Hamra* soil—c. 1 m; sandy soft *kurkar*—c. 4 m; a second *hamra* soil layer—c. 2 m; calcium carbonate nodules—0.5 m; hard *kurkar* (sandstone)—c. 4 m. Flint implements were collected from the top of the upper *hamra* layer (c. 200 m²).
Lithic finds: Lower Paleolithic.
Pottery: Byzantine.

16.   11-10/29-6   11270 10930   16270 60930
Shaᶜfat el-Mughr (M)
Shaᶜfat Umm ez-Zamilia (M)
Cemetery on a *kurkar* hill (c. 10 dunams), 800 m N of the Arab village Sumsum. On the E edge, in a natural section, two quarries of *kurkar* stones. On S slope and on flat top, 22 burial caves hewn in a hard *kurkar* layer mostly in the same manner: A narrow vertical shaft (1 x 1 m, 1–2 m deep) leads to a square entrance (0.8 x 0.8 m), installed in a smoothed facade.

Some of the entrances have marginal linear decorations around three of the edges. Each burial cave consists of a chamber (average size 2.5 x 3 m, height 2 m); some caves have additional niches. On the W side of the hill, a burial cave of a different style: A central chamber (4 x 2 m) and six cells (2 x 1 m each), arranged symmetrically, three on each side of the long wall.

The upper part of this cave has collapsed. Most of the burial caves were robbed, leaving dense scatters of pottery sherds near the entrances.
Pottery: Roman and Byzantine.

17.	11-10/39-1	11305 10995	16305 60995
Gevarᶜam Kurkar Ridge Reserve
Hewn rock cave (c. 20 x 18 m, 2 m height) on S cliff of a hill, located on the Gevarᶜam-Nirᶜam *kurkar* ridge. The roof is supported by four hewn pillars. Used initially as a stone quarry and converted later to an enclosure for sheep and goats. Light scatter of pottery sherds inside the cave and near the entrance.
Pottery: Byzantine and Ottoman.

18.	11-10/39-2	11310 10980	16310 60980
Gevarᶜam Kurkar Ridge Reserve
Several concentrations of flint implements (c. 1 dunam) on a spur of a hill composed of alternating layers of *hamra* and *kurkar*. Flint artifacts included cores, choppers, handaxes, scrapers, and denticulates. Some of the tools were produced using the Levallois technique.
Lithic finds: Lower Paleolithic.

19.	11-10/39-3	11365 10960	16365 60960
Gevarᶜam Kurkar Ridge Reserve
Bell-shaped cistern, partly blocked, on moderate NE slope of a *kurkar* hill. Diameter: 2.5 m, visible depth: 3 m. Moderate scatter of pottery sherds (c. 100 m²).
Pottery: Byzantine.

20.	11-10/39-4	11335 10940	16335 60940
Gevarᶜam Kurkar Ridge Reserve
Bell-shaped cistern on top of a *kurkar* hill. Built of cemented fieldstones. Diameter: 2 m, depth: 4 m. Moderate scatter of pottery sherds (c. 100 m²).
Pottery: Byzantine.

21.	11-10/39-5	11350 10915	16350 60915
Kh. el Babliya (M)
Settlement remains (c. 3 dunams) on moderate SW slope of a *kurkar* hill and adjacent plain. Three bell-shaped cisterns, partly blocked, diameter 2.5–3 m, built of small cemented *kurkar* stones. Foundations of a structure (8 x 4 m), built of cemented fieldstones, preserved c. 0.8 m high. On NW edge, several recent ruined dwellings arranged on both sides of a narrow passage-way. These structures were built mainly of stones from the ancient settlement. Broken architectural elements are embedded in the walls. Scatter of marble fragments, broken basalt grinding stones, fragments of glass vessels, tesserae, and pottery sherds.
Pottery: Roman, Byzantine, Early Islamic, medieval, Ottoman, and modern.
Identification: Babilliya is the name of a village enumerated in the list of taxpayers from the year 1596/97 (Hütteroth and Abdulfattah 1977:147).

22.	11-10/39-6	11380 10920	16380 60920
Kh. el Babliya (M)
Well on flat terrain, 250 m E of Kh. el Babliya, near a tributary of Nahal Bror. Diameter: 2.20 m, built of dressed rectangular *kurkar* stones, reinforced with iron bars. Some 25 m to N, a concrete block (c. 1.8 x 1.8 x 1.5 m) intended to hold a pumping engine. The modern concrete was poured on an existing foundation built of cement strengthened with potsherds of the Byzantine period. It seems that the well was excavated in this period and renovated later in the twentieth century. If so, this would account for many other such wells elsewhere. Moderate scatter of pottery sherds around the well (c. 100 m²).
Pottery: Byzantine, Early Islamic, medieval, Ottoman, and modern.

23.	11-10/49-1	11450 10970	16450 60970
Nahal Bror (Wadi Shaqafat)
Collapsed structure (3 x 3 m) on a *kurkar* hill, built of small cemented stones. Scatter (c. 200 m²) of plaster fragments, coarse tesserae (2 x 2 cm), and pottery sherds.
Pottery: Byzantine.

1.

2.

Figure 5.17: Site 17

Figure 5.18: Site 22

24.   11-10/49-2   11450 10955   16450 60955
Nahal Bror (Wadi Shaqafat)
Scatter of flint implements (c. 400 m²) on hilltop. Two *hamra* layers and a *kurkar* layer between them were discerned. The artifacts were collected from the top of the upper *hamra* layer.
Lithic finds: Lower Paleolithic.

25.   11-10/49-3   11460 10950   16460 60950
Nahal Bror (Wadi Shaqafat)
Scatter of flint implements (c. 200 m²) on a *kurkar* hill with a *hamra* layer, for the most part eroded, on top. On some flakes the use of the Levallois technique was noted.
Lithic finds: Lower Paleolithic.

26.   11-10/49-4   11450 10940   16450 60940
Nahal Bror (Wadi Shaqafat)
Scatter of flint implements (c. 1.2 dunams) on a *kurkar* hill. The uppermost level, in which the artifacts were found, was a *hamra* layer, almost completely eroded as on the neighboring hills.
Lithic finds: Lower Paleolithic.

27.   11-10/49-5   11430 10930   16430 60930
Nahal Bror (Wadi Shaqafat)
Collapsed structure (c. 2 x 3 m) on W slope of a *kurkar* hill. Large vaulted architectural fragments of cemented fieldstones enabled the identification of a tomb here. Moderate scatter of potsherds around the building (c. 100 m²).
Pottery: Byzantine.

28.   11-10/59-1   11510 10980   16510 60980
Nahal Heletz (Wadi el Qaʾa)
Moderate scatter of flint implements (c. 300 m²) eroded by water, on W slope of a *kurkar* hill. Here, too, erosion processes removed the *hamra* layer, leaving the flint tools on the *kurkar* deposits.
Lithic finds: Lower Paleolithic.

29.   11-10/59-2   11540 10970   16540 60970
Nahal Heletz (Wadi el Qaᵓa)
Heap of medium-sized *kurkar* stones (3 m diameter, 1 m high), on eastern slope of a *kurkar* hill, west of a tributary of Nahal Heletz. A similar heap exists close to a *kurkar* stone quarry (site 93 below). Here, no quarry was discerned, probably due to the dense vegetation. Light scatter of pottery sherds around the piled stones (c. 100 m²).
Pottery: Byzantine.

30.   11-10/59-3   11530 10960   16530 60960
Nahal Heletz (Wadi el Qaᵓa)
Light scatter of flint implements (c. 200 m²) on W slope of a *kurkar* hill covered by a thin layer of *hamra*.
Lithic finds: Lower Paleolithic.

31.   11-10/59-4   11550 10925   16550 60925
Bureir (S)
Bureir (M)
Foundations of structures and wall segments built of dressed stones (c. 800 m²) some 600 m NE of the village center, at the location of the village school. Scatter of pottery sherds.
Pottery: Ottoman and modern (Mandatory).

32.   11-10/59-5   11590 10910   16590 60910
Bureir (S)
Bureir (M)
Remains of a structure (c. 5.5 x 6 m) built of small cemented *kurkar* stones. The northern wall stands to a height of 1.2 m.
    The structure is located at the N edge of Bureir village (site 58). Dense scatter (c. 1 dunam) of marble fragments, broken basalt grinding stones, tesserae, and sherds.
Pottery: Roman, Byzantine, Early Islamic, medieval, Ottoman, and modern.

33.   11-10/69-1   11635 10920   16635 60920
Nahal Heletz
Light scatter of fieldstones, pebbles, and pottery sherds (c. 100 m²) on a flat field W of Nahal Heletz (Wadi Shaqafat).
Pottery: Byzantine.

34.   11-10/79-1   11705 10910   16705 60910
Kh. el Ghayada (M)
Ruins of settlement (c. 3 dunams) on a hill, some 800 m E of Bureir village. Recent quarrying activity has revealed a cistern (diameter 4 m, depth 7 m). Another smaller, ruined cistern was noted in an artificial section. Both cisterns were built of small cemented fieldstones. On the hill slopes, a dense scatter of marble fragments, tesserae, fragments of glass vessels, and potsherds.
Pottery: Roman, Byzantine, Early Islamic medieval, Ottoman, and modern.
Reference: Petrie 1891:52.

35.   11-10/89-1   11810 10995   16810 60995
Nahal Heletz (Wadi el Qaᵓa)
Settlement ruins (c. 1 dunam) on top and S slope of a low hill covered by loess. Two complete bell-shaped cisterns (c. 2 m in diameter, 3 m deep). Scatter of broken building stones, kiln waste, slag, and pottery sherds.
Pottery: Byzantine.

36.   11-10/08-1   11090 10885   16090 60885
Nahal Revaiya (Wadi Hirbiya)
Group of four ruined dwellings on hill spur facing Nahal Revaiya. The largest structure (4 x 8 m) is built of fieldstones consolidated with mud. The three others (c. 3 x 4 m each) built of sun-dried bricks. Nearby, a well, partly blocked (diameter 2.5 m, visible depth 10 m); lined with properly dressed *kurkar* blocks. Scatter of pottery sherds (c. 500 m²).
Pottery: Byzantine, Ottoman, and modern.

37.   11-10/08-2   11045 10870   16045 60870
Kh. Hirbiya (M)
Remains of settlement (c. 20 dunams) on elongated spur, part of a *kurkar* ridge, covered by loessic soil, located between two tributaries of Nahal Revaiya (designated on Mandatory maps [Survey of Palestine, Sheet 11-10, Bureir] and Wadi Hirbiya, presumably following the name of the ruin).

Ruined structure (c. 6 x 6 m), the walls (0.60 m wide) are built of cemented fieldstones preserved 1.8 m high. On S slope, foundations of additional structures. Scatter of marble fragments, broken basalt grinding stones, tesserae, and potsherds. On NE edge of the site, dense scatter of kiln bricks, slag, and concentrations of kiln waste, consisting mainly of jars. These finds indicate the existence of a pottery workshop.
Pottery: Roman, Byzantine, Early Islamic, medieval, and Ottoman.

38.   11-10/08-3   11010 10860   16010 60860
Nahal Revaiya (Wadi Hirbiya)
Scatter of flint implements (c. 800 m²) on series of small *hamra* hills sloping downward from east toward Nahal Revaiya. Among the flint tools: scrapers, denticulates, and burins. Some of the implements were made in the Levallois technique.
Lithic finds: Lower Paleolithic.

39.   11-10/08-4   11010 10810   16010 60810
Nahal Shiqma (Wadi el Hesi)
Lithic assemblage collected from a clay layer deposited in a depression created by erosion. Farther to the S, the depression turns into a short tributary that joins Nahal Shiqma. Flint implements were eroded away from a *hamra* hill nearby (triangulation point 352).
Lithic finds: Lower Paleolithic.

40.   11-10/08-5   11040 10810   16040 60810
Nahal Shiqma (Wadi el Hesi)
Disturbed structures, foundations (contour unclear) built of cemented fieldstones and pebbles (probably brought from the Shiqma riverbed). These foundations are similar to structural foundations at other sites, dated to the Byzantine period (see site 41 below). On W slope of this hill, on top of a *hamra* layer, light scatter of flint implements (c. 400 m²).
Lithic finds: Lower Paleolithic.
Pottery: Byzantine.

Figure 5.19: Site 37

41.   11-1-/08-6   11050 10800   16050 60800
Nahal Shiqma (Wadi el Hesi)
Structural foundations on W slope of a *hamra* hill, built of cemented fieldstones. Nearby, three *kurkar* stone heaps (average size: diameter 2 m, height 0.5 m). On hilltop, light scatter of flint implements (c. 100 m²).
Lithic finds: Lower Paleolithic.
Pottery: Byzantine.

42.   11-10/18-1   11135 10860   16135 60860
Nahal Shiqma (Wadi el Hesi)
Light scatter of flint implements (c. 250 m²) on *hamra* hill (+79 m).
Lithic finds: Lower Paleolithic.

43.   11-10/18-2   11110 10840   16110 60840
Nahal Shiqma (Wadi el Hesi)
Stones quarries along a length of 250 m, in a natural cliff of a *kurkar* ridge located W of small tributaries of Nahal Shiqma. Here, the *kurkar* sandstone is arranged in horizontal layers (according to the deposition pattern of the ancient dunes that traversed the petrifaction process). A number of stone blocks left behind allow for reconstructing the quarrying activity: Large blocks were removed from a horizontal sandstone layer and were processed by cutting and chiseling.
     Moderate scatter of pottery inside the small chambers and cells created by the hewers indicates that the quarries were used over a long period. On NW slope of the *kurkar* ridge, light scatter of flint implements (c. 400 m²).
Lithic finds: Lower Paleolithic.
Pottery: Roman, Byzantine, Early Islamic, medieval, Ottoman, and modern.

44.   11-10/18-3   11105 10800   16105 60800
Nahal Shiqma (Wadi el Hesi)
Moderate scatter of flint implements (c. 200 m²) on W slope of a *kurkar* hill, partly covered by *hamra* soil. Some of the flint tools were knapped using the Levallois technique.
Lithic finds: Lower Paleolithic.

45.   11-10/28-1   11215 10895   16215 60895
Nahal Sumsum (Wadi el Badawiya)
Bell-shaped cistern on a *kurkar* hilltop (diameter 3 m, depth 5 m) E of Nahal Sumsum. Built of cemented fieldstones. Nearby, a light scatter of pottery sherds (c. 100 m²).
Pottery: Byzantine.

46.   11-10/28-2   11260 10890   16260 60890
Sumsum
Bell-shaped cistern (blocked) on S slope of a *kurkar* hill, recognized only by its opening. Diameter 2.5 m. Light scatter of pottery sherds (c. 100 m²).
Pottery: Byzantine.

47.   11-10/28-3   11240 10880   16240 60880
Sumsum
Bell-shaped cistern (blocked) on flat terrain. Ruined remains of a clay pipe system (length of each section 80 cm, diameter 10 cm) that branched out from the cistern to lower elevations nearby. Moderate scatter of pottery sherds (c. 100 m²).
Pottery: Byzantine.

48.   11-10/28-4   11240 10870   16240 60880
Sumsum
Burial structure NE of the remains of the Arab village Sumsum (see below, site 52). Built of cemented small-sized fieldstones. The vaulted roof of the main central chamber (2 x 3 m) has partly collapsed. Adjacent to the NW corner of this chamber is an entrance (0.6 x 0.6 m) leading to a smaller room (1.5 x 2.5 m.). The location of this room makes it possible to reconstruct the symmetrical plan of the structure and to determine its similarity to other burial systems in the region (see sites 67, 95).
     Moderate scatter of potsherds (c. 100 m²).
Pottery: Roman and Byzantine.
Reference: Huster and Sion 2006:61–64, Table 1 no. 67.

Figure 5.20: Site 49

49.   11-10/28-5   11280 10870   16280 60870
Sumsum
Cemetery of the village on a sandy hill, over an area of c. 2 dunams. Concentrations of fieldstones.
   Larger stones arranged at regular distances as grave markers. On the hilltop, a small structure (1.2 x 2.2 m, height 1.4 m), built of hewn *kurkar* stones, consolidated by recent concrete. Moderate scatter of pottery sherds.
Pottery: Roman, Byzantine, Early Islamic, medieval, Ottoman, and modern.

50.   11-10/28-6   11215 10860   16215 60860
Sumsum
Well (diameter 2 m, depth c. 25 m) and nearby built pool (c. 5 x 5 m, 1.2 m deep), on slope of sandy hill, E of Nahal Sumsum and c. 500 m W of the ruins of the village Sumsum. The well was lined with properly dressed *kurkar* stones. Two fragments of columns, one of marble and the other of granite, were placed on the uppermost part of the well and served to support the rope friction during water drawing (leaving behind deep slits). The pool was built of small fieldstones, consolidated by a light-colored cement. On large sections of the walls, both interior and exterior faces, thick layers of red color plaster remain. It seems that the installation was used over a long period without change.
   Moderate scatter of pottery sherds (c. 200 m²).
Pottery: Roman, Byzantine, Early Islamic, medieval, Ottoman, and modern.

51.   11-10/28-7   11230 10860   16230 60860
Sumsum
Bell-shaped cistern on loessic hill spur (width of opening 1.8 m, depth 4 m), built of small fieldstones consolidated by light-colored cement. Moderate scatter of pottery sherds (c. 200 m²).
Pottery: Byzantine, Early Islamic, medieval, Ottoman, and modern.

1. Site 50 pool and well

2. Site 50 well

Figure 5.21: Site 50

52.　　11-10/28-8　　11280 10850　　16280 60850
Simsim (S)
Sumsum (M)
Abandoned and ruined Arab village on S slopes of hilly area, some 100 m N of Nahal Bror (Wadi Shaqafat), a tributary of Nahal Shiqma (Wadi el Hesy). Within the limit of the ruins (c. 60 dunams), a small area with dense scatter of architectural elements, fragments of marble, basalt broken vessels, basalt grinding stones, building stones, and potsherds. At the S edge of the village, an ancient well (diameter 1.8 m, depth c. 25 m), built of well-dressed stones. Nearby, two bell-shaped cisterns (opening 2 m wide, 3–4 m deep).
Pottery: Hellenistic, Roman, Byzantine, Early Islamic, medieval, Ottoman, and modern.

53.　　11-10/38-1　　11310 10870　　16310 60870
Sumsum
Group of ruined dwellings on a *kurkar* hill c. 350 m NE of the village, built of small fieldstones joined with mud. The largest unit consists of a central yard (6 x 8 m) surrounded by small rooms (c. 3 x 3 m each) on three sides. Walls preserved 2.0 m high. Dressed *kurkar* building stones scattered around. On the E slope, a well (diameter 2.5 m, c. 25 m deep), built of high quality dressed stones. The walls are reinforced by iron bars. Close to the well, a concrete block intended for holding a pumping engine. Water was elevated to a pool (3 x 3 m, width of walls 0.6 m, depth 1.5 m). Along three walls are water troughs. Scatter of pottery sherds (c. 500 m²).
Pottery: Ottoman and modern.

54.　　11-10/48-1　　11460 10835　　16460 60835
Nahal Bror (Wadi Shaqafat)
Ruined structure (c. 3 x 4 m) on a *kurkar* hill, built of fieldstones joined with mud. The walls are preserved to a height of 1.5 m. On SW slope, light scatter of flint implements (c. 100 m²).
Lithic finds: Lower Paleolithic.
Pottery: Ottoman and modern.

55.　　11-10/48-2　　11445 10810　　16445 60810
Nahal Bror (Wadi Shaqafat)
Remains of a dam (4 m long, 3 m wide at bottom, preserved 0.5 m high) in a shallow wadi (a tributary of Nahal Bror). Built of small fieldstones joined with a gray-colored mortar, attributed to the Byzantine period. It seems that part of the dam was covered by sediment.
Light scatter of pottery sherds (c. 50 m²).
Pottery: Byzantine.

56.　　11-10/58-1　　11560 10890　　16560 60890
Bureir (M)
Dense concentration of kiln waste, scatter of slag, and pottery sherds (c. 2 dunams), on W edge of the ruined village Bureir (strong evidence of the existence of a pottery workshop).
Pottery: Roman and Byzantine.

57.　　11-10/58-2　　11565 10890　　16565 60890
Bureir (M)
Remains of a vaulted underground burial structure, partly filled by alluvium. A rectangular chamber (c. 2 x 4 m) with two small adjacent rooms (c. 1.5 x 2 m) were noted. Built of cemented small fieldstones. This structure is identical to others clearly identified as burial systems (see below, sites 62, 64, 67, and 95). Some 30 m to E, a blocked well (diameter 2.5 m, visible depth 5 m), built of dressed stones strengthened by iron bars placed widthwise, and a pool (c. 3 x 3 m; walls 0.70 m wide) preserved to a height of 2 m. Nearby, foundations of a large structure (c. 6 x 8 m), with large fragments of modern grinding stones (diameter: 1.4 m) within and around. Mandatory maps indicate the existence of a modern mill here (Survey of Palestine, Sheet 11-10, Bureir). Scatter of pottery sherds (c. 500 m²).
Pottery: Roman, Byzantine, Early Islamic, medieval, Ottoman, and modern.
Reference: Huster and Sion 2006:61–64, Table 1 no. 68 (wrong coordinates there).

58.　　11-10/58-3　　11590 10890　　16590 60890
Bureir (M)
Ruins of Arab village (c. 250 dunams) covering ancient remains, in an area surrounded by abandoned orchards, on a low elevation W of Nahal Heletz. The intentional destruction of the dwellings left a debris layer 2–3 m thick. Between the ruins are ancient and modern cisterns, one with columbarium niches. Several heaps of building stones (from the dismantled structures), including jambs, doorsteps, and column fragments. Dense scatter of pottery sherds over the entire area.
Pottery: Hellenistic, Roman, Byzantine, Early Islamic, medieval, Ottoman, and modern.
References: Robinson and Smith 1841, II:370–71, 386–88; Guérin 1869:293.

59.   11-10/58-4   11580 10870   16580 60870
Bureir (M)
Structural foundations (4 x 6 m) built of dressed *kurkar* stones, E of the open water pool of the village that consists of a round shallow artificial depression (diameter 40 m). Dense scatter of potsherds (c. 400 m²).
Pottery: Roman, Byzantine (the majority), Early Islamic, medieval, Ottoman, and modern.

60.   11-10/58-5   11595 10865   16595 60865
Bureir (M)
Remains of an ancient road, S of the village ruins, under an existing earth path. A section (40 m long, 3 m wide) was revealed by occasional strong winds that removed the upper dust. Margins paved with dressed limestone blocks and the inner part with *kurkar* stones. As limestone is uncommon in this area, the stones were probably brought from farther east. It seems that the paved section is a remnant of the Roman Beit Guvrin-Gaza road, in use until the end of the nineteenth century. Light scatter of pottery (c. 100 m²).
Pottery: Roman, Byzantine, Early Islamic, medieval, and Ottoman.

61.   11-10/58-6   11500 10840   16500 60840
Tel Bror
Tell el Mashnaga (M)
Natural *kurkar* hill (c. 10 dunams) with local deep *hamra* pockets, elevated c. 5–6 m above the surrounding plain. Several rock-hewn caves (probably shaft graves), filled with *hamra* soil; one contained a complete jar, pottery sherds, and a bronze dagger (length 15 cm). It seems that during the Middle Bronze I period the hill served as a cemetery. In later periods, building activities were carried out on the flat top of the hill: In the center, foundations of a structure (c. 3 x 4 m), paved with cemented pottery sherds laid in vertical position, covered by a plaster layer. This technique was in use mainly in winepresses of the Byzantine period throughout the region. On NE side of the hill, remains of a burial structure (c. 2 x 4 m) with a vaulted roof, composed of one single chamber (see site 62 below). On the SW side of the hill, over a large area, a scatter of kiln bricks, slag, and enormous heaps of pottery sherds, pointing to the existence of a major pottery workshop.
Extraordinary finds: Marble bust (height 0.6 m, width 0.5 m).
Pottery: Middle Bronze I, Roman, Byzantine, and Ottoman.
Reference: Huster and Sion 2006:61–64, Table 1 no. 73.

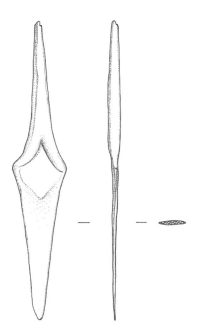

Figure 5.22: Middle Bronze Age I bronze dagger from site 61 (scale 1:2)

1.

2.

Figure 5.23: Site 62

62.　　　11-10/68-1　　　11610 10895　　　16610 60895
Bureir (M)
Cemetery visible in a narrow channel (flow direction N-S, length 200 m), created by water erosion, which joins Nahal Heletz. Three tombs were built on the W section of the wadi. The northern tomb is completely collapsed and its outline is unclear. The southern, at a distance of c. 60 m, is composed of a single chamber (2 x 3 m) with a vaulted roof. Between them, the third is composed of a central space (2 x 3.6 m) and four rooms (1.5 x 2 m each), arranged symmetrically. In the main chamber, fragmentary segments of decorated plaster (incised and painted) remain on the walls. Nearby, heaps of pottery sherds.
Pottery: Roman, Byzantine (the majority), Early Islamic, medieval, Ottoman, and modern.
Reference: Huster and Sion 2006:61–64, Table 1 nos. 69–71.

63.　　　11-10/68-2　　　11610 10880　　　16610 60880
Bureir (M)
Completely collapsed remains of the village mosque, on a moderate elevation. Dense concentration of building stones, lintel fragments, and a threshold (of hard limestone). Some 10 m to the W, in a shallow depression in the ground, a baptismal basin was observed. It was formed in the shape of a cross (outer measurements c. 1 x 1 m), built of cemented fieldstones; the inner surface was plastered in several layers, while the outer was made of modern cement with embedded sherds of black Gaza Ware. Nearby, a monolithic stone (of limestone), also chiseled in a cross form, probably the *baptisterium* cover. An intentional cross-section made at this spot revealed a mosaic pavement about 1.3 m below the surface. Some 40 m W of the mosque ruins, three marble columns.
Pottery: Roman, Byzantine, Early Islamic, medieval, Ottoman, and modern.

64.　　　11-10/68-3　　　11620 10870　　　16620 60870
Bureir (M)
Burial structure on flat terrain SE of the village ruins. Built of cemented fieldstones. The structure consists of a central chamber (c. 2 x 4 m) and four smaller rooms (c. 2 x 2 m each), two on each side of the chamber's long walls. The vaulted roof has collapsed. Pottery scatter (c. 100 m²).
Pottery: Roman, Byzantine, Early Islamic, medieval, Ottoman, and modern.
Reference: Meron 1975:37; Huster and Sion 2006:61–64, Table 1 no. 72.

65.　　　11-10/68-4　　　11625 10865　　　16625 60865
Bureir (M)
Collapsed remains of the village well, a large heap of building stones including fragments of architectural elements. An intentional channel was dug some 100 m W of the well (see site 63 above), revealing a fragment of an Arabic inscription from the second half of the fifteenth century A.D. that commemorates the well's construction or repair (Sharon 2004:xlviii–l). Several travelers referred specifically to the village well and chose the place for camping overnight.
Pottery: Byzantine, Early Islamic, medieval, Ottoman, and modern.
References: Robinson and Smith 1841, II:370–71; Guérin 1869:293; Conder and Kitchener 1881–83, III:259.

66.　　　11-10/68-5　　　11690 10880　　　16690 60880
Nahal Bror (Wadi Shaqafat)
Light scatter of fieldstones, pebbles, and potsherds (c. 200 m²), on flat terrain N of Nahal Bror.
Pottery: Byzantine and Ottoman.

67.　　　11-10/68-6　　　11620 10850　　　16620 60850
Bureir (M)
Cemetery on flat terrain (c. 3 dunams), some 200 m SE of the ruined village Bureir. Dense scatter of building stones, *kurkar* stones, and pebbles. Some stones remained in their original upright position (as grave markers), making it possible to discern cist tombs (c. 1 x 2 m). According to Mandatory maps (Survey of Palestine, Sheet 11-10, Bureir), this is the village cemetery. Light scatter of pottery sherds.
Pottery: Roman, Byzantine, Early Islamic, medieval, Ottoman, and modern.

68.　　　11-10/68-7　　　11670 10860　　　16670 60860
Bureir (M)
Well on flat terrain N of Nahal Bror. Diameter 4 m, visible depth 5 m. Built of dressed *kurkar* stones. Light scatter of pottery sherds (c. 100 m²).
Pottery: Ottoman and modern.

69.   11-10/68-8   11640 10880   16640 60880
Bureir (M)
Dense scatter of cemented and plastered sherds over a small area (100 m²) in an agricultural field. Probably an installation (winepress?) damaged by deep plowing.
Pottery: Byzantine.

70.   11-10/68-9   11660 10850   16660 60850
Nahal Bror (Wadi Shaqafat)
Strip of cemented and plastered sherds on flat terrain (1.5 x 40 m) N of Nahal Bror.
Pottery: Byzantine.

71.   11-10/68-10   11670 10805   16670 60805
Nahal Bror (Wadi Shaqafat)
Bell-shaped cistern partly blocked (diameter 2.5 m, visible depth 2.5 m), on moderate slope SE of Nahal Bror. Built of cemented fieldstones. Light scatter of pottery sherds (c. 100 m²).
Pottery: Byzantine.

72.   11-10/68-11   11690 10808   16690 60808
Nahal Bror (Wadi Shaqafat)
Bell-shaped cistern on moderate slope S of Nahal Bror, partly filled by eroded earth. Diameter 3 m, visible depth 2 m. Light scatter of pottery sherds (c. 100 m²).
Pottery: Byzantine.

73.   11-10/68-12   11695 10810   16695 60810
Nahal Bror (Wadi Shaqafat)
Collapsed remains of a cistern. Light scatter of pottery sherds (c. 100 m²).
Pottery: Byzantine.

74.   11-10/78-1   11700 10815   16700 60815
Nahal Bror (Wadi Shaqafat)
Collapsed remains of a blocked cistern. Light scatter of pottery sherds (c. 100 m²).
Pottery: Byzantine.

75.   11-10/78-2   11710 10815   16710 60815
Nahal Bror (Wadi Shaqafat)
Structural foundations (5 x 8 m): wall segments (0.9 m wide), built of cemented fieldstones. The structure was damaged by erosion. Scatter of building stones, limestone tiles (0.2 x 0.4 m), broken clay pipes (diameter 10 cm), square and round fired clay tiles (pilae tiles), and pottery sherds.
    These elements can be attributed to the underfloor heating system of a bath. Water was probably supplied from nearby cisterns (see sites 71–74 above).
Pottery: Byzantine.

76.   11-10/98-1   11940 10810   16940 60810
Nahal Shiqma (Wadi el Hesi)
Light scatter of small pebbles (c. 100 m²), near the E bank of a shallow tributary of Nahal Shiqma. One arrowhead.
Lithic finds: Neolithic.

77.   11-10/98-2   11980 10800   16980 60800
Nahal Shiqma (Wadi el Hesi)
Light scatter of flint implements (c. 200 m²) on S slope of a *kurkar* hill, cut by gullies that join up with Nahal Shiqma.
Lithic finds: Lower Paleolithic.

78.   11-10/07-1   11005 10770   16005 60770
Nahal Shiqma (Wadi el Hesi)
Collapsed and blocked cistern (diameter 2.5 m) adjacent to Nahal Shiqma, without indicative potsherds. As cisterns dated to the Byzantine period and built of the same materials were found in the vicinity, this cistern was also attributed to the Byzantine period.

79.   11-10/07-2   11080 10750   16080 60750
Kh. Umm Qallum (M)
Ruins of settlement (c. 20 dunams) on flat agricultural field N of Nahal Shiqma. Dense scatter of small marble fragments, small fieldstones, broken kiln bricks, slag, tesserae, and pottery sherds. On N side, a structure (3 x 4 m) with walls (0.60 m width) preserved 1.5–2 m high; built of cemented fieldstones.

Inside the structure, a pile of *kurkar* stones, some dressed, and marble and basalt fragments, probably cleared from the adjacent agricultural field in recent times. Nearby on the N side, a cistern (diameter 2 m, depth 3.50 m).
Pottery: Roman, Byzantine, Early Islamic, medieval, and Ottoman.

80.   11-10/07-3   11090 10700   16090 60700
Nahal Shiqma (Wadi el Hesi)
Lime kiln (diameter c. 2 m, depth 2.5 m) on slope of a *kurkar* hill S of Nahal Shiqma. The kiln was cut during work to widen a dismantled old railway track, built at the very end of the Ottoman period (i.e., 1917). The location of the lime kiln in a well-dated artificial section leads to the conclusion that it was built somewhere between the years 1917 and 1948.
For the railway track, see Sasson and Huster 2010:95–102.

81.   11-10/17-1   11180 10725   16180 60725
Nahal Shiqma (Wadi el Hesi)
Collapsed and blocked cistern; details not visible. Light scatter of pottery sherds (c. 100 m²).
Pottery: Byzantine.

82.   11-10/37-1   11380 10700   16380 60700
Nahal Shiqma (Wadi el Hesi)
Settlement remains (c. 40 dunams) on flat terrain, N of and close to Nahal Shiqma. Accumulation of rubble and silt caused the place to be elevated some 1.5 m above the flat fields around. Scatter of broken building stones, small fieldstones, marble fragments, basalt grinding stone fragments, and pottery sherds.
Pottery: Roman, Byzantine, Early Islamic, medieval, and Ottoman.
Identification: Kh. Qamsa. On June 22, 1867, C. Warren, who was surveying the plain of Philistia for the Palestine Exploration Fund, planned a direct route E from Nigid (Najd) to Dwaime (Dawayima) (Warren 1871:95). Leaving Nigid at 7:10 a.m. he stopped at the top of the first hill, left it at 7:45, headed E on the *kurkar* ridge ("through hills of indurated shells") until he arrived at Kh. Kums at 8:07, left at 8:10, was on Wadi Mehowre at 8:11, and came to Kh. Jelameh (Jalama) at 8:22. The immediate conclusion from Warren's description is that a certain Kh. Kums was situated a short distance W of Kh. Jalama, either on the S or the N bank of Wadi Hesi, and very close to the confluence of Wadi Mehowre (a corruption of Mahawir, the name of the northern section of Wadi Raml) with Wadi Hesi. In the Mandatory period, the Survey of Palestine designated a wide flat area north of Wadi Hesy as Qamsa, on the topocadastral map of Bureir (Sheet 11-10). This designation reflects the traditional name and boundaries of agricultural lands as in other cases in the map (e.g., the designation Bureir for the land of that village, or Sha^crata for the land of a former settlement bearing the same name—site 112 below). It seems that the original location of Kh. Kums/Qamsa was eventually lost, possibly due to the fact that the site was partly covered with sediment as result of frequent flooding in Wadi Hesi. In 1930 Ory visited a site named Kh. Qamsa and described it as located "on low ground, on the Wadi Ruml, south of Kh. Jalameh" (report N° S. 1078, February 4 1930, Kh. Qamsa file). In 1944 Kh. Qamsa was included in the Mandatory list of archaeological sites (1944 Schedule:1297). The remains were described as rubble cisterns, a well, and surface pottery, and the location fixed near the intersection of coordinates 114-105. This description and the general location given by Ory lead to the E edge of sites 130 and 131 (see below), a disturbed area with only a few surface sherds of the Byzantine period. Later, the place of the site was marked officially by the Department of Antiquities at the intersection of coordinates 11460-10565, but repeated visits by the author and other surveyors to the place yielded not even a handful of sherds, so that the existence of a site there should be rejected. On the other hand, during a visit to site 82 in December 2010, more medieval (Mamluk and Early Ottoman periods) sherds, as well as imported Italian pottery dated to the sixteenth to seventeenth centuries, were collected. Qamsa (Camsa) is one of fourteen villages listed in Crusader period documents from 1256–57 relating to a geographical region located east and southeast of Ashkelon. This Crusader village has been identified by several researchers with Kh. Kamas/Kemas (preferably Qimas), E of Ashkelon and NW of Kaukaba (e.g., Rey 1883:406; Röhricht 1887:240; Conder 1890:31; Prawer, 1958:235), at coordinates 1167-1164. Indeed, Kh. Kemas/Kamas/Qimas is noteworthy for its large twelfth- and thirteenth-century occupation and is therefore a possible candidate for the Crusader village under discussion (see Allen in *Ashkelon 1*, p. 50). Despite these arguments, the identification of site 82 as the Crusader Camsa is preferable, both for linguistic reasons (since the equation Qamsa=Camsa is more exact) and geographical reasons, as Qamsa is located in a territorial cluster of five settlements listed in the same Crusader period document(s), along with Saarethe (site 112), Semsem (site 52), Zeite (site 9), and Beitderas seconde (Beit Daras, at coordinates 1095-1086; see Yalqut HaPirsumim 1964:1451). The village name appears again in the sixteenth-century Ottoman *defters*: Qamsa was enumerated in the list of taxed villages in 1596, as part of Liwa (the district of) Gaza (Hütteroth and Abdulfattah 1977:149). Reference: Huster and Blakely, in press.

83.   11-10/47-1   11495 10720   16495 60720
Nahal Shiqma (Wadi el Hesi)
Well (partly blocked, diameter c. 2 m, visible depth 10 m) on flat terrain N of Nahal Shiqma. Nearby, a pool (c. 3 x 3 m). Both installations were built of modern cement blocks.
Pottery: Ottoman (late) and modern.

84.   11-10/57-1   11565 10730   16565 60730
Nahal Shiqma (Wadi el Hesi)
Light scatter of fieldstones, fragments of glass vessels and pottery sherds (c. 400 m²) on elevated terrain. Recent active cemetery.
Pottery: Byzantine.

85.   11-10/77-1   11780 10780   16780 60780
Nahal Shiqma (Wadi el Hesi)
Light scatter of flint implements (c. 1 dunam) on *hamra* hill (+90 m), N of Nahal Shiqma. The assemblage includes handaxes, scrapers, points, and blades.
Lithic finds: Lower Paleolithic.

86.   11-10/77-2   11750 10770   16750 60770
Nahal Shiqma (Wadi el Hesi)
Light scatter of flint implements (c. 200 m²) on moderate S slope of *hamra* hill covered by a thin loess layer.
Lithic finds: Lower Paleolithic.

87.   11-10/77-3   11735 10740   16735 60740
Nahal Shiqma (Wadi el Hesi)
Burial structure (1.6 x 2.4 m) on moderate slope of loessic hill, 600 m N of Kh. Shaᶜrata (site 112 below). Built of small fieldstones bonded with mud cement. The entrance (0.8 x 0.8 m), in the E side, was sealed by a monolithic stone. Remains of human bones and pottery sherds.
Pottery: Byzantine.
Reference: Huster and Sion 2006:61–64, Table 1 no. 79 (there, wrong coordinate).

88.   11-10/77-4   11950 10700   16950 60700
Nahal Shiqma (Wadi el Hesi)
Remains of ancient settlement (c. 12 dunams) on a low elevation, near a tributary of Nahal Shiqma: Layers of dark loess soil containing pebbles, flint flakes, flint sickle blades, and pottery sherds.
   Near the wadi bed, several heaps of stones cleared from the site containing limestone mortar fragments and basalt grinding stones.
Lithic finds and pottery: Late Bronze.

89.   11-10/06-1   11080 10690   16080 60690
Tell Magharat Ghazza (M)
Light scatter of flint implements (c. 400 m²) on slopes of a *kurkar* hill (and not a tell as marked on Mandatory maps), S of Nahal Shiqma.
   On S, *kurkar* stone quarries on natural cliff.
Lithic finds: Lower Paleolithic.

90.   11-10/06-2   11045 10685   16045 60685
Nahal Shiqma (Wadi el Hesi)
A bell-shaped cistern (diameter 3 m, depth 4 m) on N slope of a *kurkar* hill. Built of small stones mortared with lime cement. Scatter of pottery sherds (c. 200 m²)
Pottery: Byzantine.

91.   11-10/06-3   11090 10600   16090 60600
Nahal Mardim (Wadi Mardin)
Ancient settlement remains (c. 4 dunams) on top and slopes of a *kurkar* hill E of Nahal Mardim. On E slope, a rock-hewn cave (c. 4 x 5 m, 2 m high), probably a stone quarry. On E moderate slope, structural foundations, built of cemented fieldstones.
   Nearby, remains of a coarse tiled mosaic floor (c. 2 x 2 m). Dense concentration of pottery sherds.
Pottery: Roman and Byzantine.

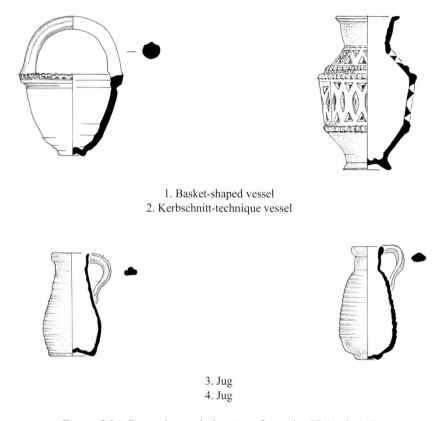

1. Basket-shaped vessel
2. Kerbschnitt-technique vessel

3. Jug
4. Jug

Figure 5.24: Byzantine period pottery from site 87 (scale 1:5)

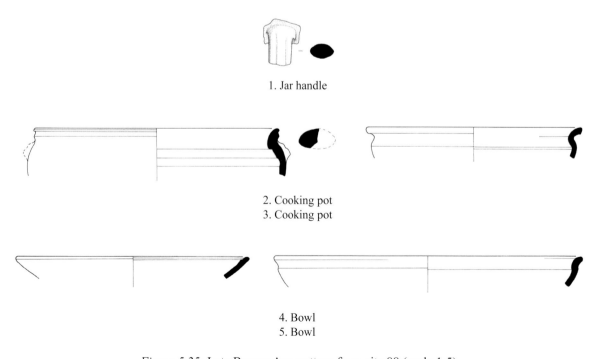

1. Jar handle

2. Cooking pot
3. Cooking pot

4. Bowl
5. Bowl

Figure 5.25: Late Bronze Age pottery from site 88 (scale 1:5)

Figure 5.26: Late Bronze Age flint sickle blade from site 88 (scale 1:2)

Figure 5.27: Site 91

92.   11-10/16-1   11170 10690   16170 60690
Nejed (S)
Najd (M)
Ruins of Arab village (c. 40 dunams) on hills E of Wadi el Khirba. Among the ruined dwellings, ancient remains: Building stones, column fragments, broken basalt grinding stones, and pottery sherds. On W moderate slope, a well (diameter 2.5 m, depth 16 m) and nearby pool (4 x 4 m). To the SE, a cemetery (c. 1 dunam), recognized by arranged gravestones. Farther to E, collapsed building built of dressed *kurkar* stones. South of the village, remains of abandoned orchards delineated by stone and cactus fences.
Pottery: Hellenistic, Roman, Byzantine, Early Islamic, medieval, Ottoman, and modern.
References: Guérin 1869:292; Conder and Kitchener 1881–83, III:260; Petrie 1891:53.

93.   11-10/16-2   11190 10660   16190 60660
Najd
Sandstone quarry on natural cliff of a *kurkar* hill, S of the village ruins, c. 100 m long. In front of the quarry, several stone heaps. Light scatter of pottery sherds.
Pottery: Byzantine, Early Islamic, medieval, Ottoman, and modern.

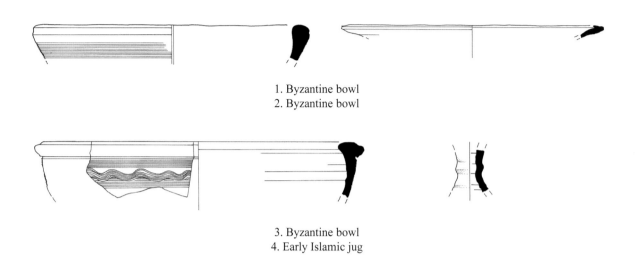

1. Byzantine bowl
2. Byzantine bowl

3. Byzantine bowl
4. Early Islamic jug

Figure 5.28: Pottery from site 93 (scale 1:5)

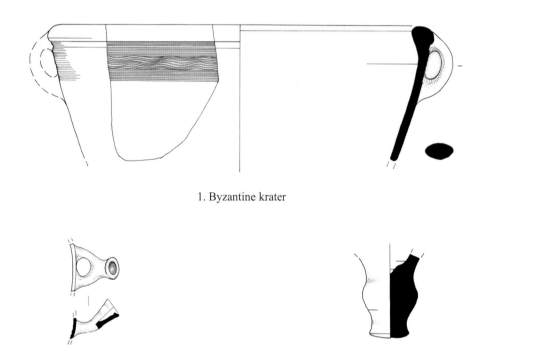

1. Byzantine krater

2. Byzantine cooking pot handle
3. Early Islamic jug

Figure 5.29: Pottery from site 94 (scale 1:5)

94.   11-10/16-3   11140 10630   16140 60630
Kh. Umm Tabun (M)
Remains of settlement on prolonged and narrow *kurkar* ridge (c. 100 x 400 m), between two tributaries of Nahal Shiqma (Wadi Mardin and Wadi el Khirba). On the summit, four cisterns (now mostly blocked, diameter 2.5–3 m, depth 4–5 m). On E slope, remains of a structure (3 x 4 m) built of *kurkar* stones. Nearby, two monolithic large stones (beam weights of an olive press). On W slope, structural foundations and scattered building stones. On the N edge of the site, rock-hewn caves created by quarrying. On the S end, a flat artificial elevation (c. 1 dunam). Fragmentary remains of a large building (c. 15 x 20 m) containing a cistern, surrounded by scattered marble fragments, pieces of plaster, pottery sherds, and small tesserae.
Pottery: Hellenistic, Roman, Byzantine, Early Islamic, medieval, Ottoman, and modern.
References: Guérin 1869:293; Conder and Kitchener 1881–83, III:287; Petrie 1891:53.

95.   11-10/16-4   11170 10620   16170 60620
Kh. Umm Tabun
Burial system on W moderate slope of a *kurkar* hill. Built of small fieldstones bonded with mud cement. Composed of a main chamber (c. 2 x 4.5 m) and four rooms (c. 2 x 2 m each), arranged symmetrically. The inner faces of the walls of the main room are plastered and decorated with geometric patterns, plants, and fourteen human images placed in rounded medallions. Dated to the Byzantine period.
References: Tsafrir 1968; Michaeli 1990; Huster and Sion 2006:61–64, Table 1, no. 74.

96.   11-10/26-1   11240 10660   16240 60660
Nahal Shiqma (Wadi el Hesi)
Light scatter of flint implements (c. 100 m²) on S slope of *hamra* hill.
Lithic finds: Lower Paleolithic.

97.   11-10/26-2   11270 10660   16270 60670
Nahal Shiqma (Wadi el Hesi)
Light scatter of flint implements (c. 200 m²) on E slope of a *kurkar* hill covered by a thin layer of *hamra*. Some tools were made using the Levallois technique.
Lithic finds: Lower Paleolithic.

98.   11-10/26-3   11280 10650   16280 60650
Nahal Shiqma (Wadi el Hesi)
Scatter of flint implements (c. 100 m²) eroded away by water from an eroded hill. Two geological layers were noted: The upper, sandy layer is composed of soft *kurkar*, while the lower is of hard petrified sandstone. On W side, a sandstone quarry, located in a natural cliff. Nearby, a moderate scatter of pottery sherds (c. 100 m²).
Lithic finds: Lower Paleolithic.
Pottery: Byzantine.

99.   11-10/26-4   11260 10620   16260 60620
Nahal Nir^cam (Wadi Najd)
Light scatter of flint implements (c. 100 m²) on moderate slope of a *kurkar* hill (+90 m), S of triangulation point 295. Use of Levallois technique.
Lithic finds: Lower Paleolithic.

100.   11-10/26-5   11290 10610   16290 60610
Nahal Nir^cam (Wadi Najd)
Dense concentration of flint implements (c. 500 m²) on E slope of *kurkar* ridge, descending toward Nahal Nir^cam. Several handaxes. Cores produced using the Levallois technique.
Lithic finds: Lower Paleolithic.

101.   11-10/36-1   11340 10690   16340 60690
Nahal Shiqma (Wadi el Hesi)
Light scatter of flint implements on a *kurkar* hill (triangulation point 14Y; c. 100 m²). Here, the ancient dunes, now forming a *kurkar* ridge, caused a sharp bend in the course of Nahal Shiqma.
Lithic finds: Lower Paleolithic.

1. Core, Zevallois technique
2. End Scraper

Figure 5.30: Lithics from the Lower Paleolithic period from site 99 (scale 1:2)

102.   11-10/36-2   11305 10670   16305 60670
Nahal Nir^cam (Wadi Najd)
Ruinous structure on top of a *kurkar* hill (c. 3 x 3 m), erosion by water caused its destruction and the scatter of fieldstones, plaster fragments, coarse tesserae, and pottery sherds over the W slope, where flint implements were also collected.
Lithic finds: Lower Paleolithic.

Pottery: Byzantine.
103.   11-10/36-3   11330 10660   16330 60660
Nahal Nir^cam (Wadi Najd)
Concentration of small fieldstones (c. 50 m²) on top of a *kurkar* hill. Light scatter of pottery sherds.
Pottery: Byzantine.

104.   11-10/36-4   11335 10650   16335 60650
Nahal Nir^cam (Wadi Najd)
Ruinous structure (c. 2 x 4 m) on W moderate slope of *kurkar* ridge, E of wadi bed (Nahal Nir^cam). Built of fieldstones bonded with a lime cement. Collapsed vaulted segments demonstrate that this was a burial structure. Few fragments of pottery.
Pottery: Byzantine.
Reference: Huster and Sion 2006:61–64, Table 1 no. 76.

105.   11-10/36-5   11310 10630   16310 60630
Nahal Nir^cam (Wadi Najd)
Ruins of a small deserted Arab village (c. 10 dunams). About twelve dwellings, some preserved 2 m high, built of sun-dried mudbricks. On E edge, a well (at present blocked) and a pool (c. 3 x 3 m, 1.3 m deep).
Pottery: Modern.

106.   11-10/36-6   11375 10615   16375 60615
Nahal Hoga (Wadi er Raml, Wadi el Mahawir)
Cistern (blocked) in flat terrain, at present in a citrus grove. Scatter of pottery (c. 400 m²).
Pottery: Byzantine.

107.   11-10/37-7   11380 10610   16380 60610
Nahal Hoga (Wadi er Raml, Wadi el Mahawir)
Cistern (blocked) in a citrus grove. Light scatter of pottery sherds (c. 100 m²).
Pottery: Byzantine.

Figure 5.31: Site 105

Figure 5.32: Winepress at site 108

108.   11-10/46-1   11450 10650   16450 60650
Hurvat Gluma
Kh. Jelameh (S)
Kh. Jalama (M)
Settlement remains (c. 20 dunams) on low elevation (caused by accumulation of debris), on S bank of Nahal Shiqma. Two cisterns (blocked), collapsed remains of a square structure (c. 4 x 4 m) built of cemented fieldstones, and remains of an agricultural installation (3 x 4 m), composed of three cells (c. 1.1 x 2.5 m each), paved with coarse tesserae placed on foundations built of vertical pottery sherds—probably a winepress. Fragment of a marble column (length c. 2 m) bearing an Arabic inscription dated to the end of the seventh century A.D. (M. Sharon, pers. comm.). Scatter of marble fragments, dressed and undressed building stones, and dense scatter of pottery sherds. The identification of the site with Jalama of the sixteenth-century Ottoman *defters* (Hütteroth and Abdulfattah 1977:149) seems positive.
Pottery: Roman, Byzantine, Early Islamic, medieval, and Ottoman.
References: Guérin 1869:294; Conder and Kitchener 1881–83, III:282.

109.   11-10/46-2   11425 10615   61425 60615
Beʾer Gluma
Bir Jalama (M)
Well in flat terrain (diameter 3 m, blocked at present), close to Nahal Hoga (Wadi er Raml, indicated on Mandatory maps as Wadi Mahawir at a short section before it joins Nahal Shiqma/Wadi el Hesi; Survey of Palestine, Sheet 11-10, Bureir). Built of dressed *kurkar* stones. No indicative pottery sherds, but the construction style indicates a date in the late nineteenth century.

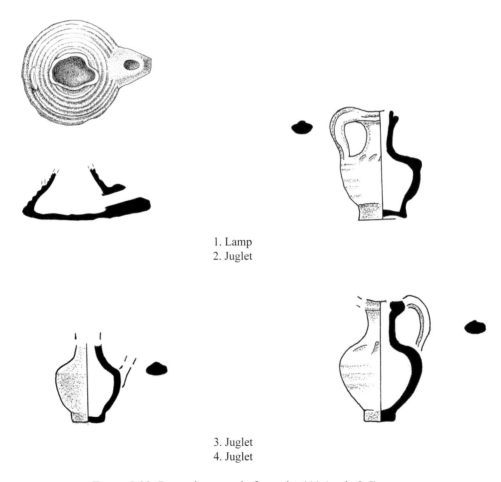

1. Lamp
2. Juglet

3. Juglet
4. Juglet

Figure 5.33: Byzantine vessels from site 111 (scale 2:5)

110.   11-10/56-1   11530 10650   16530 60650
Nahal Shiqma
Light scatter of fieldstones, pebbles, patches of ashy soil, and pottery sherds (c. 200 m²) on flat land N of Nahal Shiqma.
Pottery: Byzantine.

111.   11-10/66-1   11660 10600   16660 60600
Kh. Beit Tafa (M)
Scatter of building stone fragments, roof tiles, glass vessels, small tesserae, and pottery sherds on flat ground, N of and close to Nahal Shiqma (c. 10 dunams). The site size may in fact be larger, obscured by the fact that the ground here was flooded in the past due to its proximity to the narrow river channel.

During the installation of a pipeline at a point 200 m from the site's center, ancient remains were raised from a depth of 1.5 m, underneath a clay layer (among the finds: kiln waste, slag, and many pottery sherds, indicating the existence of a pottery workshop).

Beit Tafa does not appear as a village in the sixteenth-century Ottoman *defters*; instead, it seems to have been a *mazraᶜa* (a sown field, typically the lands of an abandoned village). The lands of the *mazraᶜa* Beit Tafa are described in a *waqfiyya* (deed) dated to 1560, and were S of the Wadi Hesi (Natsheh 2000:1014, 1060) and therefore S of the *khirbeh*. The Ottoman pottery collected must therefore represent temporary settlement or activity at the site, perhaps seasonal habitation related to planting or harvesting the *mazraᶜa*.
Pottery: Roman, Byzantine, Early Islamic, medieval, and Ottoman.

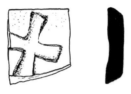

1. Decorated Byzantine sherd

2. Byzantine lamp
3. Byzantine lamp

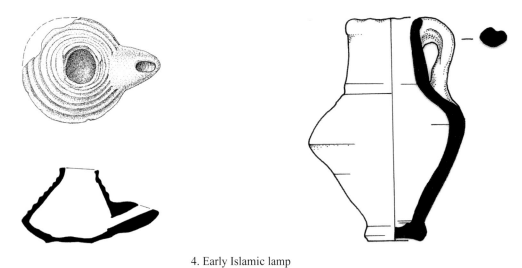

4. Early Islamic lamp
5. Early Islamic jug

Figure 5.34: Pottery from site 112 (scale 2:5)

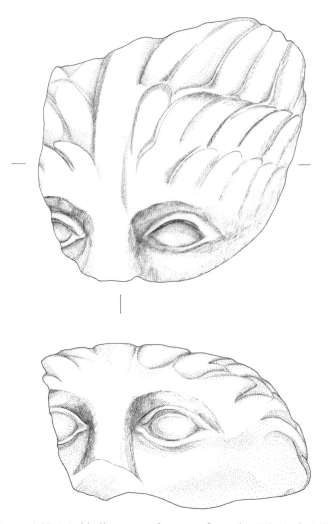

Figure 5.35: Marble lion statue fragment from site 112 (scale 1:2)

112.   11-10/76-1   11740 10660   16740 60660
H. Kefar Se^cora
Kh. Sha^crata (S)
Kh. Sha^carta; Kh. Sha^cratta (M)
Settlement remains (c. 40 dunams) on flat terrain N of Nahal Shiqma. Accumulation of debris caused the place to be elevated some 2 m above the flat fields around. Two bell-shaped cisterns, segments of structural foundations, scatter of building stones, basalt grinding stone fragments, tesserae, and pottery sherds. On E side, kiln waste, slag, and large accumulation of pottery sherds. At the site's center, marble capitals, broken pillars, two marble chancel screen posts, and a fragment of a marble chancel screen decorated with a cross. These finds indicate that a church of the Byzantine period stood here. Kh. Sha^crata was first visited by Conder and Kitchener (1881–83, III:285; see also Survey of Western Palestine, Sheet XX, Fw; Palmer 1881:374). In the late nineteenth century it was identified by Clermont-Ganneau with Kefar Se^carta, where the monk Zeno settled in a monastery toward the end of his life (Clermont-Ganneau 1896:437; 1897:15–16). This identification seems definite not only because of the name, but especially because of the distance from Gaza. Kefar Se^carta was mentioned in two works composed by John Rufus in the sixth century: *Plerophoriae* and the *Life of Peter the Iberian*. The latter source indicates also the distance, "about fifteen miles from Gaza." Fifteen Roman miles are equivalent to c. 24 km. The direct distance from Gaza to Kh. Sha^crata is 18 km. The direction of the customary main route to Beit Guvrin was initially northeast with the objective to cross Wadi el Hesi (probably on a bridge), then, on the northern bank of the wadi it turned to the east, passing through Najd, Sumsum, and Bureir. Kh. Sha^crata is located c. 2.5 km southeast of Bureir. Considering this detour, one may assume that the total length of the way is in accordance with the distance in the text. It is worth mentioning the existence of another ruin named Kh. Sha^carta (also called Kh. el Qutshan), that may represent the village of Kefar Se^carta. The remains are typical of the Byzantine period and include finds which suggest that a church stood there also (Hirschfeld 2004:72–73; Hirschfeld has identified the church at the southern Kh. Sha^carta with the monastery of Zeno). This place is situated in the Besor region of the western Negev exactly 10 km (c. 6.25 Roman miles) south of Gaza. Since this distance is not close to that given by John Rufus, and the direction is not mentioned in the text, the identification of Se^carta with the southern Kh. Sha^carta should be rejected. Clermont-Ganneau (1897:15–16) also suggested that site 112, the northern Kh Sha^crata, should be identified as Saarethe, a Crusader village that belonged in 1256 to the Hospitallers; Prawer's identification is the same (1958:235–36). The site is also identified as *Sha^carta al-Kubra* (*Tabi Burayr*) of the sixteenth-century Ottoman *defters* (Hütteroth and Abdulfattah, 1977:144). Pottery: Roman, Byzantine, Early Islamic, medieval, and Ottoman.

113.   11-10/76-2   11755 10640   16755 60640
Nahal Shiqma (Wadi el Hesi)
Bell-shaped cistern on a flat field N of Nahal Shiqma and some 300 m S of Kh. Sha^crata. Built of cemented fieldstones (diameter 3 m, visible depth 2 m). Moderate scatter of pottery sherds (including sherds of the Late Bronze Age moved here from site 114 by modern agricultural activity).
Pottery: Byzantine and Early Islamic.

114.   11-10/76-3   11780 10630   16780 60630
Nahal Shiqma (Wadi el Hesi)
Settlement remains (c. 10 dunams) on raised area among flat fields, N of Nahal Shiqma. Patches of ashy soil, fragments of basalt grinding stones, flint implements (mainly sickle blades), and pottery sherds.
Pottery: Chalcolithic (few) and Late Bronze.

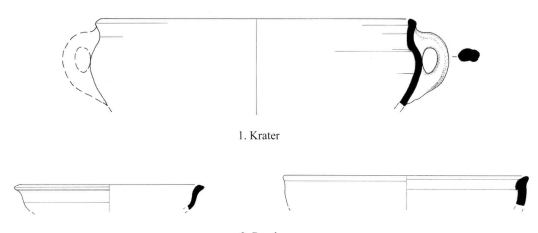

1. Krater

2. Bowl
3. Cooking vessel

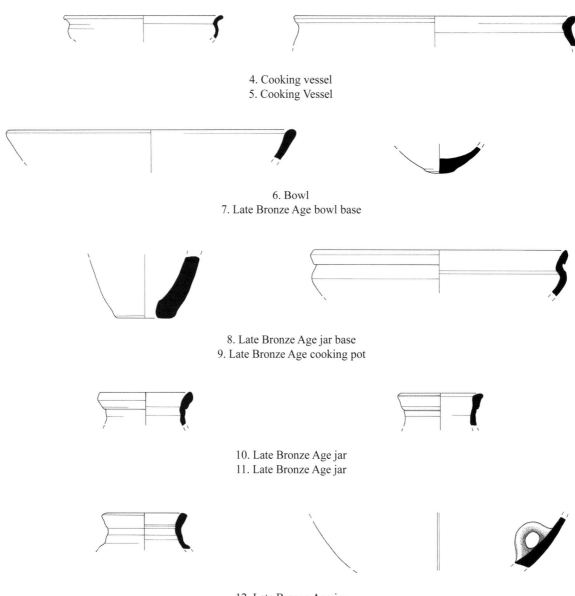

4. Cooking vessel
5. Cooking Vessel

6. Bowl
7. Late Bronze Age bowl base

8. Late Bronze Age jar base
9. Late Bronze Age cooking pot

10. Late Bronze Age jar
11. Late Bronze Age jar

12. Late Bronze Age jar
13. Late Bronze Age inner handle of spinning bowl

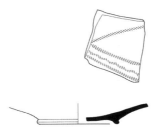

14. Late Bronze Age decorated bowl

Figure 5.36: Pottery from site 114 (scale 1:5)

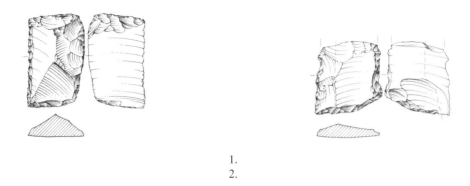

1.
2.

Figure 5.37: Late Bronze Age flint sickle blades from site 114 (scale 1:2)

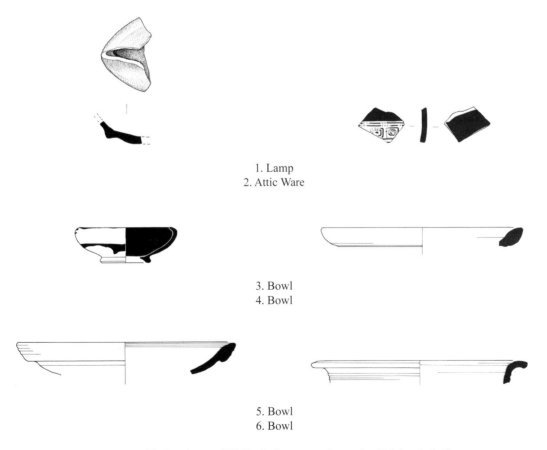

1. Lamp
2. Attic Ware

3. Bowl
4. Bowl

5. Bowl
6. Bowl

Figure 5.38: Persian and Hellenistic pottery from site 115 (scale 1:5)

115.   11-10/76-4   11750 10600   16750 60600
Nahal Shiqma (Wadi el Hesi)
Settlement remains on flat terrain N of Nahal Shiqma (c. 4 dunams). Patches of ashy soil, scatter of pebbles, fieldstones, burned bone, and pottery sherds.
Pottery: Persian and Hellenistic.

116.   11-10/96-1   11960 10690   16960 60690
Nahal Hatzav (Wadi El Khanazir)
Ruins of dwellings from the late Ottoman and Mandatory periods on flat terrain E of Nahal Hatzav (Wadi el Khanazir), a tributary of Nahal Shiqma. The group of structures is dispersed over an area of c. 15 dunams. One large structure (4 x 6 m), built of sun-dried mudbricks bonded by mud with straw. Other structures have smaller dimensions; in some, the western wall was built of stones, probably because this is the main direction of the wind (and rain). Nearby, abandoned orchards (c. 50 dunams).
Pottery: Late Ottoman and Mandatory.

117.   11-10/96-2   11980 10630   16980 60630
Nahal Hatzav
Well (partly blocked, diameter 2.8 m, visible depth c. 5 m) on flat land, close to a gully, a tributary of Nahal Hatzav. Built of dressed *kurkar* stones. Nearby, a collapsed pool (3 x 3 m), a square pillar base (1 x 1 m), and a burnt wood beam, all indicating that water was drawn by means of a "Persian wheel" (*saqiye*).
Pottery: Late Ottoman and Mandatory.

118.   11-10/96-3   11940 10635   16940 60635
Nahal Shiqma (Wadi el Hesi)
Ruinous structure (c. 8 x 10 m) on a *kurkar* hill, S of Nahal Shiqma. Ashlar-built outer walls preserved 1.8 m high. Inner dividing walls built of sun-dried mudbricks, preserved 5–6 courses high. At foot of hill to W, remains of an additional structure (c. 4 x 4 m), built of sun-dried mudbricks, except the western wall which was built of fieldstones bonded by mud with straw, preserved 4–5 courses high.
Pottery: Late Ottoman and Mandatory.

119.   11-10/96-4   11940 10610   16940 60610
Nahal Shiqma (Wadi el Hesi)
Well (3.0 m diameter, c. 20 m depth) in sandy valley between low *kurkar* hills S of Nahal Shiqma. Built of dressed *kurkar* stones. No signs of use, nor indicative finds. Nearby, an artificial sand pile suggests that the well was abandoned shortly after it was excavated, probably at the end of the Mandatory period.

120.   11-10/96-5   11910 10600   16910 60600
Nahal Shiqma (Wadi el Hesi)
Light scatter of flint implements (c. 400 m²) in area of small *hamra* hills S of Nahal Shiqma. Many flakes produced by the use of the Levallois technique.
Lithic finds: Lower Paleolithic.

121.   11-10/05-1   11020 10590   16020 60590
Nahal Mardim (Wadi Mardin)
Bell-shaped cistern (diameter 2.5 m, depth 4 m) on moderate slope descending W from a *kurkar* hill, toward Nahal Mardim. Built of cemented small fieldstones. Nearby, dense scatter of pottery sherds (c. 100 m²). Sherds and flint implements also on hilltop and slopes.
Lithic finds: Lower Paleolithic.
Pottery: Byzantine.

122.   11-10/05-2   11060 10580   16060 60580
Nahal Mardim (Wadi Mardin)
Foundations of two structures (2 x 2 m and 2 x 2.5 m) and remains of fieldstone fences, preserved 3–4 courses high, on a *kurkar* hill partly covered by *hamra* soil, located between two tributaries of Nahal Mardim. Dense scatter of pottery sherds (c. 400 m²).
Pottery: Byzantine.

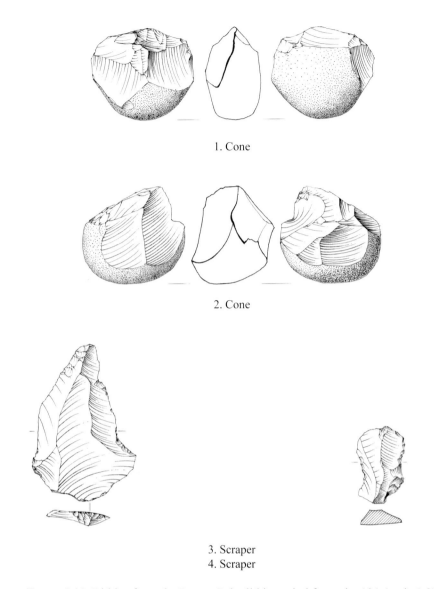

1. Cone

2. Cone

3. Scraper
4. Scraper

Figure 5.39: Lithics from the Lower Paleolithic period from site 121 (scale 1:2)

123.   11-10/05-3   11020 10510   16020 60510
Nahal Kosses (Wadi el Makkus)
Structural foundations (3 x 3 m) on a *kurkar* hilltop E of Nahal Kosses. Built of fieldstones bonded with lime cement. Nearby, dense scatter of pottery sherds (c. 200 m²). On N slope, light scatter of flint implements.
Lithic finds: Lower Paleolithic.
Pottery: Byzantine.

124.   11-10/05-4   11050 10530   16050 60530
Nahal Mardim (Wadi Mardin)
Light scatter of flint implements (c. 500 m²) on a *kurkar* hill (+119 m). A natural section enables the distinction of alternating strata of *kurkar* and *hamra* soil formations. The flint tools originated in the upper *hamra* layer.
Lithic finds: Lower Paleolithic.

125.   11-10/05-5   11070 10510   16070 60510
Nahal Mardim (Wadi Mardin)
Light scatter of flint implements (c. 400 m²) on E slope of a *kurkar* hill descending toward Nahal Mardin.
Lithic finds: Lower Paleolithic.

126.   11-10/25-1   11205 10555   16205 60555
Nahal Nir^cam (Wadi Najd)
Bell-shaped cistern (diameter 2.8 m, depth 4 m) on moderate slope of a *kurkar* hill covered by loess soil, facing Nahal Nir^cam on the E. Nearby, scatter of plaster fragments, tesserae, and pottery sherds (c. 100 m²).
Pottery: Byzantine.

127.   11-10/25-2   11210 10510   16210 60510
Kh. Nejed (S)
Kh. Najd (M)
Remains of settlement (c. 20 dunams) on elongated spur of *kurkar* ridge covered by loess, N of Nahal Tal (Wadi el Jabali) and W of Nahal Nir^cam (Wadi Najd). Remains of several installations: Five bell-shaped cisterns—three in the site's center, two on the edges. On the E, a well (2.5 m diameter, partly blocked) and a pool (5 x 5 m) nearby. The pool was built of small *kurkar* stones bonded with lime cement and the walls were lined with pinkish-colored plaster (cf. site 50 above). To the W of the pool (c. 40 m), remains of a rectangular installation (c. 4 x 4 m) surrounded by rough tesserae, probably a winepress. On S edge, a collapsed burial system that includes a small rectangular central chamber and four cells, each of them covered with a vaulted roof. On E side, a curved wall (0.8 m thickness, 4–5 courses preserved). Nearby, a scatter of dressed stones, fragments of marble architectural elements, and pottery sherds.
Pottery: Roman, Byzantine, Early Islamic, medieval, and Ottoman.
References: Conder and Kitchener 1881–83, III:285; Huster and Sion 2006:58 and no. 77.

Figure 5.40: Collapsed burial system from site 127

128.   11-10/35-1   11380 10595   16380 60595
Nahal Hoga (Wadi er Raml, Wadi el Mahawir)
Two bell-shaped cisterns (diameter 2.5–2.8 m, apparent depth 2–2.5 m) on a *kurkar* hill covered by a loess layer W of Nahal Hoga, constructed of small stones mortared with lime cement; the walls are lined with plaster. Nearby, many scatters of rough tesserae and pottery sherds.
Pottery: Byzantine.

129.   11-10/35-2   11395 10580   16395 60580
Nahal Hoga (Wadi er Raml, Wadi el Mahawir)
A bell-shaped cistern (diameter 2.8 m, apparent depth 4 m) on moderate slope descending to the E. Built of small stones mortared with lime cement. Scatter of pottery sherds (c. 100 m²).
Pottery: Byzantine.

130.   11-10/45-1   11405 10580   16405 60580
Nahal Hoga (Wadi er Raml, Wadi el Mahawir)
A bell-shaped cistern on moderate slope. Scanty remains (currently in a citrus orchard). Scatter of pottery sherds (c. 100 m²).
Pottery: Byzantine.

131.   11-10/45-2   11410 10580   16410 60580
Nahal Hoga (Wadi er Raml, Wadi el Mahawir)
Collapsed remains of a structure (c. 2 x 3 m) on hill slope descending toward Nahal Hoga. Vaulted blocks built of small stones mortared with lime cement. The extant features point to a burial system. Mandatory maps (Sheet 11/10, Bureir, Scale 1:20,000) indicate a tomb here. Few pottery sherds (c. 100 m²).
Pottery: Byzantine.
Reference: Huster and Sion 2006:61–64, Table 1 no. 75 (wrong coordinate there).

132.   11-10/65-1   11660 10570   16660 60570
Nahal Shiqma (Wadi el Hesi)
Remains of settlement (c. 2 dunams) on plain, close to S bank of Nahal Shiqma. Scatter of pebbles, fieldstones, and potsherds, revealed mainly in ashy dumps within brown-colored loess soil.
Pottery: Byzantine and Early Islamic.

133.   11-10/65-2   11690 10560   16690 60560
Nahal Shiqma (Wadi el Hesi)
Scatter of pebbles, fieldstones, fragments of basalt grinding stones, and pottery sherds (c. 800 m²) on a plain S of Nahal Shiqma.
Pottery: Byzantine.

134.   11-10/65-3   11640 10510   16640 60510
Nahal Shiqma (Wadi el Hesi)
Light scatter of flint implements (c. 400 m²) on moderate slope of *hamra* hill descending N to Nahal Shiqma.
Lithic Finds: Lower Paleolithic.

135.   11-10/75-1   11750 10580   16750 60580
Nahal Shiqma (Wadi el Hesi)
Scatter of small pebbles, fieldstones, fragments of lime tiles, roofing tiles, and pottery sherds (c. 1 dunam) on plain, along S bank of Nahal Shiqma.
Pottery: Roman and Byzantine.

136.   11-10/75-2   11790 10580   16790 60580
Nahal Shiqma (Wadi el Hesi)
Remains of a pottery kiln (diameter 1.8 m) on the bank of a tributary of Nahal Shiqma. Fired mudbricks, slag, and dense concentration of pottery sherds were exposed by runoff. This installation seems to be part of a pottery workshop located in the industrial area of an ancient settlement (see site 138).
Pottery: Byzantine.

Figure 5.41: Well from site 138

137.   11-10/75-3   11780 10570   16780 60570
Kh. el Marashan (S)
Kh. Sawabta (M)
Collapsed remains of a structure on the hillside, c. 100 m N of Kh. el Marashan, revealed as a result of recent quarrying activity. The structure was built of large hard *kurkar* stones (0.5 x 0.8 x 1.0 m). Few sherds around the structure.
Pottery: Roman and Byzantine.

138.   11-10/75-4   11790 10580   16790 60580
Kh. el Marashan (S)
Kh. Sawabta (M)
Remains of an ancient settlement beneath the ruins of an Arab village (each c. 10 dunams). Located on a series of low *kurkar* and *hamra* hills. On top of the central hill, a well (diameter 2.5 m, depth 25 m) with a rectangular structure with water troughs built over it. Nearby, a cistern (diameter 4 m; apparent depth 5 m), built of small stones bonded with lime cement. Scatters of building stones (some dressed), fragments of marble, glass vessels, and pottery sherds. On W slope, runoff exposed a shaft containing human bones and broken pottery vessels. At the bottom of the adjacent wadi, the same finds were observed.
　　Around the end of the Ottoman period or the beginning of the Mandatory period, Arab farmers settled here (neither Conder and Kitchener nor Petrie mention an Arab village). Ruins of some twenty dwellings were observed.
Pottery: Middle Bronze, Roman, Byzantine, Early Islamic, medieval, Ottoman, and modern.
References: Conder and Kitchener 1881–83, III:284; Petrie 1891:52.

139.   11-10/75-5   11760 10550   16760 60550
Kh. el Marashan (S)
Kh. Sawabta (M)
Ancient remains (c. 500 m²) on small *hamra* hill, 200 m W of Kh. el Marashan. Fragmentary structural foundations. An underground space (2 x 3 m, depth 2 m) containing fragments of a collapsed mosaic floor that covered it (probably a crypt). A bell-shaped cistern (diameter 3 m; depth 3 m) built of small stones bonded with lime cement. Scatter of *kurkar* building stones, fragments of marble, glass vessels, roof tiles, pottery sherds, and tesserae.
Pottery: Roman, Byzantine, Ottoman, and modern.

140.   11-10/75-6   11770 10510   16770 60510
Nahal Zedim (Wadi el Manyasa)
Light scatter of flint implements (c. 200 m²) on low *hamra* hill covered by a loess layer. Two dwellings (4 x 3 m, 4 x 4 m) built of unfired mudbricks.
Lithic finds: Lower Paleolithic.
Pottery: Modern.

141.   11-10/85-1   11870 10570   16870 60570
Nahal Zedim (Wadi el Manyasa)
Group of five dwellings on spur of a *kurkar* hill covered by a loess layer, N of Nahal Zedim, a tributary of Nahal Shiqma. Built of unfired mudbricks, except western walls which were built of small stones bonded with mud (preserved 1.8–2 m high). Nearby, two round enclosures (diameter c. 10 m), built of *kurkar* stones, some dressed, probably brought from the adjacent ruins of Kh. el Marashan.
Pottery: Modern.

142.   11-10/85-2   11890 10550   16890 60550
Nahal Zedim (Wadi el Manyasa)
Group of four ruined dwellings on a sandy *kurkar* hill N of Nahal Zedim. Built of unfired mudbricks, preserved 1.5–1.7 m high.
Pottery: Modern.

143.   11-10/85-3   11850 10520   16850 60520
Nahal Zedim (Wadi el Manyasa)
Group of three ruined dwellings (c. 3 x 4 m each) on moderate slope of loess hill, located between two tributaries of Nahal Zedim. Walls (preserved 1.8–2 m high) built of unfired mudbricks, except western walls, which were built of small stones bonded and plastered with mud.
Pottery: Modern.

144.   11-10/04-1   11020 10480   16020 60480
Nahal Kosses (Wadi el Makkus)
Scatter of flint implements (c. 100 m²) eroded from a *hamra* layer on a *kurkar* hill. Use of the Levallois technique.
Lithic finds: Lower Paleolithic.

145.   11-10/04-2   11070 10470   16070 60470
Nahal Tal (Wadi en Nada)
Light scatters of implements (c. 200 m²) in deep gorges close to Nahal Tal. Tools made by use of the Levallois technique.
Lithic finds: Lower Paleolithic.

146.   11-10/04-3   11060 10450   16060 60450
Nahal Tal (Wadi en Nada)
Dense concentrations of flint implements (c. 600 m²) on a *kurkar* hill (+110 m) covered by a *hamra* layer. Numerous flakes produced by use of the Levallois technique, together with tools, suggest that knapping activity took place at the site.
Lithic finds: Lower Paleolithic.

147.   11-10/04-4   11040 10430   16040 60430
Nahal Tal (Wadi en Nada)
Light scatter of flint implements (c. 100 m²) on slopes of a *kurkar* hill, covered by a thin layer of *hamra*.
Lithic finds: Lower Paleolithic.

148.   11-10/04-5   11060 10400   16060 60400
Nahal Tal (Wadi en Nada)
Light scatter of flint implements (c. 100 m²) on S and E slopes of a *kurkar* hill, W of Wadi el Bi, a small tributary of Wadi en Nada.
Lithic finds: Lower Paleolithic.

149.   11-10/14-1   11140 10460   16140 60460
Sderot (Wadi el Jabali)
Settlement remains (c. 5 dunams, now destroyed due to the construction of a neighborhood in Sderot). In the past, the site included two bell-shaped cisterns, a scatter of building stones, tesserae, and pottery sherds.
Pottery: Roman and Byzantine.

150.   11-10/24-1   11290 10485   16290 60485
Nahal Nir^cam (Wadi Najd)
Ancient remains (c. 500 m²) E of Nahal Nir^cam in a eucalyptus wood plantation. Scatter of fieldstones, coarse tesserae, and pottery sherds.
Pottery: Byzantine.

151.   11-10/24-2   11265 10430   16265 60430
Nahal Nir^cam (Wadi Najd)
Ancient cemetery on N slope of a *kurkar* hill, E of Nahal Nir^cam and some 700 m SE of Kh. Najd. Three cist tombs containing skeletons and small objects were excavated. Nearby, an infant burial in a jar was exposed.
Pottery: Roman and Byzantine.
Reference: Neder Ory, field diary 1991.

152.   11-10/34-1   11380 10470   16380 60470
Nahal Hoga (Wadi er Raml, Wadi el Mahawir)
Light scatter of flint implements (c. 100 m²) on slope descending to E toward Nahal Hoga.
Lithic finds: Lower Paleolithic.

153.   11-10/34-2   11350 10450   16350 60450
Nahal Hoga (Wadi er Raml, Wadi el Mahawir)
Ancient remains (c. 300 m²) in a eucalyptus wood plantation. Scatter of building stones, coarse tesserae, and pottery sherds.
Pottery: Byzantine.

154.   11-10/44-1   11450 10420   16450 60420
Nahal Hoga (Wadi er Raml, Wadi el Mahawir)
Scatter of flint implements (c. 400 m²) on area of small loess hills and in the channel of Wadi el Hadd. To E, concentration of pottery sherds.
Lithic finds: Lower Paleolithic and Chalcolithic.
Pottery: Byzantine.

155.   11-10/64-1   11635 10490   16635 60490
Nahal Nigraf (Wadi el Jurf)
Scatter of flint implements (c. 200 m²) on *hamra* hill E of Nahal Nigraf, a southern tributary of Nahal Shiqma.
Lithic finds: Lower Paleolithic.

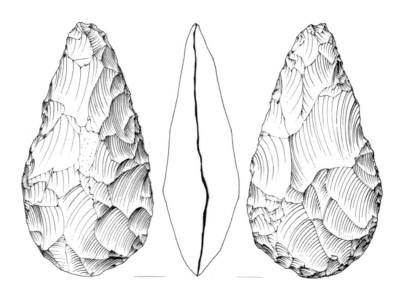

Figure 5.42: Handaxe from the Lower Paleolithic period from site 156 (scale 1:2)

156.   11-10/64-2   11640 10460   16640 60460
Nahal Nigraf (Wadi el Jurf)
Scatter of flint implements (c. 100 m²) on *hamra* hill (+106 m), E of Nahal Nigraf.
Lithic finds: Lower Paleolithic.

157.   11-10/64-3   11610 10480   16610 60480
Nahal Nigraf (Wadi el Jurf)
Scatter of flint implements (c. 200 m²) in badlands created as result of undermining of short eastern tributaries of Nahal Nigraf.
Lithic finds: Lower Paleolithic.

158.   11-10/74-1   11750 10420   16750 60420
Nahal Marashan (Wad Iweida)
Ancient remains (c. 200 m²) in eroded ground close to Nahal Marashan. Scatter of small pebbles, tesserae, and pottery sherds.
Pottery: Byzantine.

159.   11-10/84-1   11820 10410   16820 60410
Nahal Zedim (Wadi el Manyasa)
Some flint implements (c. 100 m²) on *hamra* soil eroded by runoff near Nahal Zedim, a tributary of Nahal Shiqma.
Lithic finds: Lower Paleolithic.

160.   11-10/84-2   11890 10440   16890 60440
Nahal Zedim (Wadi el Manyasa)
Ancient remains (c. 600 m²) on W moderate slope of a *kurkar* hill S of Nahal Zedim. Scatter of small pebbles, broken fired mudbricks, slag, and pottery sherds.
Pottery: Byzantine.

161.   11-10/03-1   11020 10380   16020 60380
Nahal Tal (Wadi el Bi, Wadi en Nada)
Light scatter of flint implements (c. 200 m²) in area of small *kurkar* hills, SW of Wadi el Bi.
Lithic finds: Lower Paleolithic.

162.   11-10/03-2   11060 10310   16060 60310
Nahal Tal (Wadi el Bi, Wadi en Nada)
Ancient remains (c. 1 dunam), on slope of *hamra* hill, covered by a thin layer of loess. Stains of dark soil and patches of gray color containing small *kurkar* stones, coarse tesserae, and pottery sherds.
Pottery: Byzantine.

163.   11-10/13-1   11110 10380   16110 60380
Nahal Tal (Wadi el Bi, Wadi en Nada)
Light scatter of flint implements (c. 100 m²) on W slope of a *kurkar* hill descending from E toward Wadi el Bi. Now a built area.
Lithic finds: Lower Paleolithic.

164.   11-10/23-1   11240 10350   16240 60350
Nahal Nirᶜam (Wadi Najd)
Flint implements (200 m²) on *hamra* soil eroded by water from a hill toward Nahal Nirᶜam.
Lithic finds: Lower Paleolithic.

165.   11-10/43-1   11450 10380   16450 60380
Nahal Hoga (Wadi er Raml, Wadi el Mahawir)
Flint implements in area of badlands and gullies (c. 200 m²) S of Wadi el Hadd, a tributary of Nahal Hoga.
Lithic finds: Lower Paleolithic.

166.   11-10/43-2   11435 10330   16435 60330
Nahal Hoga (Wadi er Raml, Wadi el Mahawir)
Findspot of a single arrowhead in a gully of Nahal Hoga.
Lithic find: Neolithic.

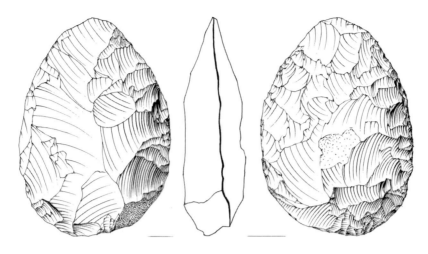

1. Handaxe

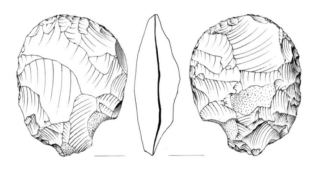

2. Handaxe

Figure 5.43: Lithics from the Lower Paleolithic period from site 167 (scale 1:2)

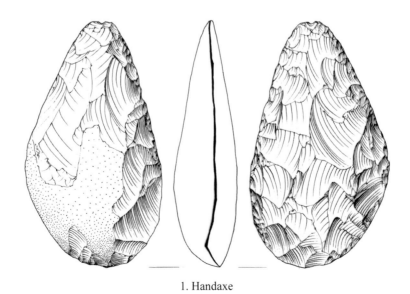

1. Handaxe

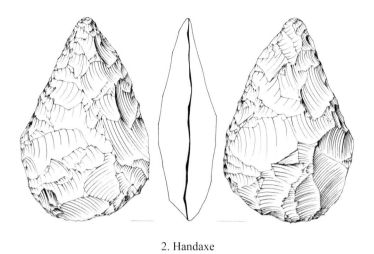

2. Handaxe

Figure 5.44: Lithics from the Lower Paleolithic period from site 168 (scale 1:2)

167.   11-10/53-1   11510 10380   16510 60380
Nahal Hoga (Wadi er Raml, Wadi el Mahawir)
Scatter of flint implements in area of badlands and gullies between Wadi el Hadd and Wadi er Rada, tributaries of Nahal Hoga. Extreme erosion processes in the past caused the removal of the *hamra* layer, spreading the artifacts over a large area.
Lithic finds: Lower Paleolithic.

168.   11-10/83-1   11870 10330   16870 60330
Nahal Dov (Wadi en Namus)
Scatter of eroded flint implements (c. 200 m²) on W slope of *hamra* hill, close to the N bank of Nahal Dov. Among the tools: Flakes, scrapers, and handaxes.
Lithic finds: Lower Paleolithic.

169.   11-10/02-1   11040 10250   16040 60250
Nahal Mefalsim (Wadi Lisin)
Settlement remains (c. 5 dunams) on low hill, E of a tributary of Nahal Mefalsim. Two bell-shaped cisterns (now blocked) and patches of gray soil containing *kurkar* stones, pebbles, and potsherds.
Pottery: Roman, Byzantine, and Early Islamic.

170.   11-10/02-2   11070 10210   16070 60210
Nahal Mefalsim (Wadi Lisin)
Settlement remains (c. 10 dunams) on low hill and flat terrain E of a tributary of Nahal Mefalsim. Two blocked bell-shaped cisterns. Dense concentrations of burnt bricks, kiln wasters, slag, and pottery sherds.
Pottery: Roman, Byzantine, Early Islamic, and medieval.
References: Schuster 2000b; Seriy 2010.

171.   11-10/22-1   11255 10205   16255 60205
Nahal Azur (Wadi el Ghazawiya)
Settlement remains (c. 3 dunams) on top of hill (triangulation point 339W) and on NE slope, close to Wadi el Amayir, a tributary of Nahal Azur. Scatter of pottery sherds. Nearby, three stone heaps (diameter 3–4 m) containing *kurkar* stones and marble fragments.
Pottery: Byzantine, Early Islamic, and medieval.

172.   11-10/32-1   11310 10230   16310 60230
Nahal Azur (Wadi el Ghazawiya)
Light scatter of flint implements (c. 200 m²) on slopes of *hamra* hill (triangulation point 340W, +94 m).
Lithic finds: Lower Paleolithic.

173.   11-10/32-2   11360 10215   16360 60215
Kh. Tell edh Dhahab

Abandoned olive orchard, (two remaining trees, partly enclosed with cactus fences). No visible ancient remains except some sherds of the Byzantine period.

Kh. Tell edh Dhahab appears in the Mandatory list of archaeological sites (1944 Schedule:1249), placed near the intersection of coordinates 114-102 (OIG); meanwhile, the 1964 Schedule of Monuments and Sites (Yalqut HaPirsumim 1964:1452) places the site within the square km of coordinates 113-102. Both the archaeological context and geographical features of this area, however, demonstrate that this placement is in error. Guérin described the site of Tell Dahab (also called Tell Ahmar) as a little elevated oblong hill, whose summit and slopes were covered by large quantities of pottery sherds, while the fields around included many bell-shaped cisterns (Guérin 1869:291–92). None of these features is in accordance with the finds in the abandoned orchard and in the (almost) flat fields around. A comprehensive analysis of Guérin's itinerary on June 11, 1863 not only removes the actual placement of Kh. Tell edh Dhahab at 113-102, but points to the site's exact location. Guérin left Gaza at 1:15 p.m. Setting out on a heading ENE, he arrived at Kh. Beit Durdis (coordinates 10715-10170) at 2:30. He then rode NE for 15 minutes and arrived at Tell Dahab at 2:45. Note that the distance between the abandoned orchard and the village of Huj is 500 m, while Guérin's ride from Tell Dahab to Huj lasted 1 hour and 30 minutes, as he arrived at Huj at 4:15. Furthermore, on Guérin's map the distance from Tell Dahab to Huj is more than twice the distance from Beit Durdis to Tell Dahab. Guérin's track from Gaza to Huj, including the deviation to Tell Dahab, lasted 3 hours. Twenty-five years earlier (May 21, 1838), Robinson rode from Gaza to Huj on the same route (Robinson and Smith 1841, II:384): He left Gaza at 12:20 p.m., passed Beit Dirdis at 1:30, and reached Huj at 2:55. Robinson did not indicate any notable site between Beit Durdis and Huj.

For the reasons mentioned above, Tell edh Dhahab should be located northeast of Beit Durdis, at a distance equivalent to a ride of 15 minutes. The German geographer H. Kiepert calculated the rate of Robinson's travels, and found that the distance traveled in one hour on horseback should be 2.8–3 geographical miles on level areas such as the plains E of Gaza (Kiepert 1841:31). As the length of a geographical mile is equivalent to 1852–55 m, the average distance should be 5.2–5.5 km per hour. Guérin's calculated rate was almost the same. Applying these calculations to Guérin's travels, we would expect Tell edh Dahab to be roughly 1.3–1.4 km NE of Beit Durdis. Indeed, at a distance of c. 1.5 km NE of Beit Durdis, there is an elevated area called El Ahmar that has the additional name of Tell Dahab (Survey of Palestine, Sheet 10-10, Beit Hanun). Its exact position is derived from the measurements carried out by van de Velde from the hill Ali Muntar (van de Velde 1858:115). He provided a bearing to Tell ed-Daheb of 68° 30', pointing to a *hamra* hill at coordinates 10760-10330.

174.   11-10/32-3   11395 10220   16395 60220
Esh Sheikh Mansur (M)

Abandoned orchard enclosed by cactus fences with the foundations of a rectangular structure, partly covered by a large stone heap. Probably the location of a sheikh's tomb.
Pottery: Medieval, Late Ottoman, and Mandatory.

175.   11-10/42-1   11420 10220   16420 60220
Huj (S)
Huj (M)

Ruins of Arab village (c. 45 dunams) on slope of low hill, W of Wadi el Balad, a tributary of Nahal Hoga (Wadi er Raml). Outline of planned streets under ruined structures built of mudbricks. To the E, a ruinous and blocked well. Nearby, a collapsed pool. Scatter of pottery sherds.
Pottery: Byzantine, Early Islamic, medieval, Ottoman, and modern.
References: Robinson and Smith 1841, II:384–86; Guérin 1869:292; Conder and Kitchener 1881–83, III:275.

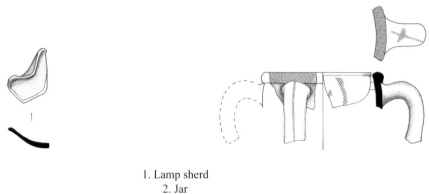

1. Lamp sherd
2. Jar

Figure 5.45: Pottery from site 176 (scale 1:5)

176.   11-10/42-2   11470 10200   16470 60200
H. Hoga
En Nabi Huj (M)
Islamic cemetery of the village of Huj (c. 1.5 dunams) on low *hamra* hill. Ancient remains over a larger area (c. 40 dunams). Several bell-shaped cisterns. Scatter of building stones, fragments of architectural elements, roof tiles, marble, and pottery sherds. A mosaic floor (4 x 5 m) and a burial system were documented in the past.
Pottery: Iron II, Persian, Hellenistic, Roman, Byzantine, Early Islamic, medieval, Ottoman, and modern.

177.   11-10/52-1   11510 10245   16510 60245
Nahal Dorot (Wadi er Raml, Wadi el Mahawir)
Settlement remains on flat terrain, NE of Kh. Hoga, near the junction of Wadi es Sallaqa and Nahal Hoga. The site is covered by a thick layer of silt (c. 1.2 m), resulting from constant flooding in the adjacent wadis. In 1992, torrential rains caused the partial removal of the silt coverage, exposing part of the site (c. 200 m²) for a short time: Scatter of pebbles, *kurkar* stones, fragments of basalt grinding stones, bone, flint implements, and pottery sherds.
Lithic finds and pottery: Late Bronze and Iron I.

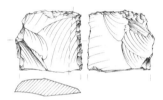

Figure 5.46: Late Bronze Age flint sickle blade from site 177 (scale 1:2)

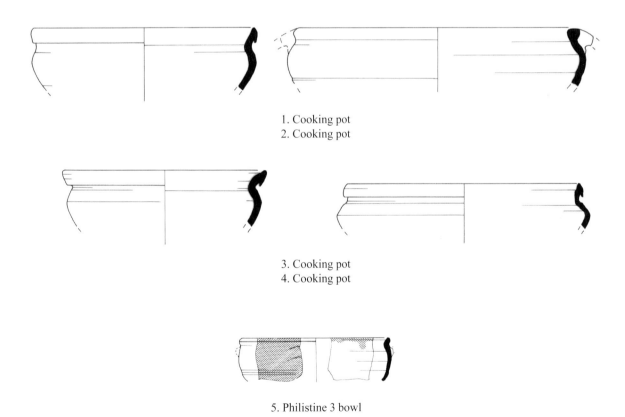

1. Cooking pot
2. Cooking pot

3. Cooking pot
4. Cooking pot

5. Philistine 3 bowl

Figure 5.47: Late Bronze Age and Iron Age I pottery from site 177 (scale 1:5)

Figure 5.48: Site 177

Figure 5.49: Site 181

178.   11-10/62-1   11630 10210   16630 60210
Nahal Dorot (Wadi er Raml)
Scatter of flint implements on *hamra* hill (c. 1 dunam, triangulation point 588, +116 m).
Lithic finds: Lower Paleolithic.

179.   11-10/62-2   11690   16690 60210
Nahal Ruhama (Wadi Abu Rashid)
Findspot in the bed of Nahal Ruhama. A single arrowhead, probably eroded by water from the ascent of the wadi to the west.
Lithic find: Neolithic.

180.   11-10/72-1   11740 10210   16740 60210
Nahal Ruhama (Wadi Abu Rashid)
Settlement remains on flat terrain (c. 500 m²) on N bank of Nahal Ruhama. Patches of gray soil containing pebbles, small fieldstones, burned bone, flint implements, and pottery sherds.
Lithic finds and pottery: Chalcolithic.

181.   11-10/82-1   11890 10260   16890 60260
H. Berekha
Kh. en Namus (M)
Remains of two rectangular burial systems on low hill (triangulation point 597), each composed of a main chamber (3.5 x 5.5 m and 2 x 4 m) with a vaulted roof. Built of small fieldstones bonded with lime cement. Few pottery sherds.
Pottery: Byzantine and modern.

182.   11-10/92-1   11940 10230   16940 60230
H. Berekha
Kh. en Namus (M)
Settlement remains (c. 60 dunams) on moderate slope descending to S toward Nahal Ruhama. During development work carried out here in 1962 with heavy machinery, many ancient remains were raised to the surface: Dressed *kurkar* stones, flooring marble and lime tiles, marble columns, and capitals. These finds enable us to determine that the center of H. Berekha/Kh. en Namus should be located 300 m SE of triangulation point 597 and that both localities (sites 181 and 182) are part of one large settlement (IAA archive, Kh. Berekha file, reported by Ram Gophna, 1962). As a result of an additional survey (Lamdan et al. 1977:185), more ancient remains were noted: On the N, dense concentrations of kiln waste, slag, and pottery sherds, mainly Gaza jar fragments. On the SE, ruins of a large structure (c. 10 x 10 m), walls 1–1.2 m wide, built of fieldstones, preserved 2.0 m high. This is a two-story structure. The lower story is partly buried by rubble, but still visible. The building features suggest that it served as a bath. If so, it correlates with the existence of a certain Kh. el Hammam ("the ruin of the bath"), known also as Kh. Umm Rujum, in this area. Kh. el Hammam was described in the Mandatory list of sites and monuments (1944 Schedule:1260) and later recorded under paragraph 97 in the 1964 Schedule of Monuments and Sites (Yalqut HaPirsumim 1964:1453).

In both publications general coordinates were given for the location: 120-103 (OIG). It was also marked on Mandatory maps (Survey of Palestine, Sheet 12-10, Ruhama), with more details that enable the fixing of the site at the intersection of coordinates: 12035-10360, some 1.1 km NE of Kh. en Namus and c. 2.5 km N of Kh. Jammama; however, the only ancient remains found at this location were a single burial system (Huster and Sion 2006:no. 80). Guérin, meanwhile, mentioned a place called Kh. el Hammam SE of Kh. Jammama (1869:295), as opposed to the Survey of Western Palestine which placed Kh. el Hummam NW of Jammama, apparently at the same location as Kh. en Namus (Sheet XX, Fw). The site was mentioned in the *Memoirs* in connection with Kh. Jamamma and described twice, the first time as Kh. el Hummam, the second as Kh. Umm Rujum, with little difference between the two descriptions (Conder and Kitchener 1881–83, III:281–82, 287).

Furthermore, the adjacent wadi name and the additional name of the *khirbeh* are identical: Umm Rujum. Petrie, who visited the site in 1890 (1891:53), mentioned a Roman ruin southeast of the *khirbeh* (probably the large structure) and described a well that had fallen out of use. The labeling of the site as Kh. en Namus occurs only on Mandatory maps. This name is likely derived from the owner of the land at the time: Many sites and wadis were named by the British surveyors according to land owners, and the agricultural fields in this area are still known as "Namusa's land." The site was named Kh. Berekha ("the ruin of the pool"), meanwhile, because of the existence of modern water installations (now out of use) on its N edge since 1947 (Braslavi 1956:459). Considering all of the details above, it is reasonable to assume that the site should be identified as Kh. el Hammam.
Pottery: Roman, Byzantine, Early Islamic, medieval, and Ottoman.

Figure 5.50: Site 182

183.　　11-10/92-2　　　11970 10220　　　16970 60220
Nahal Ruhama (Wadi Abu Rashid)
Ancient remains on loess hill (c. 200 m²) N of Nahal Ruhama. Disturbed structural foundations (only north wall remained), built of small *kurkar* stones bonded with lime cement. Nearby to the S, two blocked cisterns, and the screw weight of a wine-press. Dense scatter of pottery sherds.
Pottery: Byzantine.

184.　　11-10/92-3　　　11970 10210　　　16970 60210
Nahal Ruhama (Wadi Abu Rashid)
Ruinous structure (5 x 7 m) on moderate slope descending to S toward Nahal Ruhama. The outer walls were built of field-stones bonded with mud, while the inner walls were built of sun-dried mudbricks. Few pottery sherds.
Pottery: Modern.

185.　　11-10/01-1　　　11080 10150　　　16080 60150
Kh. Lasan (S)
Kh. Lasan (M)
Ancient cemetery (c. 20 dunams) on loess hill, 400 m NE of Kh. Lasan. Salvage excavations revealed dozens of cist tombs, built of dressed *kurkar* stones and covered mainly with *kurkar* slabs.
Pottery: Roman and Byzantine.

186.　　11-10/11-1　　　11130 10120　　　16130 60120
Kh. Lasan (S)
Kh. Lasan (M)
Settlement remains (c. 60 dunams) on loess hill and on moderate slopes descending to SW, toward Nahal Mefalsim (Wadi Lisin). Six bell-shaped cisterns (now blocked) built of cemented small fieldstones. Architectural elements: pillars, capitals, fragments of marble chancel screen posts, and panels. On W slope, remains of an olive press, winepresses, kiln waste, slag, and dense concentrations of pottery sherds. Farther to W, on flat terrain near Nahal Mefalsim, concentration of marble frag-ments and clay pipes (bath?).
Pottery: Roman, Byzantine, Early Islamic, medieval, and Ottoman.

187.   11-10/11-2   11140 10160   16140 60160
Kh. Lasan (S)
Kh. Lasan (M)
Group of five bell-shaped cisterns on moderate slope of loess hill, 400 m N of Kh. Lasan. Built of cemented small *kurkar* stones. Light scatter of pottery sherds (c. 800 m²).
Pottery: Byzantine, Early Islamic, and medieval.

188.   11-10/11-3   11180 10110   16180 60110
Nahal Mefalsim (Wadi Lisin)
Two bell-shaped cisterns, now blocked, on loessic spur descending W toward Nahal Mefalsim. Light scatter of pottery sherds (c. 200 m²).
Pottery: Byzantine.

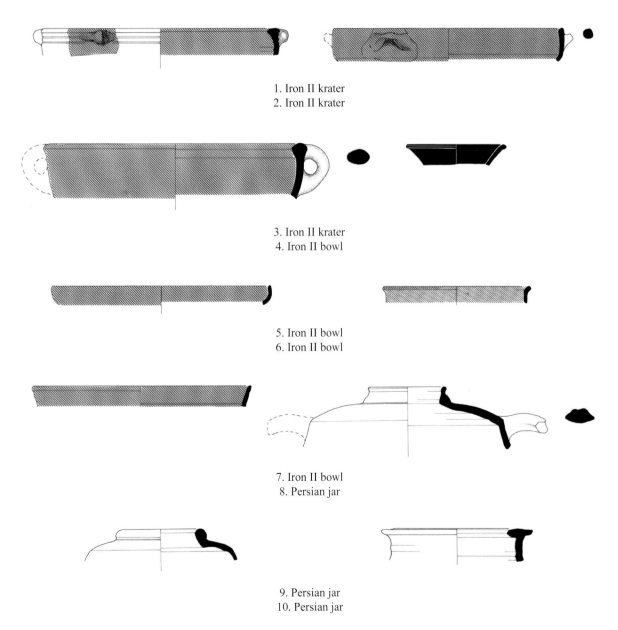

1. Iron II krater
2. Iron II krater

3. Iron II krater
4. Iron II bowl

5. Iron II bowl
6. Iron II bowl

7. Iron II bowl
8. Persian jar

9. Persian jar
10. Persian jar

Figure 5.51: Pottery from site 189 (scale 1:5)

189.   11-10/41-1   11460 10195   16460 60195
H. Hoga
Kh. Huj; Neby Huj (S)
Kh. Huj; En Nabi Huj (M)
Remains of large settlement (c. 120 dunams) on a series of mounds and in valleys between them.
   The nucleus of the settlement was located on the flat top of one of the hills (c. 5 dunams, labeled Sheikha Fatma tomb on Mandatory maps). Here, the base of a structure (c. 50 x 50 m) built of mudbricks was unearthed (Porat 1976). Its exact date and function are unclear, although it seems that it was established during the tenth century B.C. Nearby, further remains from the Persian and Hellenistic periods were excavated. Settlement remains were also observed around the excavated area, including several cisterns, segments of two mosaic floors, and a burial system. On the S, slag and dense concentrations of pottery sherds, evidence of a ceramic workshop. Dense scatter of building stones, marble fragments, and fragments of ceramic and glass vessels.
Pottery: Iron II, Persian, Hellenistic, Roman, Byzantine, Early Islamic, medieval, Ottoman, and modern.

190.   11-10/61-1   11670 10140   16670 60140
Nahal Dorot (Wadi el Majnuna, Wadi er Raml)
Scatter of flint implements on a series of *kurkar* hills, some covered by a thick layer of *hamra*, close to the W bank of Nahal Dorot. The *hamra* layer is constantly being eroded. Flint implements are often removed during this process. Among the tools: scrapers, burins, denticulates, and handaxes.
Lithic finds: Lower Paleolithic.

191.   11-10/71-1   11770 10170   16770 60170
Tell Shega
Tell el Majnuna (M)
Natural *hamra* hill (not a tell), N of Nahal Dorot (Wadi el Majnuna). Light scatter of flint implements (c. 200 m²) on N slope. Two hundred and fifty m to the NE, on the S bank of Nahal Ruhama, a well (diameter 2.5 m, visible depth c. 15 m), built of dressed *kurkar* stones. Nearby, a ruined pool (3 x 3 m). The informal name of the spot is Bir Abu Rashid (Abu Rashid's well). Light scatter of late Ottoman sherds.
Lithic finds: Lower Paleolithic.

192.   11-10/71-2   11750 10125   16750 60125
Nahal Dorot (Wadi el Majnuna, Wadi er Raml)
Light scatter of flint implements (c. 100 m²) on hill spur descending to a tributary of Nahal Dorot.
Lithic finds: Lower Paleolithic.

193.   11-10/81-1   11850 10190   16850 60190
Nahal Ruhama (Wadi Abu Rashid)
Settlement remains (c. 1.2 dunams) on flat land N of Nahal Ruhama. Patches of gray-colored soil containing pebbles, fieldstones, burnt animal bones, flint implements, and pottery sherds.
Lithic finds and pottery: Chalcolithic.

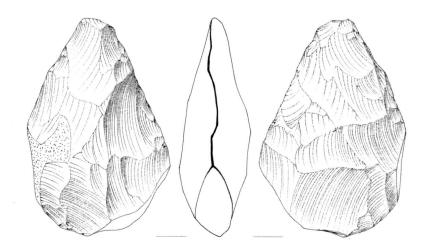

Figure 5.52: Handaxe from the Lower Paleolithic period from site 192

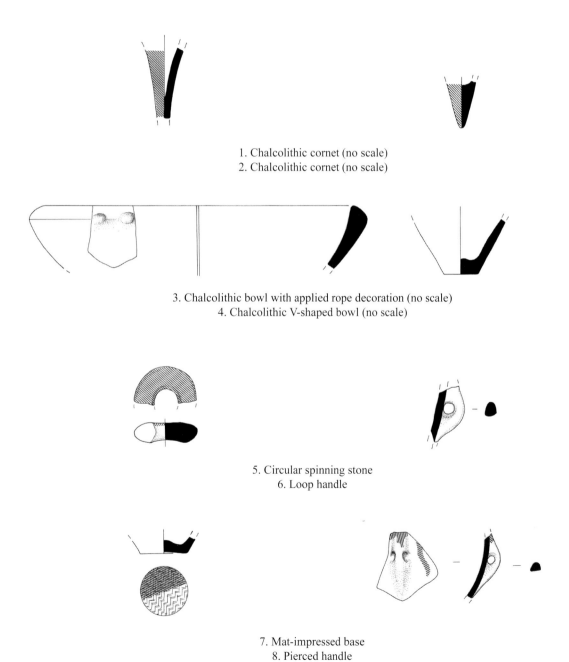

1. Chalcolithic cornet (no scale)
2. Chalcolithic cornet (no scale)

3. Chalcolithic bowl with applied rope decoration (no scale)
4. Chalcolithic V-shaped bowl (no scale)

5. Circular spinning stone
6. Loop handle

7. Mat-impressed base
8. Pierced handle

Figure 5.53: Pottery and stone from site 193 (scale 1:5)

194.   11-10/81-2   11880 10190   16880 60190
Nahal Ruhama (Wadi Abu Rashid)
Ancient remains (500 m²) on loessic plain N of Nahal Ruhama and near its bank. Scatter of bone, flint implements, and pottery sherds.
Lithic finds and pottery: Chalcolithic.

195.   11-10/91-1   11920 10180   16920 60180
Nahal Ruhama (Wadi Abu Rashid)
Settlement remains (c. 2.5 dunams) on moderate slope and on flat terrain adjacent to S bank of Nahal Ruhama. In this unplowed field, a concentration of large rounded patches of gray earth visible on the brown loessic soil. The patches are c. 30–40 m apart, and contain pebbles, fieldstones, flint implements, and pottery sherds.
Lithic finds and pottery: Chalcolithic.

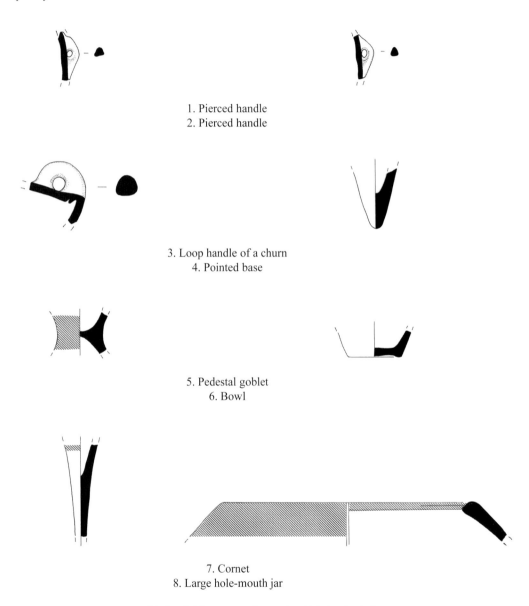

1. Pierced handle
2. Pierced handle

3. Loop handle of a churn
4. Pointed base

5. Pedestal goblet
6. Bowl

7. Cornet
8. Large hole-mouth jar

Figure 5.54: Chalcolithic pottery from site 194 (scale 1:5)

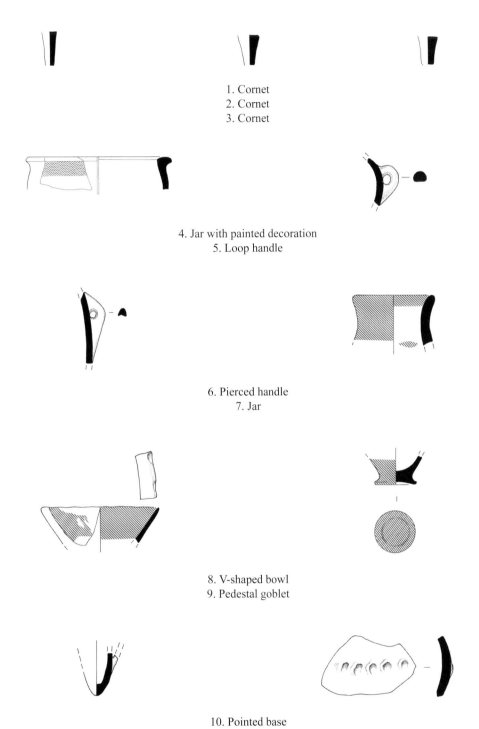

1. Cornet
2. Cornet
3. Cornet

4. Jar with painted decoration
5. Loop handle

6. Pierced handle
7. Jar

8. V-shaped bowl
9. Pedestal goblet

10. Pointed base
11. Body sherd with impressed decoration

Figure 5.55: Chalcolithic pottery from site 195 (scale 1:5)

196.   11-10/91-2   11905 10160   16905 60160
Nahal Ruhama (Wadi Abu Rashid)
Remains of a rectangular structure: segments of a fine tiled mosaic floor (white color, 4 m² exposed), ornamented with a cross (red tesserae). Nearby, three cisterns, partly blocked. Dense scatter of pottery sherds (c. 200 m²).
Pottery: Byzantine.

197.   11-10/91-3   11960 10170   16960 60170
Nahal Ruhama (Wadi Abu Rashid)
Ancient remains on small *hamra* hill (c. 800 m²). In the center, segments of structural foundations and scatter of rough white tesserae (4 x 4 cm). Four bell-shaped cisterns, three N of the structure and one S of it (diameter 2.5–3 m). Nearby, a rectangular structure (c. 3 x 4 m) built of sun-dried mudbricks bonded with mud, dated to the Late Ottoman or Mandatory period.
Pottery: Byzantine and modern.

198.   11-10/91-4   11970 10120   16970 60120
Nahal Ruhama (Wadi Abu Rashid)
Scatter of flint implements (c. 200 m²) on N slope of a *kurkar* hill.
Lithic finds: Lower Paleolithic.

199.   11-10/00-1   11050 10090   16050 60090
Nahal Mefalsim (Wadi Lisin)
Findspot on N bank of Nahal Mefalsim. Round clay tablet (diameter 10 cm), with incised inscription in ancient Hebrew letters.
Pottery: Iron II.
References: David Keidar (pers. comm.); Department of Antiquities registration no. R4675.

200.   11-10/50-1   11570 10060   16570 60060
Nahal Hoga (Wadi er Raml, Wadi Abd el Aziz)
Settlement remains (c. 1 dunam) on loessic plain, close to N bank of Nahal Hoga. Scatter of pebbles, fieldstones, burnt animal bones, flint implements, and pottery sherds.
Lithic finds and pottery: Chalcolithic.

201.   11-10/70-1   11735 10080   16735 60080
Nahal Hoga (Wadi er Raml, Wadi Abu Ali)
Ruined structure (c. 5 x 5 m) W of Wadi Abu Ali, a tributary of Nahal Dorot (Wadi el Majnuna). Built of sun-dried mudbricks (preserved 1.2–1.3 m high).
Pottery: Late Ottoman and Mandatory.

202.   11-10/70-2   11750 10070   16750 60070
Nahal Hoga (Wadi er Raml, Wadi Abu Ali)
Ancient remains (c. 400 m²) on W bank of Wadi Abu Ali, a tributary of Nahal Dorot. Light scatter of pebbles, fieldstones, flint implements, and pottery sherds.
Lithic finds and pottery: Chalcolithic.

203.   11-10/70-3   11780 10020   16780 60020
Nahal Hoga (Wadi er Raml, Wadi Abu Ali)
Two dwellings (4 x 4 and 5 x 5 m) on moderate slope descending to N toward Wadi Abu Ali, a tributary of Nahal Dorot. Built of sun-dried bricks. Walls preserved 1.2–1.5 m.
Pottery: Late Ottoman and Mandatory.

204.   11-10/70-4   11740 10010   16740 60010
Nahal Hoga (Wadi er Raml, Wadi Abu Ali)
Ruined structure (c. 3 x 4 m) on slope descending to E toward Wadi Abu Ali, a tributary of Nahal Dorot. Built of sun-dried mudbricks bonded with mud (preserved 2 m high).
Pottery: Late Ottoman and Mandatory.

205.   11-10/80-1   11840 10050   16840 60050
Nahal Dorot (Wadi el Majnuna, Wadi er Raml)
Light scatter of flint implements (c. 300 m²) on NW slope of *hamra* hill (+130 m).
Lithic finds: Lower Paleolithic.

206.   11-10/90-1   11990 10095   16990 60095
H. Herev
Kh. el Haj Harb (M)
Settlement remains (c. 10 dunams) on a *kurkar* hill (+180 m). Structural foundations, two cisterns (one bell-shaped, the second rectangular with a vaulted roof). In an artificial section created by the widening of an adjacent road, a coarse tiled mosaic floor (10 m length). Nearby, remains of a curved wall and segments of a fine tiled mosaic floor. Scatter of pottery sherds.
Pottery: Byzantine, Early Islamic, medieval, and Ottoman.

207.   11-10/90-2   11980 10030   16980 60030
H. Buta
Kh. Umm Buteih (M)
Bell-shaped cistern (2 m diameter) built of small cemented stones. This is the NW edge of a sizeable ancient settlement located some 400 m to the SE. Also a ruined structure (c. 4 x 5 m) built of fieldstones and mudbricks.
Pottery: Byzantine and modern.

BIBLIOGRAPHY

Abel, Félix-Marie
1938   *Géographie de la Palestine*. Vol. 2. Paris: Gabalda.

Abu-Khalaf, Marwan F.
1983   Khan Yunus and the Khans of Palestine. *Levant* 15:178–86.

Aharoni, Yohanan
1979   *The Land of the Bible: A Historical Geography*. Translated by A. F. Rainey. Revised and enlarged ed. Philadelphia: Westminster.

Aja, Adam J.
2009   Philistine Domestic Architecture in the Iron Age I. Ph.D. diss., Harvard University.

al-Dabbāgh, Mustafa Murad
1975   *Biladuna Filastin: 2.9 Fī Bait al Maqdis*. Beirut: Dār aṭ-Ṭalīᶜa.

al-Din, Mujir
1876   *Histoire de Jérusalem et d'Hébron depuis Abraham jusqu'à la fin du XVe siècle de J.-C.: Fragments de la Chronique de Moudjir-ed-Dyn*. Translated by H. Sauvaire. Paris: E. Leroux.

Allen, Mitchell J.
1997   Contested Peripheries: Philistia in the Neo-Assyrian World-System. Ph.D. diss., University of California.
2008   Regional Archaeological Survey. In *Ashkelon* 1: 21–65. Winona Lake, Ind.: Eisenbrauns.

Al-Maqdisi
1886   *Description of Syria, including Palestine*. Translated by G. Le Strange. London: Palestine Exploration Fund.
1906   *Ahsan al-taqasim fi Maᶜrifat al al-Aqalim*, ed. M. de Goeje. Leiden: Brill

Amiran, David H. K.
1953   The Pattern of Settlement in Palestine. *IEJ* 3:65–78, 192–209, 250–60.

Antl-Weiser, Walpurga
2007   Die Studien des Oberleutnants Josef Bayer in Palästina in den Jahren 1917 und 1918. *Mitteilungen der Anthropologischen Gesellschaft in Wien* 136/137:145–71.

Al-Swarieh, Noufan
2008   Gaza during the first half of the tenth century/the first half of the sixteenth century (A.D.)—its political administration, demography and system of taxation [in Arabic]. *Jordan Journal for History and Archaeology* 2/3:117–82.
2009   Economic life of Gaza in the first half of the tenth century/sixteenth century [in Arabic]. *Jordan Journal for History and Archaeology* 3/3:33–74.

Archives
1944   Schedule: Schedule of Historical Monuments and Sites. Supplement No. 2. *Palestine Gazette Extraordinary*, No. 1375.
1964   Schedule of Monuments and Historical Sites [in Hebrew]. In *Reshumot. Yalqut HaPirsumim*, No. 1091 [English index of sites]. Jerusalem.
1976   Department of Antiquities Geographical List of the Mandatory Records Files. Jerusalem.

Avissar, Miriam, and Edna J. Stern
2005   Pottery of the Crusader, Ayyubid, and Mamluk Periods in Israel. IAA Reports 26. Jerusalem: Israel Antiquities Authority.

Avi-Yonah, Michael
1940   *Map of Roman Palestine*. 2d ed. London: Oxford University Press.

Avi-Yonah, Michael, Rudolph Cohen, and Asher Ovadiah.
1993   Churches. In *NEAEHL*, ed. E. Stern, 1:305–14. Jerusalem: Israel Exploration Society.

Avshalom-Gorni, Dina
2008   A Complex Winepress from Mishmar Ha-ᶜEmeq: Evidence for the Peak in the Development of the Wine Industry in Eretz Israel in Antiquity. ᶜ*Atiqot* 58:49–66, 65*–67*.

Bailey, Donald M.
1999   Sebakh, Sherds and Survey. *JEA* 85:211–18.

Baker, Jill L.
2006   The Funeral Kit: A Newly Defined Canaanite Mortuary Practice Based on the Middle and Late Bronze Age Tomb Complex at Ashkelon. *Levant* 38:1–31.
2010   Form and Function of Mortuary Architecture: The Middle and Late Bronze Age Tomb Complex at Ashkelon. *Levant* 42/1:5–16.

Barako, Tristan
2008   Amphoras through the Ages. In *Ashkelon* 1:429–62. Winona Lake, Ind.: Eisenbrauns.

Barel, Amir
1999   Ashqelon, Afridar [in Hebrew]. *HA* 110:120.

Bar-Yosef, Ofer
1970a   Prehistoric Sites near Ashdod, Israel. *PEQ* 102: 52–64.
1970b   Gisements épipaléolithiques près de Ashdod—Israël. *Bulletin de la Société royale belge d'anthropologie et de préhistoire* 81: 5–27.

Barzilay, Eldad
2004   Geological and Geomorphological Setting of the EB Site at Afridar. ᶜ*Atiqot* 45:331–35.

Baumgarten, Yaᶜaqov
1996 Ashkelon, Haṭayyasim Street. *ESI* 15:99–100.
1999 Givᶜati Junction [in Hebrew]. *HA* 107:115.
2000 Evidence for the Byzantine city at Tel Ashdod. *ᶜAtiqot* 39:69–74.
2004 An Excavation at Ashqelon, Afridar—Area J. *ᶜAtiqot* 45:161–84.
2006 Ashqelon. *HA-ESI* 118. [http://www.hadashot-esi.org.il/report_detail_eng.asp?id=374&mag_id=111 (6.7.2006)]

Baumgarten, Yaᶜaqov, Amir Gorzalczany, and Alexander Onn
2008 Petura. In *NEAEHL*, ed. E. Stern, 5:1995. Jerusalem: Israel Exploration Society.

Bayer, Yosef
1919 Der Kulturverlauf im Steinzeitalter: Nach den Ergebnissen der prähistorischer Forschungen im Orient. *Zeitschrift für Ethnologie* 51:163–79.

Ben-Shlomo, David
2003 The Iron Age Sequence of Tel Ashdod: A Rejoinder to "Ashdod Revisited." *TA* 30:83–107.
2006 *Decorated Philistine Pottery: An Archaeological and Archaeometric Study*. BARIS 1541. Oxford: Archaeopress.

Berman, Ariel, and Leticia Barda
2005 *Map of Nizzanim-West (87), map of Nizzanim-East (88)*. Jerusalem: Israel Antiquities Authority.

Berman, Ariel, Leticia Barda, and Harley Stark
2005 *Map of Ashdod (84)*. Jerusalem: Israel Antiquities Authority.

Berman, Ariel, Harley Stark, and Leticia Barda
2004 *Map of Ziqim (91)*. Jerusalem: Israel Antiquities Authority.

Bintliff, John, and Anthony Snodgrass
1988 Off-Site Pottery Distributions: A Regional and Interregional Perspective. *CA* 29:506–13.

Biran, Avraham
1993 Ẓippor, Tel. In *NEAEHL*, ed. E. Stern, 4:1526–27. Jerusalem: Israel Exploration Society.

Biran, Avraham, and Ora Negbi
1966 The Stratigraphical Sequence of Tel Ṣippor. *IEJ* 16:160–73.

Bird, James H.
1973 Of Central Places, Cities and Seaports. *Geography* 58:105–18.

Birney, Kate and Ely Levine
2011 Balance Weights. In *Ashkelon* 3:473–92. Winona Lake, Ind.: Eisenbrauns.

Bosworth, Clifford Edmund
1995 Sabīl. In *The Encyclopaedia of Islam*, vol 8, ed. C. E. Bosworth, E. van Donzel, W. P. Heinrichs, and G. Lecomte, 679–83. Leiden: E. J. Brill.

Brand, E.
2001 Agricultural Device in Ashkelon Coast [in Hebrew]. In *Ashkelon: A City on the Seashore*, ed. A. Sasson, Z. Safrai, and N. Sagiv, 203–11. Ashkelon: Ashkelon Academic College.

Brandl, Baruch
1992 Evidence for Egyptian Colonization of the Southern Coastal Plain and Lowlands of Canaan during the Early Bronze I Period. In *The Nile Delta in Transition: 4th–3rd millennium B.C.: Proceedings of the Seminar held in Cairo, 21–24 October 1990, at the Netherlands Institute of Archaeology and Arabic Studies*, ed. E. C. M. van den Brink, 441–76. Tel Aviv: van den Brink.

Brandl, Baruch, and Ram Gophna
1993 Ashkelon, Afridar. *ESI* 12:89.

Braslavi, Joseph
1956 *Do You Know The Land?* Vol. 2, *The Land of the Negev* [in Hebrew]. Tel Aviv: Hakibbutz Hameuchad.

Braun, Eliot, and Ram Gophna
2004 Excavations at Ashqelon, Afridar—Area G. *ᶜAtiqot* 45:185–241.

Bronson, Bennet
1977 Exchange at the Upstream and Downstream Ends: Notes toward a Functional Model of the Coastal State in Southeast Asia. *Michigan Papers on South and Southeast Asia* 13:39–52.

Bull, Ian D., Phillip B. Betancourt, and Richard P. Evershed
2001 An Organic Geochemical Investigation of the Practice of Manuring at a Minoan Site on Pseira Island, Crete. *Geoarchaeology* 16:223–42.

Bulliet, Richard W.
1979 *Conversion to Islam in the Medieval Period: An Essay in Quantitative History*. Cambridge, Mass.: Harvard University Press.

Bunce, Michael
1982 *Rural Settlement in an Urban World*. New York: St. Martin's.

Burghardt, Andres F.
1971 A Hypothesis about Gateway Cities. *Annals of the Association of American Geographers* 61: 269–85.

Burgoyne, Michael Hamilton, and Donald Sidney Richards
1987 *Mamlūk Jerusalem: An Architectural Study*. Buckhurst Hill, England: Scorpion.

Burke, Aaron A.
2007 *Magdalūma, Migdālîm, Magdoloi*, and *Majādīl*: The Historical Geography and Archaeology of the Magdalu (Migdāl). *BASOR* 346:29–57.
2008 *"Walled up to Heaven": The Evolution of Middle Bronze Age Fortifications Strategies in the Levant*. Winona Lake, Ind.: Eisenbrauns.

Canaan, Tawfiq
　　1927　*Mohammedan Saints and Sanctuaries in Palestine*. London: Luzac.

Carmi, Israel, et al.
　　2008　Dating Ancient Water Wells Using Radiocarbon and Ceramics. In *Ashkelon* 1:127–30. Winona Lake, Ind.: Eisenbrauns.

Cherry, John F.
　　1983　Frogs around the Pond: Perspectives on Current Archaeological Survey Projects in the Mediterranean Region. In *Archaeological Survey in the Mediterranean Area*, ed. D. R. Keller and D. W. Rupp, 375–416. BARIS 155. Oxford: British Archaeological Reports.

Chisholm, Michael
　　1968　*Rural Settlement and Land Use: An Essay in Location*. London: Hutchinson.

Christaller, Walter
　　1933　*Die zentralen Orte in Süddeutschland eine ökonomisch-geographische Untersuchung über die Gesetzmäßigkeit der Verbreitung und Entwicklung der Siedlungen mit städtischen Funktionen*. Jena: Gustav Fischer.
　　1966　*Central Places in Southern Germany*. Englewood Cliffs, N.J.: Prentice Hall.

Clermont-Ganneau, Charles
　　1884　*Mission en Palestine et en Phénicie: Entreprise en 1881: Cinquième Rapport*. Paris: Imprimerie Nationale.
　　1887　Notes d'épigraphie et d'histoire arabes. *Journal Asiatique* (8ème serie) 9:485–91.
　　1896　*Archaeological Researches in Palestine During the Years 1873–1874*. Vol. II. Translated by J. Macfarlane. London: Palestine Exploration Fund.
　　1897　Sur quelques localités de Palestine mentionnées dans la Vie de Pierre l'Ibére. In *Études d'Archéologie Orientale*, vol. 2, 1–22. Paris: Émile Bouillon.

Cohen, Meir
　　1993　*Between the Besor and Shiqma: Settlement Distribution in Selected Periods* [in Hebrew]. Jerusalem [no publisher].
　　2010　The Climate [in Hebrew]. In *Sderot: The Human Landscape*, ed. A. Sasson, 17–24. Jerusalem: Makom.

Cohen, Susan
　　2002　*Canaanites, Chronologies, and Connections: The Relationship of Middle Bronze IIA Canaan to Middle Kingdom Egypt*. Winona Lake, Ind.: Eisenbrauns.

Collier, Peter, and Rob Inkpen
　　2001　Mapping Palestine and Mesopotamia in the First World War. *The Cartographic Journal* 38: 143–54.

Conder, Claude R.
　　1877　The Moslem Mukams. *PEFQS*, 89–103.
　　1890　Norman Palestine. *PEFQS* 22:29–37.

Conder, Claude R., and Horatio H. Kitchener
　　1880　*Map of Western Palestine, Sheets I–XXVI*. London: Palestine Exploration Fund.
　　1881–1883　*The Survey of Western Palestine: Memoirs of the Topography, Orography, Hydrography, and Archaeology*. Vols. 1–3. London: Palestine Exploration Fund.

Cross, Frank M., and Lawrence E. Stager
　　2006　Cypro-Minoan Inscriptions Found in Ashkelon. *IEJ* 56:129–59.

Dagan, Yehuda
　　1992　*Map of Lakhish (98)*. Jerusalem: Israel Antiquities Authority.
　　n.d.　Archaeological Survey of Israel. [http://www.antiquities.org.il/article_Item_eng.asp?sec_id=33&subj_id=75#MMMas (5.8.2011)].

Dalman, Gustaf H.
　　1903　Epigraphisches und Pseudepigraphisches. *Mitteilungen und Nachrichten des Deutschen Palaestina-Vereins* 9:17–32.

Dauphin, Claude M.
　　1998　*La Palestine Byzantine: Peuplement et Populations*. BARIS 726. Oxford: Archaeopress.

de Hamme, Liévin
　　1887　*Guide-indicateur des Sanctuaires et Lieux Historiques de la Terre-Sainte*. 3d ed. Jerusalem: Imprimerie des P. P. Franciscains.

Dever, William G.
　　1987　The Middle Bronze Age: The Zenith of the Urban Canaanite Era. *BA* 50:148–77.

Dimashqi, Shams al-Din Muhammad ibn Abi Talib
　　1866　*Nukhbat al-Dahr Fi Adjaᵓib al-Barr Wa al-Bahr. Cosmographie de Chems-Ed-Din Abou Abdullah Muhammad El-Dimichqui*, ed. M. A. F. Mehren. St. Petersburg: l'Académie Impériale des sciences.

Di Segni, Leah
　　2008　A Greek Inscription from Tel Ashdod: A Revised Reading. ᶜ*Atiqot* 58:31*–36*.

Dorsey, David.
　　1991　*The Roads and Highways of Ancient Israel*. Baltimore: Johns Hopkins University Press.

Dothan, Moshe
　　1971　*Ashdod*. Vol. II–III, *The Second and Third Seasons of Excavations, 1963, 1965, Soundings in 1967*. ᶜAtiqot English Series 9–10. Jerusalem: Department of Antiquities and Museums.
　　1993　Ashdod. In *NEAEHL*, ed. E. Stern, 1:93–102. Jerusalem: Israel Exploration Society.

Dothan, Moshe, and David Ben-Shlomo
2005 *Ashdod.* Vol. VI, *The Excavations of Areas H and K (1968–1969).* IAA Reports 24. Jerusalem: Israel Antiquities Authority.

Dothan, Moshe, and David N. Freedman, eds.
1967 *Ashdod.* Vol. I, *The First Season of Excavations, 1962.* ᶜAtiqot English Series 7. Jerusalem: Department of Antiquities and Museums.

Dothan, Moshe, and Yehoshua Porath.
1982 *Ashdod.* Vol. IV, *Excavation of Area M, The Fortifications of the Lower City.* ᶜAtiqot 15. Jerusalem: Department of Antiquities and Museums.
1993 *Ashdod.* Vol. V, *Excavation of Area G; The Fourth-Sixth Seasons of Excavations 1968–1970.* ᶜAtiqot 23. Jerusalem: Israel Antiquities Authority.

Dussaud, René
1912 *Les Monuments Palestiniens et Judaïques: Moab, Judée, Philistie, Samarie, Galilée.* Paris: E. Leroux.

Ein Gedy, Miki
2002 Ashkelon, El-Jura [in Hebrew]. *HA* 114:110.

Elᶜad, Amikam
1982 The Coastal Cities of Palestine during the Early Middle Ages. *The Jerusalem Cathedra,* vol. 2, 146–67. Jerusalem: Yad Ben Zvi.

Elitzur, Yoel
2004 *Ancient Place Names in the Holy Land: Preservation and History* [in Hebrew]. Jerusalem: Magnes.

Elitzur, Yoel, and C. Ben-David
2007 Deir in Hebrew, Aramaic, and Arabic and Toponyms of the "Deir-X" Type. *Cathedra* 123: 13–38.

Etkes, Haggay
2012 The Impact of Employment in Israel on the Palestinian Labor Force. *Peace Economics, Peace Science, and Public Policy* 18/2:1–36.

Eusebius
1870 *Eusebii Onomasticon Urbium et Locorum Sacrae Scripturae,* ed. P. Lagarde. Gottingae: A. Rente
1904 *Eusebius Das Onomastikon der biblischen Ortsnamen,* ed. E. Klostermann. Leipzig: J. C. Hinrichs.

Fabian, Peter, Pirhiya Nahshoni, and Miki Ein Gedy
1994 Ashqelon, Ḥammama. *ESI* 14:110–11.

Fargo, Valerie M.
1979 Settlement in Southern Palestine during Early Bronze III. Ph.D. diss., University of Chicago.

Finkelstein, Israel
1994 The Archaeology of the Days of Manasseh. In *Scripture and Other Artifacts: Essays on the Bible and Archaeology in Honor of Philip J. King,* ed. M. Coogan, J. Exum, and L. Stager, 169–87. Louisville, Ky: Westminster John Knox.
1996a The Philistine Countryside. *IEJ* 46:225–42.
1996b The Territorial-Political System of Canaan in the Late Bronze Age. *UF* 28:221–55.

Finkelstein, Israel, and Lily Singer-Avitz
2001 Ashdod Revisited. *TA* 28:231–59.
2004 "Ashdod Revisited"—Maintained. *TA* 31:122–35.

Fischer, Moshe, Itamar Taxel, and David Amit
2008 Rural Settlement in the Vicinity of Yavneh in the Byzantine Period: A Religio-Archaeological Perspective. *BASOR* 350:7–35.

Garfinkel, Yosef, and Doron Dag
2008 *Neolithic Ashkelon.* Qedem 47. Jerusalem: Institute of Archaeology, Hebrew University.

Garstang, John
1921a The Fund's Excavation of Askalon. *PEFQS* 12–16.
1921b The Excavation of Askalon, 1920–1921. *PEFQS* 73–75.
1922 The Excavations at Askalon. *PEFQS* 112–19.
1924 Askalon. *PEFQS* 24–35.

Gatt, Georg
1884 Verzeichniss der bewohnten Ortschaften der Kaimakāmīje Gaza. *ZDPV* 7:293–98.

Gavish, Dov
2005 *A Survey of Palestine under the British Mandate, 1920–1948.* Trans. J. Shadur. London: RoutledgeCurzon

Garfinkel, Yosef
1999 Ashqelon, Afridar. *HA-ESI* 110:71*–72*.

Gazit, Dan
1996 *Map of Urim (125).* Jerusalem: Israel Antiquities Authority, Archaeological Survey of Israel.

Gershuny, Lilly
1996 Migdal Ashqelon. *ESI* 15:131–32.
1997 Ashqelon, Migdal North. *ESI* 16:141.
1999 Ashqelon, Givᶜat Ziyyon. *ESI* 19:108*.

Gibson, Shimon
1995 Landscape Archaeology and Ancient Agricultural Field Systems in Palestine. Ph.D. diss., University College, London.

Gibson, Shimon, F. Vitto and L. Di Segni
1998 An Unknown Church with Inscriptions from the Byzantine Period at Khirbet Makkûs near Julis. *Liber Annus* 48:315–34.

Gitin, Seymour
1995 Tel Miqne-Ekron in the 7th Century B.C.E.: The Impact of Economic Innovation and Foreign Cultural Influences on a Neo-Assyrian Vassal City-State. In *Recent Excavations in Israel: A View to the West,* ed. S. Gitin, 61–79. Dubuque, Iowa: Kendall/Hunt.
2003 The Philistines: Neighbors of the Canaanites, Phoenicians and Israelites. In *100 Years of American Archaeology in the Middle East: Proceedings*

of the American Schools of Oriental Research Centennial Celebration. Washington, D.C., April 2000, ed. D. R. Clark and V. H. Matthews, 57–85. Boston: American Schools of Oriental Research.

Gitin, Seymour, and Trude Dothan
1987   The Rise and Fall of Ekron of the Philistines: Recent Excavations at an Urban Border Site. *BA* 50:197–222.

Golani, Amir
1996   A Persian Period Cist Tomb on the Ashqelon Coast. ᶜ*Atiqot* 30:115–19.
1997   Ashqelon, Hajar ᶜId. *ESI* 16:122.
2004   Salvage Excavations at the Early Bronze Age Site of Ashqelon—Area E. ᶜ*Atiqot* 45:9–62.
2005a   Ashqelon, Barneᶜa B–C. *HA-ESI* 117. [http://www.hadashot-esi.org.il/report_detail_eng.asp?id=134&mag_id=110 (3.28.2005)]
2005b   Ashqelon, Ha-Tayyasim St. *HA-ESI* 117. [http://www.hadashot-esi.org.il/report_detail_eng.asp?id=282&mag_id=110 (12.29.2005)]
2007   Ashqelon, Barneᶜa B–C. *HA-ESI* 119 (11.6.2007). [http://www.hadashot-esi.org.il/report_detail_eng.asp?id=533&mag_id=112 (6.11.2007)]
2008   The Early Bronze Site of Ashqelon, Afridar—Area M. ᶜ*Atiqot* 60:19–51.

Golani, Amir, and Ianir Milevsky
1999   Ashqelon, Afridar (A). *ESI* 19:82*–83*.

Goodenough, Erwin Ramsdell
1953   *Jewish Symbols in the Greco-Roman Period*. Vol. 1. New York: Pantheon.

Gophna, Ram
1963   "Haserim" Settlements in the Northern Negev [in Hebrew]. *Yediot* 27:173–80.
1964   Beer Zeᵓelim, An Iron Age Site [in Hebrew]. *HA* 11:24.
1965   Beit Jurja [in Hebrew]. *HA* 14:14
1966   Iron Age I Haserim in Southern Philistia [in Hebrew]. ᶜ*Atiqot* 3:44–51.
1970   Some Iron Age II Sites in Southern Philistia [in Hebrew with English summary]. ᶜ*Atiqot* 6:25–30, 3*.
1977   Fortified Settlements from the Early Bronze and Middle Bronze II at Tel Poran [in Hebrew]. *EI* 13:87–90.
1981   The Boundary Between Judah and the Kingdoms of Gaza and Ashkelon in the Light of the Archaeological Survey in Nahal Shiqma [in Hebrew]. *Proceedings of the Seventh World Congress of Jewish Studies: Held at The Hebrew University of Jerusalem, 7–14 August 1977*. Vol. 2, *Studies in the Bible and the Ancient Near East*, ed. Y. Gutman, 49–52. Jerusalem: World Union of Jewish Studies.
1990   The Early Bronze I settlement at ᶜEn Besor Oasis. *IEJ* 40:1–11.
1992a   A Faience Statuette from ᶜEn Besor. *EI* 23:45–47.
1992b   Early Bronze Age Fortification Wall and Middle Bronze Age Rampart at Tel Poran. *TA* 19:267–73.
1992c   The Contacts between ᶜEn Besor Oasis, Southern Canaan, and Egypt during the late Predynastic and the Threshold of the First Dynasty: A Further Assessment. In *The Nile Delta in Transition: 4th–3rd millennium B.C.: Proceedings of the Seminar held in Cairo, 21–24 October 1990, at the Netherlands Institute of Archaeology and Arabic Studies*, ed. E. C. M. van den Brink, 385–94. Tel Aviv: van den Brink.
2002a   Afridar 1968: Soundings in an EB I Occupation of the "Erani C Horizon". In *Aharon Kempinski Memorial Volume: Studies in Archaeology and Related Disciplines*, ed. S. Ahituv and E. D. Oren, 129–37. Beersheba: Ben-Gurion University of the Negev Press.
2002b   Elusive Anchorage Points Along the Israel Littoral and the Egyptian-Canaanite Maritime Route During the Early Bronze Age I. In *Egypt and the Levant: Interrelations from the 4th through the Early 3rd Millennium B.C.E.*, ed. E. C. M. van den Brink and T. E. Levy, 418–21. London: Leicester University Press.
2004   Excavations at Ashqelon, Afridar—Introduction. ᶜ*Atiqot* 45:1–8.

Gophna, Ram, and Nurit Feig
1993   A Byzantine Monastery at Kh. Jemameh. ᶜ*Atiqot* 22:98–108.

Gophna, Ram, and Dan Gazit
1985   The First Dynasty Egyptian residency at ᶜEn Besor. *TA* 12:9–16.

Gophna, Ram, and Nili Lipschitz
1996   The Ashkelon Trough Settlements in the Early Bronze Age I: New Evidence of Maritime Trade. *TA* 23:143–53.

Gophna, Ram, and Dov Meron
1963   Survey of the south to the southern edge of Nahal Shiqma [in Hebrew]. *HA* 7:22.
1970   An Iron Age Tomb between Ashdod and Ashkelon [in Hebrew with English summary]. ᶜ*Atiqot* 6:1–5, 1*.

Goren, Haim
2002   Sacred, but Not Surveyed: Nineteenth-Century Surveys of Palestine. *Imago Mundi* 54:87–110.

Green, John D. M.
2009   Archaeology and Politics in the Holy Land: The Life and Career of P. L. O. Guy. *PEQ* 141: 167–87.

Grossman, David
1992   *Rural Process-Pattern Relationships: Nomadization, Sedentarization, and Settlement Fixation*. New York: Praeger.
2010   The Arab Settlement in the Region before the Establishment of the State [in Hebrew]. In *Sderot: Nof-adam ba-Merhav*, ed. A. Sasson, 71–84. Jerusalem: Makom.

Gudovitch Shlomo
  2006   Remains of a Monastery at the Foot of Tel
          Ashdod [in Hebrew with English summary].
          ᶜ*Atiqot* 51:1*–2*, 233.

Guérin, Victor
  1857   Description des ruines d'Ascalon. *Bulletin de la
          Société de Géographie* (4th series) 13:81–95.
  1869   *Description géographique, historique et ar-
          chéologique de la Palestine*. Tome Deuxième,
          Judée. Paris: Imprimerie Impériale.

Guy, Philip Langstaffe Ord
  1937   British School of Archaeology in Jerusalem. *PEQ*
          69:19–30.
  1938   British School of Archaeology in Jerusalem, Re-
          port for the Season 1936–37. *PEQ* 70:11–17.

Hachlili, Rachel
  2001   *The Menorah, The Ancient Seven-armed Cande-
          labrum: Origin, Form and Significance*. Leiden:
          Brill.

Haiman, Mordechai
  2010   Givᶜati Junction. *HA-ESI* 122. [http://www.
          hadashot-esi.org.il/report_detail_eng.aspx?
          id=1321&mag_id=117 (1.17.2010)]
  2011   Ashqelon. *HA-ESI* 123. [http://www.hadashot-esi.
          org.il/report_detail_eng.aspx?id=1721&mag_
          id=118 (7.12.2011)]

Haimi, Yoram
  2007   Ashqelon, el-Qabu. *HA-ESI* 119. [http://www.
          hadashot-esi.org.il/report_detail_eng.aspx?
          id=677&mag_id=112 (12.24.2007)]
  2008a   Ashqelon, Barneᶜa *HA-ESI* 120. [http://www.
          hadashot-esi.org.il/report_detail_eng.aspx?
          id=953&mag_id=114 (11.23.2008)]
  2008b   Mavqiᶜim HA-ESI 120. [http://www.hadashot-
          esi.org.il/report_detail_eng.aspx?id=751&mag_
          id=114 (4.2.2008)]
  2009   Ashqelon. *HA-ESI* 121. [http://www.hadashot-esi.
          org.il/report_detail_eng.aspx?id=1016&mag_
          id=115 (1.12.2009)]

Hall, Kenneth R.
  1985   *Maritime Trade and State Development in Early
          Southeast Asia*. Honolulu: University of Hawaii
          Press.

Hamilton, R. W., ed.
  1933   Schedule of Historical Monuments and Historical
          Sites [Additions]. *Official Palestine Gazette Ex-
          traordinary* 387.

Hartmann, Martin
  1883   Die Ortschaftenliste des Liwa Jerusalem in
          dem türkischen Staatskalendar für Syrien auf
          das Jahr 1288 der Flucht (1871). *ZDPV* 6:
          102–52.
  1910   Die Strasse von Damaskus nach Kairo. *Zeitschrift
          der Deutschen Morgenländischen Gesellschaft*
          64:665–702.

Haselgrove, Colin
  1986   Central Places in British Iron Age Studies: A
          Review and Some Problems. In *Central Places,
          Archaeology, and History*, ed. E. Grant, 3–12.
          Sheffield: University of Sheffield Department of
          Archaeology and Prehistory.

Hirschfeld, Yizhar
  1990   List of the Byzantine Monasteries in the Judean
          Desert. In *Christian Archaeology in the Holy
          Land*, ed. G. C. Bottini, et al., 1–90. Jerusalem:
          Franciscan Printing Press.
  1997   Farms and Villages in Byzantine Palestine.
          Dumbarton Oaks Papers 51:33–71.
  2004   The Monasteries of Gaza: An Archaeological
          Review. In *Christian Gaza in Late Antiquity*, ed.
          B. Bitton-Ashkelony and A. Kofsky, 61–88. Je-
          rusalem Studies in Religion and Culture, vol. 3.
          Leiden: Brill, 2004.

Hoffman, Tracy
  2003   Ascalon ᶜArus al-Sham: Domestic Architecture
          and the Development of a Byzantine-Islamic City.
          Ph.D. diss., University of Chicago.

Horowitz, Aharon
  1979   *The Quaternary of Israel*. New York: Academic
          Press.

Huehnergard, John, and Wilfred van Soldt
  1999   A Cuneiform Lexical Text from Ashkelon with a
          Canaanite Column. *IEJ* 49:184–92.

Humbert, Jean-Baptiste et al.
  2000   Mukheitem à Jabaliyah, un site Byzantin.
          Gaza Méditerranéenne, 121–26. Paris: Errance.

Huster, Yaakov
  2007   Ashqelon. *HA-ESI* 119. [http://www.hadashot-
          esi.org.il/report_detail_eng.aspx?id=570&mag_
          id=112 (8.14.2007)]

Huster, Yaakov and Jeffrey A. Blakely
  In press The Wadi el-Hesi Region in 1256/7: An Interpre-
          tation of John of Ibelin's Contract with the Hospi-
          tal of Saint John. *Crusades* 15.

Huster, Yaakov, and Ofer Sion
  2006   Late Roman and Byzantine Period Vaulted Tombs
          in the Southern Coastal Plain [in Hebrew]. *Jerusa-
          lem and Eretz-Israel* 3:49–67.

Hütteroth, Wolf-Dieter, and Kamal Abdulfattah
  1977   *Historical Geography of Palestine, Transjordan
          and Southern Syria in the Late 16th Century*.
          Erlanger Geographische Arbeiten, Sonderband 5.
          Erlangen, Germany: Frankische Geographische
          Gesellschaft.

Ibrāhim, Abd al-Lateef
  1961   Sutlan Qaytbay Document: Study & Analysis,
          Madrasa in Jerusalem and Mosque in Gaza. *Gaza,
          the Third Conference for Archaeology in Arab
          Countries*, 389–434.

İnalcik, Halil
1991 Ottoman Galata (1453–1553) [in Turkish]. In *Varia Turcica*, vol. 13, ed. E. Eldem, 17–137. Istanbul: Editions ISIS.

Ipsirli, Mehmed, and Muhammad Dawud al-Tamimi
1982 *The Muslim Pious Foundations and Real Estates in Palestine* [in Arabic]. Istanbul: Research Centre for Islamic History, Art, and Culture.

Israel, Yigael
1993 Ashqelon [in Hebrew]. *HA* 100:88.
1995a Ashqelon. *ESI* 13:100–5.
1995b The Economy of the Gaza-Ashkelon Region in the Byzantine Period in the Light of the Archaeological Survey and Excavations of the "3rd Mile Estate" near Ashqelon [in Hebrew with English summary]. *Michmanim* 8:16*–17*, 119–32.
2006 Black Gaza Ware from the Ottoman Period [in Hebrew]. Ph.D. diss., Ben-Gurion University of the Negev, Beersheba.

Israeli, Shoshana
1997 Ashkelon, Afridar (B) [in Hebrew]. *HA* 107: 120–22.

Issar, Arie
1968 Geology of the Central Coastal Plain of Israel. *Israel Journal of Earth Sciences* 17:16–29.

Issar, Arie S., and Mattanyah Zohar
2007 *Climate Change: Environment and History of the Near East*. Berlin: Springer.

Jasmin, Michaël
2006 The Political Organization of the City-States in Southwestern Palestine in the Late Bronze Age IIB (13th Century BC). *"I Will Speak the Riddles of Ancient Times": Archaeological and Historical Studies in Honor of Amihai Mazar on the Occasion of his Sixtieth Birthday*, ed. A. M. Maeir and P. de Miroschedji, 161–91. Winona Lake, Ind.: Eisenbrauns.

Johnson, Barbara L., and Leon Levy
2008 *Ashkelon*. Vol. 2, *Imported Pottery of the Roman and Late Roman Periods*. Winona Lake, Ind.: Eisenbrauns.

Johnson, Barbara L., and Lawrence E. Stager
1995 Ashkelon: Wine Emporium of the Holy Land. In *Recent Excavations in Israel: A View to the West*, ed. S. Gitin, 95–109. Archaeological Institute of America Colloquia and Conference Papers 1. Dubuque, Iowa: Kendall/Hunt.

Johnson, Gregory A.
1987 The Changing Organization of Uruk Administration on the Susiana Plain. In *The Archaeology of Western Iran: Settlement and Society from Prehistory to the Islamic Conquest*, ed. F. Hole, 107–39. Washington, D.C.: Smithsonian Institution.

Karmon, Yehuda
1960 An Analysis of Jacotin's Map of Palestine. *IEJ* 10:155–73, 244–53.

Katz, Ofer
2012 Horbat Lasan. *HA-ESI* 124. [http://www.hadashot-esi.org.il/report_detail_eng.aspx?id=2130&mag_id=119 (12.17.2012)]

Kempinski, Aharon, and Isaac Gilead
1991 New Excavations at Tel Erani: A Preliminary Report of the 1985–1988 Seasons. *TA* 18: 164–91.

Khalaily, Hamoudi
2004 An Early Bronze Age Site at Ashqelon, Afridar—Area F. *ᶜAtiqot* 45:121–59.

Khalaily, Hamudi and Z. Wallach
1998 Ashqelon, Ha-Tayysim Street. *ESI* 18:100–1.

Khalidi, Walid
1992 *All That Remains: The Palestinian Villages Occupied and Depopulated by Israel in 1948*. Washington, D.C.: Institute for Palestine Studies.

Khalilieh, Hassan S.
1999 The *Ribāt* System and its Role in Coastal Navigation. *JESHO* 42:212–25.

Kiepert, Heinrich
1841 Memoir on the Maps Accompanying This Work. In *Biblical Researches in Palestine, Mount Sinai and Arabia Petraea: A Journal of Travels in the Year 1838*, vol. 3, by E. Robinson, First Appendix, 29–55. Boston: Crocker & Brewster.

Kitchen, Kenneth A.
1993 *Ramesside Inscriptions: Translated and Annotated*. Vol. 1. Oxford and Cambridge, Mass.: Blackwell.

Kletter, Raz
1999 Pots and Polities: Material Remains of Late Iron Age Judah in Relation to its Political Borders. *BASOR* 314:19–54.

Knudtzon, J. A.
1915 *Die El-Amarna-Tafeln*. Leipzig: J. C. Hinrichs.

Kogan-Zehavi, Elena
1997 Ashqelon. *ESI* 16:123.
1999a Late Roman–Byzantine Remains at Ashqelon. *ᶜAtiqot* 38:113*–26*, 230–31.
1999b A Painted Tomb of the Roman Period at Migdal Ashqelon. *ᶜAtiqot* 37:181–209, 179*–81*.
2006 Ashqelon, el-Jura. *HA-ESI* 118. [http://www.hadashot-esi.org.il/report_detail_eng.aspx?id=391&mag_id=111 (2.8.2006)]
2007 Ashqelon, the Barzilay Hospital. *HA-ESI* 119. [http://www.hadashot-esi.org.il/report_detail_eng.aspx?id=547&mag_id=112 (6.28.2007)]

Kohl, Heinrich, and Carl Watzinger
  1916   *Antike Synagogen in Galilea.* Leipzig: J. C. Hinrichs.

Kol-Ya^cakov, Shlomo, and Yoav Farhi
  2012   Ashqelon (al-Nabi Hussein): Evidence for the Burial of Jews, Christians and Pagans in a Late Roman-Period Burial Ground? [in Hebrew]. ^cAtiqot 70:87–111.

Kol-Ya^caqov, Shlomo and Yoab Shor
  1999   Ashqelon, Nabi Husein [in Hebrew]. *HA* 110:94.

Koucky, Frank L.
  2008   Early Maps and Records. In *Ashkelon* 1:17–20. Winona Lake, Ind.: Eisenbrauns.

Lamdan, Mordechai, Daniel Ziffer, Yaakov Huster, and Avraham Ronen
  1977   *A Prehistoric Archaeological Survey in Nahal Shiqma* [in Hebrew]. Sha^car Hanegev: Regional Council of Sha^car Hanegev.

Lass, Egon
  2008   The Survey of Wells. In *Ashkelon* 1:107–26. Winona Lake, Ind.: Eisenbrauns.

Leibner, Uzi
  2009   *Settlement and History in Hellenistic, Roman, and Byzantine Galilee.* Texts and Studies in Ancient Judaism, 127. Tübingen: Mohr Siebeck.

Le Strange, Guy
  1890   *Palestine Under the Moslems: A Description of Syria and the Holy Land from* A.D. *650 to 1500.* London: Alexander P. Watt.

Levin, Noam, Ruth Kark, and Emir Galilee
  2009   Maps and the Settlement of Southern Palestine, 1799–1948: An Historical/GIS Analysis. *Journal of Historical Geography* 30:1–21.

Levy, Thomas E.
  1995   Cult, Metallurgy and Rank Societies—Chalcolithic Period (ca. 4500–3500 BCE). In *The Archaeology of Society in the Holy Land*, ed. T. E. Levy, 226–44. London and Washington: Leicester University Press.

Levy, Yossi
  2005   The Necropolis of the Middle Bronze IIA–B Period from the Area of the Rishon LeZion Sands. In *Yavneh, Yavneh-Yam, and Their Neighborhood: Studies in the Archaeology and History of the Judean Coastal Plain*, ed. M. Fischer, 59–68. Tel Aviv: Eretz and Tel Aviv University.
  2008   Rishon le-Ẕiyyon: The Middle Bronze Age II Cemetery. In *NEAEHL*, ed. E. Stern, 5:2018–20. Jerusalem: Israel Exploration Society.

Litt, Thomas, Christian Ohlwien, Frank H. Neumann, Andreas Hense, and Mordechai Stein
  2012   Holocene Climate Variability in the Levant from the Dead Sea Pollen Record. *Quaternary Science Reviews* 49:95–105.

Luckenbill, Daniel David
  1924   *The Annals of Sennacherib.* Chicago: University of Chicago Press.

Masarwa, Yumna
  2006   From a Word of God to Archaeological Monuments: A Historical-Archaeological Study of the Umayyad Ribāts of Palestine. Ph.D. diss., Princeton University, Princeton, N.J.

Martin, Mario A. S.
  2008   Egyptian at Ashkelon? An Assemblage of Egyptian and Egyptian-Style Pottery. *Ägypten und Levante* 18:245–74.
  2011   *Egyptian-Type Pottery in the Late Bronze Age Southern Levant.* CCEM 29. Vienna: Verlag der Österreichischen Akademie der Wissenschaften.

Master, Daniel M.
  2009   The Renewal of Trade at Iron 1 Ashkelon. *EI* 29:*111–22.

Mayer, Leo A.
  1934   Satura Epigrahica. Arabica III, *QDAP* 3:24–25.

Mayer, Leo A. and Jacob Pinkerfield
  1950   *Some Principle Muslim Religious Buildings in Israel.* Jerusalem: Government Printer.

Mayerson, Philip
  1993   The Use of Ascalon Wine in the Medical Writers of the Fourth to the Seventh Centuries. *IEJ* 43:169–73.

Mazar, Amihai
  1985   *Excavations at Tell Qasile II: The Philistine Sanctuary: Various Finds, the Pottery, Conclusions, Appendixes.* Qedem 20. Jerusalem: Institute of Archaeology, Hebrew University.

Meri, Josef W.
  2002   *The Cult of Saints Among Muslims and Jews in Medieval Syria.* Oxford: Oxford University Press.

Meron, Dov
  1969   Horvat Hoga [in Hebrew]. *HA* 28/29:19.
  1975   Bror Hayil, Tomb [in Hebrew]. *HA* 56:37.
  1983   Ashkelon [in Hebrew]. *HA* 82:61.

Meron, Dov, and Yosef Ginat
  1963   Hurvat Hoga, A Tomb from the Sixth-Seventh Centuries C.E. [in Hebrew]. *HA* 7:21.

Meyer, Martin A.
  1907   *History of the City of Gaza: From the Earliest Times to the Present Day.* New York: Columbia University Press.

Michaeli, Talila
  1990   The Pictorial Program of the Tomb near Kibbuz Or-ha-Ner [in Hebrew with English summary]. M.A. thesis, Tel Aviv University.
  2001   Painted Tombs in Ascalon [in Hebrew]. In *Ashkelon, A City on the Seashore*, ed. A. Sasson, Z.

Safrai, and N. Sagiv, 175–202. Ashkelon: Ashkelon Academic College.

Milevski, Ianir, and Yaakov Baumgarten
2008   Between Lachish and Tel Erani: Horvat Ptora, A New Late Prehistoric Site in the Southern Levant. In *Proceedings of the 5th International Congress on the Archaeology of the Ancient Near East: Madrid, April 3–8, 2006*, vol. 3, ed. J. M. Córdoba et al., 609–26. Madrid: Ediciones Universidad Autónoma de Madrid.

Milevski, Ianir and Alexander Krokhmalnik
2010   Ashqelon, Barneᶜa B–C. *HA-ESI*. [http://www.hadashot-esi.org.il/report_detail_eng.aspx?id=1395&mag_id=117 (5.10.2010)]

Mills, Eric
1932   *Census of Palestine 1931: Population of Villages, Towns and Administrative Areas*. Jerusalem: Greek Convent and Goldberg Presses.

Moorey, Peter Roger Stuart
1987   On tracking cultural transfers in prehistory: the case of Egypt and lower Mesopotamia in the fourth millennium B.C. In *Centre and Periphery in the Ancient World*, ed. M. Rowlands, M. Larsen and K. Kristiansen, 36–46. New Directions in Archaeology. Cambridge: Cambridge University Press.

Musil, Alois.
1907a   *Arabia Petraea*. Vol. 2, *Edom*, part 1. Wien: Hoelder.
1907b   *Arabia Petraea*. Vol. 2, *Edom*, part 2. Wien: Hoelder.
1907c   *Karte von Arabia Petraea*. Wien: Hoelder.
1908   *Arabia Petraea*. Vol. 3, *Ethnologischer Reisebericht*. Wien: Hoelder.

Naᵓaman, Nadav
1979   The Brook of Egypt and Assyrian Policy on the Border of Egypt. *TA* 6:68–90.
1995   The Debated Historiocity of Hezekiah's Reform in the Light of Historical and Archaeological Research. *ZAW* 107:105–17.
1998   Two Notes on the History of Ashkelon and Ekron in the Late Eighth-Seventh Century B.C.E. *TA* 25:219–27.

Nahshoni, Pirhiya
1996   Ashqelon [in Hebrew]. *HA* 106:172–73.
1999   Ashqelon, Migdal (North). *ESI* 19:81*–82*.
2001   Ashqelon, Khirbet Khiṣaṣ. *HA-ESI* 113:109*–10*.
2009a   Ashqelon. *HA-ESI* 121. [http://www.hadashot-esi.org.il/report_detail_eng.aspx?id=1041&mag_id=115 (2.16.2009)]
2009b   Ashqelon, Industrial Zone (North). *HA-ESI* 12. [http://www.hadashot-esi.org.il/report_detail_eng.aspx?id=1262&mag_id=115 (11.26.2009)]

Nahshoni, Pirhiya, and Yossi Nagar
2002   Khirbet Lasan [in Hebrew]. *HA-ESI* 114:145.

Natsheh, Yusuf
2000   Architectural Survey. In *Ottoman Jerusalem: The Living City, 1517–1917*, part II, ed. S. Auld and R. Hillenbrand, 657–1085. London: Altajir World of Islam Trust.

Negbi, Ora
1966   *A Deposit of Terracottas and Statuettes from Tel Ṣippor*. ᶜAtiqot English Series 6. Jerusalem: Department of Antiquities and Museums.

Netser, Michael
1994   The Climatic Changes During the Holocene Stage and their Effect on the Formation of the Landscape in Gush-Dan (Israel) and on the Human Settlement in this Region [in Hebrew]. Ph.D. diss., Bar-Ilan University.

Neumann, Frank H., Elisa J. Kagan, Suzanne A. G. Leroy, and Uri Baruch
2010   Vegetation History and Climate Fluctuations on a Transect along the Dead Sea West Shore and their Impact on Past Societies over the Last 3500 Years. *Journal of Arid Environments* 74:756–64.

Nikolsky, Vlada
2010   Ard el Mihjar. *HA-ESI* 122. [http://www.hadashot-esi.org.il/report_detail_eng.aspx?id=1452&mag_id=117 (9.5.2010)]

Nir, Dov and Bar-Yosef, Ofer
1976   *Quaternary Environment and Man in Israel* [in Hebrew]. Jerusalem: Society for the Protection of Nature in Israel.

Noy (Yizraeli), Tamar
1967   A Lower Paleolithic Site at Holon. *IEJ* 17:144–45.
1976   Ziqim. *IEJ* 26:49.
1977   The Neolithic Sites in the Western Coastal Plain [in Hebrew with English Summary]. *EI* 13:18–33, *290–*91.
1993   Ziqim. In *NEAEHL*, ed. E. Stern, 4:1527–28. Jerusalem: Israel Exploration Society.

Noy, Tamar, and Ariel Berman
1974   Prehistoric Site Near Ashkelon. *IEJ* 24:132.

Oppenheim, A. L.
1969   Babylonian and Assyrian Historical Texts. *ANET³*, 265–317.

Oren, Eliezer and Yuval Yekutieli
1992   Taur Ikhbenieh—Earliest Evidence for Egyptian Interconnections. In *The Nile Delta in Transition: 4th–3rd Millennium B.C.: Proceedings of the Seminar held in Cairo, 21–24 October 1990, at the Netherlands Institute of Archaeology and Arabic Studies*, ed. E. C. M. van den Brink, 361–84. Tel Aviv: van den Brink.

Ory, J.
1939   A Painted Tomb near Ashcalon. *QDAP* 8:38–44.

Ovadiah, Asher, and Carlos Gomez de Silva
1981   Supplementum to the Corpus of the Byzantine Churches in the Holy Land. *Levant* 13:200–62.
1982   Supplementum to the Corpus of the Byzantine Churches in the Holy Land. *Levant* 14:122–70.
1984   Supplementum to the Corpus of the Byzantine Churches in the Holy Land. *Levant* 16:129–65.

Palestine Survey
1931   British Mandate: Survey of Palestine (1:20,000). *Topocadastral Series.* Jaffa.
1939   War Office, Survey of Palestine (1:100,000). London.

Palmer, Edward H.
1881   *The Survey of Western Palestine: Arabic and English Name Lists.* London: Palestine Exploration Fund.

Paoli, Sebastiano
1733   *Codice Diplomatico del Sacro Militare Ordine Gerosolimitano Oggi di Malta.* Lucca: For Salvatore and Giandomenico Marescandoli.

Paran, Nir-Shimson
2007   Ashqelon. *HA-ESI* 119. [http://www.hadashot-esi.org.il/report_detail_eng.aspx?id=628&mag_id=112 (12.12.2007)]
2009   Givᶜati Junction. *HA-ESI* 121. [http://www.hadashot-esi.org.il/report_detail_eng.aspx?id=1204&mag_id=115 (9.1.2009)]

Patrich, Joseph
1988   The Glass Vessels. In *Excavations at Rehovot-in-the-Negev: The Northern Church*, ed. Tsafrir Yoram, 134–49. Jerusalem: The Institute of Archaeology, The Hebrew University of Jerusalem, 1988.

Peretz, Ilan
2008   Khirbat el-Hannuna *HA-ESI* 120. [http://www.hadashot-esi.org.il/report_detail_eng.aspx?id=829&mag_id=114 (7.20.2008)]
2011   Khirbat Lasan: Final Report. *HA-ESI* 123. [http://www.hadashot-esi.org.il/report_detail_eng.asp?id=1662&mag_id=118 (4.17.2011)]

Perrot, Jean
1955   Ashkelon. *IEJ* 5:270–71.

Perrot, Jean, and Avi Gopher
1996   A Late Neolithic Site near Ashkelon. *IEJ* 46:145–66.

Petersen, Andrew
1994   Ottoman Terracotta Vaulting Tubes. *Orient Express* 3:89–91.
2001   *A Gazetteer of Buildings in Muslim Palestine.* Oxford: Oxford University Press.
2005   *The Towns of Palestine under Muslim Rule:* A.D. *600–1600.* Oxford: Archaeopress.

Petrie, W. M. Flinders
1891   *Tell el Hesy (Lachish).* London: Pub. for the Committee of the Palestine Exploration Fund by A. P. Watt.

Phythian-Adams, William J.
1921   Askalon Reports: Stratigraphical Sections. *PEFQS*:163–69.
1923   Report on the Stratification of Askalon. *PEFQS*: 60–84.

Piphano, Shlomo
1990   *Ashdod Sea in Byzantine Period Israel* [in Hebrew]. Ashdod: Society for the Protection of Nature in Israel.

Porat, Yosef
1975   The Gardens of Caesarea [in Hebrew]. *Qadmoniyot* 8:90–93.
1976   Hurvat Hoga [in Hebrew]. *HA* 59/60:41–42.

Porat, Yosef, and Dov Meron
1977   Carmiyeh [in Hebrew]. *HA* 51/52:36.

Porter, Josias L.
1858   *A Handbook for Travellers in Syria and Palestine.* Part I. London: John Murray.

Posener, Georges
1940   *Princes et pays d'Asie et de Nubie.* Brussels: Fondation Égyptologique Reine Élisabeth.

Post, George E.
1891   Essays on the Sects and Nationalities of Syria and Palestine. *PEFQS*:99–147.

Prawer, Yehoshua
1951   Colonization Activities in the Latin Kingdom of Jerusalem. *Revue belge de philologie et d'histoire* 29:1063–118.
1956   Ascalon and the Ascalon Strip in Crusader Politics [in Hebrew]. *EI* 4:231–48.
1958   The City and Duchy of Ascalon in the Crusader Period [in Hebrew]. *EI* 5:224–37.

Press, Michael D.
2007   Philistine Figurines and Figurines in Philistia in the Iron Age. Ph.D. diss., Harvard University.

Pye, Kenneth, and Haim Tsoar
2009   *Aeolian Sand and Sand Dunes.* Berlin: Springer.

Raban, Avner
1991   The Philistines in the Western Jezreel Valley. *BASOR* 284:17–27.

Raban, Avner and Tur-Caspa, Y.
2008   Underwater Survey, 1985–1987. In *Ashkelon* 1: 67–96. Winona Lake, Ind.: Eisenbrauns.

Renfrew, Colin
1975   Trade as Action at a Distance: Questions of Integration and Communication. In *Ancient Civilization and Trade*, ed. J. A. Sabloff and C. C.

Lamberg-Karlovsky, 3–59. Albuquerque: University of New Mexico Press.

Rey, Emmanuel-Guillaume
1862   *Étude historique et topographique de la tribu de Juda*, Paris: A. Bertrand.
1871   *Étude sur les monuments de l'architecture militaire des Croisés en Syrie et dans l'île de Chypre.* Paris: Imprimerie Nationale.
1883   *Les colonies franques de Syrie aux XIIme et XIIIme siècles.* Paris: A. Picard.

Richardson, Robert
1822   *Travels along the Mediterranean and Parts Adjacent; in Company with the Earl of Belmore, During the Years 1816–17–18: Extending as far as the Second Cataract of the Nile. Jerusalem, Damascus, Balbec, &c. &c.* London: Printed for T. Cadell, in the Strand; and W. Blackwood, Edinburgh.

Richmond, E. T., ed.
1929   Schedule: Provisional Schedule of Historical Sites and Monuments. *Official Palestine Gazette Extraordinary.*

Robinson, Edward, and Eli Smith
1841   *Biblical Researches in Palestine, Mount Sinai and Arabia Petraea: A Journal of Travels in the Year 1838.* 3 vols. Boston: Crocker & Brewster.

Röhricht, Reinhold
1887   Studien zur mittelalterlichen Geographie und Topographie Syriens. *ZDPV* 10:195–345.
1893   *Regesta Regni Hierosolymitani.* Oeniponti: Libraria Academica Wagneriana.

Ronen, A., D. Gilead, E. Shachnai, and A. Saull.
1972   Upper Acheulean in the Kissufim Region. *Proceedings of the American Philosophical Society* 116:68–96.

Rosen, Arlene Miller
2008   Site Formation. In *Ashkelon* 1:101–4. Winona Lake, Ind.: Eisenbrauns.

Rosen-Ayalon, Miriam
2006   *Islamic Art and Archaeology in Palestine.* Walnut Creek, Calif.: Left Coast.

Rust, Alfred
1936   Das Askalonien in Palästina. In *Festschrift zur Hundertjahrfeier des Museums vorgeschichtlicher Altertümer in Kiel*, ed. G. Schwantes, 12–17. Neumünster: Wacholtz.

Sasson, Avi
2002   Water for the Sojourner: Introduction to the history and typology of "sabils" (water fountains) in the Land of Israel in the late Ottoman period. In *Cura Aquarum in Israel*, ed. C Ohlig, Y. Peleg, T. Tsuk, and Y. Eren, 113–25. Schriften der Deutschen Wasserhistorischen Gesellschaft 1. Siegburg: Deutsche Wasserhistorische Gesellschaft.

Sasson, Avi, ed.
2010   *Sderot: Nof-adam ba-Merhav* [in Hebrew]. Jerusalem: Makom.

Sasson, Avi, and Yaakov Huster
2010   The Engine Whistle—The Railroad Section from Deir Suneid to Huj in the First World War [in Hebrew]. In *Sderot: Nof-adam ba-Merhav*, ed. A. Sasson, 95–102. Jerusalem: Makom.

Schaefer, Jerry
1979   The Ecology of Empires: An Archaeological Approach to the Byzantine Communities of the Negev Desert. Ph.D. diss., University of Arizona.

Schiffer, Michael B., Alan P. Sullivan, and Timothy C. Klinger
1978   The Design of Archaeological Surveys. *World Archaeology* 10:1–28.

Schloen, J. David
2008a   Early Explorations. In *Ashkelon* 1:143–52. Winona Lake, Ind.: Eisenbrauns.
2008b   British and Israeli Excavations. In *Ashkelon* 1: 153–63. Winona Lake, Ind.: Eisenbrauns.

Scholz, Johann Martin Augustin
1822   *Reise in die Gegend zwischen Alexandrien und. Parätonium, die libische Wüste, Susa, Egypten, Palaestina u. Syrien, in den Jahren 1820 und 1821.* Leipzig and Sorau: Bei Friedrich Fleischer.

Schulman, Alan R.
1993   A Ramesside Queen from Ashdod. In *Ashdod V: Excavation of Area G, The Fourth–Sixth Seasons of Excavations, 1968–1970*, by M. Dothan and Y. Porath, 111–14. ᶜ*Atiqot* 23. Jerusalem: Israel Antiquities Authority.

Schumacher, Gottlieb
1886   Researches in Southern Palestine. *PEQ* 18/4: 171–97.

Schuster, Yishai
2000a   Horbat Herev [in Hebrew]. *HA-ESI* 112:133–35, 193–95.
2000b   Nirᶜam Junction [in Hebrew]. *HA-ESI* 112:135–38, 196–200.

Seriy, Gregory
2010   Nirᶜam Junction: Preliminary Report. *HA-ESI* 122. [http://www.hadashot-esi.org.il/report_detail_eng.asp?id=1511&mag_id=117 (5.10.2010)]
2012   Ashqelon, Neve Yam Daled. *HA-ESI* 124. [http://www.hadashot-esi.org.il/report_detail_eng.aspx?id=2164&mag_id=119 (12.31.2012)]

Sethe, Kurt
1926   *Die Ächtung feindlicher Fürsten, Völker und Dinge auf altägyptischen Tongefässcherben des Mittleren Reiches.* Berlin: Verlag der Akademie der Wissenschaften.

Sharon, Moshe

1997   *Corpus Inscriptionum Arabicarum Palaestinae.*
        Vol. 1, A. Handbuch der Orientalistik, Erste Ab-
        teilung, Nahe und der Mittlere Osten 30. Bd.
        Leiden: Brill.

1999   *Corpus Inscriptionum Arabicarum Palaestinae.*
        Vol. 2, B–C. Handbuch der Orientalistik, Erste
        Abteilung, Nahe und der Mittlere Osten 30. Bd.
        Leiden: Brill.

2004   *Corpus Inscriptionum Arabicarum Palaestinae.*
        Vol. 3, D–F. Handbuch der Orientalistik, Erste
        Abteilung, Nahe und der Mittlere Osten 30. Bd.
        Leiden: Brill.

2008   An Arabic Inscription Engraved with Crusader
        Shields. In *Ashkelon* 1:405–26. Winona Lake,
        Ind.: Eisenbrauns.

2007   *Corpus Inscriptionum Arabicarum Palaestinae*,
        Addendum. Handbuch der Orientalistik. Erste
        Abteilung, Nahe und der Mittlere Osten 30. Bd.
        Leiden: Brill.

2009   *Corpus Inscriptionum Arabicarum Palaestine.*
        Vol. 4, G. Handbuch der Orientalistik. Erste Ab-
        teilung, Nahe und der Mittlere Osten 30. Bd.
        Leiden: Brill.

2013   *Corpus Inscriptionum Arabicarum Palaestinae.*
        Vol. 5, H–I. Handbuch der Orientalistik. Erste
        Abteilung, Nahe und der Mittlere Osten 30. Bd.
        Leiden: Brill.

Shavit, Alon

2003   Settlement Patterns in Israel's Southern Coastal
        Plain during the Iron Age II. Ph.D. diss., Tel Aviv
        University.

2008   Settlement Patterns of Philistine City States. In
        *Bene Israel: Studies in the Archaeology of Israel
        and the Levant during the Bronze and Iron Ages
        in Honour of Israel Finkelstein*, ed. A. Fantalkin
        and A. Yasur-Landau, 135–64. Leiden and Boston:
        Brill.

Shavit, Alon, and Assaf Yasur-Landau

2005   A Bronze and Iron Age Settlement at Netiv Ha-
        ͨAsara. In *Salvage Excavation Reports*. No. 2, ed.
        B. Sass and I. Roll, 59–92. Tel Aviv: Sonia and
        Marco Nadler Institute of Archaeology, Tel Aviv
        University.

Sion, Ofer

2008   Ashqelon, Barneͨa. *HA-ESI* 120. [http://www.
        hadashot-esi.org.il/report_detail_eng.aspx?
        id=782&mag_id=114 (5.27.2008)]

2009   Ashqelon, el-Qabu. *HA-ESI* 121. [http://www.
        hadashot-esi.org.il/report_detail_eng.aspx?
        id=1105&mag_id=115 (6.2.2009)]

2012   A Roman-period farmstead at el-Qabu, south of
        Ashqelon [in Hebrew with English summary].
        ͨ*Atiqot* 711:1–12, 111*.

Sion, Ofer, Yehudah Rapuano, Lihi Habas and Leah Di Segni

2010   Barqa. *HA-ESI* 122. [http://www.hadashot-esi.org.
        il/report_detail_eng.aspx?id=1480&mag_id=117
        (9.5.2010)]

Smith, Kevin P., and Jeffrey R. Parsons

1989   Regional Archaeological Research in Iceland:
        Potential and Possibilities. In *The Anthropology
        of Iceland*, ed. E. P. Durrenburger and G. Páls-
        son, 179–202. Iowa City: University of Iowa
        Press.

Smith, Monica L.

2005   Networks, Territories, and the Cartography of An-
        cient States. *Annals of the Association of Ameri-
        can Geographers* 95/4:832–49.

Snodgrass, Anthony M.

1987   *An Archaeology of Greece: The Present State and
        Future Scope of a Discipline.* Berkeley: Univer-
        sity of California Press.

Socin, Albert

1879   Alphabetisches Verzeichnis von Ortschaften des
        Pashalik Jerusalem. *ZDPV* 2:81–101.

Stager, Lawrence E.

1993   Ashkelon. In *NEAEHL*, ed. E. Stern, 1:103–12.
        Jerusalem: Israel Exploration Society.

1995   The Impact of the Sea Peoples in Canaan (1185–
        1050 B.C.E.). In *The Archaeology of Society in the
        Holy Land*, ed. T. E. Levy, 332–48. New York:
        Facts on File.

2001   Port Power in the Early and the Middle Bronze
        Age: The Organization of Maritime Trade and
        Hinterland Production. *Studies in the Archaeology
        of Israel and Neighboring Lands in Memory of
        Douglas L. Esse*, ed. S. R. Wolff, 625–38. SAOC
        59. Chicago: Oriental Institute.

2002   The MB IIA Ceramic Sequence at Tel Ashkelon
        and Its Implications for the "Port Power" Model
        of Trade. In *The Middle Bronze Age in the Le-
        vant: Proceedings of an International Confer-
        ence on MB IIA Ceramic Material, Vienna, 24th–
        26th of January 2001*, ed. M. Bietak, 353–62.
        CCEM 3. Vienna: Österreichische Akademie der
        Wissenschaften.

2006   Chariot Fittings from Philistine Ashkelon. In *Con-
        fronting the Past: Archaeological and Historical
        Essays on Ancient Israel in Honor of William G.
        Dever*, ed. S. Gitin, J. E. Wright, and J. P. Dessel,
        169–76. Winona Lake, Ind.: Eisenbrauns.

2008   Ashkelon. In *NEAEHL*, ed. E. Stern, 5:1578–86.
        Jerusalem: Israel Exploration Society.

Stager, Lawrence E., Daniel M. Master, and J. David
        Schloen, eds.

2011   *Ashkelon*. Vol. 3, *The Seventh Century* B.C. Wi-
        nona Lake, Ind.: Eisenbrauns.

Stager, Lawrence E., and J. David Schloen

2008   Introduction: Ashkelon and Its Inhabitants. In
        Ashkelon 1:3–10. Winona Lake, Ind.: Eisenbrauns.

Stager, Lawrence E., J. David Schloen, and Daniel M.
        Master, eds.

2008   *Ashkelon*. Vol. 1, *Introduction and Overview
        (1985–2006)*. Winona Lake, Ind.: Eisenbrauns.

Stager, Lawrence E., J. David Schloen, Daniel M. Master, Michael D. Press, and Adam J. Aja
2008   Stratigraphic Overview. In *Ashkelon* 1:215–323. Winona Lake, Ind.: Eisenbrauns.

Stern, Ephraim
2001   *Archaeology of the Land of the Bible*. Vol. II, *The Assyrian, Babylonian, and Persian Periods, 732–332 B.C.E.* New York: Doubleday.

Stern, Ephraim, ed.
1993   *The New Encyclopedia of Archaeological Excavations in the Holy Land*, 4 vols. Jerusalem: Israel Exploration Society.
2008   *The New Encyclopedia of Archaeological Excavations in the Holy Land*, vol. 5. Jerusalem: Israel Exploration Society.

Sukenik, Eleazar L.
1935   *The ancient synagogue of El-Ḥammeh (Ḥammath-by-Gadara): an account of the excavations conducted on behalf of the Hebrew University, Jerusalem.* Jerusalem: R. Mass.

Tadmor, Hayim
1971   Fragments of an Assyrian Stele of Sargon II. In *Ashdod*. Vol. II–III, *The Second and Third Seasons of Excavations, 1963, 1965, Soundings in 1967.* ᶜAtiqot English Series 9–10. Jerusalem: Department of Antiquities and Museums.

Talis, Svetlana
2010   ᶜAd Halom Interchange *HA-ESI* 122. [http://www.hadashot-esi.org.il/report_detail_eng.aspx?id=1347&mag_id=117 (2.22.2010)]
2011   Ashqelon North, Khirbat Khaur el-Bak. *HA-ESI* 123. [http://www.hadashot-esi.org.il/report_detail_eng.aspx?id=1703&mag_id=118 (6.16.2011)]

Talmon, Rafi
2004   19th Century Travelers on Palestinian Arabic: Western travellers' testimony. *Jerusalem Studies in Arabic and Islam* 29:210–80.

Tamari, Shmuel
1987   Khân Yûnis—historical-architectural and urbanistic comments (regarding a potential conservation and restoration project). *Saggi in onore di Guglielmo de Angelis d'Ossat*, ed. S. Benedetti and G. M. Mariani, 135–44. Rome: Multigrafica.

Toueg, Ron
2009   Ashqelon, Barneᶜa. *HA-ESI* 121. [http://www.hadashot-esi.org.il/report_detail_eng.aspx?id=1316&mag_id=115 (12.30.2009)]
2010   Ashqelon: Final Report. *HA-ESI* 122. [http://www.hadashot-esi.org.il/report_detail_eng.asp?id=1401&mag_id=117 (5.26.2010)]

Trigger, Bruce G.
1967   Settlement Archaeology—Its Goals and Promise. *AmAnt* 32:149–60.

Tsafrir, Yoram
1968   A Painted Tomb at Or ha-Ner. *IEJ* 18/3:170–80.

Tsafrir, Yoram, Leah Di Segni, Judith Green, Israel Roll, and Tsvika Tsuk.
1994   *Tabula Imperii Romani; Judaea-Palaestina: Eretz Israel in the Hellenistic, Roman, and Byzantine Periods: Maps and Gazetteer.* Jerusalem: Israel Academy of Sciences and Humanities.

Tsoar, Haim
2000   Geomorphology and Paleogeography of Sand Dunes That Have Formed the Kurkar Ridges in the Coastal Plain of Israel. *Israel Journal of Earth Sciences* 49:189–96.

Tzaferis, Vassilios
1967   Ashkelon-Barnea. *IEJ* 17:125–26
2006   A Greek Inscription from Tel Ashdod. ᶜ*Atiqot* 51: 3, 233–34.

Tzaferis, Vassilos and Lawrence E. Stager
2008   The Church by the Jerusalem Gate. In *Ashkelon* 1:393–404. Winona Lake, Ind.: Eisenbrauns.

Van Berchem, Max
1915   La chaire de la Mosquée d'Hébron et le martyrion de la tête de Husain à Ascalon. In *Festschrift Eduard Sachau*, ed. G. Weil, 298–310. Berlin: Georg Reimer.

Van de Velde, Charles William Meredith
1858   *Memoir to Accompany the Map of the Holy Land.* Gotha: Justus Perthes.

Varga, Daniel
1999   Horbat Hoga. *HA-ESI* 110:69*–70*.
2001   Ashkelon [in Hebrew]. *HA-ESI* 113:177.
2002   Ashqelon, Afridar and Barneᶜa (B) [in Hebrew]. *HA-ESI* 114:108–9.
2003   Ashqelon (B) [in Hebrew]. *HA-ESI* 115:80.
2005   Tel Ashdod. *HA-ESI* 117. [http://www.hadashot-esi.org.il/report_detail_eng.aspx?id=200&mag_id=110 (6.19.2005)]
2007   Ashqelon, Barneᶜa. *HA-ESI* 119. [http://www.hadashot-esi.org.il/report_detail_eng.aspx?id=462&mag_id=112 (1.7.2007)]

Wachmann, Shelley
2008   Underwater Survey, 1996–1997. In *Ashkelon* 1: 97–100. Winona Lake, Ind.: Eisenbrauns.
2010   Ashqelon, Barneᶜa (north). *HA-ESI* 122. [http://www.hadashot-esi.org.il/report_detail_eng.aspx?id=1368&mag_id=117 (3.15.2010)]

Wallach, Zvi
2000   Ashqelon, el-Jura. *ESI* 20:120*–21*.
2003   Ashqelon (A) [in Hebrew]. *HA-ESI* 115:77–79

Warren, Charles
1871   The Plain of Philistia. *PEFQS* 3:82–96.

Weinstein, James M.
1984   The Significance of Tell Areini for Egyptian-Palestinian Relations at the Beginning of the Bronze Age. *BASOR* 256:61–69.

Weiss, Ehud, and Mordechai E. Kislev
2004 Plant Remains as Indicators for Economic Activity: A Case Study from Iron Age Ashkelon. *JAS* 31:1–13.

Weiss, Ehud, Mordechai E. Kislev, and Yael Maher-Slasky
2011 Plant Remains. In *Ashkelon* 3:591–614. Winona Lake, Ind.: Eisenbrauns.

Wilkinson, Tony J.
1982 The Definition of Ancient Manured Zones by Means of Extensive Sherd-Sampling Techniques. *JFA* 9:323–33.
1989 Extensive Sherd Scatters and Land-Use Intensity: Some Recent Results. *JFA* 16:31–46.
2003 *Archaeological Landscapes of the Near East.* Tuscon: The University of Arizona Press.

Wilkinson, Toby A. H.
1999 *Early Dynastic Egypt.* London: Routledge.

Yalçinkaya, Sinan
2006 The Sanjaq of Gaza in 1548 According to the Tahrir Defter Numbered 265 [in Turkish]. Ph.D. diss., Fırat Üniversitesi, Elazığ, Turkey.

Yasur-Landau, Assaf, and Alon Shavit
1999 Netiv Ha-ᶜAsara. *HA-ESI* 110:80*–81*.

Yāqūt Ibn-ᶜAbdallāh ar-Rūmī.
1866–1873a *Muᶜdjam al-buldān. Jacut's Geographisches Wörterbuch*, vol. 1, ed. F. Wüstenfeld. Leipzig: Brockhaus.
1866–1873b *Muᶜdjam al-buldān. Jacut's Geographisches Wörterbuch*, vol. 2, ed. F. Wüstenfeld. Leipzig: Brockhaus.
1866–1873c *Muᶜdjam al-buldān. Jacut's Geographisches Wörterbuch*, vol. 3, ed. F. Wüstenfeld. Leipzig: Brockhaus.
1866–1873d *Muᶜdjam al-buldān. Jacut's Geographisches Wörterbuch*, vol. 4, ed. F. Wüstenfeld. Leipzig: Brockhaus.

Yazbak, Mahmoud
2011 The Muslim Festival of Nabi Rubin in Palestine: From Religious Festival to Summer Resort. *Holy Land Studies* 10/2:169–98.

Yeivin, Efrat T., and Yaakov Olami
1979 Nizzanim: A Neolithic Site in Nahal Evtah; Excavations of 1968–1970. *TA* 6:99–113.
1980 Nizzanim—Nahal Evtah: A Site from the Pottery Neolithic Period; Excavations in 1968–1970 [in Hebrew]. In *Dedicated to the Memory of Efrat-Tirzah Yeivin; 1930–1975*, ed. S. Yeivin, 9–46. Tel Aviv: Institute of Archaeology, Tel Aviv University.

Yeivin, Shmuel
1961 *First Preliminary Report on the Excavations at Tel Gat (Tell Sheykh ᵓAhmed el-ᶜAreyny). Seasons 1956–1958.* Jerusalem: The Gat Expedition.

Yeivin, Shmuel, and Aharon Kempinski
1993 ᶜErani, Tel. In *NEAEHL*, ed. E. Stern, 2:417–22. Jerusalem: Israel Exploration Society.

Yekutieli, Yuval, and Ram Gophna
1994 Excavations at an Early Bronze Age Site near Nizzanim. *TA* 21:162–85.

Zadok, Ran
1995–97 A Preliminary Analysis of Ancient Survivals in Modern Palestinian Toponymy. *Mediterranean Language Review 9*, 93–171.

Zbenovich, Vladimir G.
2004 The Flint Assemblage from Ashkelon, Afridar—Area E. *ᶜAtiqot* 45:63–84.

Zelin, Alexey
2001 Ashqelon, Barneᶜa. *HA-ESI* 113:108*–9*.
2002 Ashkelon, Barneᶜa [in Hebrew]. *HA-ESI* 114:104.

Zissu, Boaz
1996 Ziqim. *ESI* 15:100–1.